Merger Control in Latin America

A Jurisdictional Guide

Presentation by
Ivo Gagliuffi

Foreword by
Cani Fernández

Editors
Paulo Burnier da Silveira
Pamela Sittenfeld

106 West 32nd Street, Suite 144 New York, NY, 10001, USA
www.concurrences.com
book@concurrences.com

First Printing, October 2020
978-1-939007-22-3
LCCN: 2020946388

Cover: Yves Buliard, www.yvesbuliard.fr
Book Design and Layout implementation: Nordcompo

Concurrences Books

Liber Amicorum

Laurence Idot – Liber Amicorum
Christophe Lemaire, Francesco Martucci (ed.), 2021

Eleanor Fox – Liber Amicorum
Nicolas Charbit, Sonia Ahmad (ed.), 2021

Herbert Hovenkamp – Liber Amicorum
Nicolas Charbit, Sonia Ahmad (ed.), 2021

Albert Foer – A Consumer Voice in the Antitrust Arena
Nicolas Charbit, Sonia Ahmad (ed.), 2020

Richard Whish – Taking Competition Law Outside the Box
Nicolas Charbit, Sonia Ahmad (ed.), 2020

Frédéric Jenny – Standing Up for Convergence and Relevance in Antitrust, Vol. I & II
Nicolas Charbit, Sonia Ahmad (ed.), 2019 & 2021

Wang Xiaoye – The Pioneer of Competition Law in China
Adrian Emch, Wendy Ng (ed.), 2019

Douglas H. Ginsburg – An Antitrust Professor on the Bench, Vol. I & II
Nicolas Charbit, et al. (eds), 2018 & 2020

Ian S. Forrester – A Scot Without Borders, Vol. I & II
Assimakis Komninos et al. (ed.), 2015

William E. Kovacic – An Antitrust Tribute, Vol. I & II
Nicolas Charbit et al. (ed.), 2013 & 2014

Practical Books

Competition Law Dictionary
Deborah Healey, William Kovacic, Pablo Trevisan, Richard Whish (ed.) 2021

Competition Law & Environmental Sustainability
Simon Holmes, Dirk Middelschulte, Martijn Snoep (ed.), 2021

Perspectives on Antitrust Compliance
Anne Riley, Andreas Stephan, Anny Tubbs (ed.), 2021

Information Exchange and Related Risks – A Practical Guide
Eric Meiring, Marcio Dias Soares (ed.), 2021

State Aid & National Enforcement
Jacques Derenne, Denis Jouve, Christophe Lemaire, Francesco Martucci (ed.), 2021

Merger Control in Latin America – A Jurisdictional Guide
Paulo Burnier da Silveira & Pamela Sittenfeld (ed.), 2020

Competition Inspections under EU Law
Nathalie Jalabert-Doury, 2020

Competition Digest – A Synthesis of EU, US and National Leading Cases, 4th ed.
Frédéric Jenny (ed.), 2020

Gun Jumping in Merger Control – A Jurisdictional Guide
Catriona Hatton, Yves Comtois, Andrea Hamilton (ed.), 2019

Choice – A New Standard for Competition Analysis?
Paul Nihoul et al., 2016

PhD Theses

The Role of Media Pluralism in the Enforcement of EU Competition Law
Konstantina Bania, 2019

Buyer Power in EU Competition Law
Ignacio Herrera Anchustegui, 2017

General Interest

Women & Antitrust – Voices from the Field, Vol. I & II
Evelina Kurgonaite & Kristina Nordlander (ed.), 2020

Conference Proceedings

Antitrust in Emerging and Developing Countries, Vol I & II
Eleanor Fox, Harry First (ed.), 2015 & 2016

Global Antitrust Law – Current Issues in Antitrust Law and Economics
Douglas Ginsburg, Joshua Wright (ed.), 2015

Competition Law on the Global Stage: David Gerber's Global Competition Law in Perspective
David Gerber, 2014

e-Book versions available for **Concurrences+** subscribers

PRESENTATION

IVO GAGLIUFFI*

Former President of the Peruvian Competition Authority (Instituto Nacional de Defensa de la Competencia y de la Protección de la Propiedad Intelectual)

It is my greatest pleasure to write a short presentation to *Merger Control in Latin America: A Jurisdictional Guide* edited by Pamela Sittenfeld and Paulo Burnier da Silveira. Both editors are leading competition experts in the region and they have managed to put together an excellent list of authors to write the chapters of this book.

The book provides a comprehensive overview of merger control in Latin America, which has today 17 merger control regimes. Each one of these jurisdictions is subject to a detailed analysis through the chapters of this book. In addition, a final chapter provides a glance at merger control in the Caribbean countries, completing the full picture of the topic in the region.

The publication is also very timely: many jurisdictions in the region are still in their early days of merger control. The introductory chapter written by the co-editors highlights this recent proliferation of merger regimes in the region. It is also the case that Peru, my home country, adopted new legislation in 2019 which is expected to enter into effect during 2021.

The adoption of merger control represents a great challenge for the countries of the region. This includes challenges for governments and competition authorities related to the implementation of the new legislation, as well as to companies that will have to comply with the new rules. In this context, the book also provides useful reflections on the rules and practices of competition authorities, which may add to efforts around the world to promote greater convergence in the field of competition law.

---

* Ivo Gagliuffi is former president of the Peruvian Competition Authority (Instituto Nacional de Defensa de la Competencia y de la Protección de la Propiedad Intelectual – INDECOPI). He holds a law degree from the University of Lima and a postgraduate degree in corporate law from the University of Salamanca, specialising in competition law and intellectual property.

Furthermore, because of the economic crisis generated by the COVID-19 pandemic, there is an expectation that a lot of businesses will have to leave markets, increasing concentrations and making merger control assessment harder for the competition authorities. Moreover, it is feasible that, to survive, undertakings will seek to merge with companies in stronger positions, thus stepping up the number of operations to review. Likewise, I think that authorities would address more frequently "failing firm defences" in their merger control cases, which will require an incredibly careful analysis.

In sum, the book offers a complete jurisdictional guide to practitioners and any other interested audience. It is a must-read for anyone who wishes to understand or learn more about merger control in Latin America and the Caribbean.

I wish you a great read!

FOREWORD

CANI FERNÁNDEZ
President, National Commission for Markets and Competition (CNMC, Spain)

Competition enforcement benefits significantly from international cooperation among agencies – thanks to forums such as the OECD or ICN, or the ECN at a more regional level – an unstoppable trend witnessed over the last two decades in all enforcement areas, particularly mergers. Cooperation among national competition authorities has become essential to ensure consistency in our respective decisions, allowing for the creation of a global level playing field.

In our increasingly interconnected world, with the explosion of the digital economy, international cooperation in the analysis of merger control is more necessary than ever before, given the scope, dynamism and scale of the digital revolution. I am convinced that sharing the experience gained in the enforcement of competition policy and advocacy in this area, in a timely and fluid way, will also benefit companies operating globally.

Many of the issues that digital mergers raise are not entirely new; it is often the actual scale and the speed of change that can be challenging. In this regard, features such as multisided markets, network effects and economies of scale are not new, but digitalisation greatly broadens their scope. The same can be said for innovation, which often plays a very relevant role in these markets and can be a key parameter for competition. In this context, there is enormous potential for competition authorities – regardless of their respective size and level of maturity – to join forces in sharing approaches, best practices, studies and experiences on competition enforcement issues.

The experience of international cooperation at a regional level gained by the Member States of the European Union, between themselves and with the EU Commission, provides food for thought, from the perspective of both the formal and informal mechanisms of cooperation.

In the area of merger control, cooperation under the framework of the EU Merger Regulation and, in particular, through the referral system within the EU has been extremely useful in overcoming some of the challenges that characterise digital mergers. Referrals give flexibility to the European system, where merger review at EU level coexists with national merger reviews, allowing for the best-placed authority to undertake the analysis of the transaction, even when the authority did not have initially jurisdiction to do so. This is, for instance, the case of the acquisition by Apple of Shazam, which did not meet the EU merger control threshold but was referred to the European Commission for review by a number of national competition authorities, whose merger control regimes captured the transaction under market-share thresholds, and decided to refer the case to the European Commission in view of its cross-border effects[1].The referral mechanism also allows the notifying parties themselves to request that a case be referred. One such case was *Facebook/WhatsApp*[2]; again, the case met market-share thresholds in certain Member States and the parties requested the merger review to be referred to the EU Commission during the pre-notification phase.

For all competition matters, the European Competition Network (ECN) constitutes the main cooperation framework between the EU national competition authorities and the Commission for the enforcement of EU competition policy. It also provides a good forum for more informal but continuous cooperation.

In this context the ECN+ Directive – adopted on 11 January 2019, and to be transposed into national legislation of Member States by 4 February 2021 – will empower the competition authorities of Member States with the means to apply the rules on competition more effectively and guarantee the proper functioning of the internal market, helping to consolidate a level playing field through equivalent powers of enforcement of EU (and, consequently, national) competition law.

On a broader international level, both the OECD and the ICN have played a decisive role in facilitating cooperation between competition authorities, creating fertile forums for discussion and promotion of best practices.

Merger control in Latin America and the Caribbean will certainly benefit from closer cooperation between their competition authorities – either by sharing public information at different stages of an investigation, sharing theories of harm, obtaining appropriate waivers or studying the most suitable remedies to apply, or even adopting consistent best practices. Some of the merger control regimes in the region are quite young, and their authorities will certainly learn from the experience of more established ones. Getting to know and understand the characteristics, similarities or differences of other neighbouring regimes will help not only companies, but authorities as well, paving the way for consistent merger control in the region. To this end, this work I have the honour to introduce is a timely, useful and necessary tool: a thorough, practical and complete view provided by knowledgeable professionals of the actual status of merger control regimes in the region.

---

1 *Apple/Shazam* (Case M.8788) Commission Decision C(2018) 5748 final

2 (Case Comp/M.7217) Commission Decision C(2014) 7239 final.

Contributors

Cynthia Andino
Independent Consultant

Favio Batres P
BLP

Paula Bauer
C.R. & F. Rojas Abogados

Paulo Burnier da Silveira
OECD

Virginia Campás Alcalde
Creel, García-Cuéllar, Aiza y Enriquez

Vinicius Marques de Carvalho
Vinicius Marques de Carvalho Advogados

Camila Chamorro Poma
DiezCanseco

Luis Diez Canseco Núñez
DiezCanseco

Marvin Francisco Discua Singh
Commission for the Defence and Promotion of Competition

Alejandro Gallotti
LEĜA

Luis García Santos Coy
Creel, García-Cuéllar, Aiza y Enriquez

Marc Jones
CARICOM Competition Commission

Natalia Jul
Uruguayan Competition Authority

Luciana Macedo
Uruguayan Competition Authority

Pablo Márquez
Márquez Barrera Castañeda Ramírez

Marcela Mattiuzzo
Vinicius Marques de Carvalho Advogados

Carlos Mena Labarthe
Creel, García-Cuéllar, Aiza y Enriquez

Jorge Molina Mendoza
Fabrega Molino

Darío Morales Herrera
DiezCanseco

Angélica Noboa Págan
Noboa Pagán Abogados / Baker McKenzie

Ernesto Rizo Pallais
BLP

Diego Rojas
C.R. & F. Rojas Abogados

Maria Eduarda Scott
Vinicius Marques de Carvalho Advogados

Mauricio Serralde Rodríguez
Creel, García-Cuéllar, Aiza y Enriquez

Pamela Sittenfeld
Ministry of Trade of Costa Rica

David A. Sperber Vilhelm
AntiTrust Consultores & Abogados

Taimoon Stewart
The University of West Indies

Pablo Trevisán
IDC – Instituto de Derecho de la Competencia

Regina Vargas
Competition Authority of El Salvador

Uri Weinstok
BLP

Mario Ybar
Garrigues

TABLE OF CONTENTS

INTRODUCTION

Pamela Sittenfeld*

(Ministry of Trade of Costa Rica)

Paulo Burnier da Silveira**

(OECD)

---

* Pamela Sittenfeld is an attorney. She graduated from the Universidad de Costa Rica, and has an Msc in Regulation and Competition from the LSE in London. She is an adviser to the Ministry of Foreign Trade of Costa Rica, and coordinator of the national team in charge of presenting to the Competition Committee of the OECD in the accession process of Costa Rica. She has been a consultant for Central American companies and international organisations at the local law firm BLP. She was also a Professor of Competition Law at La Salle University, a member of the board of the National Regulator of Public Services (ARESEP) and the National Council for the Supervision of the Financial System (CONASSIF). She was also executive director of and legal adviser to the Costa Rican Commission to Promote Competition (COPROCOM).

** Paulo Burnier da Silveira is a Senior Competition Expert at the Organization for Economic Co-operation and Development (OECD) and a Visiting Professor at Sciences Po Paris. He is also a former Commissioner at the Brazilian Competition Authority (CADE), former chief editor of the Brazilian Competition Journal, and a Professor at the University of Brasilia (currently on leave). He holds a PhD from the University of Paris and has several publications in the field of competition law including *Global Competition Enforcement* (Kluwer 2019) and *Competition Law and Policy in Latin America* (Kluwer 2017).

This chapter intends to provide an overview of merger control in Latin America and the Caribbean. It also highlights the main particularities of merger control in the region and sheds light on the following 18 chapters of this book, which gather contributions from local competition experts.

I. Overview of Merger Control in the Region

As of 2020, there are **17 merger control regimes in Latin America**[1], in addition to **three merger control regimes in the Caribbean** countries[2]. This corresponds to around 20% of merger control regimes worldwide[3]. The table indicates the number and the year when these merger control regimes were first introduced in Latin America and the Caribbean[4]:

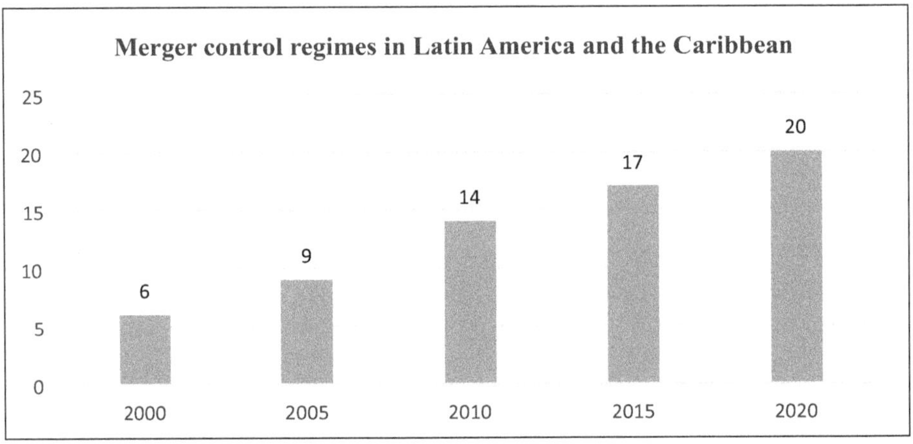

Source: Authors'contributions to this book

It is possible to note a sharp and recent increase in the number of merger control regimes in the region. Most countries have adopted their regime in the last 15 years. Until the beginning of this century, only Argentina, Brazil, Colombia, Costa Rica, Mexico and Panama had general merger control legislation[5].

1 Argentina, Bolivia, Brazil, Chile, Colombia, Costa Rica, Dominican Republic, Ecuador, El Salvador, Honduras, Mexico, Nicaragua, Panama, Paraguay, Peru, Uruguay and Venezuela.

2 Barbados, Trinidad & Tobago and Curaçao.

3 Estimations of total merger control regimes worldwide vary between 110 and 126 jurisdictions. See, for instance: Jones Day "Global Merger Control Update" (*Jones Day*, May 2017) <www.jonesday.com/en/insights/2017/05/global-merger-control-update> accessed 15 July 2020; Latham & Watkins, "Global Merger Regimes" (Latham & Watkins, 2020) <www.lw.com/bookofjargon-apps/global-merger-regimes> accessed 15 July 2020.

4 Jamaica was not included in the table, as it does not constitute a genuine merger control regime. Its merger control mechanism is rather based on an important precedent, which enables *ex post* merger control through the general provisions of anticompetitive practices.

5 In some countries, a merger control system existed for certain sectors, often based on a specific legislation of that sector. This is, for instance, the case in Peru, in which merger control was limited to the electricity sector since 1997 until 2019.

Moreover, there are currently draft laws under discussion in certain jurisdictions, which indicates a possible increase in the number of merger control regimes in the next few years[6]. One should also note that Jamaica has a de facto merger control mechanism based on an interesting precedent from 2017, in which the Jamaican Fair Trading Commission applied its general prohibition of anticompetitive practices to review a merger[7].

These numbers indicate the importance of understanding merger control in Latin America and the Caribbean, in particular for global transactions that may trigger the notification thresholds in many of these jurisdictions.

The following chapters of this book offer a detailed explanation of the merger control regime in each of these jurisdictions, so this introduction will rather focus on certain common features and particularities of merger control in the region.

II. Particularities of Merger Control in the Region

1. *Evolution From Ex Post to Ex Ante Regimes*

Many jurisdictions of the region have started with an *ex post* merger control regime, then shifted to an *ex ante* merger control regime in a moment. This happened, for instance, in Argentina (*ex post* in 1999, then *ex ante* in 2019), Brazil (*ex post* in 1994, *ex ante* in 2012), Chile (*ex post* in 2004, *ex ante* in 2016), Uruguay (*ex post* in 2007, *ex ante* in 2020), and Costa Rica (*ex post* in 1994, *ex ante* in 2012).

As of 2020, some Latin American jurisdictions have an *ex post* regime, which may be shifted to an *ex ante* regime in the future. This is the case, for example, in Panama, Paraguay and Venezuela. Jamaica also has a de facto regime based on *ex post* assessments. In addition, Curaçao has an *ex post* notification system in which transactions exceeding certain thresholds must be notified. However, it does not constitute a proper system of merger control since the purpose of these notifications is merely to monitor concentrations and their effects[8].

This shift seems a natural evolution for merger control regimes since pre-merger (*ex ante*) systems require much greater resources, including budget and staff. The current effort of Peru, which has recently adopted a pre-merger control legislation expected to take effect in March 2021, is an example of the resources required to manage a pre-merger

---

6 For instance, there are draft laws that contain merger control provisions in the Bahamas, Belize and Suriname.

7 The case was then confirmed by the Privy Council of the United Kingdom, which still serves as the final court of judicial review in Jamaica. Case ID JCPC 2016/0059, *Fair Trading Commission v Digicel Jamaica Limited and another* [2017] UKPC 28.

8 Pursuant to Article 5.2 of the Curaçao Competition Act (Landsverordening inzake concurrentie, a concentration of undertakings (in the meaning of Article 5.1 of the CCA) is subject to notification where (i) the combined worldwide turnover of the parties involved in the previous calendar year exceeded ANG 125 million (approximately €60 million) and (ii) at least two of the parties achieved a turnover in Curaçao of ANG 15 million (approximately €7 million) or more in the previous calendar year. A concentration must also be notified if as a result thereof the parties involved would create or reinforce a market share of 30% or more on any of the relevant markets in Curaçao.

review system. The Peruvian INDECOPI has indeed increased budget and hired staff to be dedicated exclusively to the new pre-merger control regime.

At the same time, this transition from *ex post* to *ex ante* regimes also seems adequate to prepare both competition authorities and the local private sector to the principles and benefits of a merger control. Companies should see merger control as an additional tool to assure fair competition and maintain a level playing field in their countries, rather than a burden imposed to local business.

2. *Special Provisions to Certain Economic Sectors*

Another feature that deserves highlighting concerns the frequent existence of special provisions to certain sectors of the economy. This may take the form of an exemption from merger control legislation or a specific framework for merger review in certain sectors. At least seven jurisdictions have special provisions. They concern mostly the telecoms and finance sectors.

In Mexico, the telecoms sector is subject to exclusive review of a specific competition authority, the Instituto Federal de Telecomunicaciones (IFT). The IFT has exclusive competence to oversee and promote competition in the telecommunications and broadcasting sectors in Mexico, including merger review. The Comisión Federal de Competencia Económica (COFECE) remains the main competition authority of the country, competent to review mergers in other sectors of the economy. Similarly, Costa Rica also has a specific merger control regime for telecommunications. Whereas the Superintendencia de Telecomunicaciones (SUTEL) enforces competition rules in the telecoms sector, including merger control, the Comisión para Promover la Competencia (COPROCOM) remains the main competition authority for the rest of the economy.

In Colombia, the aeronautical and finance sectors also have special provisions related to merger control. The Superintendencia de Industria y Comercio (SIC), the Colombian competition authority, has a complementary and not mandatory power in the financial sector, and no powers to review certain types of transactions in the aeronautical sector. In both sectors, SIC may provide a non-binding opinion to sector regulators who retain the final word to authorise these transactions.

In the Dominican Republic, merger control is limited to telecoms (since 2005) and energy (since 2002). It does not exist as a general regime for the rest of the economy. Likewise, in Bolivia, merger control is limited to certain regulated sectors. The following sectorial legislations have merger control provisions: electricity law, telecommunications law, hydrocarbons law, bank and financial institutions law, and insurance law. Merger control does not exist for the rest of the economy. In Peru, merger control was limited to the electricity sector (since 1997). The new merger control legislation, expected to take effect in March 2021, expands merger control to the entire economy.

Trinidad and Tobago has a general merger control regime, but the financial and telecoms sectors are exempt from its application, and therefore they are not submitted to a competition-based review. Similarly, in Nicaragua the competition authority (PROCOMPETENCIA) plays a limited role in mergers within regulated sectors, issuing only a non-binding opinion to the sector regulator that makes the determination in all such cases.

3. Tailored Provisions Related to Small Economies

Most of the jurisdictions of the region are small countries and have a relatively small economy. Only Brazil and Mexico have a Gross Domestic Product (GDP) larger than US$ 1 trillion. As for the size of the population, only Brazil, Mexico, Colombia, Argentina, Peru and Venezuela have more than 20 million people each.

This is a feature of the region and might explain some elements contained in their legislation, including merger control laws. One example concerns the type and the levels of thresholds for merger notification.

Although international best practices indicate a preference for notification criteria based on the annual turnover of the merging parties, many jurisdictions from the region still contain a criterion based on market share – either solely or alternatively. Indeed, this seems to be also present in other small countries across the globe such as Israel and Portugal.

The market-share criterion for merger notification is thus present, in some shape or form, in several jurisdictions of the region including: Barbados, Ecuador, Nicaragua, Paraguay, Honduras, and Uruguay (until 2019).

Panama also has an interesting merger control regime, which reflects its size, priorities and trade policy. The country has a small economy and it is highly dependent in the commercial activities related to the Panama Canal, including banking and tourism. The merger control is carried out by the judicial branch based on an *ex post* review, and the notification of transactions is not mandatory. Nevertheless, merging parties may choose to notify the Autoridad de Protección al Consumidor y Defensa de la Competencia (ACODECO) on a voluntary basis, in order to seek a formal clearance know by the procedure of *verification*. A favourable opinion from ACODECO means that the transaction cannot be challenged before the judiciary, providing thus an incentive for a voluntary notification even if no sanction is applied in case of non-notification.

4. Procedural Differences in Assessing Simple Transactions

Last, there are procedural differences when comparing the merger control regimes of the region, including nuances while assessing simple transactions.

Only a few jurisdictions, such as Argentina, Brazil, Colombia and Mexico, have fast-track procedures to review simple transactions. Costa Rica does not have such procedural option, but the legislation allows for secondary regulations to list the circumstances in which a case will have a presumption of not negatively affecting the market. This presumption, depending on how the authority applies it, can have similar effects to a fast-track proceeding.

Furthermore, other procedural difference may be observed in relation to the existence of a formal distinction between phase 1 and phase 2. While some jurisdictions have a two-phased procedure, which allows a faster approval of certain cases (i.e. Argentina, Chile, Colombia, Costa Rica and Nicaragua), other jurisdictions do not make this procedural distinction (i.e. Brazil, Honduras and Panama).

These procedural distinctions seem particularly important to consider for the coordination of transnational mergers, when notifiable to several competition authorities of the region. Of course, the competition impacts of a given transnational transaction may vary from one jurisdiction to another, with consequences for the use of the fast-track proceedings, as well as phase 1 and phase 2 when applicable.

III. Future Perspectives

An increase of case law in the region will likely take place in the next few years, adding to legal certainly in merger review and to the overall expertise of competition authorities across the region. In fact, the current backlog of case law remains relatively low in the region, despite of the increasing number of merger control regimes. One reason for this is that merger legislations require time to be implemented, often depending on a governmental decree and additional regulations. This is precisely the case of Uruguay, which lacks enforcement track record and still awaits internal regulations to apply merger control in practice.

Another reason that may also explain the low number of cases relates to current notification thresholds, which seem quite low in certain jurisdictions. Nicaragua, El Salvador, and Paraguay, for example, only reviewed two transactions each in 2019, which suggest that the bar is set relatively high for notification. In any case, time will likely enable jurisdictions from the region to increase their backlog of merger cases, adding to legal certainly and overall expertise in these competition agencies.

This feature of merger control in the region also offers an opportunity for regional cooperation in the next few years. In this context, Brazil, Colombia and Mexico emerge as the main jurisdictions of the region in terms of merger control experience and corresponding case law. Brazil, Colombia and Mexico, for instance, review hundreds of transactions every year, which give them a sufficient enforcement experience to share with neighbour countries from the region if needed. In addition, supranational merger control regimes still seem far to take form in practice, but some initiatives raise this topic as a possible future development, in particular within the Caribbean Community (CARICOM).

Furthermore, most legislation of the region establishes general standards for merger review, including the prohibition of transactions that result in "anticompetitive effects" or similar expressions. These expressions leave room for interpretation to competition authorities, who often hold dissimilar views on the substance including in relation to theories of harm. In this context, a greater convergence in the substantive analysis would be welcome in future years, in particular vis-à-vis the smaller and less experienced competition authorities of the region.

Last, another area of potential development concerns digital filings of merger transactions. This is already a reality in Brazil and Mexico, where practitioners may electronically complete a merger notification. Chile has also adopted an online filing system during the Covid-19 crisis. This may become a trend around the world, including in Latin America and the Caribbean. The restrictions imposed by the Covid-19 crisis may also intensify this process of digitalisation of merger control in the region.

ARGENTINA

Pablo Trevisán*
(IDC – Instituto de Derecho de la Competencia)

Abstract

Did everything change so nothing changes? Argentina's merger control system was substantially reformed in May 2018. Since then, that question resonates insistently: did everything change so that nothing changes? The new Competition Law 27,442 (LDC) established in 2018 a real pre-merger control system, in order to properly align the incentives and objectives of this type of control. Unfortunately, the LDC established a transition period that will last up to one year after the coming into operation of the new National Competition Authority (ANC). As long as the transition period lasts, Argentina will continue to have an ex post control system that, as a result of some regulation of the law that violates the spirit of the LDC, will also probably be the most ex post system of all the merger control systems in the antitrust world. The ANC, as at the date of writing, has not yet been designated. Everything is yet to be seen.

---

* Pablo Trevisán is the founder of the IDC – Instituto de Derecho de la Competencia. Until February 2020, he was Commissioner of the Argentine Competition Authority (CNDC). Drafter of the Argentine Competition Act 27,442, enacted in May 2018.

I. Introduction

1. Brief Overview

The defence of competition has constitutional status in Argentina, which derives from several of the National Constitution provisions and declarations of rights and guarantees but, in particular, by the provisions of section 42 of the National Constitution that establishes that the authorities will provide "for the defence of competition against any kind of market distortion" and "to the control of natural and legal monopolies".

Argentina has had some kind of competition law for almost a century. In 1923, the first antitrust law was enacted following the model of the US Sherman Act. That law was amended in 1946. Neither of them had a significant application.

In 1980, the first comprehensive competition law was introduced through Law 22,262, which created the National Commission for the Defence of Competition (CNDC) and established criminal penalties. An important reform took place in 1999, through the enactment of Law 25,156, which created an independent authority, the Tribunal of Defence of Competition (TDC) – which never came into operation – and introduced a merger control system in Argentina. An unfortunate reform took place in 2014, through Law 26,993, which abolished the TDC and introduced some inconvenient reforms to Law 25,156.

The new Competition Law 27,442[1] (LDC) was passed on 9 May 2018. On 23 May, the Executive Branch promulgated the LDC through Decree 480/2018[2]. The LDC entered into force on 25 May 2018[3].

The new LDC introduces important changes and, without a doubt, constitutes the main reform of the Argentine antitrust system of recent decades. As a result of these changes, our country once again has solid legislation on the matter. Among the most important changes, the following should be highlighted:

a) Better and greater institutionalism, through (i) the creation of a new authority, the National Competition Authority (ANC), more independent and with renewed powers, and (ii) the creation of a specialised chamber in defence of competition within the Federal Court of Appeals on Civil and Commercial Matters for judicial review of the ANC's decisions.
b) Greater deterrence towards anticompetitive behaviours, through (i) the updating and significant increase of the applicable sanctions, with a more burdensome criteria for determining them than those established by its predecessor, Law 25,156; (ii) the creation of a modern leniency programme; and (iii) the establishment of new standards for the repair of damages caused as a result of anticompetitive behaviour.

---

1 LDC, Law 27,442 *<http://servicios.infoleg.gob.ar/infolegInternet/anexos/310000-314999/310241/norma.htm>* accessed 30 November 2019.

2 Decree 480/2018 *<http://servicios.infoleg.gob.ar/infolegInternet/anexos/310000-314999/310663/norma.htm>*, accessed 30 November 2019.

3 See Pablo Trevisán, *Defensa de la Competencia: Nullius in Verba,* RDCO 292 (Thomson Reuters La Ley 2018), 527, for a detailed description of the drafting and discussion of Law 27,442.

c) Greater optimisation of resources, through (i) the establishment of a real pre-merger control system, which shall properly align the incentives and objectives of this type of control; and (ii) updating and improvement to the method of calculating the notification thresholds of said concentrations, which will allow the ANC to concentrate its efforts only on those operations that may really have an impact on the general economic interest, also allowing it to concentrate efforts in the fight against anticompetitive behaviour.

The LDC is the product of great efforts and political consensus[4], being the best possible law that our country could have in its current economic – political context and in the state of development of the matter.

For future discussions, questions will remain as if it would be advisable to reinstate specific criminal sanctions for certain anticompetitive behaviours in our country[5]; or if the institutional design[6] should enjoy greater independence from the central administration, to name two issues that probably deserve further treatment and analysis in the near future.

The rationale of the Argentine merger control is to prevent mergers that may result, with high probability, in a detriment to the general economic interest. Section 8 of the LDC[7] establishes that an economic concentration, the object or effect of which is or could be to restrict or distort competition, out of which damage to the general economic interest may result, shall be prohibited.

Legal sources for merger control in Argentina are the LDC, Decree 480/2018[8], Resolution 359/2018 of the Secretary of Commerce[9], Resolution 26/2006 of former Secretary of Technical Coordination[10], and Resolution 40/2001 of former Secretary of Competition and Consumer Defence[11], which provide the procedural regulation for merger control. The applicable thresholds are determined annually by the ANC, currently the secretary of interior commerce; and its last determination was published on 28 January 2020, which established the Mobile Unit (UM) at ARS 40.61. The secretary of commerce issued the "Guidelines for Merger Control Proceedings", on 11 April 2018.

---

4 Pablo Trevisán, "Rebuilding the Argentine Antitrust House While Living in It: A View from the Trenches", in Nicolas Charbit, Carolina Malhado and Ellie Yang (eds), *Douglas H Ginsburg, An Antitrust Professor on the Bench – Liber Amicorum Volume I* (Institute of Competition Law 2018).

5 Opinion favourable to their incorporation in the LDC is anticipated. In fact, the first draft of the LDC, under the responsibility of this author, included prison sanctions for up to three years, for cases of cartelisation in public tenders, but incorporation into the LDC was not accepted.

6 There are several models of antitrust agency around the world, some more independent than others. We consider with special interest the Chilean model, where the investigating authority, the National Economic Prosecutor's Office, is located within the orbit of the executive, whereas the ruling body, the Tribunal, it is outside the executive, its resolutions being appealable to the Supreme Court of Justice of Chile.

7 LDC, n 1.

8 See n 2.

9 Resolution 359/2018, *<http://servicios.infoleg.gob.ar/infolegInternet/anexos/310000-314999/311717/norma.htm>*.

10 Resolution 26/2006, *<http://servicios.infoleg.gob.ar/infolegInternet/anexos/115000-119999/118103/norma.htm>*.

11 Resolution 40/2001, *<http://servicios.infoleg.gob.ar/infolegInternet/anexos/65000-69999/66243/norma.htm>*.

2. Institutional Set-Up

The institutional system is one of the main innovations of the LDC[12]. It created the ANC, an autarchic authority within the scope of the executive power, which will replace the current two-tier system of the CNDC and the secretary of interior commerce.

The ANC will be formed by the Tribunal for the Defence of Competition, as a collegiate decision-making body, and two secretariats, one for conducts and one for concentrations, who will investigate the cases. Each will have a term of five years, and the renewals would be staggered.

The system by which the members of the ANC will be elected is transparent and contains all necessary elements to preclude the possibility of arbitrary appointments or appointments of members that may be considered to be accommodating to political power.

The selection process of the ANC's members went through and was almost completed during 2019, until the Executive Power informed its proposed candidate. After the change of government in Argentina in December 2019, the new elected president decided to withdraw from the Senate the candidates proposed by his predecessor. At the time of writing, it is not clear which will be the fate of the new ANC.

It is worth mentioning here the importance that the appropriate institutional design has in the due process that must be respected by a competition law authority. The history and the legal, political and economic culture of a country will play a leading role in deciding the institutional model of a competition authority[13].

But there are some specific deficiencies, common to certain institutional designs, that provide grounds to identify other options that can contribute to improving performance and the sense of legitimacy. Some of the problems attributable to institutional design are manifested in due process and institutional performance.

In general terms, we can say that there are three basic models of competition agency worldwide: (i) the bifurcated judicial model, where the competition authority has to go to court for the application of antitrust law, for example, the US Department of Justice; (ii) the bifurcated agency court model, where the authority goes to a specialised court for enforcement, as in Canada, South Africa and Chile; and (iii) the integrated agency model, where a commission within the agency performs the first level of adjudication, for example, the European Commission, US Federal Trade Commission (FTC) or the Argentine CNDC, among others.

Integrated institutions, such as the European Commission and the US FTC, raise concerns that the integration of investigation, enforcement and adjudication functions creates bias or lack of objectivity, or the appearance of it. The integration of these functions can cause agencies to be considered "judges in their own cause".

---

12 Luis Berenguer, *Voluntary Peer Review of Competition Law and Policy – Argentina*, UNCTAD 28, 2017.

13 Eleanor M Fox and Michael J Trebilcock, *The Design of Competition Law Institutions* (OUP 2013) 4; the authors explain, and we agree, that there should be no preconceptions of a better model for effective and procedurally fair systems of enforcement of competition rules.

There are ways by which these concerns can be and have been addressed. In this sense, the new LDC establishes that the ANC will have separate investigative functions from the decision and adjudication functions, through the creation of two separate secretariats, which will investigate conducts and economic concentrations, respectively, and a tribunal, which will decide the cases.

Ideally, the decision-maker in a competition authority should be legally independent of the investigator. Without a separation to maintain the distance between the investigative and decision-making functions, the official conducting the investigation would be required to determine if his or her efforts have been successful or if their existence is justified.

Related to this, we consider that Decree 972/2018 – when establishing different ranks and hierarchies among the members of the ANC – incurred a serious error. The potential for an unfair result is evident, if the referred provision under Decree 972/2018 is not modified, since those who investigate would have lower ranks than those who resolve, resulting in the former having some dependence on the latter, something undesired by the LDC and going against the spirit and institutional design projected under the LDC. This increases the risk that competition authorities can weigh the ends over the means, especially when the ends are measured in the total annual fines that enter the treasury of the government on duty[14].

It is also worth mentioning that the LDC created a specialised court of appeals that will decide on competition cases. Such court, the Specialized Chamber on Competition Issues, would work as one of the chambers of the Federal Civil and Commercial Court of Appeals. The objective is to have specialised judges on antitrust and competition law cases.

3. Type of Merger Control

Under reasonable merger control systems, agencies can carry out an *ex ante* control, that is, prior to the completion of the operation. The central idea is that blocking or restoring competition once an anticompetitive concentration has been carried out is, like when trying to unscramble the eggs, too complex, if not impossible.

The problem with a control system that works *ex post* – as in practice happened in Argentina, the product of a misapplication of section 8 of Law 25,156 and other systemic failures, such as the direct and indirect consequences of never putting in place the independent tribunal created in 1999 – is that it introduces a large part of the costs and eliminates, to a large extent, the benefits of a preventive or *ex ante* prospective procedure, making the procedure less attractive and inefficient, and in many cases useless.

Under a genuine *ex ante* control system, the parties have important incentives to cooperate, since the delay in providing the relevant information to the agency runs at their expense, as until the competition authority's approval is issued, the transaction in question

---

14 J Mark Gidley and Maxwell J Hyman, "The Emergence of Due Process following the Growth of International Antitrust Enforcement" (Concurrences Conference on Antitrust in Emerging and Developing Countries, NYU, October 2015).

cannot close or consummate. That is, the companies involved pay for any delay resulting from lack of information and full collaboration with the enforcement authority.

In an *ex post* control system, costs increase and delays in procedures are frequent, largely because there are no necessary incentives for the procedure to conclude in a short time, thus increasing private costs and, worse, the public costs of an *ex post* control procedure.

One of the main benefits, then, is to prevent anticompetitive concentrations by preserving the status quo prior to the concentration, a situation that is not verified with the possible high costs that adopting structural remedies would imply – after the consummation of the transaction under analysis – which can be costly for the parties and society in general. After the firms are integrated, it would be costly, if not impossible, to impose a structural remedy after, for example, the closure of a factory, the discontinuity of production of certain products, the joint use of distribution networks or any other of these measures that might be impossible to roll back.

We believe that under the new LDC, prior to the establishment of a full *ex ante* merger control, two serious avoidable errors have been committed:

The first consists of the introduction of a transitory scheme of subsistence, until one year after the start of operations of the new ANC[15] of an even more *ex post* system[16] than the previous merger control system applicable under Law 25,156.

In this regard, we consider that there were no sufficient or well-founded reasons to include such a scheme in the new LDC. During the discussion of LDC's draft bill, some voices argued that the inclusion of said transitory regime was necessary, due to the long resolution times of merger control cases of the enforcement authority under the previous Law 25,156. On the contrary, we repeatedly sustained that it was important to make an immediate change, leaving aside the harmful *ex post* control, and turn to a real *ex ante* control, considering that the conditions were absolutely given for it.

In sustaining this, we indicated two factual arguments that are absolutely verifiable: one, what happened in Brazil, whose economy is significantly larger than that of Argentina, and where, at the time of the reform of its merger control system in 2012 towards an *ex ante* system, their statistics and experiences were very similar to those of Argentina in 2015; and, mainly, what happened in Argentina between the end of 2015 and May 2018, when the new law was passed.

In Brazil, despite the ominous warnings from an important part of the Brazilian business sector at that time, from 2012 onwards the Brazilian competition authority managed to significantly reduce the times of its merger control processes, to the point that – to date – Brazil has a review average for this type of cases of no more than 25 days, from beginning to end, comparable to the best international practices.

---

15 LDC, s 81: "The regulation of this law shall establish the conditions under which the processing of the files initiated shall continue under the terms established in chapter III of Law 25,156."

16 As we comment further afterwards, due to other issues introduced by Section 84 of Decree 480/2018, the current transitional merger review system is definitely an ex post control system, while under the former Law 25,156, although it has been understood as mostly ex post in practice, there was always an open and not defined discussion due to the wording and reach of Section 8 of Law 25,156.

On the other hand, in Argentina, even under the application of Law 25,156, whose thresholds were absolutely out of date, the enforcement authority managed to very significantly reduce the review periods for these procedures: from an average of more than three and a half years, in December 2015, to an average of just over six months, in December 2019.

That is, like Brazil in 2012 but with the advantage that it had already significantly improved the indicators before sanctioning the new LDC, Argentina was already prepared to go directly to an *ex ante* control, without the need for a transitional *ex post* regime.

Secondly, and – unnecessarily – complicating matters even more, Decree 480/2018 introduces, through the last sentence of its section 84, a change that may have gone unnoticed by some but that further deepens the issue by suspending the application of the third paragraph of section 9 of Law 27,442[17]. Beyond considering that in this point Decree 480/2018 may have exceeded its scope by modifying a law promulgated by the National Congress, in practice, it means that in Argentina – and until a year after the new ANC is put in place – we will have an *ex post* merger control system as never seen in our country, with all the previously mentioned inconvenience. Based on the provisions of section 84 of the Decree, the notifying parties, without doubt, may from then on not only close transactions, but also consummate them, previously and independently of the intervention of the competition authority. An unnecessary absurdity, in our opinion.

Under the previous legislation, Law 25,156, it was provided that the notification could be filed up to a week after the takeover of the company in question. *Contrario sensu* of the recurrent interpretation made by the enforcement authority in this point, we have always maintained[18] that the wording of the first paragraph of section 8 of Law 25,156 was procedural in nature, and indicated when the procedural formality should be complied with to notify a concentration transaction. However, the second sentence of section 8, which was of a substantive nature, provided that the operation brought to the attention of the enforcement authority could not have an effect between the parties and with respect to third parties until the authority resolves in this regard. That is, although under an unfortunate wording, former Law 25,156 allowed the closure of the operation prior to notification, but, in light of the second sentence of section 8, it did not allow the consummation of such operation, until the authority's resolution.

Regrettably, even though the intention of the LDC is clearly to go towards an *ex ante* concentration control, during the transition phase an *ex post* control will be applied that is extremely more *ex post* than the position that existed during the validity of Law 25,156. Undoubtedly, we consider that this will be one of the main immediate challenges that will have to be dealt with under the new LDC, until the ANC is put into operation and the *ex ante* control is fully operational.

---

17 LDC, s 9, third paragraph: "The acts of economic concentration that are concluded in breach of the provisions of this section, as well as the consummation of the takeover without the prior approval of the Competition Tribunal, shall be sanctioned by said Tribunal as an infraction, under the terms of section 55, paragraph d) of this law, without prejudice to the obligation to reverse them and remove all its effects in the case in which it is determined that it has been reached by the prohibition of section 8 of this law."

18 Pablo Trevisán, "Rebuilding the Argentine Antitrust House While Living in It: A View from the Trenches", *Douglas H. Ginsburg | An Antitrust Professor on the Bench – Liber Amicorum – Volume I*, 2018.

II. Scope of Application

1. Definition of Notifiable Transaction

Pursuant to section 7 of the LDC, transactions would be considered to be economic concentrations subject to LDC's merger control regime, when the following acts would take control of one or several companies: (a) the merger between companies; (b) the transfer of goodwill; (c) the acquisition of the property or any right over shares or capital shares or debt securities that give any type of right to be converted into shares or capital shares or to have any type of influence in the decisions of the person who issues them when such acquisition grants the acquirer control of, or substantial influence over itself; (d) any other agreement or act that transfer the assets of a company in a factual or legal manner to a person or economic group or gives it decisive influence in the decision-making of ordinary or extraordinary administration of a company; (e) any of the acts of subparagraph c) above, that implies the acquisition of substantial influence in the competitive strategy of a company.

2. Material Scope

LDC's rules of merger control apply to all economic sectors and activities, without exemptions. This iswithout prejudice to other possible authorisations that might be required by certain sector regulators (e.g., ENACOM in the communications sector, CNV in the capital markets sector, BCRA in the banking sector, etc.).

3. Geographical Scope

Pursuant to its section 4, the LDC follows an effect-based approach. Therefore, economic concentrations that may produce effects in Argentina or involve parties who had sales in Argentina are subject to merger control by the ANC.

4. Thresholds

In accordance with section 9 of the LDC, acts indicated in section 7, when the sum of the total business volume of the group of affected companies exceeds in the country a sum equivalent to 100 million UM, must be notified to the ANC for examination.

Pursuant to section 11(e) of the LDC, certain transactions would be exempt from the section 9 notification, when the amount of the operation and the value of the assets located in Argentina that are absorbed, acquired, transferred or controlled, do not exceed, each of them, respectively, a sum equivalent to 20 million UM, except that within the previous 12-month period their overall operations would have exceeded said amount, or the sum equivalent to 60 million UMs during the last 36 months, provided that in both cases it is the same market.

As mentioned above, the thresholds are annually determined by the ANC, through the determination of the value of each UM (at the time of writing, each UM equals ARS 40.61).

III. Procedure

1. Launch of Procedure

As mentioned above, the LDC established a pre-merger control, but also a transitional period that will continue to apply the former *ex post* system, until a year after the new authority (i.e., the ANC) is operational.

Consequently, during the transitional period, a notification has to be filed in advance or no later than a week after the takeover of the company in question.

The parties are responsible for making the notification, although the seller's notification is non-mandatory, unless the ANC expressly requests the seller's participation in the proceedings.

The LDC establishes that certain transactions would go through a fast-track procedure. Although regulation of this accelerated procedure is still pending, the CNDC has been applying an *ex officio* fast-track procedure since 2016, which – in general terms – applies to most conglomerate transactions and to those transactions where joint market shares would not exceed 20%, among others.

The LDC provides that the parties might have to pay a filing fee that would range from 5,000 to 20,000 UM. The fee has not yet been established, so – at the time of writing – no fee currently applies, in practical terms.

Resolution 40/2001[19], passed by the former Secretary of Competition and Consumer Defence, regulates the content of the notification and the respective forms that need to be complied with during the procedure.

The investigation file is kept accessible only to the notifying parties. The decision of the ANC is public, although the parties may request and/or the ANC may order that certain parts of the file be deemed confidential[20]. Section 13 of the LDC establishes that the regulation must provide a procedure so that each act of economic concentration notified to the ANC takes public status and any interested party may formulate the manifestations and oppositions that it deems appropriate. If there are oppositions, they must be notified to the notifying parties.

2. Development of Procedure

The merger regulation entails two phases. The LDC establishes that the ANC must decide within 45 business days of the notification of the respective transaction (Phase 1). Notwithstanding, in practice and until the ANC in operation, it is worth mentioning that the CNDC makes several interruptions of the terms during the merger control proceedings, resulting in much longer terms applied to the files until the CNDC

---

19 Resolution 40/2001, <*http://servicios.infoleg.gob.ar/infolegInternet/anexos/65000-69999/66243/norma.htm*>.

20 Notwithstanding the fact that the Fiscalía Nacional Económica (FNE) from Chile can order, either *ex officio* or at the request of the interested party, that certain parts of the file be deemed confidential.

issues its opinion, followed by the final resolution of the case by the Secretariat of Commerce (SCI).

Should the notified transaction raise concerns, in accordance with section 14 of the LDC, the ANC (i.e., the CNDC/SCI during the transitional period) should issue a Statement of Objections and summon the parties for a special hearing to consider eventual remedies to the objections raised by the ANC. The time to resolve, in these cases, is extended for up to 120 additional business days (Phase 2).

In order to share information with foreign competition authorities, the ANC requires waivers from the merging parties.

The notifying parties can submit to the ANC an offer of mitigation measures that they deem appropriate to mitigate the competition risks at any time of the investigation.

3. Conclusion of Procedure

In accordance with section 14 of the LDC, the ANC may:

a) Authorise the concentration, unconditionally;
b) Authorise the concentration, subject to conditions that the ANC may establish; or
c) Reject the authorisation of the concentration, when it considers that it harms the general economic interest.

Section 66 of the LDC establishes that decisions issued by the ANC may be judicially reviewed when they impose a conditional authorisation or reject the authorisation of the economic concentration subject to merger control. The appeal must be filed and reasoned within 15 days after the resolution of the ANC is notified to the parties.

Unfortunately, the ANC lacks a special unit in charge of monitoring compliance with its decisions and, in particular, remedies or conditions that might be imposed to the notifying parties[21].

4. Sanctions

Those who do not comply with the provisions of section 9 (i.e., gun-jumping – when the full pre-merger system enters into force – and/or late filing) will be liable to a fine of a daily sum of up to 0.1% of the consolidated turnover at national level registered by the economic group to which offenders belong, during the last financial year. In case the previous criterion cannot be applied, the fine may be up to a sum equivalent to 750,000 UM per day.

Also, the ANC may impose daily fines of 500 UM to those who obstruct or hinder an investigation or do not comply with the requirements of the ANC.

---

21 See Pablo Trevisán, "Argentina" in Ronan P Harty and Nathan Kiratzis (eds), *GCR Insight, Merger Remedies Guide* (Law Business Research 2019), 181, for further analysis on this specific issue.

IV. Substance

1. Competition Analysis

The criteria of the substantive test for merger control is stated under section 8 of the LDC, that establishes that economic concentrations whose object or effect is or may be to restrict or distort competition, so that it may be detrimental to the general economic interest, are prohibited.

There are no specific provisions under the LDC regarding non-competition issues or specific elements of public interest that must be analysed by the ANC.

The traditional analysis criteria used by the ANC (i.e., CNDC/SCI until the ANC is operational) would be similar to the following: determination of the relevant markets affected, estimate of the market shares of the market participants, concentration indexes, assessment of entry conditions, determination of unilateral and coordinated risks for competitions, and their counterbalancing factors – mainly efficiencies.

The Guidelines for Control of Economic Concentrations, published under Resolution 208/2018 of the Secretary of Commerce, state that the existence of efficiency gains and the impact that these have on the consumers of Argentina may determine that a concentration does not harm the general economic interest, although it may increase the probability of exercising market power.

2. Statistics

During 2019, 93 merger control investigations were resolved:

a) 46 of them were subject to the simplified procedure.
b) All the concentrations were unconditionally approved.

3. Case Law Illustration

Cablevisión – Telecom[22]

No doubt the most relevant concentration case in recent years was the merger between Telecom Argentina SA and Cablevisión SA, mainly due to the size of the companies involved, the amount of the operation, and the general concern aroused by the integration of two of the main companies that make up the communications sector in Argentina.

The transaction was implemented as absorption of Cablevisión by Telecom, although in fact the controlling group of the new integrated company became the one that, prior to the operation, controlled Cablevisión (that is, the Clarín Group). This gave the Telecom service portfolio a series of new commercial activities, such as the provision of

---

22 See Resolución RESOL-2018-374-APN-SECC#MP, 29/06/2018, in re Cablevisión SA, Cablevisión Holding SA, Telecom Argentina SA, Fintech Media LLC y Fintech Telecom LLC S/Notificación Art.8 Ley No 25.156 (CONC. 1507). Available at <*https://www.argentina.gob.ar/sites/default/files/resolucion_y_dictamen.pdf*>.

pay-TV, and made the merged entity the first Argentine company with the capacity to offer extensive service packages of the type "quad play", which includes fixed telephony, mobile telephony, internet and subscription television.

The case was decided by a divided vote, with a majority vote by four commissioners and a minority vote by one commissioner[23]. The markets in which a greater horizontal overlap was detected and, consequently, with greater competition problems generated by the merger, were a series of local markets for fixed broadband internet service, in which the operation left an important set of customers without alternative independent providers.

The CNDC's majority vote considered this occurred essentially in a set of 29 locations, in which Telecom was the almost exclusive provider of fixed telephony, Cablevisi6n was the leading provider of cable television, and the networks of both companies were virtually the only ones that could be used to offer access to residential broadband internet customers.

To alleviate the competition problems in the mentioned locations, the parties presented a structural commitment, for which they committed to transfer a total of 143,464 residential customers from the residential internet service previously provided by Telecom (through of its Arnet brand) to an independent provider (the company Universo Net SA), which already had a background as a provider of cable television and internet in other locations. The customers' transfer was complemented by the assignment of the right of use of the Arnet brand in the localities involved, and the physical access to the Telecom network (which was the one used to access the customers in question, and that Telecom would continue to use concomitantly to provide fixed telephone service).

The provider that would take care of the divestment services was a company belonging to the so-called "Valentini Group". The referred group presented to the CNDC its background as a provider of telecommunications and broadcasting services, as well as its business plan and the contracts signed between Universo Net and Telecom that, among other things, intended to ensure the provision of the service with a certain level of quality, and to deploy an alternative fibre-optic network.

From the analysis of the information provided by Telecom and Universo Net, the majority vote of the CNDC concluded that the Valentini Group had the necessary experience, economic capacity and knowledge to perform as an effective telecoms competitor in the locations in which it was entering, so the majority of the CNDC approved the structural commitment as presented.

The minority vote of the CNDC, on the contrary, considered that the operation under study could be included in the prohibition of section 7 of Law 25,156, and that the commitments offered were not sufficient to clear doubts regarding their potential to restrict competition and generate damage to the general economic interest.

The minority vote considered that the remedy offered by the parties was neither effective, nor suitable or proportionate, among other issues, due to the indirect corporate relationship

---

23 This author was a commissioner at CNDC at the time this case was decided and voted for the minority.

that existed between Valentini Group and Clarín Group, as both economic groups had been long-term partners in a cable-television operating company, CV Berazategui, in Berazategui (Buenos Aires province) even until some months after the Telecom/Cablevisión transaction was closed and notified to the CNDC. The minority vote also highlighted some problems in the agreement proposed by the parties, which made it difficult to produce a true "competition in quality of services" between Telecom and Universo Net.

A second sector in which the CNDC detected possible competition problems was that of mobile telephony, in which Telecom (through its Personal brand) had a nationwide market share of just over 31%, while Cablevisión (through its Nextel brand) owned a share of approximately 3%. Although in the market in question there are two large additional suppliers with high market shares (AMX, through its Claro brand, with a market share of 34%, and Telefónica, through its Movistar brand, with a market share of 32%), the main problem of competition in this case had to do with the great increase that occurred in the concentration of the radio spectrum that was left to Telecom as a result of the operation under analysis (which happened to be more than 49%).

The aforementioned spectrum concentration, however, had already been analysed by the National Communications Agency (ENACOM), which had provided that the merged entity should return 80 MHz of radio spectrum (equivalent to 20% of the total spectrum). Some additional recommendations addressed to ENACOM and the Ministry of Modernization, related to the return process and future use of the radio spectrum, were included in the CNDC's opinion. These recommendations sought to enable a number of companies with their own infrastructure to make reference offers as virtual mobile operators, under non-exclusive and non-discriminatory conditions.

An additional issue had to do with the possibility that Telecom began offering the "quad play" service package, and that this could serve as a tool to displace competitors from the markets involved in said package (i.e., fixed telephony, mobile telephony, internet and subscription television). This point was included in the commitment offered by Telecom and Cablevisión, through a clause whereby the parties agreed not to jointly market the pay-TV and mobile communications services until mid-2019, or until the possibility of requesting the satellite subscription television registration by all telecommunications service operators is enabled.

After an analysis that took into account the different possible effects of the concentration and the commitments offered in the different markets and market segments affected, the CNDC, by a majority vote, ended up approving of the operation, subject to the structural and behavioural commitments offered.

Looking ahead, it will be interesting to analyse the results obtained from CNDC's evaluation of the impact of the conditions imposed.

BOLIVIA

Paula Bauer[*]
Diego Rojas[**]
(C.R. & F. Rojas Abogados)

Abstract

The Bolivian Constitution dated 7 February 2009 provides the legal framework for competition, prohibition of monopolies and private oligopolies, and any kind of association or agreement between national or foreign individuals or legal entities that is meant to exercise control or create exclusive manufacturers or suppliers of goods or services in the country. Certain regulations regarding mergers and joint ventures can be found in the Electricity Law, Telecommunications Law, Hydrocarbons Law, Bank and Financial Institutions Law and Insurance Law. The authorities called to administrate and enforce said regulations are the supervisory and control authorities for each relevant sector. Mergers and acquisitions in non-regulated sectors are not subject to merger control rules, but are subject to supervision, control and inspection in relation to corporate governance, competition defence, restructuring and trade registration by the Companies Control Authority. Regulated sectors are subject to merger control. Law 1600, dated 28 October 1994, which prohibits carrying out economic concentration operations that have the effect of establishing, promoting and consolidating a dominant position within a relevant market, contemplates a pre-merger voluntary consultation regime to allow agents to ensure that a prospective transaction is not prohibited.

---

[*] Paula Bauer initially joined C.R. & F. Rojas Abogados in 2002 until 2007, and rejoined in early 2013. Mrs Bauer obtained her law degree in 2000 from Universidad Católica Boliviana "San Pablo" in La Paz. She earned a number of diplomas in intellectual property law on courses hosted by the World Trade Organization (WTO), and she is currently a member of Bolivian Industrial Property Association. Mrs Bauer attended several IP conferences and seminars, and contributed to the World Bank's publication *Doing Business in 2006: Creating Jobs*.

[**] Diego Rojas is managing partner at C.R.&F. Rojas Abogados. He studied at Marlborough College, before obtaining his law degree with an honours distinction from Universidad Católica Boliviana Law School. He was admitted to practice in 1997. Diego holds a postgraduate degree in corporate law from the Universidad Andina Simón Bolivar, a postgraduate degree in oil and gas law from the Universidad Privada de Santa Cruz de la Sierra, a postgraduate degree in conciliation and arbitration from the Universidad Aquino de Bolivia, and holds an LLM from the University of Chicago Law School, where he won an award for negotiation skills.

I. Introduction

1. Brief Overview

There are no specific laws or regulations related to competition in Bolivia.

The general scope is provided by the Bolivian Constitution, which sets out the legal framework for competition, prohibition of monopolies and private oligopolies, and any kind of association or agreement between national or foreign individuals or legal entities, that is meant to exercise control or create exclusive manufacturers or suppliers of goods or services in the country.

Certain regulations mentioning mergers and joint ventures can be found in Electricity Law, Telecommunications Law, Hydrocarbons Law, Bank and Financial Institutions Law and Insurance Law. The authorities called to administrate and enforce said regulations are the supervisory and control authorities for each relevant sector. Mergers and acquisitions in non-regulated sectors are not subject to merger control rules, but are subject to supervision, control and inspection in relation to corporate governance, competition defence, restructuring and trade registration by the Companies Control Authority (AEMP).

Certain laws referring to competition are:

- Supreme Decree No 29519 dated 16 April 2008, regulates competition and defence of competitors[1];
- Regulations Governing Competition (Ministerial Resolution No 190/2008)[2];
- Administrative Resolutions, regulating some specific matters on competition[3];
- Decision No 608 of the Andean Community of Nations (CAN), applicable to matters having specific effects in the territory of all the member countries[4].

2. Institutional Set-Up

As previously mentioned, certain regulations regarding mergers and joint ventures can be found in the Electricity Law, Telecommunications Law, Hydrocarbons Law, Bank and Financial Institutions Law and Insurance Law.

The structure of each administrative supervisory and control authority is stated in each sector's regulation, and a general structure has been settled by Supreme Decree No. 0071 of 9 April 2009[5].

---

1 Supreme Decree No 29519, 16 April 2008, regulates competition and defence of competitors: <https://www.lexivox.org/norms/BO-DS-29519.html>.

2 Ministerial Resolution No 190/2008, May 29, 2008: <file:///Users/MARCAS/Downloads/Resolucion%20Ministerial%20N%20190.pdf>.

3 *<https://www.autoridadempresas.gob.bo/direccion-tecnica-de-defensa-de-la-competencia-y-desarrollo-normativo/resoluciones>*.

4 Decision No. 608 of CAN, 29 March 2005: <http://www.sice.oas.org/trade/junac/Decisiones/DEC608s.asp>.

5 Supreme Decree No. 0071, 9 April 2009: *<https://www.lexivox.org/norms/BO-DS-N071.html>*.

The regulatory authorities of public services are part of the executive body and have the power to regulate markets, avoid monopolistic and anticompetitive practices, and establish effective mechanisms for the resolution of conflicts between regulated companies and users.

In accordance with the Bolivian Constitution and within the new State policies, Supreme Decree No. 29894 of 7 February 2009 determines the extinction of the superintendencies that were part of the sector regulation system. Article 138 of the Supreme Decree establishes the name change of the Hydrocarbons Superintendency to the National Hydrocarbons Agency.

Article 3 of Supreme Decree No. 0071 of 9 April 2009 creates the Supervisory and Social Control Authorities for: Telecommunications and Transportation, Water and Basic Sanitation, Forests and Land, Pensions and Insurance, Electricity and Companies. This Supreme Decree also establishes that the "Authority for the Supervision and Social Control of Companies will regulate, control, supervise and regulate the activities of companies in relation to corporate governance, defence of competition, restructuring of companies and registration of trade considering Law No. 2427 of 28 November 2002 and its regulations, as long as they do not contradict the provisions of the CPE."

The Supervisory and Social Control Authorities are technical and operational public institutions, with legal status and their own assets, administrative, financial, legal and technical independence, dependent of the minister head of each sector.

The structure of each Supervisory and Social Control Authority has the following levels of organisation:

- Executive: Executive Director.
- Advisory: Council with social participation.
- Technical – operational: Sectorial, departmental technical directions, administrative and legal directions, and internal audit.

According to Supreme Decree 0071, executive directors must meet three requirements, in addition to those established in the Political Constitution of the Plurinational StateBolivian Constitution. These are: having Bolivian nationality, having a national professional title, and possessing "recognised suitability and professional experience".

3. Type of Merger Control

As previously mentioned, mergers and acquisitions in non-regulated sectors are not subject to merger control rules. Mergers of Bolivian corporations are regulated by the Bolivian Commercial Code, which requires that the companies involved in a merger give notice to their creditors and shareholders regarding the proposed merger, and such creditors and shareholders may object through a judicial procedure before a civil court.

Regulated sectors are subject to merger control. Law 1600 of 28 October 1994, which prohibits carrying out economic concentration operations that have the effect of establishing, promoting and consolidating a dominant position within a relevant market, contemplates a pre-merger voluntary consultation regime to allow agents to ensure that a prospective transaction is not prohibited.

Regarding banking and finance, mergers are subject to a pre-approval regime granted by the Financial System Supervisory Authority (ASFI), which assesses the potential formation of a private monopoly or oligopoly. However, and as stated in the relevant regulation, there is neither triggering threshold nor a specific notification procedure.

If the merger will result in a foreign direct investment into Bolivia, then such investment must be registered with the Bolivian Central Bank as a result of the recently approved Investment Promotion Law[6].

To trigger regulatory intervention, mergers must typically involve the change of effective control over the relevant regulated company. There are no general thresholds in terms of economic importance that would determine whether a merger is subject to regulatory scrutiny or not. As discussed above, the mergers that will be subject to regulatory scrutiny and, in certain cases, prior authorisation, are dependent on sector-specific regulations.

Also, the AEMP has the legal authority to monitor, control and supervise companies with regard to corporate governance, antitrust, corporate restructuring and the commercial register. It promotes "fair competition" between existing companies in a national market, thus guaranteeing a harmony between the companies and generating an efficient market structure.

II. Scope of Application

1. Definition of Notifiable Transaction

As previously explained, mergers and acquisitions in non-regulated sectors are not subject to merger control rules.

Sectorial Regulation Law 1600 of 28 October 1994, which prohibits carrying out of economic concentration operations that have the effect of establishing, promoting and consolidating a dominant position within a relevant market, and contemplates a pre-merger voluntary consultation regime to allow agents to ensure that a prospective transaction is not prohibited, refers to Regulated sectors.

Mergers in the banking and finance sectors are subject to a pre-approval regime granted by the ASFI, which assesses the potential formation of a private monopoly or oligopoly.

A merger that results in a foreign direct investment into Bolivia must be registered with the Bolivian Central Bank as a result of the requirements of Investment Promotion Law.

Based on the foregoing, no party is obliged to notify any authority about a specific transaction: there is no notification term and there is no approval required before closing any transaction. Transactions that result in foreign direct investment in Bolivia do not need to be notified. As a consequence these transactions do not need to wait for any deadline to be cleared, and may thus be implemented.

---

6 Law No. 516, 4 April 2014, Investment Promotion Law: *<http://www.planificacion.gob.bo/uploads/marco-legal/LEY%20N%20516%20LEY%20DE%20PROMOCION%20DE%20INVERSIONES.pdf>*.

The Bolivian Commercial Code, which requires that companies involved in the merger give notice to their creditors and shareholders regarding the proposed merger, regulates mergers of Bolivian corporations and such creditors and shareholders may object through a judicial procedure before a civil court[7].

Companies that have outstanding instruments issued in public securities markets must inform the markets and the ASFI of any relevant change regarding the company, including mergers and joint ventures.

2. Material Scope

Telecommunications and transportation, water and basic sanitation, forests and land, pensions and insurance, electricity and companies: as regulated sectors according to Law of the Sectorial Regulation system (SIRESE), are relevant sectors that must comply with regulations regarding an effective antitrust and merger control. Specifically, Supreme Decree 29519 states a list of absolute anticompetitive conducts, such as:

- Setting, raising, arranging or manipulating the sale or purchase price of goods or services at which they are offered or demanded in the markets, or exchanging information with the same object or effect;
- Establishing the obligation not to produce, process, distribute, market or acquire a restricted or limited quantity of goods, or the provision or transaction of a restricted or limited number, volume or frequency of services;
- Dividing, distributing, assigning or imposing portions or segments of a current or potential market for goods and services, through customers, suppliers, or specific or determinable times or spaces; or
- Establishing, arranging and coordinating bids or abstention in tenders, contests and public auctions.

Participating in such absolute anticompetitive conducts leads to administrative penalties without prejudice to the criminal and civil liability that may result.

If a natural or legal person does consider the existence of possible anticompetitive practices, they must formalise their complaint by letter or filing a writ, containing a statement of facts and specifically stating the anticompetitive activity that the company participated in, as established in Supreme Decree No 29519.

On the other hand, there also exists the possibility that the AEMP starts an investigation *ex officio* for anticompetitive behaviour.

In addition, Decision 608 of CAN states the following activities as restrictive behaviours to competition:

a) Setting prices, directly or indirectly, or other marketing conditions;
b) Restricting the supply or demand for goods or services;
c) Distributing the market of goods or services;

---

7 Decree 14379 of 25 February 1977 with force of law through which the Commercial Code is approved: <http://www.oas.org/juridico/spanish/mesicic3_blv_codcomer.pdf>.

d) Preventing or hindering the access or permanence of current or potential competitors in the market; or
e) Establishing, arranging or coordinating positions, abstentions or results in public tenders, contests or auctions.

Said Decision also states behaviours of abuse of a dominant position in the market, such as:

a) Predatory pricing;
b) The fixing, imposition or unjustified establishment of the exclusive distribution of goods or services;
c) The subordination of the conclusion of contracts to the acceptance of supplementary benefits that, due to their nature or arrangement for commercial use, are not related to the object of such contracts;
d) The adoption of unequal conditions in relation to similarly contracted third parties, in the case of benefits or equivalent operations, placing them at a competitive disadvantage;
e) The unjustified refusal to satisfy purchase or acquisition demands, or to accept offers of sale or provision, of products or services;
f) Incitement to third parties not to accept the delivery of goods or the provision of services; to prevent their provision or acquisition, or not to sell raw materials or supplies, or provide services, to others; and
g) Those behaviours that impede or hinder the access or permanence of current or potential competitors in the market for reasons other than economic efficiency.

If the result of the investigation establishes the presence of the aforementioned conducts, the General Secretariat may order the immediate cessation of the restrictive conduct and, if warranted, the application of corrective and/or sanctioning measures.

The corrective measures may include the cessation of the practice within a certain period or the imposition of certain conditions, obligations or fines on the offender. With regard to sanctioning measures, the severity of the facts, the benefit obtained, the procedural conduct of the parties and the level of damage caused to free competition in the Andean Community should be considered.

3. Geographical Scope

The Bolivian Constitution of 2009 established the prohibition of monopolies and private oligopolies, as well as any kind of association or agreement between national or foreign individuals or entities, intended to exercise control over or create the sole and exclusive manufacturers or suppliers of goods and services in the national territory.

Absolute and relative anticompetitive conducts are sanctioned by the General Secretariat of CAN within CAN Member Countries (Bolivia, Colombia, Ecuador and Peru).

4. Thresholds

There are no general thresholds in terms of economic importance that would determine whether a merger is subject to regulatory scrutiny or not. As discussed above, mergers that will be subject to regulatory scrutiny and, in certain cases, prior authorisation, are dependent on sector-specific regulations.

Regarding banking and finance, mergers are subject to a pre-approval regime granted by the ASFI, which assesses the potential formation of a private monopoly or oligopoly. However, and as stated in the regulation, there is neither triggering threshold nor a specific notification procedure. To trigger regulatory intervention, mergers must typically involve the change of effective control over the relevant regulated company.

Within 30 business days of the signing date of the merger commitment, the supervised entities must file an authorisation request with the ASFI for authorisation to sign the definitive merger agreement. Once the authority evaluates the documentation and the supervised entities have corrected any observation, the authority will issue the administrative resolution authorising or rejecting the merger of supervised entities within 30 business days. The full text of the authorisation or rejection resolution will be published on the ASFI website, www.asfi.gob.bo.

On the other hand, the AEMP will initiate an investigation *ex officio* or following a complaint by a third party in cases of certain behaviours, include possible anticompetitive practices, by any company.

III. Procedure

1. Launch of Procedure

Law No 393 of Financial Services prohibits monopoly and private oligopoly or the search for them through mergers between financial entities that harm competition, as well as any monopolistic practice and the search by a financial entity to maintain a dominant position over time, such as any other form of association or agreement of private natural or legal persons, Bolivian or foreign, that seek control or exclusivity in the provision of certain financial services through the commission of anticompetitive practices in the financial system[8].

The ASFI has the exclusive power to execute financial regulation and supervision, in order to ensure the healthy functioning and development of financial entities and preserve the stability of the financial system, within the framework of financial policy, provided for in the Bolivian Constitution.

2. Development of Procedure

Within this scope, ASFI has issued the regulation for the merger of supervised entities, where the requested steps for the authority to accept a merger are clearly stated[9].

---

8 Law No 393, 21 August 2013, regulates Financial Services: *https://servdmzw.asfi.gob.bo/circular/Leyes/Ley-393ServiciosFinancieros.pdf.*

9 Resolution ASFI No 865/2015, 21 October 2015, regulations for the merger of supervised entities: *http://servdmzw.asfi.gob.bo/circular/circulares/ASFI_344.pdf.*

The Board of Directors or equivalent body of each supervised entity must present before the respective extraordinary general shareholders' meeting or extraordinary general assembly of partners or ssociates, the financial studies, the information and the relevant documentation for the possible merger, in order for said entity to consider the same and, if applicable, authorise the subscription of the merger commitment.

After the merger commitment is signed, and whithin 30 business days, the supervised entities must file authorisation reuqest and obtain authorisation to sign the definitive merger agreement.

3. Conclusion of Procedure

Once the documentation is evaluated and duly corrected if any observation arised, the authority, within 30 business days, will issue the administrative resolution authorising or rejecting the merger of supervised entities. The full text of the authorisation or rejection resolution will be published on the ASFI website, www.asfi.gob.bo.

4. Sanctions

As previously stated, within 30 business days of the signing date of the merger commitment, the supervised entities must an authorisation request with the ASFI for authorisation to sign the definitive merger agreement. If there are observations, a term will be established so that the supervised entities that participate in the merger process can correct them. The ASFI may request any additional documentation it deems pertinent in order to evaluate the application for authorisation to sign the final merger agreement.

The only sanction indicated by the competent authority is to reject the application for authorisation to subscribe to the definitive merger agreement. It is specifically given in the event that the supervised entities do not amend the observations raised by ASFI within the period established for it, and that the plan for the merger by integration of the supervised entities does not support the viability or convenience of the project.

If in the analysis of the merger application to obtain an authorisation to subscribe a definitive merger agreement, the authority states that any of the anticompetitive practices detailed in Supreme Decree 29519 exist, then the AEMP can initiate a sanction process, according to Administrative Resolution RA/AEMP/DTDCN/No 071/2014[10].

In order to apply the penalties provided in the regulations on defence of competition, the severity of the infraction must be established on the basis of the criteria set out in article 35 of the Regulation of Competition, within the framework of Supreme Decree No 29519:

- Minor infringement: relative anticompetitive conduct that has not generated economic damage to the relevant market, the consumer, or the competition between economic agents in said market, and that the conduct is also subject to amendment and regularisation.

10 Administrative Resolution RA/AEMP/DTDCN/No 071/2014, 17 July 2014, regulation for the graduation of infractions and application of sanctions within the framework of Supreme Decree No 29519 and its regulations: *https://www.autoridadempresas.gob.bo/phocadownload/competencia/RAI-AEMP-DTDCDN-071-2014.pdf.*

- Medium severity infringement: absolute or relative anticompetitive conduct based on the evaluation of its components and criteria contained in Annex 1 of Administrative Resolution RA/AEMP/DTDCN/No 071/2014.
- Maximum severity infringement: contravention of the applicable regulations in the matter of defence of the competition that implies a sanction greater than the fine, based on the evaluation of the criteria of seriousness of the facts, acts or omissions constituting the infraction described in the Annex 1 of Administrative Resolution RA/AEMP/DTDCN/No 071/2014.

In accordance with the aforementioned degrees of severity, the applicable sanctions are as follows:

- Relative anticompetitive behaviours: warning.
- Relative or absolute anticompetitive practices, medium severity: fine.
- Relative or absolute anticompetitive practices, maximum severity: definitive or temporary suspension for the signing of contracts with the public sector.

IV. Substance

1. Competition Analysis

In the case of Bolivia, regulators usually rely on consumer welfare and competition assessment when reviewing mergers, according to Supreme Decree 29519.

Collusive conducts are included among the "absolute anticompetitive practices" (horizontal agreements). Absolute anticompetitive behaviours are acts, contracts, agreements, arrangements or combinations between competing economic agents whose purpose or effect is any of the following:

- Joint price-fixing;
- Establishing limitations to produce, process, distribute, market or acquire;
- Market distribution; or
- Establishing, arranging or coordinating positions in tenders, contests or public biddings.

Supreme Decree No. 29519 states the following analysis criteria[11]:

- Absolute anticompetitive conducts: per se analysis.
- Relative anticompetitive conducts: efficiency gains.

The following criteria should be considered to determine if an economic agent has substantial power in the relevant market:

- Market share and ability to unilaterally fix prices or restrict output in the relevant market, without having competitors that are able to outweigh such power;

---

11 Articles 10–13, Supreme Decree No 29519, 16 April 2008.

- Existence of barriers to entry and other elements that could foreseeably modify the entry requirements or output by other competitors;
- Existence of competitors and their market power in the relevant market;
- Access to supply sources by the economic agent and its competitors; and
- Recent behaviour.

The concept of abuse of a dominant position is included in the "relative anticompetitive" conducts.

The following are deemed to be relative anticompetitive conducts:

- Exclusive distribution or marketing of goods or services based on the subjects, geographic location or time period;
- The imposition of the obligation not to produce goods or supply services for a period of time;
- Fixing price and other conditions that a distributor or provider must comply when selling or distributing goods or providing services;
- Making the conclusion of contracts subject to the condition not to use, acquire, sell, commercialise or provide goods or services produced, processed, distributed or commercialised by third parties;
- Unilateral refusal to sell, commercialise or provide goods or services available and usually offered to third parties;
- Predatory pricing;
- Granting of discounts, rebates or bonuses to buyers with the condition not to use, acquire, sell, commercialise or provide goods or services produced, processed distributed or commercialised by third parties, or the purchase, subject to the condition not to sell, commercialise or provide the same goods or services to third parties;
- Using the profits related to a good or service to cover the losses of another good or service;
- Price discrimination; and
- The action of one or more economic agents whose object or effect is to increase costs, hinder the productive process or reduce the demand faced by its competitors.

2. Case Law Illustration

As of 1 April 2019, after complying with all legal processes, Industrias de Aceite SA (FINO), Sociedad Aceitera del Oriente SRL (SAO) and Alicorpgroup Inversiones Bolivia SA, have completed the merger that will allow them to operate under the name of Industrias de Aceite SA.

On 15 January 2019, a preliminary merger by incorporation agreement was signed in the city of Santa Cruz, which became effective in the second quarter of 2019.

The operation will consolidate an estimated equity of BOB 1,661,784,175 (USD 240.5 million, approx., corresponding to the combined value of the three companies).

According to Alicorp's CEO Alfredo Pérez Gubbins report to the Bolivian portal "Página Siete", the merger will allow the reorganisation of Bolivian operations, to take advantage of the potential synergies detected and undertake a growth plan[12].

12 "Alicorp anuncia fusión de sus tres empresas en Bolivia" (Página Siete, 17 January 2019) <https://www.paginasiete.bo/economia/2019/1/17/alicorp-anuncia-fusion-de-sus-tres-empresas-en-bolivia-206287.html> accessed 12 August 2020.

BRAZIL

Vinicius Marques de Carvalho[*]
Marcela Mattiuzzo[**]
Maria Eduarda Scott[***]
(Vinicius Marques de Carvalho Advogados)

Abstract

This paper intends to provide an overview of merger control proceedings in Brazil. In 2012, the Brazilian competition authorities went through significant shifts in its regulations and established the pre-merger review system in Brazil. This paper will go through each of the main aspects of the current Brazilian merger control system, including an explanation of CADE's organisational structure and competences, a practical guide to the aspects of filing a transaction before CADE and the main criteria that influence the competitive assessment of a concentration act, among several other aspects that have raised discussions among antitrust practitioners. To properly illustrate how CADE has been shaping its decisions, this paper intends to give examples of relevant cases of the past eight years.

---

[*] Vinicius Marques de Carvalho is the founding partner of Vinicius Marques de Carvalho Advogados (VMCA) and Professor of Commercial Law at the University of São Paulo. He is a former President of the Brazilian Competition Authority (CADE), former Secretary of the Brazilian Secretariat of Economic Law and former commissioner of CADE. He holds a bachelor's degree in law from the University of São Paulo and PhDs in law from the University of São Paulo and the University of Paris-1 (Panthéon-Sorbonne).

[**] Marcela Mattiuzzo is partner at VMCA. She holds a master's degree in constitutional law from the University of São Paulo and is currently pursuing a PhD in commercial law at the same institution. She was adviser and chief of staff at the Office of the President at CADE.

[***] Maria Eduarda Scott is an associate of VMCA. She holds a bachelor's degree in law from the University of São Paulo and a bachelor's degree in public administration from Fundação Getulio Vargas.

I. Introduction

1. Brief Overview

The Brazilian antitrust authority's history dates back to 1962, when the Administrative Council for Economic Defense (CADE) was created as a body of the Ministry of Justice. Until the early 1990s, however, the council had very limited power to prevent abuse of economic power. On 11 June 1994, CADE was completely restructured by Law No 8,884/94 and became an independent agency reporting to the Ministry of Justice. Under this structure, CADE was in charge of ruling on administrative proceedings related to anticompetitive conduct and of assessing mergers subject to its post-merger review system. In this structure, CADE was in charge of ruling on proceedings, but it was the Secretariat for Economic Law (SDE) and the Secretariat for Economic Monitoring (SEAE) who carried out investigations. Whereas the SDE was primarily focused on anticompetitive conduct investigations, the SEAE carried out merger review. Both authorities would issue non-binding opinions and CADE would later judge the proceedings.

2. Institutional Set-Up

In 2011, Law No 12,529/2011 was responsible for a restructuring of the Brazilian Competition Defense System (SBDC), which shifted things significantly[1]. The main institutional shifts included a new set-up of the SBDC, which is now comprised of CADE and the Secretariat for Economic Monitoring (SEAE) of the Ministry of Finance (the SEAE ceased to instruct proceedings and stated acting solely on competition advocacy). CADE is now responsible for both investigating and ruling on cases, which required a new organisation at the authority in two main bodies: the General Superintendence (GS), in charge of investigations, and the Administrative Tribunal, responsible for rulings.

In order to preserve independence, these two bodies have two separate heads, the general superintendent and the president of the tribunal, respectively. They are autonomous from one another and equal in hierarchical standing.

The general superintendent is appointed by the president of the republic, after being approved by the Federal Senate, as the head of the GS for a two-year term, which can be renewed once. The GS's main functions are to investigate and instruct cases, as detailed in article 13 of Law No 12,529/2011. To do so, it is organised in units, the so-called Merger and Antitrust Units (CGAA). There are nine CGAAs, which are supervised by two deputy superintendents[2]. One of the deputies supervises merger control and unilateral conduct activity, and the other supervises collusive practices. CGAAs 1 to 4 are responsible for examining non-fast-track proceedings (divided by economic sector) and

1 The translation to Law No 12,529/2011 can be found on CADE's website: <<http://www.cade.gov.br/assuntos/internacional/legislacao/law-no-12529-2011-english-version-from-18-05-2012.pdf/view>>.

2 Each CGAA is composed of a head of department, a coordinator and a team of case handlers.

the investigation of unilateral conducts[3]. CGAA5, also known as the screening unit, is responsible for the first contact with every merger case notified to CADE and for, as the name suggests, screening which cases qualify for fast-track proceedings. CGAA5 deliberates on whether the information provided about the notified transaction is sufficient and proceeds to either assessing the fast-track proceedings or forwarding non-fast-track cases to Units 1–4. CGAAs 6–8 are anti-cartel units, and CGAA9 receives all complaints related to unilateral and collusive anticompetitive conducts and carries out a preliminary assessment of whether such complaints should proceed to further investigation.

One of the procedural changes that followed the new law and the pre-merger review system relates to how cases are assessed at the GS. Before 2012, any merger that went through the system necessarily had to be reviewed by CADE's tribunal. That meant a large portion of commissioners' work involved reassessing fast-track proceedings, that presented no particular competition concern. Naturally, this process was inefficient, for it occupied the tribunal with a workload of merger review that made it difficult for more complex anticompetitive practices to be analysed. The new structure allows for a much smaller number of mergers to be reviewed by the tribunal, which means that the GS is, in many instances – notably for fast-track cases – the main body responsible for the assessment.

> CADE's Administrative Tribunal, the ruling body at the authority, is composed of a president[4] and six commissioners, all of which are appointed by the President of the Republic and subject to a non-renewable four-year term. The main functions of the tribunal related to merger control are: (i) to judge merger cases with recommendation from the GS for remedies or for disapproval; (ii) to claim and judge merger cases approved without restriction by the GS; (iii) to approve concentration act agreements (ACC) and appoint the GS to monitor the fulfilment of these agreements; and (iv) to elaborate and approve CADE's Internal Regulations (RICADE), which organise CADE's function, rules of procedure, means of deliberation and internal services. Therefore, unlike the merger control procedure under Law No 8884/1994, only merger cases challenged either by the GS itself, by third parties or by commissioners are assessed by the tribunal.

The Administrative Tribunal gathers in trial sessions, which are publicly available (except in cases that demand confidential treatment) and have their agenda defined by CADE's president at least 120 hours in advance. Each case deliberated in trial sessions is voted collectively and won by the majority vote[5]. Given that CADE's tribunal is comprised of

---

3 The unit segmentations are: (i) CGAA1 reviews non-fast-track proceedings that involve differentiated goods, pharmaceuticals, agribusiness and technology; (ii) CGAA2 reviews non-fast-track proceedings related to services in general, education, healthcare, financial and retail markets; (iii) CGAA3 reviews non-fast-track proceedings related to base industry, chemical, petrochemical and other commodities; and (iv) CGAA4 reviews non-fast-track proceedings involving regulated markets, such as telecommunications, energy, oil and gas and transportation.

4 The specific functions of the president of the tribunal include representing the authority and responding for its administrative management; chairing the trial sessions and distribution sessions (in which the proceedings are assigned to commissioners by drawing lots); and determining the organisation of the tribunal's agenda.

5 The Judgment Sessions calendar can be found at: <http://www.cade.gov.br/cade_english/topics/sessions>.

seven members, the minimum quorum for deliberation is four members. The distribution sessions are open to the public and carried out by CADE's president, and both types of session may also occur extraordinarily, upon summons.

3. Type of Merger Control

In addition to Law No 12,529/2011, the body of legislation from the SBDC has been complemented by several regulations issued by CADE through the years. Between May 2012 and March 2020, CADE issued 25 resolutions[6], some of which deserve to be highlighted: (i) Resolution No 02/2012 provides the general framework for the filing forms pertaining to merger review procedures; (ii) Resolution No 17/2016 establishes the specific circumstances for the notification of associative contracts; (iii) Resolutions Nos 13/2015 and 24/2019 establish the rules for gun-jumping investigations; and (iv) Resolution No 22/2019, which is the latest version of CADE's Internal Regulations.

As has been highlighted by many, the main change provided by the new law was the introduction of a mandatory pre-merger review system, which will be discussed throughout this chapter. Up until 2012, merger review did exist in Brazil, but it followed an *ex post* approach. The difficulties associated with post-merger review are well known: it ties authorities' hands, for it imposes the analysis of the operation after closing, making any attempt to impose remedies and mitigate competitive risk much more costly and, sometimes, unfeasible. This diagnosis, combined with the maturity of the competition system in Brazil, is what led the law to change and the rules currently in force to be conceived.

II. Scope of Application

1. Definition of Notifiable Transaction

Pursuant to the Brazilian Competition Law, the following transactions are considered concentration acts: (i) the merger between two or more independent companies; (ii) a direct or indirect acquisition by one or more companies of control or parts of one or more companies, by purchase or exchange of stocks, shares, bonds or securities convertible into stocks or assets, whether tangible or intangible, by contract or by any other means or way; (iii) the incorporation, by one or more companies, of another company or companies; (iv) the constitution of an associative agreement, consortium or joint venture, by two or more companies[7].

With regards to the acquisition of shares, Resolution No 02/2012[8] sets additional criteria for mandatory notification. Acquisition of minority interests should be submitted to CADE in case of: (i) the acquisition of an interest of at least 20%, if the acquirer and

---

6 For the complete list of CADE's resolutions, see: <http://www.cade.gov.br/assuntos/assuntos/normas-e-legislacao/normas_legislacao/resolucao>.

7 The only exception is for joint ventures specifically created to take part in public bids, which are not subject to CADE's merger control.

8 Resolution No 02/2012: <http://www.cade.gov.br/assuntos/normas-e-legislacao/resolucao/resolucao-2_2012-analise-atos-concentracao.pdf/view>.

target are not active in horizontally or vertically related markets; or (ii) the acquisition of an interest of at least 5%, in cases where the acquiring and target companies are competitors or active in vertically related markets.

Additionally, as mentioned, associative agreements are transactions that must be submitted to the antitrust authority for analysis. Because the idea of an associative agreement is naturally broad, they have been the object of a series of discussions and uncertainties concerning the specific criteria for characterising such mandatory filing.

In order to clarify such discussions, CADE issued Resolution No 17/2016, which entered into force on 25 November 2016, and provided additional information as to which sorts of contracts would amount to an associative agreement for purposes of mandatory filing. This resolution states that agreements with the duration of two years or more that establish a joint enterprise shall be considered as associative agreement, provided, cumulatively, that the parties involved are competitors in the relevant market subject to the agreement and that the agreement foresees the sharing of the risks and results of the underlying economic activity. Notably, CADE does not consider vertical agreements to be of mandatory notification since the issue of Resolution No 17/2016. Other cases disqualified as associative agreements will be further detailed below.

CADE has reviewed a number of associative agreements since Resolution No 17/2016 entered into force, but it has yet to properly define clear concepts for what a "common enterprise" is and what configures the "sharing of risks and results" for mandatory notification purposes. Recent case law has helped to shape CADE's understanding and allows us to reach a number of conclusions related to associative agreements. For instance, in the merger review of the associative agreement between Tim Celular and Oi Móvel, Commissioner João Paulo Resende stated the following impressions concerning the classification of "common enterprise", and was followed by the majority of the tribunal:

> CADE's recent decisions have demanded that the underlying activity should be developed independently from the parties and that there is a governance structure to jointly deliberate over the parties' decisions. That is, CADE tends to distinguish cases in which the parties decide solely where and how to operate their assets, from cases in which such activities are held commonly (contractually or actually)[9].

In relation to the sharing of risks and results, the commissioner reinforced that the sharing should be interpreted from the contractual clauses, and not directly relate to profit- and cost-sharing. This means that agreements that establish pricing and usual payment conditions that do not result in sharing of risks or results are more likely to be disregarded as associative agreements.

Such is the case of Concentration Act No 08700.002194/2019-11, between Novelis and Recicla Group. The transaction comprised a supply agreement by which the Recicla Group would supply Novelis with recycled products made from aluminium. Despite having agreed

---

9 Concentration Act No. 08700.002276/2018-84, §36 of the commissioner vote.

on a contractual "guarantee of minimum results and common commitments" to reduce costs, the parties clarified that the pricing of products had been previously established, which means that one party would not participate on the results obtained by the other. CADE's GS concluded therefore that the associative agreement did not qualify as a concentration act, as it did not establish either a common enterprise or the sharing of risks and results.

Other examples of transactions submitted to CADE and not qualified as associative agreements include: code-share agreements[10], distribution, licence and supply agreements[11] and other agreements that did not result in common enterprises with the sharing of risks and results.

Therefore, it is worth highlighting that CADE is constantly subject to new cases regarding associative agreements, and as such it is to be expected that its case law will undergo new developments and come to new and clearer interpretations. In any case, given the particular aspects of this kind of filing, parties should always be attentive to new decisions by the competition authority.

2. Material Scope

Concentration Acts are subject to CADE's approval, regardless of the economic sector involved. As per the OECD's classification, in Brazil there is no economic sector that has antitrust immunity – that means that even public-owned companies must file and wait for CADE's approval before closing transactions. Examples include: (i) Petrobras and Trident Energy, concerning the acquisition, by Trident Energy, of assets related to oil and gas production[12]; (i) Caixa Seguridade (a publicly owned insurance company) and CNP Assurances, for the constitution of a joint venture between the companies to operate life insurance businesses[13]; (iii) Eletronorte (a publicly owned energy company) and Abengoa, regarding the acquisition of shares by Eletronorte in LVTE, an energy consortium[14].

Nonetheless, transactions in regulated sectors may need special clearance by their regulatory agencies (e.g., telecommunications, insurance, oil and gas), in addition to CADE's standard merger review – in such cases, however, these proceedings are held separately and independently. For instance, Concentration Act No 08700.004955/2019-79, between Notre Dame Intermédica and São Lucas Saúde was submitted for the approval of CADE and ANS (National Supplementary Health Agency). The transaction related to health insurance and hospital markets. It was unconditionally approved by CADE in November 2019 and further approved by ANS in January 2020.

In the telecoms market, the transaction between AT&T and Time Warner (detailed further below) was subject to the approval of both CADE and ANATEL (Brazil's National Communications Agency). Although it was conditionally approved by CADE in October 2017, it was only cleared by ANATEL in February 2020.

---

10 Concentration Acts Nos 08700.002529/2017-39 (TAM Linhas Aéreas and Qatar Airways); 08700.012314/2015-64 (OceanAir Linhas Aéreas and South African Airways).

11 Concentration Act No 08700.008484/2016-25 (Medley Farmacêutica and Aurobindo Pharma).

12 Concentration Act No 08700.003987/2019-57.

13 Concentration Act No 08700.005802/2019-49.

14 Concentration Act No 08700.005321/2014-29.

A different example is the relationship between CADE and Brazil's Central Bank (BACEN) regarding mergers in the financial sector. For years, CADE and BACEN disagreed over competence to approve transactions in the financial sector, until finally entering into an agreement in February 2018 that established that mergers in the financial sector must be submitted to both authorities. Although CADE has the powers to approve transactions in the financial sector, transactions that pose high and imminent risk to the stability of the Brazilian financial system may be unilaterally approved by BACEN and must be followed by CADE's unconditional approval.

3. Geographical Scope

The mandatory notification of a concentration act shall occur where it meets two criteria. The first one is identifying whether the transaction has an effect in Brazilian territory (even if the companies involved in such transaction are foreign). Effects in Brazil might include any transaction where the target company has assets, legal entities or revenues generated in Brazil (the amount of revenue is irrelevant to the antitrust analysis, there is no "minimum or sufficient effects" test in place for the purpose of this analysis). Effects may also be achieved through local sales representatives, local subsidiaries or distributors, or through export sales to Brazil.

Recent examples of cases notified to CADE help clarify what constitutes an effect in Brazil. In 2020, Concentration Act No 08700.000494/2020-07 was notified. It was a transaction between Celanese Corporation and Nouryon AG, in which Celanese acquired Elotex, a business unit, from Nouryon. The transaction was notified in Brazil, despite the minimal amount of sales made by Elotex in the Brazilian territory. Elotex operated exclusively through imports to Brazil, which was sufficient to trigger the mandatory filing before CADE, although the transaction was unconditionally approved.

Recent cases also led the GS to conclude that certain transactions did not have effects in Brazil, confirming and clarifying the understanding on the matter. Such was the case in Concentration Act No 08700.000686/2019-71, regarding a joint venture between Denso Corporation, Aisin Seiki and JTEKT Corporation to develop a future control software meant for global sales but produced mainly in Japan. In its decision, the GS took into consideration that the software would not be available in Brazil for the next five years and therefore it could not foresee any potential effects in Brazil related to the transaction.

4. Thresholds

The second criterion occurs if the parties meet the notification revenue thresholds. The thresholds are cumulatively met when: (i) one of the economic groups involved in the transaction registered gross revenues or volume of business in Brazil equal to or exceeding BRL 750 million in the fiscal year prior to the transaction and; and (ii) one of the other economic groups involved in the transaction registered gross revenues or volume of business in Brazil in equal to or exceeding BRL 75 million in the fiscal year prior to the transaction[15].

---

15 These values were previously set at BRL 400 million and BRL 40 million, respectively, and were updated by the Interministerial Ordinance No 994/2012.

In order to calculate revenue thresholds, CADE considers the economic groups of the merging parties. An economic group, as per CADE's understanding, means: (i) companies under common control, either internal or external; and (ii) companies in which any company in the first category owns, directly or indirectly, at least 20% of the capital stock or voting capital.

Many debates have been raised regarding the definition of "common control", given that antitrust legislation does not provide a clear definition. CADE's case law[16] has been debating what qualifies as common control, internally and externally, considering both objective aspects (e.g. number of shares owned by each controlling parties) and subjective aspects, such as corporate governance. This discussion has been summarised in a recent decision:

> In several precedents where the parties presented doubts about the control and configuration of the group, the analysis carried out by this Superintendence followed two steps, essentially: first, the analysis evaluated whether there was any shareholder with a participation above 20% in the object company, which constitutes an objective and direct analysis; to subsequently conduct the assessment on the corporate governance of the subject company, check if the minority shareholder with a participation equal to or greater than 20% had rights that would go beyond the mere protection of the investment, which would imply some serious interference in the company, with the intention of framing the majority shareholder as a unitary or other controlling shareholder, a hypothesis that would constitute a dependence on the deliberation of other shareholders to address the competitively relevant issues of the company. Obviously, if a shareholder has individual control of a company, there is no need to speak of more than one economic group, since this company will belong exclusively to the group of the controlling shareholder (unitary). In addition, as stated in the previous paragraph, this SG highlights the need to verify minority shareholders, with less than 20% of the share capital or voting, have some (shared) control power in the company in question, which is accomplished through of an analysis of corporate governance of this company, according to the provisions of item I, of § 1, of art. 4 of CADE's Resolution No 02/2012[17].

In case of investment funds, the economic group is comprised of: (i) the economic group of each shareholder that directly or indirectly holds at least 50% of the quotas of the fund involved in the transaction; and (ii) the companies controlled by the fund, as well as the companies in which such fund detains ownership interest of at least 20%, directly or indirectly.

Cases involving investment funds are also subject to debate, especially with regard to what information has to be provided, both in terms of calculating revenues threshold,

---

16 For further discussions on economic group and common control, see Concentration Act No 08700.009881/2012-9 (ABN AMRO Bank and Banco CR2) and APAC No 08700.011294/2015-12.

17 Concentration Act No 08700.002073/2018-98 (Ticket Soluções HDFGT SA and Repom SA), para 17 of the GS decision.

and in terms of the general information requested to complete filing forms[18]. Resolutions Nos 02/2012 and 09/2014 have both disciplined investment funds, in the sense that the fund manager does not integrate the economic group for revenues purposes.

This understanding, however, has been recently debated by CADE in the transaction involving an acquisition of shares by Siros FIA IE, an investment fund managed by Tarpon, in Kepler Weber[19]. The transaction was submitted to CADE despite not meeting the revenues threshold established under Resolution No 02/2012, as Siros's quota-holders with 50% or more quotas did not reach revenue of BRL 75 million. However, the notifying parties argued that the fund manager Tarpon "had the autonomy and, therefore, control over the fund's investments", which meant that the fund manager would be the actual controller of the fund. CADE's GS concluded for a "teleological approach to Resolution No 02/2012, which considers the controller as the guidance to identify economic groups", accounting Tarpon's revenues into the economic group revenue threshold calculation.

This unprecedented decision serves as a warning for future cases. Although this particular case does not shift CADE's understanding of how to assess investment funds, it signals that further debates on the matter might be ahead.

Provided that a transaction meets the abovementioned criteria, it shall be notified to CADE. In exceptional cases, CADE may trigger the filing of a transaction that does not meet such criteria, pursuant to article 88, paragraph 7 of the Brazilian Competition Law, which concedes CADE the discretionary power to require the submission of a concentration act within one year as of the respective date of consummation. Such was the case of the transaction between SM Empreendimentos and All Chemistry[20], in relation to which CADE requested a submission to the antitrust authorities (although the parties did not reach notification thresholds), under the argument that "SM Empreendimentos would be monopolising distributors and importers of pharmaceutical inputs, harming free competition"[21], after a series of non-mandatory acquisitions made by SM Empreendimentos over the years.

It is worth noting that CADE does not frequently make use of this discretionary power, but it has been frequently mentioned by academics as a potential way of addressing mergers in digital markets. Often, transactions in such markets are not of mandatory submission because they fail to reach the revenue thresholds – that was the case of Facebook/WhatsApp, for example. It remains to be seen whether the authority will resort to this provision more frequently in the future.

---

18 Resolution No 02/2012 establishes that for economic group of investment funds, the information to provide to CADE, includes: (i) all funds under common management; (ii) fund managers; (iii) quota-holders with more than 20%, directly or indirectly, of the quotas of any of the involved funds; and (iv) portfolio companies in which the funds hold directly or indirectly 20% or more of the corporate or voting capital.

19 Concentration Act No 08700.000180/2020-04 (Fundo de Investimento Multimercado Profit 1552 and Kepler Weber SA).

20 Administrative Proceeding No 08700.006355/2017-83 (All Chemistry do Brasil Ltda and SM Empreendimentos Farmacêuticos Ltda).

21 See Commissioner Polyanna Ferreira Silva Vilanova Vote on the Administrative Proceeding No. 08700.006355/2017-83. Applicants: All Chemistry do Brasil Ltda. and SM Empreendimentos Farmacêuticos Ltda.

III. Procedure

1. Launch of Procedure

As previously stated, the SBDC adopted pre-merger control in 2012. Concentration acts can fall under two categories: fast track and non – fast track (longer reviews for cases which would demand a more thorough analysis by CADE). The main practical result of a case being considered fast-track or not is the level of scrutiny it receives from the authority, which in turn can lead to a significant difference when it comes to how long the merger will be assessed by the GS. As detailed below, CADE has a deadline of 30 days to decide on fast-track proceedings, counting from the day of the submission or the final amendment of the filing form. It is worth noting that the average number of days taken to decide on fast-track cases in 2019 was 16.8 days.

Fast-track proceedings are admitted in the following cases: (i) classic or cooperative joint ventures; (ii) substitution of economic agents (i.e., the acquiring company or economic group is an entrant in the markets affected by the concentration act; (iii) horizontal overlaps in which the transaction results in a combined market share of less than 20% in the relevant market; (iv) vertical integrations in which neither of the parties involved attracts a market share equal or superior to 30% in the upstream or downstream relevant markets; (v) lack of causal link, which refer to cases in which the resulting HHI variation is below 200, provided that the transaction does not result in a market share above 50%; and (vi) other types deemed sufficiently simple, but not covered by the above categories. Cases that do not fall within such categories are qualified as non-fast-track proceedings.

CADE establishes two standard filing forms, as per Resolution No 02/2012, which provides a description of the required information for the submission of each type of proceeding. The non-fast-track (and therefore more complex) transactions must provide:

i. Detailed information about the parties involved in the transaction and their respective economic groups;
ii. Description of the transaction;
iii. Documents related to and resulting from the transaction;
iv. Description of the relevant markets affected by the transaction and the proposed definitions;
v. Detailed information about the supply structure of such markets;
vi. Detailed information about the demand structure of such markets;
vii. Detailed information about potential monopsony issues;
viii. Detailed information about rivalry and entry conditions in such markets;
ix. Detailed information about potential coordinated effects;
x. Counterfactual (description of the market scenario in case the transaction does not take place).

Fast-track proceedings usually present items (i) to (v) of the abovementioned requirements.

Regardless of the procedure, the filing fee to CADE amounts to BRL 85,000, which must be paid to the authorities before submission of the transaction and can be shared freely between the notifying parties, the common practice being division of payment among the parties. There is also no applicable deadline to the submission of the concentration act, provided that the parties submit the transaction before the final consummation. CADE's Internal Regulations (article 106, §1) describe that "the submission of a concentration act must be notified, preferably, after the signing of the formal document that binds the parties and before the consummation of any act related to the transaction". The submission occurs exclusively through CADE's digital channels.

With regard to how each of the procedures work, the fast-track proceeding starts with the submission of the notification form and the respective documents concerning the transaction to CADE[22]. The parties are required to provide a public and a confidential version of the filing form, as the public version becomes available through CADE's digital channels.

Non-fast-track proceedings are submitted differently, given their more complex nature. Before submitting the transaction through CADE's digital channels, the parties usually arrange informal contacts (conference calls or meetings) with the authorities in order to present the transaction. Such communication is referred to as pre-notification contact, which is not a requirement under Law No 12,592/2011 or other regulations, but has become common practice. The parties present the filing form beforehand so that CADE can waive initial concerns and verify if the initial information provided by the parties is sufficient. This practice intends to avoid requests for amendments by the GS or dismissal due to lack of information, as per article 53 §1 of Law No 12,529/2011.

2. Development of Procedure

Once the parties submit the concentration act before CADE, the authorities issue a public notice of the transaction in the Official Gazette – the issue of the public notice is understood as an initially positive note from the authority, indicating that it believes the information provided by the parties is sufficient for analysis. From the issue of the public notice, other parties have 15 days to qualify as interested third parties if they wish to oppose or more closely follow the concentration act. Once admitted, interested third parties can directly participate in the merger review process by preparing submissions that they wish CADE to take into account. Interested third parties can also appeal a clearance decision to CADE's tribunal.

Non-fast-track proceedings also involve the issuing of questionnaires (RFIs) to competitors, consumers and suppliers that may be affected by the transaction, as a way of understanding how other market players perceive the transaction[23]. CADE takes into account information submitted by such market players to better understand the market, particularly if it sheds light on other previously unmentioned aspects of the transaction or if it contradicts the parties' statements.

---

22 The main documents include: copy of the final version of the main contract concerning the transaction, copies of non-compete and shareholders agreement, a list of all the documents resulting from the transaction and annual reports from the parties involved in the transaction, among others.

23 This is common practice in non-fast-track proceedings but, exceptionally, fast-track proceedings can also involve questionnaires to market players affected by the concentration act.

Both fast -track and non-fast-track cases are primarily decided by the general superintendent, who can: (i) unconditionally clear the transaction; (ii) recommend its approval subject to an ACC or; (iii) recommend its rejection. Cases that have recommendations either for remedies or rejection are always further assessed by the tribunal, which will issue a final administrative decision, detailed below. As for cases unconditionally cleared, which amount for the vast majority of cases analysed by the GS in any given year, those are only assessed by the tribunal if an interested third party or a commissioner decides to appeal the decision.

As per the authorities' deadlines, CADE's Resolution No 16/2016 states that the GS must issue a decision on fast-track proceedings within 30 days of the submission of the filing form or the amendment of the case by the GS. The parties are required to wait for an additional 15 days after the GS's approval, during which period the decision may be challenged by CADE's tribunal or by third parties. For non-fast-track proceedings, the statutory period to clear a transaction is limited to 240 days – subject to extensions of 60–90 days upon request of CADE or the parties.

Exceptionally, per article 59, §1 of Law No 12,529/2011, certain transactions may be implemented before CADE's final clearance (while simultaneously not investigated for gun-jumping violations), in case one of the following requirements is met: (i) the transaction does not cause irreparable damage to the market; (ii) the acts involved are entirely reversible; and (iii) irreversible and imminent damage would be caused to the target company if an exceptional approval is not granted. This is a highly exceptional occasion, which has only been accepted once by CADE, in the case between Excelente BV and Odebrecht TransPort, concerning the acquisition of shares in the Galeão Airport in Rio de Janeiro[24].

3. Conclusion of Procedure

When a merger has to be assessed by the tribunal, the first step in the procedure is for a commissioner to be assigned to the case. That commissioner then becomes the reporting commissioner for the matter. The reporting commissioner must first decide if they believe the investigation carried out by the GS is sufficient. Though the tribunal is not the main investigative unit at CADE, commissioners can further investigate proceedings if they understand it to be necessary. In most cases, however, a commissioner's job is to reanalyse the information already collected by the GS, and rule on the matter. Rulings take place during judgment sessions, during which all commissioners express their views and either agree or disagree with the reporting commissioner's opinion. The tribunal will then either grant unconditional approval, grant approval subject to conditions or reject the transaction[25].

---

24 Concentration Act No 08700.007756/2017-51. In this particular case, the prior authorisation was given because the original investor in Galeão Airport, HNA Infrastructure (a Chinese company), did not obtain the authorisations demanded by the Chinese government to operate the Brazilian airport and hence Odebrecht conceded the right of preference to Excelente. In order to obtain CADE clearance, the parties demonstrated the financial losses that would result from the delay, which could also interrupt the airport's activities.

25 Pursuant to article 61 of Law No 12,592/2011: during the judgment of the petition for the approval of the act of economic concentration, the tribunal may fully approve it, reject it or partially approve it, in which case it will determine the restrictions to be observed as conditions to validate the act.

Conditional approval involves negotiating remedies, which can happen either directly with the GS or with the tribunal. Remedies that are successfully negotiated result in an ACC, which is further approved by the tribunal and becomes an integral part of the authority's final clearance decision (see section regarding remedies, below). Compliance with ACCs is monitored by the attorney general's office associated with CADE (ProCADE), which is responsible for promoting the judicial enforcement of CADE's decisions and sentences.

Therefore, before blocking a transaction, CADE commonly attempts to negotiate behavioural or structural remedies with the parties, with the goal of eliminating competitive concerns[26]. Structural remedies may include, for example, the sale of brands of products to competitors or the sale of assets or specific plants to a competitor. Behavioural remedies may include transparent commercial policies, prohibitions to impose exclusivity, discriminatory conditions, tying and bundling strategies.

Examples of remedies can be seen, for instance, in the merger between Praxair, Inc. and Linde AG[27], a global transaction assessed by CADE. The transaction was conditioned to the signature of an ACC which involved the obligation of divesture in several business, given the parties' combined high market shares in the relevant markets. Aside from the divesture of several business, behavioural remedies also included the commitment of non-discrimination in the supply of calcium carbide, which is exclusively manufactured by Praxair in Brazil, and the prohibition of participating in new bids to renew current agreements related to the divested assets/plants.

It is worth noting that CADE's cooperation with other authorities is particularly active in merger control, especially in cases that involve remedies. Cooperating jurisdictions include Canada, Chile, the EU, Mercosul, BRICS, Portugal, the United States, Japan, South Korea and others.

Lastly, note that the parties involved in a concentration act can withdraw the transaction from CADE's assessment at any point. In such cases, the filing fee is maintained by the authorities and the transaction is not given a final assessment[28].

4. Sanctions

CADE can impose sanctions in its merger control proceedings related to: (i) the supply of misleading or wrongful information; (ii) failure to provide information requested by CADE; and (iii) gun-jumping.

---

26 CADE, Antitrust Remedies Guidelines: <http://www.cade.gov.br/acesso-a-informacao/publicacoes-institucionais/guias_do_Cade/copy_of_GuiaRemdios.pdf>.

27 Concentration Act No 08700.007777/2017-76. Press Release, "Cade approves with restriction merger between Praxair and Linde" (15 June 2018), <http://en.cade.gov.br/press-releases/cade-approves-with-restriction-merger-between-praxair-and-linde>.

28 Such was the case of Concentration Act No 08700.009711/2014-78, between Capsugel and Genix. The transaction was assessed by GS, which concluded that it would potentially generate anticompetitive effects. The parties attempted to negotiate an ACC that would address such concerns, but it did not meet the tribunal's requirements and was still perceived as anticompetitive. Such unsuccessful negotiations led the parties to withdraw the transaction from CADE, terminating the transaction agreement.

The first type of sanction, as per article 43 of Law No 12,529/2011, refers to the provision of wrongful or misleading information, documents or statements, which shall be punishable by a fine that may vary from BRL 5,000 to BRL 5 million. If CADE concludes that its approval decision has been made based on such false information, as per article 91 of Law No 12,529/2011, such fine shall vary from BRL 60,000 to BRL 6,000,000, combined with the possibility of CADE revisiting its decision.

The sanctions regarding failure to provide information usually refer to the RFIs sent by CADE to market players in the midst of concentration acts, or additional information requested to the parties throughout its assessment. Under article 40 of Law No 12,529/2011, CADE can impose a daily fine of BRL 5,000 (which can be increased up to 20 times to guarantee the effectiveness of the punishment) in the event of a refusal, omission or tardy response to RFIs and additional questionnaires.

The last sanction refers to gun-jumping practices, which occur when the parties close the transaction before the final clearance by CADE. As previously stated, the consummation of mergers before CADE's final clearance is forbidden by article 88 §3 of Law No 12,529/2011. If companies engage in such practice, they are subject to a fine ranging from BRL 60,000 to BRL 60 million. Gun-jumping sanctions may also include making the deal null and void, as well as launching a separate administrative proceeding to analyse harm to competition.

Resolution No 24/2019 (which overtook Resolution No 13/2015) sets forth the proceedings for conducting gun-jumping investigations (Deliberation of a Concentration Act Proceeding – APAC), which apply to: (i) transactions notified and consummated before CADE's final clearance, pursuant to article 88 §3 of Law No 12,529/2011; and (ii) transactions not filed before CADE but subject to mandatory filing[29]. Gun-jumping administrative proceedings can also be determined by the GS in response to a request by CADE's tribunal or a complaint made to CADE by a third party.

Investigations that initially lead to the conclusion of a gun-jumping violation by the GS are further assessed by the tribunal, which decides (i) whether the APAC should be dismissed; (ii) the determination of mandatory filing (combined with applicable fines and the nullity of actions consummated prior to the clearance of the transaction); or (iii) to open an administrative proceeding to determine additional antitrust violations.

In addition to the resolution, in May 2015 CADE published the Gun-Jumping Guidelines[30], which provide guidance to parties involved in a proposed merger, describe the kind of conduct that might configure gun-jumping and suggest measures to mitigate the risks of gun-jumping during transaction negotiations. Among the activities that might constitute previous consummation, the Guidelines describe: (i) the exchange of information between the economic agents involved in a merger; and (ii) the definition of contractual clauses

---

29 Resolution No 24/2019 also refers to the proceedings regarding transactions that fall under article 88 §7 of Law No 12,529/2011, although such transactions do not amount to gun-jumping violations as they do not meet CADE's mandatory filing criteria.

30 See <http://www.cade.gov.br/acesso-a-informacao/publicacoes-institucionais/guias_do_Cade/guideline-gun-jumping-september.pdf>.

governing the relationship between economic agents[31]. As for the recommendation to mitigate such risks, the Guidelines describe procedures, which mainly involve the creation of an antitrust protocol and the gathering of a Clean Team and Executive Committee[32].

CADE has penalised a number of transactions for gun-jumping practices. The central case to date is the conviction of Cisco Systems Inc and Technicolor S/A with a fine of BRL 30 million , as the parties consummated the transaction in November 2015, before CADE's final clearance. In this case, the parties executed a carve-out agreement to prevent effects in jurisdictions where the transaction was not yet approved. This case led to the important statement that CADE does not accept carve-out agreements of Brazilian assets to mitigate or eliminate gun-jumping penalties[33].

In another case, CADE blocked the transaction between Mataboi Alimentos and JBJ Agropecuária (Concentration Act No 08700.007553/2016-83), after negotiating a fine of BRL 664,983 due to gun-jumping.

A recent gun-jumping assessment by CADE involved the global transaction between IBM and Red Hat[34]. The transaction was submitted to CADE in April 2019 and unconditionally approved by the GS in June, but days later CADE's tribunal appealed the case, to be further assessed. In July 2019, while the tribunal's consideration was still ongoing, the parties sent a notice to CADE to inform that the transaction had been closed globally but, in order to prevent the transaction from being consummated in Brazil, the parties established a hold-separate structure until CADE's final clearance.

The argument brought about by the parties to partially close the transaction was that, as of July 2019, CADE's tribunal was left without a seating quorum. All legal deadlines were suspended and the transaction, that had already been approved in other jurisdictions and at the GS, would be postponed indefinitely[35]. This, however, was insufficient for CADE to waive its definition of a gun-jumping violation. In its decision, Commissioner Paula Azevedo stated that global transactions are expected to face timing differences, and such challenges should not be used as excuses to violate regulatory obligations. Therefore, the tribunal concluded that, although the parties acted in good faith by giving notice to CADE of their decision, this amounted to a gun-jumping violation, leading to the imposition of a BRL 57 million fine.

---

[31] CADE does not have a precise definition of competitively sensitive information, but describes that it may contain specific data about: costs of the companies involved, capacity level and plans for expansion, marketing strategies, product pricing, main customers and deductions ensured, employees' wages, main suppliers and terms of contracts, plans for future acquisitions, research and development, and competition strategies, among others.

[32] The clean team is indicated for complex transactions where (i) there is significant concentration between the companies, (ii) it is necessary to exchange a vast amount of information or (iii) the transaction creates potential competitive risks.

[33] Concentration Act No 08700.009018/2015-86. Press Release, "Cisco and Technicolor admit practice of gun jumping in global transaction" (21 January 2016), <http://en.cade.gov.br/press-releases/cisco-and-technicolor-admit-practice-of-gun-jumping-in-global-transaction-1>.

[34] Concentration Act No 08700.001908/2019-73.

[35] This was a peculiar moment in 2019, in which three commissioners' terms of office ended, leaving the tribunal without a minimum seating quorum.

IV. Substance

1. Competition Analysis

In order to assess whether transactions will raise anticompetitive concerns, CADE conducts a competition assessment that comprises steps described in the Guidelines for the Analysis of Horizontal Concentration Merger Reviews, published by CADE in July 2016[36]. Under the Horizontal Merger Guidelines, the classic assessment of a transaction by the authorities involves a set of steps.

The first step is the relevant market definition. CADE must determine which markets are affected by the transaction, on both the product and geographic dimensions. While defining the markets, CADE usually assesses which products are substitutable by others; that is, if a product is not available, or becomes more expensive, what is its substitutability for others. In terms of geographic delimitation, CADE takes into consideration factors such as where the parties are located, where their competitors are located, where customers are located, where sales take place, etc.

The second step is measuring market power. CADE presumes the existence of a dominant position when the post-merger share of the merging parties exceeds 20%. The most common measure of market concentration is the evaluation of the Herfindahl-Hirschman Index (HHI)[37], as it also reveals if there is a causal link between the transaction and the increase of market concentration. The use of HHI, however, is not the only tool available, as CADE understands it does not properly evaluate transactions which include: (i) signs of market coordination; (ii) cases where one of the parties is a maverick firm; (iii) cases that involve an entrant company; (iv) cases where the concentration does not reflect the competitive dynamics; (v) cases where the transaction increases portfolio power; among others.

The third step of CADE's assessment involves assessing unilateral effects, that is, the market conditions that would enable the exercise of market power by the merging parties. Such aspects include: (i) assessing if the market has high barriers to entry (the most common methodology is comparing the minimum viable scale and the market growth); assessing if the market rivalry is high (CADE usually measures installed capacity and idle capacity – the remaining competitors are expected to have idle capacity in an extent sufficient to be able to absorb demand shifts caused by the merging parties' price increases – in that case, rivalry is considered high); and (iii) assessing whether the market is characterised by portfolio power.

The fourth step is assessing the existence of purchasing power. CADE evaluates whether the concentration in the inputs market generates or reinforces an asymmetry in relation to suppliers or gives the parties condition to increase their influence on market conditions.

---

36 <http://www.cade.gov.br/acesso-a-informacao/publicacoes-institucionais/guias_do_Cade/guia-para-analise-de-atos-de-concentracao-horizontal.pdf>.

37 The HHI is calculated by adding the squares of the individual firms' market shares. Both the post-merger HHI and the increase in the HHI resulting from the merger are relevant for the authority and allow it to categorise markets into three types: (i) unconcentrated markets: HHI below 1500; (ii) moderately concentrated markets: HHI between 1500 and 2500; and (iii) highly concentrated markets: HHI above 2500.

Following the assessment of purchasing power, CADE assesses coordinated effects that might arise from the merged entity's relationship with its remaining competitors. CADE considers that coordinated effects are likely to arise in markets where (i) there is a reduced number of companies (especially in cases where the four largest companies have a combined market share equal to or higher than 75%), (ii) there is reduced capacity to expand offers, (iii) the products are homogeneous, (iv) the prices are similar, (v) the orders are low and frequent, and (vi) the market technology is stable, among other factors. A thorough assessment of coordinated power was conducted in the attempted merger between Ultragaz and Liquigás (Concentration Act No 08700.002155/2017-51). CADE ultimately blocked the transaction, for the markets showed high concentration and a series of other factors that increased the probability of coordinated effects, such as homogeneous products, symmetry between the companies, stable demand conditions, low bargaining power by consumers, high barriers to entry and history of market coordination.

Lastly, in more complex cases, if CADE is not yet convinced that the merger will not cause harm to competition, it will move forward to measure efficiencies that might compensate the enhanced market power. Examples of efficiencies include scale and scope economies, introduction of new technology, externalities, etc. For their acceptance by the competition authorities, the parties must show causal link between the transaction and efficiency gains. This analysis is the most complex that can be conducted in merger review and, according to CADE's case law, reaching that point usually means the transaction likely will deserve the imposition of remedies.

In addition to the Horizontal Merger Guidelines, the statutory provision in Law No. 12,529/2011 states that "concentration acts involving the elimination of competition in a substantial portion of the relevant market, which could create or strengthen a dominant position or that can result in the domination of the relevant market of goods or services, shall be prohibited by CADE" (article 88, §5). The approval of such transactions may occur in case they create substantial efficiencies and their benefits are shared to a relevant extent with consumers.

Although the Guidelines describe the main aspects taken into consideration in the assessment of horizontal mergers, they also specifically state that the steps are not mandatory and that the authorities can take other aspects into account while assessing a concentration act.

2. Statistics

Under the pre-merger system, CADE blocked a limited number of transactions – the last one to be rejected was the attempted merger between Ultragaz and Liquigás[38], which was blocked in March 2018. Other past rejected operations include the attempted acquisition of Condor Pincéis by Tigre, the transaction between Estácio Participações and Kroton Educacional and the attempted acquisition of Alesat by Ipiranga.

In 2019, CADE analysed 433 merger transactions. Of those, 406 were unconditionally approved, five were approved with remedies, 17 were not considered concentration acts, and five withdrawn . The average amount of days for clearance was 16.8 days for

[38] Concentration Act No. 08700.002155/2017-51.

fast-track proceedings and 89.4 days for non-fast-track proceedings. Additionally, CADE opened 14 gun-jumping investigations which resulted in four convictions through agreements with the parties and three dismissals. The total amount of collected gun-jumping fines in 2019 was BRL 59.7 million.

3. Case Law Illustration

In early 2017, AT&T and Time Warner notified their proposed transaction to CADE (Concentration Act No 08700.001390/2017-14). In Brazil, AT&T is the owner of Sky, one of the main national TV service providers. Time Warner, on the other hand, owns a number of pay-TV channels, therefore was active on programming and licensing of pay-TV channels. The transaction involved the telecommunications sector and resulted in a proposed vertical integration between TV service providers and pay-TV channels.

The transaction triggered a significant number of interested third parties: Simba, ESPN, Discovery, Fox and NeoTV. Generally, the parties expressed concerns that it could lead to discrimination against other pay-TV channels from AT&T, in favour of Time Warner channels.

The GS initially rejected the transaction, by concluding that both parties had considerable market power that could create incentives for market foreclosure in the licensing/programming market and in the pay-TV market, generating competition concerns. It also concluded that the resulting company would allow Time Warner to access sensitive information from its competitors through Sky. Accordingly, AT&T would have access to the conditions negotiated by its rivals through Time Warner. In addition, the merged entity would have the ability and incentives to adopt discriminative measures against its competitors on both markets, weakening the pay-TV environment. The transaction also faced regulatory scrutiny, given that the verticalisation of the pay-TV sector is limited by the Telecommunications Act (Law No 12,485/2011).

Lastly, the GS also perceived potential coordinated effects, originated from a potential relationship between the two biggest pay-TV programmers (Globosat and Time Warner) and the two biggest operators in the sector (Net/Claro and Sky), which would significantly harm consumers and other companies operating in the pay-TV segment.

The transaction was forwarded to CADE's tribunal for further analysis and, in October 2017 (two months after the original assessment by the GS), approval was given to the signature of an ACC. Reporting Commissioner Gilvandro Araujo agreed with previously raised concerns of discrimination, given both parties' market power.

To solve the previously identified issues, the parties signed a five-year commitment which included: (i) the maintenance of Sky Brasil and Time Warner's programming channels as independent companies with their own governance and administration structures, in order to prevent the exchange of sensitive information; (ii) a commitment by AT&T to offer Time Warner's channels to non-affiliated packers and pay-TV service providers with all the programming channels offered to Sky, under non-discriminatory conditions; (iii) a commitment by Sky to not refuse the broadcasting of programming channels not affiliated to AT&T, among others. The ACC also established the hiring of an independent consultant to monitor the parties' compliance with the undertaken commitments.

CHILE

Mario Ybar*
(Garrigues)

Abstract

Chile's merger control regime has recently been modified. The reform of Decree-Law No 211 of 1973 (Antitrust Law or DL 211) by Law No 20.945 was approved on September 2016. The reform established a mandatory notification system for certain transactions which produce an effect in Chile and exceed the thresholds determined by the Fiscalía Nacional Económica (FNE). Merger control is conducted by the FNE in a two-phase investigation after which the FNE can either approve the concentration unconditionally, subject to the mitigations offered by the parties, or prohibit the transaction. Only the latter decisions can be challenged before the Tribunal de Defensa de la Libre Competencia (TDLC or Competition Court). The substantive test by which the FNE assesses the transactions is substantial lessening of competition.

---

* The author is Director of the Competition Practice at Garrigues, Chile. Previously, he was Deputy National Prosecutor and first Head of the Mergers Unit at the Chilean Competition Authority (FNE).

I. Introduction

1. Brief Overview

DL 211 is the legislation governing antitrust matters in Chile. The new Title IV, incorporated by Law No 20.945 of 2016, regulates the new mandatory merger control system[1]. Supreme Decree of the Ministry of Economy No 33, dated 1 March 2017, provides the procedural regulation for merger control. Resolution No 157 of the FNE dated 25 March 2019, sets the applicable thresholds[2].

There are the National Economic Prosecutor's Office (FNE) Guidelines on Jurisdiction[3], Remedies[4] and Thresholds Interpretation[5], all dated June 2017. Although partially repealed, the FNE still uses the Guideline on Concentrations Analysis, dated October 2012[6], as a substantive reference for horizontal mergers.

2. Institutional Set-Up

According to DL 211, there are three entities in charge of enforcing antitrust laws and regulations in Chile: the FNE, the Tribunal de Defensa de la Libre Competencia (TDLC) and the Supreme Court, whose constitutional third chamber reviews the judicial resources against the final decisions from the TDLC.

The FNE is an independent administrative entity in charge of investigating conduct that may impede, restrict or hinder competition in the markets. It represents the public interest before the TDLC and the Supreme Court of Chile. Since 2017, the FNE is responsible for the new mandatory merger control system.

The Fiscal Nacional Económico (prosecutor) leads the FNE. He is appointed by the president of Chile through a selection process composed of senior public officials. The prosecutor holds the position for a four-year term, which may be renewed only once for further four years. The prosecutor can only be removed from its duties for the following causes: a) end of the legal period of the appointment; b) voluntary resignation accepted by the president of the republic; c) destitution for manifest negligence in the performance of his or her duties; or d) incapacity[7].

---

1 Before the amendment of the Antitrust Law that established a mandatory merger control regime starting in 2017, DL 211 provided for a general system for voluntary consultation about actions, acts or contracts, which the parties to a transaction or even third parties with legitimate interest could use in order to provoke the assessment of any concentration.

2 <https://www.fne.gob.cl/wp-content/uploads/2019/03/Resoluci%C3%B3n-exenta-157.pdf>.

3 <https://www.fne.gob.cl/wp-content/uploads/2017/11/Guidelines-on-Jurisdiction.pdf> (non-official English version).

4 <https://www.fne.gob.cl/wp-content/uploads/2017/11/Guidelines-on-Remedies.pdf> (non-official English version).

5 <https://www.fne.gob.cl/wp-content/uploads/2017/10/Guia-Interpretacion-Umbrales-1.pdf>.

6 <https://www.fne.gob.cl/wp-content/uploads/2012/10/Guia-Fusiones.pdf>.

7 Removal due to the causes set forth in c) and d) will be determined by the president of the republic, with a favourable report from the Supreme Court of Chile, at the request of the Ministry of Economy, Development and Tourism. The favourable report will be issued by the court's plenary, specially convened to that effect, and must garner the satisfactory vote of the majority of its presiding members.

The TDLC is a special, independent court of law, part of the judicial branch and subject to the supervision of the Supreme Court of Chile. Its main role is to prevent, correct and sanction anticompetitive conduct, and to decide on all cases the FNE or private persons may submit to its consideration.

The TDLC is composed of five members, three of whom must be attorneys (among whom one will be designated court president) and two must hold university studies or post-graduate degrees in economics. The judges are appointed by a mixed system that entails designations by the president of the republic through a selection process carried out by the Supreme Court of Chile (president of the TDLC) and the Central Bank (one lawyer and one economist), and direct designations by the Central Bank (one lawyer and one economist).

The judges remain in their positions for six years, and can be appointed for one term only.

All final decisions from the TDLC are subject to a *Recurso de Reclamación* before the Supreme Court. The only exceptions are merger decisions in which the TDLC either confirms the FNE's prohibition decision, or approves the merger subject to the last mitigation offered by the merging parties, which do not have any judicial recourse available.

3. Type of Merger Control

Concentration operations that have an effect in Chile, which are carried out by the means established in article 47 of DL 211, and which exceed the thresholds established by the FNE, must be notified to the FNE prior to their execution.

A notified concentration operation shall be deemed suspended as of the date of notification and until the decision that resolves the relevant proceedings has become final and binding. It is thus an *ex ante* merger control system.

If the concentration operation that has an effect in Chile is carried out by the means established in article 47 of DL 211, but does not exceed the thresholds established by the FNE, the companies may voluntarily notify them to the FNE to apply for clearance, provided the transaction has not been completed by the time of the notification.

If these transactions are not notified voluntarily, the FNE may still investigate them *ex officio* within one year as of completion. In this case, the investigation will be subject to the general rules of the FNE's investigations regulated in article 39(a) of DL 211, and not to the rules and deadlines of the new Title IV of DL 211.

II. Scope of Application

1. Definition of Notifiable Transaction

For a transaction to be notifiable, either mandatorily or voluntarily, the concentration operations should be executed following any of the means detailed in article 47 of DL 211:

a) Merging, regardless of the entity resulting from the merger;
b) Acquiring an interest that allows them, individually or jointly, to exert a material influence on another firm's administration;

c) Entering into agreements, under any modality, to form an independent economic agent that carries out activities in a continuous way;
d) Acquiring control over the assets of another firm.

The acquisition of minority shares in another company is not required to be notified to the FNE under the merger control procedure, since it does not fulfil the requirement established in article 47(b) (the buyer should be able to exert material influence in the targeted company).

However, according to article 4 *bis*, a post-closing information requirement exists when a 10% interest or more is acquired in a competitor. In order to comply with this duty, the parties of the transaction should complete the model form found on the FNE's website[8].

Recent case law has demonstrated that failure to inform the FNE of minority acquisitions may result in the FNE seeking to impose fines before the TDLC[9].

2. Material Scope

DL 211 rules of merger control apply to all economic sectors and activities, without exemption. This is without prejudice to other possible authorisations required by sectorial regulation (insurance and banking law, where authorisation by the Comisión de Mercados Financieros (Chilean Financial Markets Committee) is also required).

3. Geographical Scope

DL 211 follows an effect-based approach. Therefore, only concentration operations that have an effect in Chile and involve parties who had sales in Chile the year prior to that in which the notification is made are notifiable to the FNE.

4. Thresholds

The thresholds were established by the FNE in Exempt Resolution Nº 157 of 25 March 2019, which replaced Exempt Resolution No 667 of 24 November 2017, increasing the thresholds for notification.

According to Exempt Resolution No 157, a concentration must be notified if a two-pronged test is met:

a) The aggregate turnover in Chile of all the parties involved in the transaction, during the year prior to that in which the notification is made, reach or exceed UF 2.5 million (USD 100 million in 2019); and

---

8 <http://formulario4bis.fne.gob.cl/>. The completed form should be sent to <formulario4bis@fne.gob.cl>.

9 "FNE pide multas por un total de $ 780 millones en los primeros dos requerimientos contra empresas que no notificaron su participación en competidores" (28 January 2020), <https://www.fne.gob.cl/fne-pide-multas-por-un-total-de-780-millones-en-los-primeros-dos-requerimientos-contra-empresas-que-no-notificaron-su-participacion-en-competidores/>.

b) At least two of the merging parties had an individual turnover in Chile of UF 450,000 during the year prior to that in which the notification is made (USD 18 million in 2019)[10].

The FNE published a *Practical Guideline for Threshold Application*[11] which aims to guide the concentration parties in the determination and calculation of the sales considered for the effect of the application of the thresholds.

III. Procedure

1. Launch of Procedure

The parties are bound to jointly practice the notification before closing the transaction. No fees are charged by the FNE.

The content of the notification is regulated by the regulation passed by the Ministry of the Economy, Development and Tourism[12], and in the prescribed format published by the FNE[13]. In certain circumstances[14], the precept allows the parties to perform a simplified merger notification (as opposed to the regular procedure). This allows less information to be provided when notifying the transaction.

The investigation file is kept confidential during Phase 1, and it becomes public only after the beginning of Phase 2[15]. All the FNE's final decisions are public[16].

2. Development of Procedure

The merger regulation entails two phases, both of which take place before the FNE. Phase I lasts up to 30 working days, with limited room for extension.

After Phase 1 the FNE may:

a) Approve the concentration unconditionally;
b) Approve the concentration subject to the condition that the mitigation measures offered by the notifying parties must be performed; or

---

10 These figures might include the sales of other firms of the corporate groups, depending of the way in which the concentration is effected.

11 FNE, Guía Práctica para la Aplicación de Umbrales de Notificación de Operaciones de Concentración en Chile (June 2017), <https://www.fne.gob.cl/wp-content/uploads/2017/10/Guia-Interpretacion-Umbrales-1.pdf>.

12 Reglamento sobre la notificación de una operación de concentración. Num. 33.- Santiago, 1 de marzo de 2017.<https://www.fne.gob.cl/wp-content/uploads/2017/10/Decreto-33-Aprueba-Reglamento-Operaciones-de-Concentracion-1.pdf>.

13 FNE, Formulario de Notificación Ordinario (June 2017), <https://www.fne.gob.cl/wp-content/uploads/2017/10/notificacion_ordinario.pdf>.

14 Joint market shares in any plausible relevant market below 20%; and individual or joint market shares below 30% in all the plausible markets if there is vertical integration.

15 Notwithstanding the fact that the FNE can order, either *ex officio* or at the request of the interested party, that certain parts of the file be deemed confidential.

16 FNE Investigations, <*FNE* https://www.fne.gob.cl/biblioteca/actuaciones-de-la-fne/investigaciones-de-la-fne/>.

c) Extend the investigation to Phase 2 when it considers that the notified transaction's unconditional materialisation or its implementation subject to the mitigation measures offered by the notifying party, respectively, could substantially reduce competition.

If the FNE does not make a decision by the expiration of the 30-day period, the operation will be deemed approved.

Phase 2 lasts up to an additional 90 working days, with limited room for extensions.

During Phase 2 any third party interested in the transaction, including suppliers, competitors, clients or consumers, becomes entitled to intervene in the investigation.

After Phase 2, the FNE may:

a) Approve the concentration unconditionally;
b) Approve the concentration subject to the condition that the mitigation measures offered by the notifying parties must be performed; or
c) Prohibit the concentration, when it considers that it does substantially reduce competition.

During the investigation, the FNE may apply the factors or methods set out in article 39(f), (g), (h), (j), (k), (l) and (m) of DL 211[17].

In order to share information with foreign competition authorities, the FNE requires a waiver from the merging parties. The waiver model is found in an annex of the notification form.

The notifying parties can submit to the FNE an offer of mitigation measures that they deem appropriate to mitigate the competition risks at any time of the investigation. Each submission will suspend the deadlines mentioned above for 10 or 15 working days (in Phase 1 and Phase 2, respectively).

Remedies cannot be imposed by the FNE; they should always be offered by the merging parties.

With the purpose of determining whether the mitigation measures offered by the notifying parties address the risks found by the FNE, it is allowed to carry out market tests with thirdparties.

3. Conclusion of Procedure

Approval decisions by the FNE are not subject to any recourse before the TDLC.

Only prohibition decisions by the FNE may be reviewed by the TDLC. The special review recourse against the FNE's prohibition decision must be filed exclusively by the notifying parties within 10 days of its notification.

---

17 Among others, the FNE has the power to request cooperation from public entities and regulators, request information and records from any private entity and summon to submit their verbal or written depositions to any worker from public and private entities. Any entity that, with the purpose of hindering, diverting or eluding the FNE, conceals information that has been requested or submits false information, shall be penalised with imprisonment. Any entity who is bound to comply with the information request issued by the FNE, and unjustifiably fails to do so, will be penalised with a fine.

In such cases, the TDLC may confirm the FNE's prohibition decision or approve the transaction subject to the last mitigation measures offered by the parties to the FNE. These decisions are final and not subject to any recourse.

The TDLC is also allowed to approve the transaction subject to different mitigation measures than those offered by the merging parties. In this case the mitigations are imposed and not negotiated. If this is the case, the TDLC's decision may be appealed before the Supreme Court of Chile.

Since April 2019, the FNE created a new unit (Unidad de Fiscalización) in charge of monitoring the compliance of economic agents with the decisions from the TDLC and the FNE. This unit will have as one of its main priorities verifying compliance with the mitigation measures offered by or applied to merging parties.

4. Sanctions

According to article 3 *bis* of DL 211, the following conducts may result in the same penalties as applicable to any other anticompetitive conduct: breaching the notification duty[18], closing the transaction during the suspension period, not complying with the conditions subject to which the concentration was approved, materialising a concentration that has been prohibited and notifying an operation supplying false information.

Article 26 of DL 211 regulates the sanctions that could be imposed for anticompetitive conducts: a) amendment or termination of acts or contracts; b) dissolution or modification of companies; and c) fines up to 30% of the infringer's sales corresponding to the line of products or services associated with the infraction during the period in which the infringement was being perpetrated, or up to the double of the economic benefit received as a result of the infringement.

IV. Substance

1. Competition Analysis

The substantive test for merger control is substantial reduction of competition (article 57 of DL 211). Non-competition issues are not considered in the assessment.

Although partially repealed, the Internal Guide for the Analysis of Horizontal Concentration Operations[19] provides the criteria to be followed by the FNE when evaluating horizontal concentrations. The Guidelines follow traditional analysis criteria: determination of the relevant markets affected, estimate of the market shares of the market participants, concentration indexes, assessment of entry conditions, and determination of unilateral and coordinated risks for competitions and their counterbalancing factors, mainly efficiencies.

---

18 In this case, according to article 26(d) of DL 211, the TDLC may impose, in addition, a fine of up to 20 UT for each day of delay, as from the day on which the concentration is consummated.

19 FNE, Guía para el Análisis de Operaciones de Concentración (October 2012), <https://www.fne.gob.cl/wp-content/uploads/2012/10/Guia-Fusiones.pdf>.

Case law from FNE decisions, since the beginning of the mandatory notification system, is consistent in showing that the FNE supports their unilateral risks claims with economic tests, mainly GUPPI calculations.

2. Statistics

In 2019, 41 investigations completed:

a) 25 were subject to the simplified procedure, and 16 to the ordinary procedure.
b) 38 transactions were unconditionally approved; two transactions were approved subject to mitigation measures offered by the parties; and one transaction was prohibited[20] (which was the only merger whose review moved to Phase 2 and which the parties did not challenge before the TDLC).
c) The average length of the investigations that concluded in 2019 was: 28 working days for concentrations unconditionally approved; 91 working days for concentrations approved subject to mitigation measures; and 181 working days for the prohibited merger.

3. Case Law Illustration

Decision number:

FNE Investigation Resolution No F90-2017 of 10 May 2018[21].

TDLC Ruling No 166/2018 of 27 November 2018[22].

Parties/Sector/Transaction:

Acquisition of decisive influence in its competitor Nutrabien by Ideal, the largest player in the sweet snacks industry.

Nutrabien is a company belonging to the Grupo CCU, exclusively active in the sweet snacks industry, commercialising several different products. Its main products are brownies in individual and pack format.

Ideal is a subsidiary of Grupo Bimbo, a Mexican multinational bakery manufacturing company. In Chile, it is the main producer of bread and it is also active in the sweet snacks industry.

Relevant issues discussed:

According to the FNE, the transaction implied the consolidation between the first and the third player in the relevant market with a joint market share of 50–55% of the market[23]

---

20 Prohibition decision of 9 December 2019 <https://www.fne.gob.cl/wp-content/uploads/2019/12/inproh_F178_2019-1.pdf>.

21 <https://www.fne.gob.cl/wp-content/uploads/2018/05/inpr_F90_2017.pdf>.

22 <https://www.tdlc.cl/nuevo_tdlc/wp-content/uploads/sentencias/Sentencia_166_2018.pdf>.

23 The exact market share was kept confidential.

(at least in the supermarkets channel, as opposed to small stores where the joint market share was lower).

GUPPI, IPR and CMCR calculations, built upon surveys conducted to customers, consistently suggested the existence of upward pricing pressure above 10%. The FNE supported its findings with an economic report by Massimo Motta.

The FNE denied the proposed transaction on the grounds that it substantially lessened competition through unilateral effects that were not offset by merger efficiencies, in a context of high entry barriers (namely, the brand importance).

In addition, according to the FNE, the behavioural mitigation measures offered by the parties did not fulfil the standard requirements and therefore did not offset the risks found in the investigation[24].

The parties appealed to the TDLC and the tribunal overturned the FNE's decision and cleared the transaction *pursuant* to the three-year behavioural remedies proposed by the parties.

First, the TDLC decision disagreed with the FNE's market definition, concluding that sweet cookies should have been considered part of the product relevant market. If that was the case, the market share of the merged entities was largely diluted. However, the TDLC agreed with the FNE in that Nutrabien and Ideal were direct competitors and therefore supported the idea that the merger was likely to produce significant price increases.

Nevertheless, the TDLC considered that the FNE either failed to take into account, or minimised the impact, of certain dynamic considerations, such as efficiencies[25] and entry. About the latter, the TDLC argued that the FNE wrongly ruled out the possibility of rearrangement of brands and repositioning from a remaining competitor, which is likely to produce enough competitive pressure to prevent the risks detected by the FNE[26].

---

24 Among the remedies the parties offered were: fixing price caps and quality standards of the products; prohibition of incorporating exclusive dealing or targeted rebates clauses in Nutrabien's contracts; prohibition to use more shelf space than the percentage that corresponds to its market share; and, commitment to expanding the distribution of Nutrabien products. Most of these mitigations were offered for a three-year period.

25 Namely, efficiencies in distribution logistics and raw material purchase.

26 For its part, the FNE rejected the claim that a remaining player would expand its operations and reposition its products to compete more firmly with Nutrabien products, on the grounds that it lacks the incentives to challenge the leader, especially if considered that that strategy would lead to a significant cannibalisation of its own products.

COLOMBIA

Pablo Márquez*

(Márquez Barrera Castañeda Ramírez)

Abstract

This paper provides a general overview of Colombian law with respect to merger control and economic integrations, including its institutional set-up, applicable law and guidance, as well as the basic foundations used by the competition authority – Superintendency of Industry and Commerce – to exercise its merger control analysis. As will be shown, merger control is mainly governed by the provisions of Law 155 of 1959, amended by Law 1340 of 2009. The ex ante *merger control requires undertakings to get clearance from the authority before the transaction is closed, regardless of the legal or economic structure. Fines for not notifying an economic integration subject to* ex ante *control are the same as those imposed for anticompetitive behaviour. This paper includes an analysis of a recent case to illustrate the type of conditions that are imposed by the SIC, as well as the statistics regarding merger control approval and/or rejections.*

---

* Pablo Márquez holds a PhD from Oxford University and a master's degree from Harvard University; he is a professor of law at Universidad Javeriana in Colombia and partner of Márquez Barrera Castañeda Ramírez. He has more than 20 years' experience in competition law and ICT. He was the chairman of the Commission for Communications Regulation and Superintendent for Antitrust at the Colombian Competition Authority. Pablo has won several awards, such as the Caldas Award from the Colombian Central Bank, the Medal of Merit in Telecoms from the Government of Colombia and the Robert Cooter Award in Law and Economics.

Special thanks to Diana Castiblanco and Nasser Obando for their research and support for the production of this article.

I. Introduction

1. Brief Overview

Competition law in Colombia started in 1959, with Law 155 of 1959. This law was a price-control regime enacted based on role of the state as general director of the economy. Article 4 of Law 155 established an *ex ante* merger control process that was modified by Law 1340 of 2009. Other relevant legislation includes Resolutions 10,930 of 2015, and 93,503 of 2018 from the Superintendency of Industry and Commerce (SIC). Merger review guidelines have been published by the authority in 2013[1], 2015[2] and 2018[3], where all the information regarding merger control procedure and substantive analysis is explained.

2. Institutional Set-Up

Article 6 of Law 1340 of 2009 appoints SIC as the single national competition authority, with enforcement powers for the supervision and control of anticompetitive practices, competition advocacy and merger control. By virtue of the law, no other authorities are involved in the review process of a merger. However, there are two specific sectors that have a special regime regarding merger control: the first involves mergers between financial institutions, while the second involves mergers between parties in the aeronautical sector. This special regime consists of the Civil Aviation Authority's faculty to enforce merger control between aircraft operators, pursuant to article 1866 of the Commercial Code and article 8 of Law 1340 of 2009.

According to article 1 of Decree 2153 of 1992, SIC is the government's administrative and technical agency whose principal activity is aimed at strengthening business development processes and to improve Colombian consumer satisfaction. The SIC operates under the direction of the Ministry of Commerce, Industry and Tourism.

Both the merger control system and the anticompetitive regime in general are administrative law systems, as opposed to the jurisdictional adjudication system. Administrative proceedings associated with the control of behaviour may lead to the imposition of fines for those undertakings that infringe the laws regarding anticompetitive conduct.

SIC is headed by the superintendent who is in charge of leading the authority for a period equivalent to the period of the president of the republic, four years. On the other hand, those appointed as superintendent must have a professional degree, as well as a graduate degree – master's or doctorate – related to the functions of a superintendent, in addition to at least 10 years of professional experience. The process of appointment is regulated by Decree 1817 of 2015, according to which, after a public invitation, the president of

---

1 Superintendency of Industry and Commerce, *Guía de Integraciones Empresariales'* (SIC 2013) <<https://www.sic.gov.co/sites/default/files/files/Nuestra_Entidad/Publicaciones/Guia_Integraciones_VF_Para_Publicacion.pdf>.

2 Superintendency of Industry and Commerce, *Guía de Análisis de Concentracioness Empresariales* (SIC 2015).

3 Superintendency of Industry and Commerce, *Guía de Análisis de Integraciones Empresariales (Trámites de Pre-evaluación)* (SIC 2018) <https://www.sic.gov.co/sites/default/files/files/Publicaciones/Guia_Integraciones_Empresariales_31-07-2018.pdf>.

Colombia chooses a superintendent out of those who comply with all requirements and conditions. Prior to appointment, the president may require the opinion of citizens, or social or academic organisations with regard to the good credit of the applicants, as necessary. Likewise, the president may interview some applicants.

3. Type of Merger Control

Colombian merger control system is an *ex ante* control with a compulsory duty to inform, when parties comply with the objective criteria set out in article 9 of Law 1340 of 2009. Clearance is required prior to closing, so every operation must be suspended until SIC's decision. SIC has determined that *ex ante* merger control evaluates the economic effects that will be generated as a result of the transaction with the objective of avoiding an undue restriction to competition that will affect consumers' welfare.

As SIC has defined it, *ex ante* control studies the conditions of the relevant markets affected by the transaction and how these could be affected by a merger. For its part, *ex post* control over anticompetitive practices aims to evaluate the existence of potentially anticompetitive conducts that have been carried out by market agents (agreements, acts and abuses of dominant position). The difference between *ex post* and *ex ante* control in Colombia resides in the preventive character of *ex ante* control, while *ex post* control sanctions anticompetitive conducts already conducted by market agents, suggesting that *ex ante* control does not attempt to adjust market dynamics prior to the merger[4].

II. Scope of Application

1. Definition of Notifiable Transaction

As stated above, SIC's scope on merger control is limited to the conditions established in article 9 of Law 1340 of 2009. Therefore, SIC can only investigate transactions that meet the subjective and objective criteria.

The SIC has defined "merger" or "economic integration" as any mechanism used to acquire control of one or several companies, or to acquire control of a company of another already existing company, or to create a new company in order to develop activities together. Regardless of the legal form of the transaction, an "integration" implies the combination of one or more activities in which competition between the parties to the transaction ceases after its closing[5].

Control is defined in section 4 of article 45 of Decree 2153 of 1992[6] as the possibility of directly or indirectly influencing a company's business policy, the initiation or termination of a company's activity, the variation of the company's economic activity or

---

4 Resolution 24,527 of 2014, SIC.

5 See *Productos Quaker Ltda v SIC Tribunal Administrativo de Cundinamarca*, Sección primera, subsección B, [2008], 13.

6 Decreto 2153 of 1992 (Diario Oficial, Colombia), art. 45.

the disposition of the essential assets or rights for the development of the company's activity. This definition, used by SIC in the Merger Control Guidelines, considers control to include the influence of one company over the structural elements of another and, in this sense, this influence could be exerted though veto powers or other special rights and would not necessarily require a capital stake majority.

Therefore, all transactions by which one company acquires control of another are considered mergers for the purpose of *ex ante* merger control. Thus, transactions that involve mergers and acquisitions, acquisition of assets, joint ventures and minority shareholdings, as well as operations that do not involve the transfer of shares or assets, may be subject to merger control by SIC under Colombian law.

In this regard, joint ventures require special attention since Resolution 553 of 2013[7] clarified when joint ventures are subject to merger control. This resolution states that a joint venture between competitors constitutes a merger under Colombian law if the following elements are met:

- The operation is intended as permanent and ends definitively – or in a substantial manner – the participation of a competitor in the relevant market;
- The operation does not only consist of the unification of a specific function but also involves the unification of a line of business or a market; and
- The business or entity arising from the operation has full functions in the market. It must have its own independent financial resources or, at least, the potential to operate independently in the market, like a separate business.

Nonetheless, internal restructurings or reorganisations are expressly excepted from merger control, pursuant to paragraph 3 of article 9 of Law 1340 of 2009, which states that merger operations carried out between entities that belong to the same economic group, or under the same unit of control and purpose, or controlled by the same real beneficiary are exempt from the duty to inform SIC of transaction, regardless of the legal form they adopt[8].

2. Material Scope

As a general rule, all economic sectors are subject to merger control review by SIC since article 4 of Law 1340 of 2009 expressly provides that Colombia's competition regime applies to all sectors and economic activities. However, as stated above, there are two specific sectors that have a special regime regarding merger control: mergers between financial institutions and mergers in the aeronautical sector.

Regardless of the sector in which the merger occurs, all merging parties have a duty to inform, when the proposed transaction complies with the subjective and objective criteria set out in article 4 of Law 155 of 1959. It should be noted that article 9 of Law 1340 of 2009 establishes in its last subsection that all processes regarding mergers or business reorganisations exclusively between financial institutions are reviewed by the

---

7 Resolution 553 of 2013, SIC.

8 Ley 1340, 2009 (Diario Oficial, Colombia), art. 9

Superintendence of Finance. In the aeronautical sector, the special regime consists of the Civil Aviation Authority's faculty to enforce merger control between aircraft operators, pursuant to article 1866 of the Commercial Code and article 8 of Law 1340 of 2009.

3. Geographical Scope

According to article 2 of Law 1340 of 2009, merger control provisions apply to all activities that may have an effect in national markets. Therefore, if a foreign-to-foreign merger involves activities that may have an effect in Colombian territory, such as permanent investments, imports or exports, or any business in Colombia, it should be reported to SIC[9].

There is no specific test to analyse local effects, and a formal local presence is not required in order to trigger *ex ante* merger control obligations. Therefore, all mergers that may have an effect in Colombia should be reported to SIC, provided they comply with article 9's subjective and objective criteria. By way of example, filing can be required when a target has no sales and/or assets in the jurisdiction, if the proposed operation would have an effect in any national market, such as when a Colombian company acquires a foreign target, or when a foreign target conducts any business in Colombia.

4. Thresholds

If the operation complies with the requirements established in article 9 of Law 1340 of 2009 – i.e., both subjective and objective criteria – the parties must comply with SIC's merger procedure. Operations that do not meet these requirements do not have to be reported.

Under article 9 of Law 1340 of 2009 and article 1 of Resolution 10,930 of 2015, it is mandatory to inform SIC of any operation between parties that are engaged in the same economic activity or participate in the same value chain (subjective criteria), regardless of the legal form of the transaction, if the parties comply with one of the following objective criteria:

- Jointly or individually, their revenues exceed 60,000 legal monthly minimum wages (approx USD 16 million) during the prior fiscal year; or
- Jointly or individually, the total assets exceed 60,000 legal monthly minimum wages (approx USD 16 million).

This threshold (60,000 legal monthly minimum wages) is defined annually by the SIC[10].

Asset-based thresholds, like those set out in article 9 of Law 1340 of 2009, are based on book value. On the other hand, only businesses that meet the threshold – or the business group to which it belongs – are relevant for the purpose of calculating the jurisdictional thresholds. In order to determine whether companies meet thresholds, it is necessary to include the seller's turnover with that of the target.

Thresholds are regularly calculated in a group-wide basis; one should consider the "business group" definition provided in article 28 of Law 22 of 1995, where it is stated that,

---

9 ibid, art. 2

10 Resolution 76,544 of 2019, SIC.

in order to talk about "business group", there should be a subordination link as well as a unity of purpose and direction among the entities.

As mentioned, the applicable procedure varies, depending on the market share of the intervening parties. If the combined market share of the intervening parties is less than 20%, the Notification or fast-track procedure is applicable. When combined market share is more than 20%, the applicable procedure is a prior approval or Pre-Evaluation Procedure.

For its part, there are market-share presumptions that apply to particular sectors. For example, according to article 58 of the Organic Statue of the Financial Sector[11], merger transactions that do not exceed a 25% market-share threshold are understood not to generate significant risks for the competition process and are therefore considered authorised. Similarly, the public utilities regime provides a presumption of dominant position for utility companies that serve 25% or more of users in each relevant market[12].

III. Procedure

1. Launch of Procedure

As stated above, pursuant to article 9 of Law 1340 of 2009 and article 1 of SIC Resolution 9350 of 2018, it is mandatory to inform SIC and obtain any operation between parties that are engaged in the same economic activity or participate in the same value chain (subjective criteria). The duty to inform obliges parties to start a merger review process before SIC before a transaction is closed. Proceedings' length and the depth of analysis by the authority depend on market shares of the parties. It will be a fast-track procedure (Notification) if the parties' relevant market shares (jointly or individually considered) are below the 20% threshold, and will be a full procedure (Pre-Evaluation Request) if the parties' relevant market shares exceed this threshold[13].

All the intervening parties are responsible for filing, but one party may represent the others in the merger control process before the SIC. Under article 2.2 of SIC Resolution 10,930 of 2015, a power of attorney is needed when the representation is exercised through an attorney, or the signature of the legal representative is required if the company in charge of the filing is acting directly in the process. All information needs to be submitted in Spanish, so all information must be translated into Spanish before its submission to the SIC[14].

A. Fast-Track Procedure

The fast-track procedure (Notification) applies if the parties' relevant market shares (jointly or individually considered) are below the 20% threshold. It is important to note

---

11 Ley 663, 1993 (Diario Oficial, Colombia), art. 58
12 Ley 142, 1994 (Diario Oficial, Colombia), art. 14.13
13 Ley 1340, 2009 (Diario Oficial, Colombia), art. 9
14 Resolution 10,930 of 2015, SIC, art. 2.2

that the merger transactions subject to a fast-track procedure are authorised as of the filing of the merger notification document[15].

B. Pre-Evaluation Procedure

If the economic concentration must be approved by SIC (Pre-Evaluation Request), the parties must submit detailed information related to the proposed transaction, including the parties and structure of the transaction, the parties' financial statements and other relevant information, a full description of the relevant markets, the parties' market shares, and the parties' competitors, distribution channels and customers. The details of this information are contained in Annex 1 of Resolution 10,930 of 2015[16].

If the SIC considers that the proposed transaction is complex (because the parties have high market shares or because one of the parties is vertically integrated, for example), it will require additional information with a high degree of detail, such as information regarding prices to consumers/customers, cost structures, levels of imports and exports, overall and idle capacities, and inputs and their providers. The details of this information are contained in Annex 2 of Resolution 10,930 of 2015[17].

With regard to filing fees, it is worth mentioning that article 152 of Law 2010 of 2019 orders the creation of a fee for the *ex ante* merger control by SIC. However, such fee has not been created by SIC so far. Therefore, it is understood that all filings for merger control are free.

The level of detail required in the preparation of a filing depends on the characteristics of the parties and the market(s) in which they participate (including the individual or combined operational revenues or assets, the individual or combined market shares, barriers to entry and other relevant information related to the competitive dynamics of the market). There are other specific requirements for the submission of documents – for instance, all quantitative information must be submitted in magnetic media through an electronic spreadsheet with numerical cell format, and powers of attorney must be apostilled if they come from abroad[18].

2. Development of Procedure

A. Notification or Fast-Track Procedure

Once the parties have provided the information required by article 3.2 of Resolution 10,930 of 2015, the SIC has 10 business days to issue an acknowledgement of receipt or suggest the parties to proceed to a Pre-Evaluation Procedure, if it does not agree with the methodology used by the parties to define relevant markets or estimate market shares[19].

---

15 The information that must be submitted in a notification procedure is found in s 3.2 of Resolution 10,930 of 2015.

16 The Pre-Evaluation Procedure, Annex 1 of Resolution 10,930 of 2015, provides the list of documents and information required for the submission.

17 Annex 2 of Resolution SIC 10,930 of 2015 provides the list of documents and information pertaining to Phase 2 of the Pre-Evaluation Procedure.

18 Resolution 10,930 of 2015, SIC, art. 2.2.2.

19 See Caracol/La Voz de Colombia, SIC [2018].

B. Pre-Evaluation Request

The first phase of the Pre-Evaluation Procedure starts with the intervening parties filing a document that includes the information listed in Annex 1 of Resolution 10,930 of 2015 and complies with the Pre-Evaluation Guide described in said Annex. Once this document is filed and the information is considered complete, SIC has 30 business days to decide whether to move to the second phase or terminate the proceeding in the first phase and approve the economic concentration[20].

SIC may decide to move to Phase 2 if, after the analysis of the information, considers that there were not enough elements to determine the absence of substantial risks to competition. If the SIC decides to move to Phase 2, a second request for information (RFI) is sent to the parties and includes all the information set out in Annex 2 of Resolution 10,930 of 2015. Once the parties file the reply to the RFI and the information is deemed complete, SIC has three calendar months to decide whether it approves the transaction, rejects the transaction or approves the transaction with conditions. If SIC fails to issue a decision within these three months, it is understood that the transaction has been authorised by law[21]. A second RFI in the second phase, at SIC's discretion, might restart the Phase 2 clock[22].

If the process applicable to the transaction is a Notification or fast-track procedure, it usually takes 10 business days. When the applicable procedure is a pre-evaluation, Phase 1 takes 30 business days and Phase 2 takes up to three months, but, if information is not filed in full, SIC can stop the clock[23].

In addition, if there is a motion of reconsideration (i.e., a third party files a revision of the decision), closing can only happen once the parties have been formally served with SIC's decision. This will add up to two months after the filing of the appeal, but, on average, it takes between two and four weeks to decide.

As stated previously, SIC's scope is limited to the conditions established in article 9 of Law 1340 of 2009. Therefore, SIC can only investigate transactions that meet the subjective and objective criteria.

C. Information and Confidentiality

For transactions reported through the Notification or fast-track procedure, SIC is empowered to review, within the following five years, whether the combined market share of the intervening parties was, in effect, less than 20%. If it is found that the market share presented by the parties was underestimated, the SIC may impose the sanctions described in articles 25 and 26 of Law 1340 of 2009 (maximum 100,000 legal monthly wages for legal entities and 2,000 legal monthly wages for individuals)[24].

---

20 Ley 1340, 2009 (Diario Oficial, Colombia), art. 9.

21 ibid, art. 10.

22 ibid.

23 Resolution 10,930 of 2015, SIC, art. 2.4.

24 Ley 1340, 2009 (Diario Oficial, Colombia), arts. 25 and 26.

In addition, under article 3.3 of Resolution 10,930 of 2015, if SIC has sufficient motive to believe that the information provided by the parties is misleading, an administrative investigation can be initiated, that could lead to the imposition of the fines described above. Misleading information can also be subject criminal prosecution[25].

Regarding confidentiality, it should be noted that once a Pre-Evaluation Request is filed, SIC has three business days from the receipt of the request to order the publication of the merger operation on the web page of the entity, as long the information is complete in terms of article 2.2 of Resolution 10,930 of 2015. This publication will include general information concerning the transaction, the intervening parties and the affected relevant markets, and provides an opportunity for third parties to present their observations towards the merger and/or to request to be recognised as interested third parties[26]. Article 2.2.3 of Resolution 10,930 of 2015 describes how to request the secrecy of information related to trade secrets or any other information on which there is a legal rule of secrecy or confidentiality.

The intervening parties must file a written, explicit and motivated request explaining which information contains a business secret or is reserved or confidential, and why. This shall be presented along with a non-confidential summary of the information that is considered confidential, and it is an obligation of the parties to provide such summaries[27]. If parties cannot present a non-confidential summary, either because the information for its nature cannot be summarised or because the presentation of the summary implies total or partial disclosure of the secret information, then this requirement may be waived. In such cases, SIC shall have a public file where the summaries will be kept and will maintain another confidential file for the complete documents.

It is important to note that SIC has the power to reject the confidential character of the information that is presented where there is no constitutional or legal reason to maintain the secrecy of such information. However, if public servants reveal to the public confidential information held by the powers conferred to them for the exercise of their legal functions, they are subject to fines and sanctions under Public Servants Code of Conduct[28].

D. Third Parties

Under Colombian law, third parties can intervene in the Pre-Evaluation Procedure, but not in the fast-track procedure. Article 2.2 of Resolution 10,930 of 2015 states that, upon the publication of the merger operation on the web page of the entity during Phase 1, third parties have 10 days to present their observations of the projected business merger.

If a third party wants to take part in the review process of the projected merger, and more precisely object to the merger, there is a limitation period of 10 business days to prove its position as a consumer or competitor, or to demonstrate it has an individual and direct interest in the projected merger, in order to request or contribute evidence to the

25 Ley 599, 2000 (Diario Oficial, Colombia), arts. 289, 291, 293.
26 Resolution 10,930 of 2015, SIC [2015], art. 2.3.2.3.
27 ibid, art. 2.2.3.
28 Ley 734, 2002 (Diario Oficial, Colombia), art. 34.

file. In previous years, SIC construed such intervention using the rules of third parties' intervention in administrative investigations for anticompetitive practices[29].

After SIC receives the third-party request, it reviews the evidence provided to determine if it is enough to assert that the third party is, effectively, a competitor or consumer affected by the transaction[30]. The authority then sends the third-party request document to the parties, for them to submit their opinion within the next three business days. Once the authority has received the filing from the parties, SIC has 15 business days to decide on the matter[31].

Interested third parties that are recognised as such have the same rights as the intervening parties. Therefore, any third party has the right to intervene in the procedure and to appeal any decision taken by SIC in the pre-evaluation process, so SIC can consider their observations towards the merger. In this sense, third parties are part of SIC's review process, if they actively participate by filing their observations and objections.

On the other hand, SIC has also the power to contact third parties *ex officio*. Contacting third parties by the authority is very common especially when there are problems regarding market size, market shares, entry or exit barriers, etc. This contact is made through questionnaires made by SIC. Therefore, contact between SIC and third parties normally takes place within the framework of written requests for information.

3. Conclusion of Procedure

Depending on the type of proceedings, SIC produces a different decision. In a Notification procedure, SIC only issues an "acknowledgement of receipt", as the transaction is deemed authorised as of filing. In difficult cases, where market shares are difficult to assess, SIC recommends the parties to hold closing for 10 days in order to produce a statement regarding product market definition and market shares. However, SIC can always investigate whether a market share was properly defined and start an investigation if there are solid grounds to consider that market shares were underestimated[32].

In a Pre-Evaluation Procedure, SIC issues a resolution containing all the arguments of its decision. After SIC reaches a decision, and such decision is notified/served, parties have 10 business days to file an appeal for reversal before SIC, according to article 76 of the Procedural Administrative Code. If parties are unsatisfied with SIC's appeal decision, they can file an appeal against the resolution before the administrative jurisdiction within four months of the notification of that decision[33].

In practice, several appeals formulated by intervening parties have been successful. SIC Resolution 9915 of 2018 provides an example of a successful appeal for reversal before

---

29 Law 1340 of 2009 (Diario Oficial, Colombia), art. 19

30 SIC, *Guía de Análisis de Integraciones Empresariales (Trámites de Pre-evaluación)*, note 3.

31 Resolution 10,930 of 2015, SIC, art. 2.5.3.

32 See article 3.3 of Resolution 10,930 of 2015.

33 See article 138, Law 1347 of 2011. This article expressly states the following: "Any person who believes their subjective right has been harmed may request the nullity of a particular, express or presumed administrative act, as well as his right being restored, and damages caused by the administrative act ..." Therefore, since all SIC resolutions are considered administrative acts, parties who do not agree with a reversal's decision may request the anullment of SIC's decision, as well as damages caused by that same administrative act.

SIC, where the proposed merger between Terpel and ExxonMobil, which was initially rejected, was later approved with conditions[34].

As interested third parties acquire the same rights as the intervening parties, they can also appeal SIC's decisions (and they usually do). In practice, however, there have been no cases where an interested third party has successfully appealed a clearance decision by SIC.

As SIC might impose certain obligations to monitor compliance with commitments: it might appoint external audits such as hold-separate manager to supervise/manage the remedies imposed, or a monitoring trustee to oversee the remedies imposed. Additionally, parties might be required to sign insurance contracts and to provide periodical reports. Following article 22 of Law 1340 of 2009, SIC's monitoring efforts are to be paid by the parties through a yearly contribution, which rates are fixed depending on the complexity of the remedies to be verified. This contribution cannot exceed one per thousand of the current assets of each company[35].

Finally, against the SIC's final decision, the parties can request the administrative courts to review the decision, but, as long as a preliminary decision or final decision is taken by the tribunals, SIC's decision comes into effect. It is important to highlight that, in practice, successful challenges of SIC decisions before the courts are not common. Given the fact that it takes more than five years to have a decision by the courts, a successful outcome might be useless.

4. Sanctions

As stated before, generally, clearance is required prior to closing, so every operation must be pre-conditioned to SIC's decision.

Parties must act with special diligence to avoid gun-jumping as SIC has sanctioned parties that, having been informed of the transaction, carried out proceedings that could affect the competitive behaviour in a market, without its prior approval[36]. Parties must avoid performing acts that imply union between the companies, such as the acquisition of influence over the assets or assets of the competitor, access to sensitive information of the competitor or the acquisition of influence over the governing bodies of the competitor[37].

Nevertheless, when parties do not comply with compulsory notification rules set out in article 9 of Law 1340 of 2009, or otherwise, or follow notification rules but implement

---

34 In this case, even though the merger was initially objected to by SIC, after the parties' reversal, the merger was later approved with milder conditions of behavioural and structural nature. The merger was subject to the condition of abstaining from agreeing exclusivity clauses with service stations.

35 See article 22, Law 1340 of 2009. This article expressly states: "The monitoring activities carried out by the SIC in connection with the acceptance of guarantees for the closure of the investigation for alleged restrictive practices of competition and the authorization of a business merger operation conditioned on the fulfilment of particular obligations by the interested parties will be subject to an annual monitoring fee in favour of the SIC ... The fee shall be determined by weighting the sum of the current assets of the previous fiscal year of the companies being monitored during that period, against the entity's operating expenses destined to the development of the monitoring work during the same period and may not exceed one per thousand of the current assets of each company subject to monitoring."

36 See Resolution 3703 of 2013, SIC, Resolution 31,142 of 2015, SIC, Resolution 83,882 of 2018, SIC.

37 See Resolution 49,903 of 2014, SIC.

the merger without a carve-out authorisation, SIC has the power to initiate an administrative investigation that can lead to the imposition of the sanctions in articles 26 and 27 of Law 1340 of 2009 or the reversal of the transaction. The statutory maximum fine is 100,000 monthly minimum wages (approx. USD 26 million) for companies, or a fine of up to 2,000 wages (approx. USD 530,000) for individuals.

Apart from these sanctions, the SIC may order the reversal of the transaction or divestiture when the transaction was not informed of it, or when the transaction was closed before SIC's decision if in the corresponding investigation, it determines the following:

- That the operation involves an undue restriction to free competition[38];
- That the operation would have been rejected; or
- That the conditions under which the operation was authorised were breached.

A prior breach of this obligation might adversely influence antitrust filings in the future. By way of example, in future filings related to any antitrust violation (including cartels, abuse of dominant position, mergers and anticompetitive practices), the breach of the suspensive obligation would be considered an aggravating factor when setting the fine (see article 25, Law 1340 of 2009).

In recent years, fines up to USD 100,000 for companies and up to USD 8,000 for individuals have been imposed, although these have generally related to failures to notify simple transactions with very low combined market shares, not full-length filings[39].

5. Remedies

Pursuant to merger control regulation (Law 155 of 1959, Law 1340 of 2009, SIC Resolution 10,930 of 2015), SIC has the power to approve, reject or condition the proposed transaction. Under article 11 of Law 1340 of 2009, SIC shall reject the merger when it is proven that the merger substantially lessens competition. But, according to article 11 of Law 1340 of 2009, SIC has the power to authorise a merger by subjecting it to the fulfilment of conditions when there are sufficient elements to consider that such conditions are suitable to ensure the effective preservation of competition.

According to article 10.4 of Law 1340 of 2009, intervening parties can suggest remedies/conditions during any part of the merger approval process. However, condition proposals must comply with SIC's requirements explained in their Merger Control Guidelines[40]. Hence, parties' remedies proposals must at least show the duration of the condition and the identification of the intervening parties. Also, remedies must be written in a clear and precise form and should be of a structural or behavioural nature.

SIC's Merger Control Guidelines also provide that asset divestment is a common remedy imposed on horizontal mergers, since the increase in market power can result from a divesting overlap that consists in the combination of assets for the performance of

38 See article 4, Law 155 of 1959, and article 13, Law 1340 of 2009.

39 See Resolutions 3703 of 2013, SIC; Resolution 49903 of 2014, SIC; Resolution 52782 of 2015, SIC; and Resolution 38973 of 2016, SIC.

40 SIC, *Guía de Análisis de Integraciones Empresariales*, note 2, 32.

certain activities[41]. In vertical mergers, common remedies are those of a behavioural nature, since vertical mergers may give the merged entity the power to influence the competitive process in the value chain[42].

There is no standard approach regarding the conditions and timing for divestitures or other remedies. However, under article 2.5.4 of Resolution 10,930 of 2015, SIC is compelled to inform intervening parties about possible anticompetitive effects that could derive from the proposed transaction and that are susceptible of being addressed by remedies.

The parties can complete a transaction before remedies are complied with if, by their nature, they must be fulfilled after SIC's authorisation. In this regard, an example appears in SIC's Resolution 9192 of 2007, where the competition authority imposed post-authorisation conditions on the intervening parties, such as refraining from requesting clauses that oblige customers to provide information about commercial conditions they have established with the intervening parties' competitors. SIC also has the possibility to require the intervening parties to fix a structural situation derived from the proposed transaction before its clearance.

As stated, there are no specific rules or standards for remedies. and according to the Merger Control Guidelines, parties' remedies proposals must at least show the duration of the condition and the identification of the intervening parties. Also, remedies must be written in a clear and precise form and should be of a structural or behavioural nature[43].

Concerning examples of behavioural remedies, SIC regularly considers that these remedies are aimed at preventing potentially discriminatory treatment or exploitation of purchasers/clients, or foreclosing competitors' access to clients. Behavioural remedies regularly proposed by SIC in deregulated markets, but that would also apply to the present situation, would involve commitments to reduce risks of vertical foreclosure. Although a case-by-case analysis produces the most likely remedies, in regulated or unregulated markets, behavioural remedies include but are not limited to: (i) eliminating, not applying or suppressing conditions or requirements to provide preferential treatment to certain clients with respect to other clients of essential facilities; (ii) confirming clients do not have any economic relationship with the merged entities, with equal and non-discriminatory conditions vis-à-vis the formers' affiliates, on matters such as prices and discounts, access requirements and other commercial terms, (iii) obligation to refrain from demanding or forcing clients to provide sensitive information; (iv) obligation to develop and subscribe a confidentiality protocol, through which they are obliged to not share, directly or indirectly, total or partially, the information they obtain derived from the relationship they have established with their customers, referring to sensitive information[44].

---

41 ibid.

42 ibid.

43 SIC, *Guía de Análisis de Integraciones Empresariales*, note 2, 32.

44 See Resolution 100658 of 2015, SIC. In this Resolution SIC repeated the importance of maintaining the independence of merging companies in a highly concentrated market. TERPEL would acquire the retail supply business of hydrant from Airplan in the airport José María Cordova, which would prevent any other competitor entering and participating in this market since TERPEL was a dominant participant in the market of wholesale supply of hydrants. Therefore, the transaction was initially rejected by SIC. Nonetheless, parties later proposed a mechanism through which Airplan would be independent of TERPEL and would only hire TERPEL for technical operations. SIC highlighted the importance of corporate governance rules – which include confidentiality rules and prohibitions of information exchange – as well as contract rules that could preserve independence.

In addition, intervening parties can commit to periodically submission of quarterly reports, audited by the accountant and/or auditor of the intervening companies, referring to: (i) prices, discriminated monthly, by type of service/product, indicating variables taken into account for price variations and the corresponding justification; (ii) volume of clients' service demanded, by month and measuring unit; (iii) discounts offered to clients, by month and specifying type of discount, percentage applied and discount values[45].

The parties can also commit to propose a structural remedy that oblige the parties to divest their participation in the market. This includes but is not limited to the sale of companies, branches of a company, brands, IP and any other asset that may have an impact in the relevant market.

6. Information Exchange and Cooperation

Colombia has signed several agreements regarding antitrust cooperation between countries, which form part of free trade agreements with said countries. Colombia's antitrust authority has also reached cooperation agreements for technical assistance with other antitrust authorities in the world, such as Chile, Ecuador, Mexico, Brazil, Spain and the United States, among other members of the International Competition Network. However, no agreement between authorities can serve as a means to justify information exchange between authorities without the express consent of the intervening parties, as such might be consider a violation of the Public Servants Code of Conduct[46]. In general, antitrust cooperation between authorities follows general policy matters, since most agreements reached with other countries' authorities are part of free trade agreements that include cooperation provisions.

There is only one case where SIC requested information from another country. In this case, SIC requested information from Mexico's Federal Competition Commission regarding the proposed acquisition of Pfizer's infant unit by Nestlé. The information requested was obtained pursuant to confidentiality waivers of the merging parties[47].

7. Carve-Outs

Local regulations include a formal mechanism in article 2.7 of Resolution 10,930 of 2015 that allows the intervening parties to separate or carve-out the business or assets in Colombia before clearance (not closing the transaction)[48].

---

45 See Resolution 34904, SIC, p 62. In this case, Exito and Carulla – the intervening parties – were obliged to submit a semi-annual report to SIC about the fulfilment of behavioural conditions such as refraining from agreeing exclusivity clauses in all maquila contracts. The intervening parties were also required to hire an external auditor to monitor compliance with the conditions and for the presentation of the report.

46 The exchange of information between authorities is unlikely, since article 2.2.3 of Resolution 10,930 of 2015 provides that the exchange of information requires an express and written waiver.

47 Resolution 20,968 of 2013, SIC.

48 Resolution 10,930 of 2015, article 2.7: "In the cases in which a transaction must be analysed and approved by competition authorities in from various jurisdictions, the intervening parties may propose, prior to the execution of the administrative act of [SIC], mechanisms to guarantee that transactions that were approved in other jurisdictions, does not imply a Business Merger in Colombia ... all mechanisms designed by the intervening parties shall comply with the following requirements: a) Guarantee that there will be no change in the intervening parties' corporate control; b) Guarantee the absence of competitive influence by one

For a carve-out process, parties must file a submission before SIC explaining how the carve-out structure they propose will ensure that there will be no exchange of competitively sensitive information between parties. Upon the request, SIC has five working days to approve or reject the proposal. If SIC rejects the proposal, the parties have an opportunity to submit a revised version, which SIC then has an additional five working days to consider[49]. This mechanism is generally used to implement a global closing, when the local authority has not yet reached a conclusion regarding the merger.

IV. Substance

1. Competition Analysis

The Merger Control Guidelines do not contain a defined theory of harm but do include some substantive tests to be pursued by the authority in the analysis of mergers[50]. For example, to analyse whether the proposed transaction creates a dominant position in the market, SIC often uses the Stenbacka Index, and, in order to define concentration it regularly uses the Herfindahl-Hirschman Index (HHI), which calculates the sum of the square of the merging parties' market shares in the defined relevant market.

The SIC also uses the NEE test to calculate the decrease in the number of competitors of equal size in the relevant market after a proposed merger is consummated. Other tests include LIDER, CR2 and CR4. The LIDER test represents the leader's market share in the relevant market, while CR2 and CR4 represent, respectively, the sum of the market shares of the two and four leader companies in the market[51].

For its part, SIC has recently heavily relied in the Stenbacka Index. The Stenbacka, Melnik and Shy Index (Stenbacka Index) is a dominance threshold proposed by Melnik, Shy and Stenbacka in 2008[52] which, "contrary to concentration measures such as the [HHI] that characterizes the concentration of an industry, our dominance measure suggests an approach that classifies when an individual firm has a dominant position"[53]. The Stenbacka Index is a tool that enables regulators to draw inferences about dominance of the leading firm, by determining the value from which an undertaking holds a dominant position in a particular market. In this sense, the Stenbacka Index is a single-market measure (threshold) that determines a level from which there is a risk of dominance in the market.

---

or more of the intervening companies, in the general shareholders' meeting of one or more of the other intervening parties, or in any other administrative body; c) prevent the exchange of strategic, confidential, or sensitive information between one or more of the intervening parties; d) have a vocation of permanence, in such way that the independence of the business in Colombia is guaranteed, in case of objection to the planned operation by [SIC]."

49 See article 2.7.2 of Resolution 10,930 of 2015.

50 SIC, *Guía de Análisis de Integraciones Empresariales*, note 2, 19–20.

51 ibid, 19.

52 Arie Melnik, Oz Shy and Rune Stenbacka, Rune "Assessing market dominance" [2008] 68(1) J. Economic Behavior & Organization, 63–72.

53 ibid, 1.

SIC, in its Guidelines for Analysing Mergers, establishes the use of the Stenbacka Index to identify dominance in the relevant market structure[54]:

> The STENBACKA index of dominance is a measure for identifying when a firm would be able to hold a position of dominance in the determined market. Taking into account the market share of the leader and the second most important firm, the STENBACKA index yields a threshold market share beyond which the leading firm might possible be in a dominant position.
>
> In accordance with the above, any market share above the said threshold could mean a dominant position. Nevertheless, this index constitutes a first approximation. It is necessary to analyse other elements to determine the dominant position of an enterprise[55].

The formula to calculate the Stenbacka Index is as follows:

$$S^D = g(S_1,S_2) = \frac{1}{2}\,[1 - \gamma(s_1^2 - s_2^2)]$$

Where s_1 and s_2 are the market shares of the biggest participants in the market,respectively
Where γ is a competition parameter.
SIC supposes $\gamma = 1$

According to the criteria behind this index, an undertaking will hold a dominant position if its market share (*MS*) is bigger that S^D:

$$MS > S^D$$

When assessing a transaction, the Stenbacka Index may also be useful in analysing whether the merger reinforces or weakens a dominant position. For this, the Stenbacka Index should be calculated pre-merger S^D_{pre} and post-merger S^D_{prost}, and the values compared, determining whether the Index increases, decreases or stays the same.

Comparison	Conclusion
$S^D_{pre} < S^D_{prost}$	The merger weakens a dominant position
$S^D_{pre} > S^D_{prost}$	The merger reinforces a dominant position
$S^D_{pre} = S^D_{prost}$	The merger does not strengthen or weaken a dominant position

Lastly, the KWOKA test focuses on measuring the symmetry of firms within a market, assessing the distribution pattern of agents' market shares.

2. Market Definition

For its part, relevant markets are determined through general rules of market definition which require the finding of a relevant product market as well as the relevant geographical market. According to SIC Resolution 22,624 of 2005, the geographical market

---

54 SIC, *Guía de Análisis de Integraciones Empresariales*, note 2, 22–23.

55 ibid.

corresponds to the place where companies offer their products and in which the plaintiffs are located. In this area, the conditions of competition must be similar or sufficiently homogeneous so that the area can be distinguished from other markets[56].

On the other hand, the product market requires finding the substitutability of the demand and then the substitutability of the supply. The substitutability of the demand is defined in SIC Resolution 13,815 of 2018 as the group of products that the consumer considers as substitutes. In this sense, the analysis would require assessing from the viewpoint of the consumer which attributes are considered as replaceable among the candidate goods for defining a market. In SIC Resolution 35,006 of 2010, the product market is described as products that can replace the affected product because of their usage, characteristics, applications and similar prices[57].

Finding substitute products requires a simulation where a small increase in the price of the goods is made and the possible reaction of the consumers to that variation in price is gauged[58]. Following the "small but significant and non-transitory" (SSNIP) standard (also called the Hypothetical Monopolist test), the recommended variation in the price is of 5 or 10% above the actual price of the good. If the variation of the price prompts consumers to drift away to other products, those products to which consumers drift away should be included as the substitute goods of the original product defined. This exercise is done until a set of products is determined where an increase in price would not amount to a sufficient substitution of the supply.

The Merger Control Guidelines establish that the substitutability of the supply is analysed from the perspective of the possible competitors[59]. In this sense, it is said that a supply (understood as the product that a determined company is selling in the market) is replaceable when potential competitors can access the market without incurring substantial costs of entry or investment as entry barriers.

Hence, merger control analysis in Colombia follows a pure competition system, where the competition authority analyses all possible effects that can arise with the consummation of a proposed merger. In this sense, all competition concerns are considered, such as unilateral effects, coordinated effects, conglomerate or portfolio effects, vertical concerns and the elimination of potential competition.

However, by virtue of law, SIC can only analyse competition issues that can arise in a proposed merger, since article 6 of Law 1340 of 2009 only gives SIC power to investigate and punish breaches of competition protection regulation. Therefore, in practice, there is no decision where non-competition issues such as labour law or the impact of any other political economy variables are analysed.

Economic efficiencies fall under the statutory exception provided by article 3 of Law 1340 of 2009. Under this article, SIC may authorise a transaction if the economic benefits outweigh the potential negative effects of the operation (i.e., restrictions on competition).

---

56 Resolution 22,624 of 2005, SIC, 22

57 Resolution 33,506 of 2010, SIC, 7.

58 SIC, *Guía de Análisis de Integraciones Empresariales,* note 2, 14.

59 ibid, 27.

Nevertheless, the burden to prove the merger's efficiencies lies with the intervening parties. Additionally, parties must commit themselves to passing on the positive effects to consumers.

3. Defences

It is worth noting that there are specific defences within the legal framework of merger control.

A. The Efficiency Defence

Article 12 of Law 1340 of 2009 establishes that the authority may authorise a merger or concentration that, despite the potential negative impact on competition, has benefits for consumers that outweigh the negative effects of the operation. They may also do so when, regardless of the market share that the integrated entity may obtain, the external market conditions guarantee free competition in the national territory.

Article 12. Exception of Efficiency. Modify article 51 of Decree 2153 of 1992, which will read as follows:

> The national competition authority may not object to a business integration if the interested parties demonstrate within the respective process, with studies based on methodologies of recognised technical value that the beneficial effects of the operation for consumers exceed the possible negative impact on competition and that such effects cannot be achieved by other means.
>
> In this event, the commitment that the beneficial effects will be transferred to consumers must be accompanied.
>
> [SIC] may refrain from objecting to an integration when, independent of the participation in the national market of the integrated company, the external market conditions guarantee free competition in the national territory.

However, this exception is applicable to those operations that are intrinsically problematic for free competition in the local market when the parties can demonstrate that the potential procompetitive effects are superior to their potential anticompetitive effects. This weighted analysis is carried out applying the same guidelines studied in the efficiency exception section in the framework of agreements between competitors[60].

B. The Failing Firm Defence

Hand-in-hand with the efficiency exception contained in article 12 of Law 1340 of 2009, the Colombian competition authority has developed a defence known as the "failing firm defence". This has allowed certain mergers and problematic operations that would

---

60 Resolution 10,0658 of 2015, SIC, 27–29. In this case, SIC denied the efficiency exception provided by an intervening party since despite having presented an estimate of the benefits of final consumers, these benefits were not offset by the possible impact that would derive from an increase in final fuel prices.

normally be objected to (denied) due to their anticompetitive effects, to be authorised due to the critical financial situation that some of the participants in the operation is going through[61].

In accordance with SIC doctrine, the application of this exception requires compliance with the following conditions[62]:

i. The undertaking in crisis (target) must be condemned, due to its economic problems, to abandon the market in the near future: it must be proven that market exit for the target company is imminent, i.e., in the short term, generally in less than a year. This can be evidenced, among others things, by the absence of working capital, the minimal possibility of generating profits, plans to close plants, excess debts and non-debt service.
ii. The target undertaking should have no other alternative, or any other real or achievable project that is less anticompetitive as the concentration. That is, it must be proven that there is no other possibility of acquisition by another third party that produces a less harmful outcome to competition than the projected integration.
iii. The damages to competition caused by the economic integration must be comparable to that caused by the exit from the market of the company in crisis: the situation of competition in the market is analysed under two assumptions: (a) exit from the market of the failing firm; and (b) projected business integration. If the contrast shows that the harm to the competition of carrying out the integration is less than that of the exit from the market of the company in crisis, it is possible to authorise the operation[63].

As can be seen, it is, ultimately, a weighted or balancing analysis of efficiencies that contrasts the negative consequences derived from the market exit of the failing firm and the effect derived from allowing the company to merge with a certain competitor. If the analysis shows that it is better for the market and for the competition that the company in crisis and its assets do not disappear, the authority may decide to authorise the operation, through the imposition of certain behavioural or structural conditions.

4. Statistics

As the Colombian economy grows, the number of filings increases year by year. During the last four years the total number of filings has increased by 61%, from 120 filings to 201 for the year 2019. The number of fast-track filings has increased the most, with not much growth in the full filing or pre-evaluation proceedings noted in the previous four years. This shows that most transactions have not occurred between parties in sectors where their market shares are not above 20%. 2019 was also a very odd year in merger control in the financial sector. Twelve mergers were analysed, an increase of 300% in the number of filings.

---

61 Resolution 90,622 of 2015, SIC, 12

62 Resolution 13,544 of 2006, SIC, 38

63 ibid.

Table 1. Merger Control Filings

	2019	2018	2017	2016
Total Filings	201	165	154	120
Fast-track Filings	145	126	116	75
Full Filing	44	35	35	42
Aproved	164	140	91	112
Conditioned	2	4	3	0
Objected	1	0	0	0
Withdrawn	2	3	1	3
Financial Sector Opinions	12	4	3	3
Average Days Full Filings	111	106	97	99
Maximum Days	325	331	329	281

Finally, it is important to note that during these four years only one merger has been objected to and only nine have been approved subject to conditions. However, several transactions have been withdrawn by the parties. This regularly happens when a transaction is on track for objection or conditions or when the parties have lost interest in merging. Finally, SIC has increased the number of average days to analyse mergers where parties have more than 20% of market share. Average number of days for full filing mergers was 99 calendar days in 2016 and 111 calendar days in 2019. The maximum number of days has also increased from 281 to 325 days. This might mean that parties are having more trouble providing all the information for first and second phase filings, as the maximum statutory number of days is 240, unless the parties have wrongly filed the information.

5. Case Law Illustration

Pursuant to merger control regulation (Law 1340 of 2009, SIC Resolution 10,930 of 2015), SIC has the power to approve, reject or apply conditions to the proposed transaction.

However, as explained, there is no standard approach regarding the common or most likely conditions, or the timing applicable for divestitures or other remedies. However, under article 2.5.4 of Resolution 10,930 of 2015, SIC is compelled to inform the intervening parties about possible anticompetitive effects that could derive from the proposed transaction that are susceptible of being addressed by remedies.

The parties can complete a transaction before remedies are complied with if, by their nature, they must be fulfilled after the SIC's authorisation. In this regard, an example appears in SIC's Resolution 9192 of 2007, where the authority imposed post-authorisation conditions on the intervening parties, such as refraining from requesting clauses that oblige customers to provide information about commercial conditions they have established with the intervening parties' competitors. This case was about the merger between Postobon and Projugos, through which Postobon acquired Projugos' shares. Through this resolution, SIC demonstrated that the proposed transaction could affect the following markets: (1) fruit-soft-drink market in non-returnable packing; (2) fruit-soft-drink market in returnable packing; (3) industrialised juices.

The SIC also has the possibility to require the intervening parties to fix a structural situation derived from the proposed transaction before its clearance. For example, in SIC Resolution 29,937 of 2010, SIC imposed a fix-first remedy consisting of the obligation to sell a brand of cigars before closing the transaction.

By way of another example, a recent case that is worth mentioning is the merger between Organización Terpel SA (Terpel), and ExxonMobil Colombia SA. This case, illustrated in SIC Resolution 9915 of 2018, consisted of Terpel taking control of ExxonMobil shares in the Colombian market. Through this operation, Terpel acquired the local fuel business from ExxonMobil. At first, this merger was rejected since according to Resolution 76,541 of 2017, this merger would lead to a horizontal integration in the wholesale and retail distribution markets for liquid petroleum fuels (regular gas, premium gas, and diesel). Nevertheless, Terpel's acquisition of the proposed lubricants business was approved subject to conditions[64]. SIC's initial findings were that the proposed transaction represented a horizontal merger in the markets of wholesale and retail distribution of liquid fuels derived from petroleum, as well as in the market of wholesale and retail sale of production of lubricants. In addition, SIC found that the proposed transaction represented a vertical integration since both parties are involved in different levels of the value chain[65].

Under these considerations, SIC argued that the proposed transaction could prevent the entry of other competitors or could reinforce Terpel's participation in both markets. Among other things, SIC found that the operation would allow Terpel to consolidate as the leader in the liquid fuels wholesale distribution market.

However, the intervening parties appealed SIC's first resolution, arguing that businesses regarding the wholesale and retail distribution of fuels from Terpel and ExxonMobil was not part of the Pre-Evaluation Request. In this sense, the parties argued that there is a conditioning that would prevent Terpel from acquiring control over the distribution of fuels of ExxonMobil. In particular, a fix-it-first remedy required Terpel to transfer all ExxonMobil's shares to a transitory buyer – concomitant with closing – who would acquire ownership of these shares through an irrevocable autonomous equity that would guarantee, among other things, that ExxonMobil would continue to be managed and operated consistently with past practices and by people who operated the business independently from Terpel[66].

Additionally, the intervening parties argued that some conditions prevent Terpel from competing effectively in the market, and, in addition, include obligations whose fulfilment depends on the consent of third parties. SIC decided to approve the projected transaction with milder conditions of both a structural and behavioural nature[67]. All conditions in this case are explained below:

- To guarantee the access to other wholesale distributors in conditions of non-discrimination, non-obstruction, and neutrality.

---

64 Resolution 76,541 of 2017, SIC.

65 ibid.

66 ibid.

67 Resolution 9915 of 2018, SIC.

- To maintain and respect all storage capacity lease contracts, or any other agreed figure.
- Not contracting the supply of liquid vehicles derived from petroleum with service stations that had current contracts for the distribution of this type of products with ExxonMobil. This condition was imposed for a term of 10 years.
- Not to contract the supply or distribution of lubricants with clients that had contracts for the purchase of lubricants Máxter and Máxter progresa, which are ExxonMobil brands. This condition was imposed for a term of 10 years.
- To eliminate or to refrain from imposing exclusivity clauses with service stations for a period of 4 years.
- To refrain from imposing a commercial strategy that has the purpose of directing or influencing the choice of lubricants to be distributed by service stations or any other distributor thereof.
- Lastly, it obliges Terpel to divest its investment through the sale of ExxonMobil's shares and assets to a third-party acquirer who is independent from the intervening parties.

As can be seen, contrary to several other previous transactions, SIC included several non-merger related remedies as an attempt to "fix" some of the issues in the market, using the merger as an excuse to intervene in the lubricants and gasoil markets.

COSTA RICA

Uri Weinstok*

(BLP)

Abstract

As in many other countries, Costa Rican competition laws require some mergers and acquisitions to be submitted for approval. This procedure was introduced in 2012, and from that moment it became the main activity of the authority, and that which gives rise to a large majority of its decisions. The Costa Rican Competition Authorities Strengthening Act (No 9736) that recently entered into force, completely changed the system of promotion and protection of competition in the country. This is the most ambitious reform to the competition protection system in the country since the adoption of the law almost 25 years ago. One of the areas that underwent deeper reforms was concentration control. The main changes relate to the introduction of a true previous notification system (prior to the reform the transactions could be notified after closing); a change in the calculation of thresholds; a change in the review process, moving to a two-stage procedure similar to that in other jurisdictions; a new substantive test for analysis; and creation of new infractions and increase in the fines for violation of the notification rules. The expectation is that these changes will accelerate case approval, and that the authority will focus its efforts on the cases that truly generate risks to competition in the market.

---

* Uri Weinstok is the head of the antitrust and competition practice at BLP. His experience includes filing and approval of mergers; representation in filing complaints and defending against investigations by the authorities; and the conduct of audits and compliance programs that help prevent and avoid anticompetitive behaviour. For more than 10 years he was a member of the national competition authority (Commission to Promote Competition), and he was also its President. He has been an international consultant for the Organisation for Economic Co-operation and Development (OECD), the World Bank, and the United Nations Conference on Trade and Development (UNCTAD). He obtained his law degree at the University of Costa Rica (1996), and a postgraduate diploma on EU Competition Law at King's College, University of London (2001).

I. Introduction

1. Brief Overview

The first competition law enacted in Costa Rica is the Law for the Promotion of Competition and Effective Defense of Consumers (No 7472) of 1994[1]. While this law included a definition of a "concentration"[2] and prohibited anticompetitive transactions, it did not include a merger control procedure (neither *ex ante* nor *ex post*). Instead, the law stipulated that mergers were to be investigated in a similar process as anticompetitive practices, granting the authority powers to dissolve anticompetitive mergers and impose fines for them.

During this time, the competition authority (COPROCOM) issued a "Guide for Voluntary Notification of Concentrations"[3]. This voluntary process, however, was neither implemented in any normative rule, widely communicated nor applied in practice.

This changed in 2012, when the law was amended to include a merger review process. While the definition of a concentration remained the same, transactions that met certain thresholds had to be filed no later than five days after closing. The transactions would be reviewed by COPROCOM, who could approve, apply conditions to, or reject them. Secondary rules for the review process were introduced by Decree No 37,899 (articles 38–62 specifically[4]). Also, in 2014 COPROCOM issued guidelines for the review of mergers[5].

A major legal reform to the Competition Promotion system happened in 2019, when Law No 7472 was changed substantially by the Law for Strengthening the Competition Authorities, No 9736[6]. This was a substantial reform to competition law and the agencies in charge of its application. Among several others, merger review was one of the areas in which the reform was most far-reaching. The new rules changed the definition of a concentration, set new filing thresholds and reformed the competition agency.

In parallel, in June 2008 a General Telecommunications Law was approved[7]. This law created a sector-specific competition protection system for the telecommunications sector, applied by the sector regulator. It established a pre-merger control process with a mandatory filing of all transactions (no thresholds were set). Secondary rules were also

---

1 Ley para la Promoción de la Competencia y Defensa Efectiva del Consumidor, No 7472 (1995), <<https://www.pgrweb.go.cr/scij/Busqueda/Normativa/Normas/nrm_texto_completo.aspx?nValor1=1&nValor2=26481>.

2 For the purposes of this paper, the terms "concentration" and "merger" will be used interchangeably, unless otherwise stated.

3 <<https://www.coprocom.go.cr/tramites_y_servicios/requisitos/requisitos_autorizaciones.pdf>.

4 Reglamento a la Ley para la Promoción de la Competencia y Defensa Efectiva del Consumidor, Decreto No 37899-MEIC (2013), <<http://www.pgrweb.go.cr/scij/Busqueda/Normativa/Normas/nrm_texto_completo.aspx?param1=NRTC&nValor1=1&nValor2=75696&nValor3=119695&strTipM=TC>.

5 COPROCOM, *Guía para el Análisis de Concentraciones Económicas* (2014), <<https://www.coprocom.go.cr/tramites_y_servicios/requisitos/guia_analisis_concevf.pdf>.

6 Ley de Fortalecimiento de las Autoridades de Competencia de Costa Rica, No 9736 (2019), <<http://www.pgrweb.go.cr/scij/Busqueda/Normativa/Normas/nrm_texto_completo.aspx?param1=NRTC&nValor1=1&nValor2=90054>.

7 Ley General de Telecomunicaciones, No 8642 (2008), <http://www.pgrweb.go.cr/scij/Busqueda/Normativa/Normas/nrm_norma.aspx?param1=NRM&nValor1=1&nValor2=63431&nValor3=0&strTipM=FN>.

issued to regulate application of the rules[8], and the authority also issued guidelines for the analysis of mergers[9]. The competition reform of 2019 also affected this sector, and the merger review rules are now identical to the general system, except for the lack of thresholds, and the application and control remaining within the sector regulator.

2. Institutional Set-Up

There are two competition authorities in Costa Rica: the Commission to Promote Competition (COPROCOM), and the Superintendence of Telecommunications (SUTEL). COPROCOM oversees competition in all activities except for telecommunication, and SUTEL is the competition authority for the telecommunications market.

COPROCOM is a "maximum deconcentration" body attached to the Ministry of Economy, Industry and Trade, with technical, administrative, budgetary and functional independence. It has legal personality to carry out contractual activity; to manage their resources and assets; and to enter into contracts and agreements with public and private entities, national or international.

It has powers of promotion (advocacy) and protection (enforcement) of competition. Its powers include investigation of anticompetitive conduct; reviewing of mergers; carrying out market studies; and promoting changes in laws and regulations.

Structurally, COPROCOM is divided in two: the Superior Body and the Technical Body. The Superior Body is the maximum authority. It defines policies and use of budget, issues regulations and guidelines, and more. It is the adjudication body for cases and investigations. It is composed of three members, including at least one lawyer and one economist. They are appointed for periods of six years without possibility of re-election. The appointment is made by the president and Council of Ministers and ratified by the legislative power. Members of the Superior Body may be removed from their position only for specific reasons such as: a change of circumstances making them no longer eligible, failure to comply their duties, committing a crime, or similar reasons[10].

The Technical Body is in charge of conducting the investigation and prosecuting the cases, which are adjudicated by the Superior Body. It also collaborates on the advocacy functions and provides technical support to the Superior Body to execute its tasks and pursue the objectives of the law.

SUTEL, on the other hand, is the telecommunications regulator. It combines the application of *ex ante* regulations as well as the application of the competition principles in the telecommunications sector.

---

8 Reglamento del Régimen de Competencia en Telecomunicaciones, Autoridad Reguladora de los Servicios Públicos, 2008, <http://www.pgrweb.go.cr/scij/Busqueda/Normativa/Normas/nrm_texto_completo.aspx?param1=N-RTC&nValor1=1&nValor2=64161&nValor3=74275&strTipM=TC>.

9 Dirección General de Mercados, *Guía de Análisis de Concentraciones. Sector de telecomunicaciones* (Superintendencia de Telecomunicaciones 2015), <<<https://sutel.go.cr/sites/default/files/2015_sutel_telecomunicaciones_guia.pdf>.

10 Law 9736, art. 10.

SUTEL is a "maximum deconcentration" body attached to the Regulatory Authority of Public Services. It has instrumental legal personality, sufficient to carry out the contractual activity, manage its resources and its budget, as well as to sign the contracts and agreements that it requires for the performance of its functions. It is composed of three members, appointed for a five-year periods and they may be re-elected once. The competition law functions of SUTEL are structured in the exact same way as COPROCOM, with a Superior Body (SUTEL's board) and a Technical Body, which is an internal unit. The adjudication and prosecution powers of each body are identical to those of COPROCOM. Members of SUTEL can be removed for reasons expressly established by law, all of them related to their eligibility for their positions and the compliance with their duties[11].

3. Type of Merger Control

Merger control in Costa Rica is *ex ante* with compulsory notification, according to articles 89 of Law 9736 and 56 of the General Telecommunications Law. Filings for notifiable transactions must occur before the transaction generates any legal or material effect. There is no voluntary notification for transactions that do not meet the thresholds. There is no preliminary (formal) consultation with the authority either.

All notifiable transactions are automatically suspended until they are authorised. In exceptional circumstances, the authority may allow parties to execute the transaction before the end of the process. When allowing the temporary execution, the authority may impose special conditions[12].

Since the enactment of Law 9736, the procedures and criteria followed by both authorities is identical. The main differences are that there are no notification thresholds for the telecommunications sector, and SUTEL must consult COPROCOM before issuing a final decision. Other than that, the two merger control systems are substantially identical.

II. Scope of Application

1. Definition of Concentration

The definition of a "concentration" is wide, and encompasses all transactions, regardless of their form, involving two or more previously independent economic agents that result in the acquisition of control by one over the other or others, or in the formation of a new agent under the joint control of the parties. Specifically, article 88 of Law 9736 defines it as:

a) The merger, acquisition, sale of a commercial establishment, the strategic alliance or any other act or contract, under which companies, associations, shares, equity, trusts, management powers or assets in general are concentrated;

11 Law 8660, art. 65.
12 Law 9736, art. 95.

b) Carried out between competitors, suppliers, customers or other economic agents that have been independent of each other; and
c) Result in the lasting acquisition of economic control by one of them over the other or others, or in the formation of a new economic agent under the joint control of two or more economic agents;
d) As well as any transaction by which any natural or legal person, public or private, acquires control of two or more independent economic agents.

Article 56 of the General Telecommunications Law contains a similar definition of concentration, adapted to telecommunications operators and suppliers[13].

2. Material Scope

Competition laws in Costa Rica do not exclude nor exempt any sector or activity. However, the law does exclude specific actions that are expressly permitted by special laws[14].

There are, however, two types of transactions that are exempt from the duty to notify[15]:

a) Acquisitions made as part of the normal course of business of the buyer, without the intent or the effect of integrating the operations of independent economic agents;
b) Purchases of assets, shares, or participations made transitorily and with the intention of resale, as long as the resale occurs within one year of the purchase; that the purchaser does not participate in any strategic decision of the acquired entity; and that, prior to the resale the assets, shares or participations are not subject to a subsequent concentration that must be notified.

In the telecommunications sector, the law covers transactions involving regulated operators or suppliers[16]. Conversely, all other transactions fall under the jurisdiction of COPROCOM and the application of the general competition laws. The law does not define which set of rules applies to transactions between regulated and non-regulated entities, and this has not been clarified by any secondary rule. While both authorities (SUTEL and COPROCOM) have recently signed a cooperation and information exchange agreement[17], it does not deal with this specific issue. One may assume that in a borderline case, the authorities would look into the market where the effects of the transaction occurs and

---

13 "Article 56: Concentrations: Concentration means the merger, acquisition, sale of the commercial establishment, strategic alliance, or any other act or contract, under which companies, associations, shares, capital, trusts, management powers, or assets in general, are concentrated; between network operators and telecommunications service providers independent of each other, and result in the lasting acquisition of economic control by one of them over the other or others, or in the formation of a new telecommunications operator or provider under the joint control of two or more telecom operators or providers, as well as any transaction by which any natural or legal person, public or private, acquires control of two or more independent telecommunications operators or providers."

14 Article 9 of Law 7472.

15 Article 91 of Law 9736.

16 Article 56 of Law 8642.

17 Convenio de Coordinación y Cooperación Interinstitucional em Materia de Competencia entre la Comisión para Promover la Competencia (COPROCOM) y la Superintendencia de Telecomunicaciones (SUTEL), (2019) <https://sutel.go.cr/sites/default/files/convenios_contribuciones/convenio_sutel-coprocom_2019.pdf>.

allocate their jurisdiction accordingly. However, there has not yet been a case where this has been discussed.

3. Geographical Scope

Article 9 of Law 7472 establishes that it applies to all economic agents with actions that generate effects in Costa Rica, regardless of where they occur. Hence, foreign-to-foreign transactions are covered by the law when they generate local effects. Conversely, the law would not apply to transactions involving one local entity that does not generate any effects in Costa Rica.

To be notifiable, and along with the other thresholds, article 89(a) of Law 9736 requires that a concentration must involve at least two economic operators who carry out activities with incidence in Costa Rica, or have carried out such activities at any time during the two tax periods prior to the transaction. For these purposes, Article 1(g) of Law 9736 establishes that an economic agent has activities with incidence in Costa Rica when it generates sales or keeps productive assets in the country, either directly or through third parties.

4. Thresholds

In addition to qualifying as a concentration and having a local effect, a notifiable transaction must meet two economic thresholds, both related to the size of the economic agents participating in the transaction. One is a "joint" or "collective" threshold, and the other is an individual one.

The thresholds are:

a) Jointly, all parties have, during the fiscal year prior to the transaction, combined productive assets or combined turnover in an amount to be determined yearly by COPROCOM of between 30,000 and 60,000 base salaries[18] or more.
b) Individually, at least two of the economic agents participating in the transaction have generated turnover or own productive assets in Costa Rica during the previous fiscal year in an amount equal or above the threshold set by COPROCOM within the range of 1,500 to 9,000 base salaries[19].

Notification will also be required when, considering all successive transactions that occur within a term of two years, the combined value of sales or assets reach the thresholds.

In both cases, the calculation must include the parties to the transaction, as well as all entities belonging to the same economic group[20]. However, only the turnover generated

---

18 As of the date of writing, the threshold was set at 30,000 minimum wages, which is approximately USD 2.3 million.

19 As of the date of writing, the threshold was set at 1,500 minimum wages, which is approximately USD 1,164,000.

20 Article 1(f) of Law 9736 defines "economic group" as the "grouping of companies or business entities, in fact or in law, manifested by a unit of decision, that is, the union of all or a substantial part of the elements of command or business management through an operational centre, and which is externalized by two basic

locally and the assets located in Costa Rica are to be considered. Worldwide turnover is irrelevant for the calculation of the thresholds.

In the telecommunications sector there are no thresholds. All transactions involving operators or suppliers must be notified[21].

III. Procedure

The procedure for filing and deciding on a concentration is the same for cases before COPROCOM and SUTEL, except for some specific provisions, identified below.

1. Launch of Procedure

Procedure is initiated by the notification made by the parties, which must occur at any moment between the first action towards accomplishing the transaction and before its execution in Costa Rica[22]. All parties involved in the concentration have the obligation to notify the transaction, and failure to notify may result in a fine to all of them. However, the notification made by any party will release all of them from this duty[23].

The notification of a concentration must be in writing, and contain at least the following:

a) Detailed description of the concentration: a summary of the concentration, specifying at least the economic agents involved; the type of transaction; the sectors of activity of the parties and their related entities; the markets in which the concentration will have effects; express identification of the markets in which the parties' activities overlap or relate vertically; the form and timelines expected to execute the transaction; and the strategic and economic reasons for the merger.
b) Identification of the economic agents involved: complete individualisation of the economic agents participating in the concentration, as well as natural or legal persons belonging to the same economic group and carrying out commercial activities from, or having effects in, Costa Rica.
c) Structure of the share capital: description of the structure of the share capital of the companies involved in the transaction, and those belonging to the same economic group, identifying the persons who have and will have direct and indirect control, before and after the concentration.
d) Activities of the economic agents involved: nature and description of the activities carried out by economic agents involved in the concentration and the other natural or legal persons referred to in the previous paragraph, both in Costa Rica and in other countries.

---

movements: the criteria of unity of direction, either by subordination or by collaboration between its members, or the criterion of economic dependence of its members, regardless of whether their legal personality is affected, or that their assets are transferred."

21 Article 56 of Law 8642 and article 89 of Law 9736.

22 Article 89 of Law 9736.

23 ibid.

e) Markets concerned: description of the markets affected by the transaction, their barriers to entry, their main participants and their market shares, including the market shares of the parties to the concentration.
f) Information on the criteria compliance with the notification thresholds: indication of the individual volume of gross sales or productive assets of the parties, as appropriate, in accordance with the notification threshold that is required by the transaction, in accordance with the provisions of this law and its regulations.
g) Effects of the concentration: applicants may include an analysis of the possible anticompetitive and procompetitive effects of the concentration, if any. In the latter case, a proposal for commitments may be included to counter them.
h) Any additional information that applicants deem relevant to the assessment of the case.

Through a technical regulation, the authority may specify the documents to be provided in support of the application, and the specific ways to comply with the filing requirements[24].

For cases to be decided by COPROCOM, the authority may establish a filing fee based on the criteria to be set by a technical regulation[25]. Cases filed at SUTEL do not have to pay any filing fee.

While the rules do not establish a formal electronic filing, in 2020, and because of the global pandemic of COVID-19, COPROCOM created a provisional electronic submission of documents. It is not clear yet if the electronic system will remain after the emergency measures.

2. Development of Procedure

Within the first 15 business days after filing, the authority must verify if the application is complete and, if needed, must require from the applicant all pending information, documents or clarifications. The parties will have 15 business days to complete the application. If the application is not completed properly it will be rejected and considered as if it was not filed for all legal purposes[26].

Once the application is complete, the authority will publish a notice with a brief description of the transaction, identification of the economic agents involved and the markets affected by it, and the indication that any third party may provide relevant information and documents within 10 business days[27]. Publication is typically made through the agency's website[28].

The procedure for the analysis of concentrations is composed of two phases. The purpose of the first phase is to identify whether, because of its possible effects in the market, the transaction generates risks to the competition process. In that case, the process will

24 As of the date of writing the technical regulation has not been issued.
25 As of the date of writing the technical regulation has not been issued, and no filing fee has been set.
26 Article 93 of Law 9736.
27 Article 96 of Law 9736.
28 <www.coprocom.go.cr> and <www.sutel.go.cr>.

be opened to a second phase in which the possible effects of the transaction will be analysed[29]. Since the enactment of the law establishing this two-phase process, there has been one case (out of a total of 16 notifications) that has been opened to a second-phase analysis[30].

The decision of the first phase must be issued within 30 calendar days of the day on which the application is filed or, if additional documents or information are requested, from the date on which the application was completed. If the process is opened for a second phase, the decision must be made within 90 additional calendar days. The term will not run during the time in which the applicants must submit additional documents or information, until they comply with the request. In both cases, if no decision is made within the set deadline the transaction will be deemed to be approved unconditionally.

The decision of first phase may: a) authorise the transaction; b) condition the transaction to the compliance of the commitments proposed by the parties, if such a proposal is made either with the initial filing or at any time before the decision of phase I; or c) initiate phase II of the process[31].

When the process is opened for phase II, the authority must notify the parties of the following[32]:

a) The reasons for which the transaction may potentially generate concerns to the competition process, granting a term of 10 business days to issue allegations and provide information about them.
b) The additional documents and information required to analyse the case, which must be provided within 10 business days. The additional information and documents must be related to the potential risks identified specifically for the case. The parties may also provide additional evidence to support any allegation made in support of their application.

During the process, third parties are allowed to participate and provide documents and evidence that they may deem useful for the case. Third-party allegations are regularly considered in the authority's decisions. However, the authorities have also being consistent in rejecting their standing as formal parties to the case, as well as their right to appeal or otherwise participate in the process. In 2018, a competitor that felt affected by a transaction approved by COPROCOM questioned the constitutionality of the procedure based on a violation of due process, for not giving third parties sufficient opportunities to participate. The case, which was before the reform of Law 9736 and, therefore referred to the previous process, is still pending[33].

---

29 Article 94 of Law 9736.

30 Vote No 10-2020 of 18:30h, 10 March 2020. Concentration between Baltimore Spice Central America, S.A., Grupo Kerry, and Global Spice, S.A.

31 Article 97 of Law 9736.

32 Article 98 of Law 9736.

33 File No 18-19669-0007-CO followed at the Constitutional Hall of the Supreme Court of Costa Rica.

In any stage of the process, the parties may meet with the staff of the competition authority – or the authority themselves – in order to analyse and clarify the information on file, the content of the proposals, or the concerns of the competition authority. The matters discussed during these meetings will not have any binding effects on the result of the case[34].

3. Conclusion of Procedure

The decision of second phase, once the analysis of the concentration is finished, may: a) authorise the transaction unconditionally, or subject to the conditions that the parties may have offered up until that moment of the process; b) inform the parties of its determination that the transaction may generate anticompetitive effects that may be remedied, and grant them a term of up to 30 business days to propose remedies to address them; or c) prohibit the transaction, if it determines that its negative effects in the market may not be remedied[35].

Within 30 calendar days after the proposal for remedies is received, if the parties choose to make one, the authority will determine whether the transaction is approved subject to those remedies; determine whether it imposes additional remedies as a condition to carry out the transaction; or block the transaction if the prospective anticompetitive effects cannot be remedied[36].

The decision imposing remedies must specify the specific obligations imposed upon the parties and the time frame for compliance. If the remedies imposed are different from those proposed by the parties, the authority will grant the parties a term of 20 business days to decide whether they accept the conditions or not. In a case of silence, the conditions will be deemed as rejected. Rejection of the remedies or conditions will result in a denial of the transaction by the authority.

Once the decision is firm it may not be questioned at an administrative level. However, it can be reviewed judicially.

The authority may also terminate the process in advance, and without making a determination on the merits if a) the transaction notified is not a merger which is subject to notification; b) the parties surrender their application; or c) the parties fail to respond properly to a request of information[37].

---

34 Article 106 of Law 9736.
35 Article 99 of Law 9736.
36 Article 100 of Law 9736.
37 Article 105 of Law 9736.

4. Sanctions

The following are the penalties that COPROCOM may impose in relation to concentrations[38]:

Infraction	Penalty (percentage of the gross income of the previous fiscal year)
Providing incomplete (or unjustifiably late) information when requested by the authority	0.1–3%
Filing a notification after the transaction is executed (gun-jumping)	0.1–3%
Provide false or altered information	0.1–5%
Failure to notify a concentration	0.1–5%
Breach of a condition or remedy ordered by the authority	0.1–10%
Failure to notify a concentration when, in addition, the transaction generates anticompetitive effects	0.1–10%

On the other hand, in the telecommunications sector, the penalties are set between 0.25% and 0.5% of the gross income of the telecommunications operator. In addition, in cases of gun-jumping, SUTEL will first issue a warning, requiring the parties to notify the transaction and, if this warning is not heeded, then they may open a procedure to impose the penalty[39].

In addition to the monetary penalties, both authorities may order the divestiture of a concentration that is executed without proper notification, and may also impose remedies on such transaction[40].

5. Special Note on the Financial Sector

The law contains certain provisions that apply specifically for the financial sector[41]. These mergers are reviewed and must be filed at COPROCOM. However, COPROCOM must notify the financial regulator within 3 days of filing.

The financial regulator will inform COPROCOM when, for reasons of prudential regulation, the transaction should be reviewed by them, to protect the solvency of the financial sector and avoid systemic risks. In such cases, it may require the technical opinion of COPROCOM prior to deciding on the case.

If a financial institution is being subject to an intervention process at the time of the concentration, the transaction will be exempt from any filing obligation and approval requirements.

---

38 Articles 115–119 of Law 9736.

39 Regulation for the competition provisions in Law 8642, article 27.

40 Article 109 of Law 9736

41 Article 27 *bis* of Law 7472

IV. Substance

1. Competition Analysis

The substantive test for merger review is pure competition assessment. Other elements, such as public interest, protection of jobs, or promotion of national industry are not considered. However, article 101 of Law 9736 allows for the approval of otherwise anticompetitive transactions based on "other conditions that, according to the authority, protect the interests of national consumers". These criteria have not yet been applied, but one may assume that it will be interpreted in the context of the rest of the competition law provisions, that is, seeking the benefit of consumers through market efficiency and promotion of competition in the market, without regard or consideration to other economic policies that may be adopted by different government institutions.

Prior to the 2019 reform, the competition analysis was based on whether the transaction a) created or increased market power, and as therefore displaced or limited competition; b) facilitated coordination between competitors; or c) otherwise damaged or impeded competition with respect to similar or related products[42].

Upon the approval of Law 9736, the standard of analysis changed. Under the current law, the authority will approve all concentrations "that do not have as its object or forceable effect the significant obstruction of competition in the relevant market affected by the transaction, or in other similar or substantially related markets"[43]. In the evaluation of whether the transaction affects competition in the relevant market, the authority will consider the creation or reinforcement of market power, the coordination between economic agents or other effects on consumers. The criteria for such determination will be determined by secondary regulations that have not been enacted to date.

In other words, the creation of market power or coordination between competitors are no longer the substantive issues, but rather the means by which competition in the market may be hindered. This will require from the authorities a more elaborated theory of harm, and a focus on the economic effects of the transaction in the market.

In cases where the concentration has an anticompetitive object, or is likely to have anticompetitive effects, the authority may also approve it if:

a) The transaction generates efficiencies (to be alleged and demonstrated by the applicants) that outweigh the possible anticompetitive effects.
b) The transaction is necessary to avoid the exit from the market of productive assets of the parties (i.e. in case of an unsustainable financial situation).
c) The anticompetitive effects may be countervailed by conditions imposed by the authority.
d) There are other conditions that, according to the authority, protect the interests of national consumers.

---

42 Article 16.1 of Law 7472 (now repealed by Law 9736).
43 Article 101 of Law 9736.

In addition, Article 102 of Law 9736 establishes that the authority will establish, through secondary regulation, the cases in which there will be a presumption that the transaction will not have a negative impact in the market. While this regulation has not yet been enacted, according to the previous rules this applied, for example, to transactions of minor importance, conglomerate mergers, foreign-to-foreign transactions or cases where the buyer already had partial ownership of the target.

In cases where the concentration is found to have anticompetitive object or effects, the authority may impose conditions for the authorisation to reduce or countervail such effects. These conditions may be the following[44]:

a) The mandatory sale or licensing of assets, rights, distribution services or others to a third party approved by the authority.
b) Limitations or restriction when providing certain services or selling certain assets, including geographical or to the clients to whom they can be offered.
c) The obligation to provide certain goods or services, in non-discriminatory conditions, to specific clients or to competitors.
d) The introduction, elimination, or modification of certain clauses in written or verbal agreements with clients or suppliers.
e) The separation or split of the economic agent.
f) The limitation or restriction to obtain additional concessions or authorisations.
g) Any other condition, whether structural, conduct or a combination of both, that may be necessary to impede, reduce or countervail the anticompetitive effects of the concentration.

The conditions or remedies must be complied during the term to be established by the authority, of up to 10 years, which may be extended for up to five more years. If, during that time, the conditions in the market change in such a way that the conditions are no longer necessary to eliminate any potential anticompetitive effect foreseen in the decision, then the affected party may request their revision and/or elimination.

When examining the proposals for conditions in the context of the merger filing process, the authority must consider the following[45]:

a) The purpose of the remedies is to maintain the state of competition in the market towards the foreseeable effects of the concentration, and not to improve the conditions of the market prior to the transaction.
b) The conditions must be directly related to the anticompetitive effects identified by the authority for the specific transaction.
c) If there are several different alternatives to attain similar results, then the choice must be for the one least detrimental for the implementing parties.
d) Conditions must be easy and fast to implement, and the verification of compliance must be viable and effective.
e) Conditions must be effective, considering their impact in the market, extent, and risks of implementation.

---

44 Article 103 of Law 9736.
45 Article 104 of Law 9736.

2. Statistics

The following are the number of cases decided by the authority since the establishment of a merger notification process in 2012[46]:

Year	# of cases	Cleared Unconditionally	Cleared with Conditions	Blocked	Other[47]
2013	8	8	–	–	–
2014	26	24	1	–	1
2015	24	22	1	–	1
2016	37	37	–	–	–
2017	37	31	2	–	4
2018	32	29	2	1	–
2019	10	7	2	–	1
TOTAL	174	158	8	1	7

3. Case Law Illustration

The following case was subject to remedies by COPROCOM.

Name of case

Acquisition of Aceros Abonos Agro, S.A. by Metalco, S.A., File number 096-17-CE

Decision number/year

Analysis of the transaction was decided by Vote No 16-2018 of 13:45h, 16 March 2018. Conditions were approved by Vote No 45-18 of 17:50h, 3 July 2018.

Parties

Buyer: Metalco, S.A.

Target entity: Aceros Abonos Agro, S.A.

Sellers: Agriculture Advisory Corporation and El Lagar, S.A.

Sector/Industry

Steel products

Brief description of the transaction

Buyer is an industrial entity dedicated to the import of steel bars and their transformation to manufacture steel-based construction materials.

---

46 COPROCOM, 'Notified Concentrations, <<https://www.coprocom.go.cr/concentraciones/concentraciones_notificadas.html>.

47 "Other" includes cases where the application was surrendered by the parties or the authority decided that the notification was not required.

They intended to buy 100% of the shares of target, a company in the business of importing and selling steel-based construction materials at the wholesale level.

In addition to target, sellers owned controlling interest of two of the largest hardware store chains in the country, in which they sell, among others, the products imported by target.

Relevant issues discussed

The transaction was deemed to affect six different product markets, all of them of steel-based construction products. Buyer and target were competitors in three of the relevant lines of products. Target was active in the other three relevant markets, in which buyer did not participate. The transaction was then considered to be a horizontal merger, with a conglomerate component.

COPROCOM determined that the large market shares of the parties in the two of the markets where they competed generated concerns, as they were close competitors and, after the transaction, would have a large portion of the market (46% and 52%), with very distant closer competitors.

They also identified a strong probability of portfolio effects, as clients may be inclined to purchase all their steel product needs from a distributor that holds a large participation in the different markets.

The authority also recognised efficiencies derived from the transaction. These efficiencies originated in economies of scale and scope attained by the transaction. Also, the separation between the target and the large hardware store chains affiliated to it would eliminate incentives to foreclose access to the product by other retailers.

The transaction also had an ancillary restraint, consisting of a guaranteed minimum supply agreement between the target and the related retailers (this agreement was disclosed by the parties as an ancillary restraint of the transaction, necessary to protect the value of the purchased entity).

Analysis

In its decision, COPROCOM determined that the supply agreement disclosed as an ancillary restraint was valid, but it delayed the effects of the efficiencies generated by the transaction. Hence, as a remedy, it ordered the parties to commit to hold separate the entities for a term similar to the supply agreement. This way, the negative effects of the transaction would also be delayed until such time as the efficiencies would begin to be in effect (five years).

Another condition imposed was to modify the terms of the supply agreement, to make it easier for other suppliers to access retailers and avoid any foreclosure effects of such agreement.

The decision also ordered the parties to reduce a non-compete clause to a maximum of three years, and to make certain commitments to avoid the probable conglomerate effects, such as preventing tied sales, exclusivity agreements, and other similar conditions.

Final decision

Based on the above, the parties to the transaction accepted the conditions described above and thus the transaction was approved subject to their compliance.

DOMINICAN REPUBLIC

Angélica Noboa Pagán*
(Noboa Pagán Abogados / Baker McKenzie)

Abstract

This chapter provides an overview of the merger and acquisitions regime in the Dominican Republic. Despite having a General Law for the Defence of Competition, the Dominican jurisdiction does not include a general ex ante or ex post regime for merger control. However, the sectoral laws that regulate the telecommunications and energy industries establish prior authorisation requirements for merger and acquisition operations. This chapter explains the Dominican jurisdiction institutional set-up, legal concept and category of notifiable transactions, the material and geographical scope, as well as the criteria and procedures that the telecommunications and energy regulatory bodies must follow for ex ante authorisation. The chapter also explains that there are acts of abuse of a dominant position and prohibited anticompetitive agreements, as well as ex post powers by these sectoral agencies that could render previously authorised mergers ineffective. Finally, it includes a summary of the precedents examined by two administrative entities, the Dominican Institute of Telecommunications (INDOTEL) and the Superintendency of Electricity (SIE), namely two cases of merger with prior authorisation requests and one divestiture order.

---

* Mrs. Noboa is a founding partner of the law firm Noboa Pagán Abogados of the Dominican Republic and is Knowledge Manager at Baker McKenzie Mexico, the country where she currently resides. Admitted to practice in the Dominican Republic, she has extensive practice in competition, telecommunications and energy law. She is a professor of competition law at the OMG Institute. She graduated from the Universidad Iberoamericana (UNIBE) in 1987, she is a specialist in business law and candidate for Master's in Corporate Law from the Universidad Anáhuac Mexico Norte.

I. Introduction

1. Brief Overview

Since the 19th century, the Dominican Constitution has proscribed monopolies, which may only be established on behalf of the state. Following the reform of 2010, the Constitution declared the fundamental right to free competition; proscribed anticompetitive practices; and, consigned a reservation of law to control the harmful effects of monopolies and abuses of dominant position, among other provisions that organise the productive activity and the economic system of the Dominican State[1]. The General Law for Defence of Competition[2] governs all economic agents, whether they are natural or legal persons, public or private, with or without profit, national or foreign, who carry out economic activities in the national territory. In addition, it applies to economic agents regulated by sectoral laws that contain provisions on competition in those areas in which the law is silent, unclear or ambiguous[3].

Its enactment occurred in two stages: the Draft Market Regulation Code was first submitted to Congress. This initiative was not successful. The second stage of drafting and discussion of a competition law began in 2005, because of the negotiation, signing, and enforcement of the Free Trade Agreement between the United States of America, Central America and the Dominican Republic (known by its acronym DR-CAFTA)[4]. Reference should be made to the fact that, both in the preliminary draft of the Market Regulation Code and in the preliminary draft of the General Law for Defence of Competition, provisions were set and discussed regarding the control of mergers and acquisitions that are not part of the approved legislation. This is despite the fact that in the Dominican Republic various products and services with specific bearing on the GDP are found in highly concentrated markets, according to figures obtained from the General Directorate of Internal Taxes[5].

However, two sectoral regimes, the General Telecommunications Law No 153-98, of May 27, 1998[6]: and the General Electricity Law No 125-01, its amendments and com-

---

1 10 July 2015, published in Official Gazette No 10805, <https://www.tribunalconstitucional.gob.do/servicios/publicaciones/constituci%C3%B3n-2015/>.

2 General Law for Defence of Competition, No 42-08, promulgated on 16 January 2008 and published in Official Gazette No 10458, 25 January 2008, <https://www.wipo.int/edocs/lexdocs/laws/es/do/do044es.pdf>.

3 The Law on the Rights of People in their Relations with the Public Administration and Administrative Procedure, No 107-13, enacted and published in the Official Gazette No 10722, dated 8 August 2013, supplements Law No 42-08 through general principles and procedural rules, <https://observatorioserviciospublicos.gob.do/publicaciones/miscelaneos/ley_107_13.pdf>.

4 United States, Central America and Dominican Republic Free Trade Agreement (DR-CAFTA), <http://www.sice.oas.org/Trade/CAFTA/CAFTADR/chapter1_5s.asp>.

5 General Directorate of Internal Taxes, Market Concentration in the Dominican Republic (2017), <https://dgii.gov.do/publicacionesOficiales/estudios/Documents/2017/ConcentracionMercado2017.pdf>.

6 Published in Official Gazette 9983, <https://transparencia.indotel.gob.do/base-legal-de-la-institucion/leyes/>. It establishes the basic regulatory framework to be applied throughout the national territory to regulate the installation, maintenance and operation of networks, the provision of services and the provision of telecommunications equipment. It includes among its guiding principles that of guaranteeing the satisfaction of the demand for public telecommunications services in conditions of free competition.

plementary regulations[7], have *ex ante* rules and procedures, and *ex post* attributions for merger operations based on competition law principles[8]. While the General Law of Commercial Companies and Individual Limited Liability Companies, No 479-08 and its amendments[9] establishes general rules regarding merger, divestment and transformation operations, compliance with requirements and procedures is necessary so that equity transfers may be made enforceable against third parties.

2. Institutional Set-Up

For the mergers of public telecommunications service companies, the authority in charge of its approval is the Dominican Telecommunications Institute (INDOTEL), a decentralised state body, with functional, jurisdictional and financial autonomy, its own property and legal personality. It has two levels of authority: the board of directors, which has the powers of management, judgment, decision, sanction and regulation, and the executive director, the body in charge of reviewing merger requests and which issues a report of recommendations to the board of directors, if deemed appropriate. INDOTEL's board of directors is composed of five members which are designated by the executive branch, four of which serve a fixed term of four years. The Minister of Economy, Planning and Development occupies the fifth seat. Two members are designated from a shortlist of candidates nominated each by the telephony sector and the broadcasting sector, respectively[10].

The energy sector regulations grant powers to the Superintendency of Electricity (SIE)[11] and the National Energy Commission (NEC) respectively, to rule on mergers, including takeovers[12]. Both have legal personality under public law and their own property.

---

7 Dated 26 July 2001, published in Official Gazette No 10095, 27 July 2001 and as amended by Law No 186-07 dated 6 August 2007, published in Official Gazette No 10429, 9 August 2007. Implementation Regulations, issued by Presidential Decree No 555-02 of 19 July 2002 and its modifications, <https://sie.gov.do/>. General Energy Law No 125-01, governs the production, transmission, distribution and commercialisation of electricity and the functions of the state agency related to these matters. In addition, it promotes healthy and effective competition in all those activities in which it is feasible, preventing unfair competition or abuse of a dominant position in the market.

8 The financial and banking intermediation service sectors establish the general principle of free competition and the obligation to request the prior approval of the financial authorities in the event of a merger. However, they do not establish a procedure for economic analysis of the transaction. The requirements are not those of competition law. They limit themselves to requesting a study from a firm of recognised prestige that supports the relevance and advantages that the merger would entail, but focused on the particular stability and growth of the entity that survives the merger.

9 Issued on 11 May 2008, Official Gazette No 10497.

10 They may be removed for the following reasons: a) when for any reason, not duly justified, they have missed six ordinary sessions in a year; b) when due to physical disability they have not been able to carry out their position for six months; and c) for condemnation with a final sentence of criminal penalty. Law 153-98 organises a special judicial procedure before the Supreme Court of Justice with the participation of the Office of the Attorney General of the Republic, to order the removal. Indotel's executive director is appointed by the board of directors.

11 Law No 125-01, article 31: "In addition to the functions set forth in Article 24 of the Law, the ... [SIE] shall have the following powers, including and not limited to: ... j) Authorise transfers of generation concessions and public distribution services or part thereof."

12 Law No 125-01, article 19 (amended by article 7 of Decree No 494-07 of 30 August 2007): "In addition to the powers that correspond to the NEC Board of Directors established in Article 17 of the Law: 1) Analyse and resolve through resolution, on requests for provisional concession of works of generation, transmission and distribution of electricity, as well as its expiration or revocation. 2) Decide on the approval, rejection or modification of the recommendations of the Definitive Concessions coming from the ... SIE."

A council made up of a president and two members, appointed by the executive branch and ratified by the National Congress, heads the SIE. The members of the SIE Council are designated for a term of four years and may only be removed for committing serious offences. A board of directors made up of various ministers or their representatives heads the NEC. Currently, the board is composed of representatives of the Ministries of Industry and Trade; Energy and Mines; Economy, Planning and Development; Finance; and Environment and Natural Resources.

The national competition authority, Comisión Nacional de Defensa a la Competencia (ProCompetencia)can only intervene in the *ex post* processes established in the telecommunications and energy laws, in an advisory capacity. This agency is a decentralised body of the state with legal personality, full capacity to acquire rights and contract obligations and a non-attachable, autonomous capital. It has two levels of authority: the board of directors, which has the powers of management, judgment, decision, sanction and regulation, and the executive director which is in charge of investigating and prosecuting anticompetitive behaviour. ProCompetencia's board of directors is the body in charge of issuing a non-binding opinion, in case of *ex post* control of the mergers of sectoral bodies.

ProCompetencia's board of directors is composed of five members appointed by National Congress from a proposal of 10 candidates presented by the executive power as follows:

a) Five candidates presented to the Senate of the Republic for an election of three members that, in the first period of operation of the Commission, is for a term of two years; and
b) Five candidates presented to the Chamber of Deputies of the Dominican Republic, for selection of two members for a term of five years, from the same first period of operation of the Commission.

The renewal of the directors of the Commission is done partially every three years, for a term of five years in office. In other words, three and two directors are appointed successively, in the same manner established in the law, no later than one month after the expiration date of their appointments. The members of the board of directors cannot be removed for the duration of their term, except in some specific situations provided by law[13]. The president of the board is chosen by vote from among its members, according to the procedure established in the Commission's law and the statutes.

3. Type of Merger Control

Dominican competition law has no provisions on merger and acquisition control *ex ante*. Only the aforementioned laws related to telecommunications and energy services have some prerequisites that must be exhausted before agreeing to a merger based on competition rules.

---

13 Removal or substitution causes: a) when for any reason, not duly justified, they have missed six ordinary sessions in a year; b) when due to physical disability they have not been able to carry out their duties for six months; c) for condemnation with a final sentence of criminal penalty; d) when manifest negligence is demonstrated in the fulfilment of their functions, or, in the event that, without due justification, they fail to fulfill their obligations, in accordance with the law, the regulations and the decisions of the board; and e) when they are responsible for fraudulent and illegal acts, operations, or that are clearly opposed to the purposes and interests of the institution ... (Law No 42-08, article 29).

ProCompetencia can only intervene in sectoral regimes, in a merely advisory capacity, in matters related to the application of competition law or in the event that the sectoral bodies are in the process of issuing regulations or settling a conflict affecting competition. Therefore, ProCompetencia does not have the authority to intervene in the *ex ante* procedures set forth in the telecommunications and energy laws[14].

II. Scope of Application

1. Definition of a Notifiable Transaction

An economic concentration in the telecommunications sector is the legal transaction through which a permanent and secure modification occurs regarding the control structure[15], whether direct, indirect, in whole or in part, of one or more companies providing public telecommunications services, benefiting other subjects of law that control other companies that provide public telecommunications services, with the possibility of modifying the structure and functioning of the markets of the telecommunications sector. It is also defined as a related company, any company that has a relationship of majority shareholder, parent, subsidiary, affiliate, holder, controller, controlled or dependent on another, exceeding the barrier of a simple commercial relationship[16].

The energy regime defines controlling companies as those that have the possibility of controlling, through voting stock or in the control of management, other companies. It could be either through direct or indirect majority participation, through the control of one or more companies whose added shareholding corresponds to the majority of the equity, or through any other contractual or legal mechanism that confers direct or indirect control of a company or its assets[17].

A company is a subsidiary of another company when the latter has control of the former. A company is affiliated with another or other companies when all are under common control, and two or more companies are related when they have communicating vessels through shareholders that represent at least 10% of the subscribed and paid-in capital of any of the companies, or represent as directors in economic groups with these shareholding characteristics[18].

---

14 Law 42-08, article 20: Relationship with other regulatory market entities. Administrative acts intended to dictate regulations or resolve administrative proceedings, brought before other market regulatory entities other than the Commission, provided they are related to the object of this law, must be sent to the Commission for its examination, together with the supporting documentation.

15 Control: the power to determine, directly or indirectly, the business policy, the start or end of the company's activity, the variation of the activity to which it is dedicated, or the disposition of the assets or rights essential for the development of the activity of said entity. Free and Fair Competition Regulations for the Telecommunications Sector, issued by Resolution 022-05 of 24 February 2005 by the Board of Directors of the INDOTEL, article 1.

16 Free and Fair Competition Regulations, note 16, article 1.

17 Law No 125-01, article 2.

18 ibid.

Also, the energy services regulations establish *ex post* restrictive rules on the control and connection between companies in the interconnected electricity sector. The SIE must investigate allegations of links between companies in the interconnected electric system. In order to carry out its investigations on these links, the SIE may use, among others, the following criteria:

a) A link will be considered to exist when a company is related to another, either as subsidiary, affiliate or controlling company, or through a shareholder or majority shareholder.
b) Controlling companies are those that have the possibility of controlling other companies, by means of the votes in the assemblies or in the control of the management, either through their direct majority participation, or indirectly through control of one or more companies whose added shareholding corresponds to the majority of stakeholders, or through any other contract or legal mechanism that confers direct or indirect control of a company or its assets.
c) A company is a subsidiary of another company when the latter has control of the former; a company is affiliated with another or other companies when all are under common control. In addition, two or more companies are linked when they have communicating vessels through shareholders that represent 10% or more of the subscribed and paid-in capital of any of the companies or represent as directors in economic groups with these shareholding characteristics[19].

2. Material Scope

Merger control in the telecommunications[20] sector applies to all operations of the installation, maintenance and operation of networks, the provision of services and the provision of telecommunications equipment[21]. It will apply to all public telecommunications service providers and their service resellers, particularly in relation to access to the networks and essential infrastructure for the provision of these services[22]. INDOTEL will carry out the control of economic concentrations in the telecommunications sector in order to achieve the objectives indicated in article 2[23] of the regulations and articles 3[24] and 28 of the law[25].

---

19 Law No 125-01, article 11 (amended by article 6 of Decree No 749-02 dated 19 September 2002): "In accordance with Article 11, Law, Generation Companies, Co-generators, Self-Producers and Distribution Companies, may carry out only one of the generation, transmission or distribution activities, except as provided in Paragraph I."

20 Free and Fair Competition Regulations, note 16, Chapter IV.

21 Law 153-98, article 2.

22 Free and Fair Competition Regulations, note 16, article 12.

23 Relating to the scope of the regulation, that is, it will apply to all public telecommunications service providers and their service resellers, particularly in relation to access to the networks and essential infrastructure for the provision of these services.

24 Promote the participation in the market of public telecommunications services of providers with the capacity to develop fair, effective and sustainable competition over time, which translates into a better telecommunications offer in terms of prices service quality and technological innovation.

25 Free and Fair Competition Regulations, note 16, article 12: Duty of Information.

In the case of energy service providers, without prior authorisation from the SIE, the generation or distribution concessions, or part of them, may not be transferred, whether by divestment, lease, transfer between associated persons, transformation, acquisition or merger of companies, or by any other act according to which domain or exploitation right is transferred[26]. The rule applies to all types of concessions for the generation, distribution and commercialisation rights, to avoid monopolistic practices and promote competition in the Interconnected National Electrical System (INES), as well as to avoid the threat to free competition in the Wholesale Electric Market (WEM). The energy services contemplated in the law are those related to the exploitation of electricity, coal, gas, oil and its derivatives, hydraulic, nuclear, geothermal or solar energy, unconventional energy and other energy sources, present or future[27]. In the energy sector, the transmission service is a legal state monopoly.

The NEC and SIE will take the necessary measures to guarantee that there are no horizontal integrations in the generation segment of the EINS that produce anticompetitive effects in the WEM. Furthermore, before proceeding to authorise the transfer of generation concessions, mergers or sales of shares involving generation companies, it must investigate whether the submitters themselves, or their related companies, own generation plants whose total generation capacity, including that of related companies, represents a percentage of the maximum demand of EINS, which, according to criteria established by regulation by the NEC, constitutes a threat to free competition in the WEM[28].

3. Geographical Scope

The telecommunications[29] and energy[30] regimes apply to the entire Dominican territory. By complementary application of the General Competition Law, merger or acquisition operations arranged abroad that may have effects on free competition in the national territory are also subject to control[31].

4. Thresholds

In the telecommunications regime, no thresholds are established. According to the regulations on merger and acquisitions control, the providers of public telecommunications services, as well as other persons to whom that regulation applies, must inform INDOTEL of all operations intended to carry out an economic concentration in the telecommunications sector, in order to obtain prior authorisation to proceed. Economic mergers in the telecommunications sector must be authorised by INDOTEL in accordance with the regulations, and may not have an effect on the market until such authorisation is obtained[32].

---

26 Transfer of Concessions Application Regulation, article 82.

27 Law 125-01, article 13.

28 Regulation of Application of the General Law of Electricity, article 12.

29 Free and Fair Competition Regulations note 16, Chapter IV.

30 The law does not expressly establish its geographical scope, but from its content, we can derive a national scope.

31 Law 42-08, article 3(a).

32 Free and Fair Competition Regulations note 16, articles 12.2 and 12.3.

Similarly the energy regime does not establish thresholds. Without prior authorisation from the SIE, the generation or distribution concessions or part of them may not be transferred, whether by takeover, lease, transfer between associated persons, transformation, acquisition or merger of companies, or by any other act according to which domain or exploitation right is transferred[33].

III. Procedure

1. Launch of Procedure

Merger request for public energy services companies is a procedure that is carried out in person and in written form, requiring the payment of certain fees for studies, when applicable. In the case of telecommunications services, electronic requests may be accepted. In both cases, the documents must be presented in Spanish and, if they are from a foreign source, must have corresponding consular stamps. The application must contain the corporate documents that demonstrate the by-laws, current assets and persons in charge of the control of the companies that are part of the transaction, as well as the fulfilment of their corresponding tax obligations[34].

Regarding telecommunications notifications, the request for authorisation must include the following information:

a) Identification of the individuals or companies involved in the concentration.
b) Identification of the relevant market for marketing purposes, of the product or service involved in the economic concentration.
c) Nature, development and economic impact of the operation carried out.
d) Total (and detailed) value of the sales of each of the products or services offered.
e) Total (and detailed) value of assets and initial investment to be made.
f) Estimated market share.
g) The legal instruments by which the operation is executed or sustained and the mechanisms by which the will of the parties involved is manifested.
h) Any other information required by INDOTEL in order to verify the criteria in the preceding article[35].

The extract of the application drawn up by INDOTEL must be published in a newspaper with national circulation, within seven days of INDOTEL's notification. Non-publication

---

33 Article 82, Transfer of Concessions Application Regulation, issued by Resolution No 07-02, 2 June 2000, modified by Resolution No 129-04, 22 February 2007 by the Board of Directors of INDOTEL.

34 In the case of telecommunications companies, in accordance with the formal and procedural requirements of Chapter VIII of the Concessions Regulations, Entries in Special Registries and Licenses to Provide Telecommunications Services. INDOTEL Board of Directors Resolution No 07-02, modified by Resolution No 129-04, <https://www.observacom.org/wp-content/uploads/2017/03/Reglamento-concesiones-y-licencias.pdf>.

35 Free and Fair Competition Regulations, note 16, article 13.1: Processing of the Authorisation Request.

within the period will constitute a reason for refusal of the request by INDOTEL. In the event that the application is incomplete or incorrect, the applicant may amend it within 15 calendar days of notification by INDOTEL, under penalty of rejection of the application. Once INDOTEL has authorised the publication of the merger notice, any interested person may make observations or objections, within 15 days of publication of the application extract. The applicant may respond to observations or objections within a period of 10 days, counted from the date on which the observations were notified.

Without prior authorisation from the SIE, the generation or distribution concessions, or part of them, may not be transferred, whether by transfer, lease, transfer between associated persons, transformation, absorption or merger of companies or by any other act according to which domain or exploitation right is transferred. In order to obtain said authorisation, the proposed acquirer must submit to the SIE, along with the transactional and property information[36], the documentation that accredits its technical and economic capacity, as well as any other documentation that the SIE considers pertinent for such purposes[37].

With regard to an application for the merger of energy service companies, the petitioner must have a legal domicile in the Dominican Republic, and submit the following to the SIE through his legal representative:

a) Letter/application addressed to the president of the republic, via the SIE.
b) Corporate, commercial, and financial background documentation.
c) Location of the electrical work and real estate documents of the location, with a description of the civil work.
d) Technology to be used, expected lifetime, electrical study that will contain at least the short-circuit analysis, load flow, stability of the interconnected system and commitment to any cost of compatibility.
e) Commissioning schedule, environmental impact study presented to the Ministry of Environment and Natural Resources, which must declare no objection; and,
f) Fee for study of the petition[38].

Within five business days of receiving the request, the NEC will publish it in a newspaper with national circulation, so that any interested party can present, within five business days of publication, their observations or objections[39].

2. Development of Procedure

Regarding merger authorisation requests in the telecommunications sector, once the information has been presented, the executive director of INDOTEL will have a period of 60 calendar days to rule on the authorisation, impose corrective measures or object to

---

36 Contained in the Processing Regulations for the Exploitation of Electric Works issued by the SIE.
37 Regulation of Application of the General Law of Electricity, article 82.
38 ibid.
39 ibid.

the request for authorisation to carry out the concentration operation through a reasoned resolution. Said term may be extended by INDOTEL, once, for a period of 30 calendar days. Upon expiry of the indicated period without a ruling from INDOTEL, the applicants may proceed to make the economic concentration effective, and INDOTEL loses competence to rule on it[40].

INDOTEL will review the application, which must contain at least: name of the applicant; authorised services or radio frequencies, as applicable; service zone; operation description; parties involved in the operation; and a list of other licences of which the applicant is a beneficiary[41].

In the event that the information is not complete or that INDOTEL requires additional information to carry out its analysis, it will so communicate to the applicants within the the 60-day period mentioned in the previous paragraph. In this case, the time for INDOTEL's analysis will be interrupted and will only start running again when the applicants have provided the corresponding information. INDOTEL may only request additional information once. Once the additional information has been provided, INDOTEL must decide, based on what is found in the file, if the information delivered meets the criteria of the information request. If the interested parties do not provide the additional information within 60 calendar days of the date of receipt of the request, they must withdraw from the process[42].

In the event of opposition or observations to a requested merger in the energy sector, the SIE may open a period of submission of evidence, so that, where appropriate: a) the applicant presents additional evidence to support its claims; and b) the petitioner submits the corresponding clarifications or proof of discharge. The SIE will initiate the corresponding investigation within no more than 30 working days of receiving the complaint. As part of the investigation, the SIE will request the parties to produce all documentation deemed necessary for the assessment of the complaint in question. The SIE must decide within a period not exceeding 90 working days[43].

The SIE, after studying and considering the documentation presented, will make its decision, in order to make its recommendation to the NEC in due course.

The NEC may modify and expand these criteria, in order to ensure the proper functioning of the market in the energy sector and avoid anticompetitive practices. In order to comply with the previous provision, electric companies must submit their shareholding composition to the SIE, indicating their situation with respect to control of any other companies, and the way in which said control is exercised. This shall be done every six months, specifically in June and December each year; and/or when the SIE requests it.

In the event of shareholder or control changes made before the expiry of the period, the electricity companies must notify the SIE within 15 days of the date the changes occur. The SIE may require certification of the shareholder breakdown by natural person of

---

40 Free and Fair Competition Regulations, note 16, article 13.2: Processing of the Authorisation Request.

41 In order to comply with basic rules of the Transfer of Concessions Application Regulation.

42 Free and Fair Competition Regulations, note 16, article 13.2: Processing of the Authorisation Request.

43 Regulation of Application of the General Law of Electricity, article 11, para II.

those legal entities that appear as shareholders of electricity companies, as well as documentation that proves their relationship or not with companies in the electricity sector. The SIE must keep an updated record of the investments made by and in the electricity firms in order to ensure compliance with the law and, in case of non-compliance, apply the corresponding sanctions to the offending companies in accordance with regulatory procedures.

Likewise, any market agent may make complaints of the relationship of the companies in the system, for which they must provide the SIE, at the time of making the complaint, with the documents that support their claim. The SIE will initiate the corresponding investigation within a period of no more than 30 business days from receipt of the complaint. Within this investigation, the SIE will open a process in which it will request of the parties involved all documentation it deems necessary for its construction and assessment of the complaint in question, having to resolve within a period not exceeding 90 business days[44].

Immediately after the SIE adopts its decision, it must communicate it to the parties within 10 business days. If it considers that there is a relationship, it will order the related company or companies to dispose of the corresponding investment within 120 days, warning that if they do not comply with that provision, it will be liable for fines of up to 5% of its assets, without prejudice to other sanctions that may be applied if it insists on non-compliance.

The decision adopted by the SIE may be appealed to the NEC, according to a procedure established by the NEC for this purpose. The filing of this appeal will automatically suspend the separation order, including the term of 120 days. In the event that the denounced related company does not proceed with the separation or divestment within the period, the SIE will proceed to impose the corresponding fine, in accordance with the provisions of these regulations. The income generated by this may be used for special professional education programmes in the areas of electricity market regulation, as well as for the promotion and development of technical and professional areas related to the sector[45].

3. Conclusion of Procedure

After reviewing the request and the observations of interested parties and the applicant, the INDOTEL board of directors will issue its decision by resolution, approving or rejecting the request, within 45 days. Once said term has ended, if INDOTEL has not pronounced an express rejection, the request will be considered approved. Within 20 days of the date the applicant submits its amendments or corrections, INDOTEL will advise either: a) that the request has been accepted, and the operation may continue; or b) that it does not meet the requirements, and the application has been rejected.

With respect to mergers in the energy sector, within 30 business days of receipt of the application the SIE will grant or reject the request for authorisation[46]. In any case of

44 The SIE shall establish a procedure to process the allegations of links and process the pertinent investigation, guaranteeing the constitutional right of defence of the company accused of linkage.

45 ibid.

46 Law No 125-01, Implementing Regulation, article 82

transfer, and as long as it is authorised, the acquiring company must comply with all the conditions provided by the law to be a licensee[47].

The administrative act may authorise or reject a merger, as well as a divestiture order be challenged before the Superior Administrative Court (*Tribunal Superior Administrativo*), by way of administrative judicial review and, on the merits, may request possible interim measures. The court can review INDOTEL, SIE or NCE decisions both in substance and in form and may overrule them.

4. Sanctions

The lack of information and/or request for prior authorisation of an economic concentration operation in the telecommunications and energy sector constitutes a breach that will carry corresponding sanctions, which may include payment of administrative fines, or immediate cessation of the effects of the merger or acquisition agreement.

IV. Substance

1. Competition Analysis

In accordance with telecommunications regulation on the authorisation of assignment of rights or authorisations[48], the assessment on the conformity of an economic concentration in the sector of telecommunications, with the objectives of the law and these regulations, will be based on the analysis of their restrictive, predictable and verified effects, mainly taking into account the following circumstances:

a) Delimitation of the relevant market.
b) Structure and economic agents that supply it.
c) Evolution of supply and demand.
d) Growth, elasticity, price behaviour.
e) Market entry barriers.
f) Presence of potential and active competitors, cost structures, service exploitation permits, fees.
g) The economic and financial power of companies[49].

INDOTEL may object to those operations of economic concentration in the telecommunications sector whose purpose or effect is to decrease, restrict, damage or unreasonably prevent free competition in the sector. It also may presume that an economic concentration in the telecommunications sector has the purpose or effect of unreasonably reducing, restricting, damaging or preventing free competition in the sector, in the following cases:

---

47 ibid., article 83.

48 Without prejudice to the provisions of the Regulations on Concessions, Inscriptions in Special Registries and Licenses to Provide Telecommunications Services in the Dominican Republic.

49 Free and Fair Competition Regulations, note 16, article 12.

a) When it confers (or can confer) on the economic agent resulting from the merger the power to unilaterally fix prices or substantially restrict the procurement or supply of products or services in the relevant market, without the competing agents being able to, effectively or potentially, counteract said power;
b) When it has displaced or intends to displace other existing or potential competitors, or prevent them from entering the relevant market; and,
c) When the object or effect is to substantially facilitate the exercise of restrictive or unfair competition practices by the participants[50].

The interested party, providing evidence to the contrary, may disprove these presumptions. When INDOTEL determines the existence of one or more of the presumptions, it may object to the economic concentration operation or subject its execution to the fulfilment of the necessary conditions[51].

Telecommunications regulations do not give INDOTEL powers to issue divestiture orders, as the energy regulation in does in favour of the SIE. However, in the case of a company that, because of a merger, acquires a dominant position in the telecoms market and repeatedly abuses it, committing anticompetitive practices that are classified as very serious by the Telecommunications Law[52], such companies may be subject to scrutiny by INDOTEL. An inversion in this sense could lead to revocation of the operating licence, an even more severe penalty than a divestiture order[53].

When evaluating merger notifications within the energy sector, upon recommendation of the SIE, the NCE shall investigate whether the petitioners, themselves or through related companies, own generation plants whose total capacity represents a significant percentage of EINS's maximum demand[54].

2. Statistics

INDOTEL has granted two *ex ante* authorisations and the SIE an *ex post* with a divestiture order. The precedents' names, type of transaction and duration of each procedures are:

a) Resolution No SIE-60-2003 of the SIE issued on 5 December 2003, which ordered the divestiture of AES Corporation, Ltd, in the equity participation of Empresa Generadora de Electricidad Itabo, S.A., exercised via its subsidiary AES Gener, S.A. This procedure lasted three months.
b) Resolution No 219-06 of the Board of Directors of INDOTEL issued on 30 November 2006, through authorising Verizon Dominicana, C. Por A., to transfer its shareholding control in favour of América Móvil, S.A.B. de C.V., through the corporate structure submitted for approval. This procedure lasted three years.

---

50 Free and Fair Competition Regulations, note 16, article 14.
51 ibid.
52 Abuse of dominant position or anticompetitive agreements.
53 General Telecommunications Law No 153-98, article 29 (c).
54 Law No 125-01, Implementing Regulation, article 12 paragraph II.

c) Resolution No 056-17 of the Board of Directors of INDOTEL issued on 20 September 2017, granted prior authorisation to Tricom, S.A. and Altice Hispaniola, S.A., to complete a merger by acquisition. However, through Resolution No 077-17 of 22 November 2017, regarding the appeal for reconsideration filed by *Altice* Hispaniola S.A. and Tricom, S.A., some corrective measures were modified. The procedure lasted one year and nine months.

3. Case Law Illustration

(1) On 5 December 2003, the SIE issued Resolution No SIE-60-2003, which ordered the divestiture of AES Corporation, Ltd., in the equity participation of Empresa Generadora de Electricidad Itabo, S.A., exercised via its subsidiary AES Gener, S.A. In addition to its condition as concessionaire of the distribution networks in the east of the country, the company AES Corporation Ltd had, through its affiliates and subsidiaries in the country, a global participation of 61.169% within the national generation sector. This percentage comes from a comparison of the estimated calculation of the maximum demand of the national sector for the year 2003, 1,583.3 Megawatts, with the production of AES Corporation Ltd. and its affiliates and subsidiaries in the country, a total of 968.5 Megawatts.

This last result was obtained by the sum of the combined installed capacity of the *Itabo*, *Los Minas V* and *Los Minas VI* and *Andrés Punta Caucedo* generating plants. The SIE considered that such participation quota in the national power generation sector, by a company that owns majority control of one of the concession companies in charge of power distribution, violated the provisions of its concession contract, which contemplated a capacity not greater than 15%. Furthermore, the concentration, within a single legal entity of control, of more than 50% of the generation market, and a third of the internal distribution market, constituted a dominant position in the national energy market. The decision also refers to the internal unrest in the other energy market concessionaires that seized the SIE, denouncing the abuse of a dominant position of AES Corporation Ltd, accusing it of generating an immediate harmful effect, which was not verified by the SIE. Despite the foregoing, the SIE considered that the market power of the denounced company was susceptible of generating it, a reason that also supported its decision.

(2) On 30 November 2006, through Resolution No 219-06, INDOTEL authorised Verizon Dominicana, C. Por A., to transfer its shareholding control in favour of América Móvil, S.A.B. de C.V., through the corporate structure submitted for approval. According to the application, América Móvil would maintain direct control of the Mexican company AMX Tenedora, S.A. de C.V. In turn, AMX Tenedora, would directly control the Canadian company 3146032 Nova Scotia Limited (AMX Canada), to whom the company GTE Venezuela S.a.r.l. would transfer 100% of the shares representing the capital stock of Verizon Canada Holdings Corporation, majority shareholder of the Verizon Dominicana. As provided in the resolution, Verizon Dominicana was ordered to keep its records and corporate information updated before the competent regulatory body, including information regarding its shareholders and representatives.

(3) On 20 September 2017, through Resolution No 056-17, INDOTEL granted prior authorisation to Tricom, S.A. and Altice Hispaniola, S.A., to complete a merger by acquisition. However, INDOTEL partially accepted observations and objections presented by Compañía Dominicana de Teléfonos, S.A. and Trilogy Dominicana, S.A. The authorisation granted the applicants the possibility of modifying the structure and operation of the relevant markets for mobile services (telephony and access to Internet). This included the transfer of authorisations granted for the use of segments of the radio electric spectrum, included ranges of 824–835 MHz, 845–846.5 MHz, 869–880 MHz and 890–891.5 MHz, subject to its effectiveness on compliance with all corrective measures established in the resolution.

The corrective measures ordered to prevent concentration effects resulting from the authorised operation, in the relevant markets of mobile telephony and Internet access, due to spectrum accumulation, were:

a) The return to the Dominican State of the frequencies 1850–1865 MHz and 1930–1945 MHz assigned to Tricom, S.A. with the consequent cancellation of the corresponding qualifying titles.
b) The allocation in favour of Altice Hispaniola, S.A. of the frequency segments 1720–1730 MHz and 2120–2130 MHz, for use in the provision of final public mobile telecommunications services at national level[55].
c) The publication by Altice Hispaniola S.A. of its Reference Interconnection Offer (OIR) in the terms that were presented to INDOTEL, regarding the request for authorisation of the merger operation. This included an access charge per minute for termination in the Altice Hispaniola mobile network; lower than the prices established in the interconnection contracts in force at that time of Altice Hispaniola and Tricom; and their respective OIR deposited with INDOTEL.

However, through Resolution No 077-17 of 22 November 22 2017, regarding the appeal for reconsideration filed by Altice Hispaniola and Tricom, the corrective measure contained in (a) was modified. This was replaced by *ex post* controls, so that in the use of the bands assigned to concessionaires the effects of effective competition can be equated, establishing obligations aimed at improving conditions of quality, price and technological innovation, to promote competition. The measures included actions to guarantee the coverage of mobile services, with the capacity to provide broadband to low-served provinces over a period of three years; the installation of Wi-Fi points in locations designated by INDOTEL within the same term; and a monetary contribution for the development of ICTs. In addition, Altice Hispaniola was allocated the frequency segments 1720–1730 MHz and 2120–2130 MHz, for use in the provision of final public mobile telecommunications services nationwide, as a substitute for the previously authorised frequency assignments. Finally, the inclusion of an access charge per minute for termination in the Altice Hispaniola mobile network, lower than the prices established in the Altice Hispaniola or Tricom interconnection contracts in force at that time, and their respective OIR deposited with INDOTEL.

---

55 In substitution for the frequency assignments authorised by Resolution No 007-04 of 30 January 2004 of the INDOTEL Board of Directors, with the consequent issuance of the qualifying titles in favour of said company.

ECUADOR

David A. Sperber Vilhelm*

(AntiTrust Consultores & Abogados)

Abstract

The Ecuadorian Competition Law of 2011 establishes the relevant merger control regime. It establishes an ex ante merger control when one of two thresholds are met. Informative filings that do not meet the thresholds can also be filed. The Superintendency of Control of Market Power, the national administrative competition authority, can approve, subordinate or deny a filed transaction. The Commission of First Instance can intervene in cases where a merger has or may have anticompetitive effects in the relevant market. A new fast-track procedure has been in force since April 2020. The fine for jumping the gun or "gun-jumping" is one of up to 12% of the local transaction's gross income, plus the possibility of having the transaction voided, as well as other actions and/or remedies. The Commission has the power to undo the transaction and impose additional conditions and/or measures. Correspondingly, failure to provide requested information by the transaction parties and/or third parties can be sanctioned with fines of up to USD 500,000.

---

* David A. Sperber Vilhelm is a partner at AntiTrust Consultores & Abogados, Quito, dsperber@antitrust.ec; davidspeber@hotmail.com. Before joining the firm, he served as the first National Competition Director at MIPRO. He teaches competition law at Universidad Internacional del Ecuador. He holds a Juris Doctor from Pontificia Universidad Católica del Ecuador, an LLM from Harvard Law School and a PhD from Universidad de Barcelona. The author thanks Charles Reeves and Cynthia Andino for their contributions.

I. Introduction

1. Brief Overview

The relevant antitrust legislation is the Ecuadorian Competition Law[1], also so-called Competition and Market Power Law (*Ley Orgánica de Regulación y Control del Poder de Mercado* – LORCPM), which came into effect on 13 October 2011, and the Rules that accompany that legislation[2].

From March 2009 to October 2011 Ecuador's competition rules were controlled by Andean Community Decisions 608[3] and 616[4]. Decision 608 applies to abuse of dominant position and collusive practices and restrictive agreements, but it does not cover merger control.

In 2009 the Ecuadorian government approved Executive Decree 1416 in order to directly apply Decision 608[5]. This executive decree created the first national competition authority, the Under-Secretary of Competition and Consumers at the Ministry of Industry and Productivity (MIPRO). When I led the competition team at MIPRO, we were in charge of building and creating the competition authority, and investigating cases in Ecuador applying Decision 608. We were also responsible for preparing, outlining and reaching consensus on the draft Ecuadorian Competition Law. This draft was presented to the government's president and later to Congress (Asamblea Nacional). I participated in the two debates held by the Congressional Economic Regulation Commission, where a few changes were made to the merger control section of the Competition and Market Power Law.

Ecuador's Competition Law is the first national antitrust legislation approved by the Ecuadorian legislature, which enabled for the first time all five aspects of antitrust regulation to be enforceable in Ecuador as of 2011. Until the first Superintendent of Competition was appointed, MIPRO continued to resolve the antitrust cases presented to it.

The following are the five main areas regulated by the Competition and Market Power Law:

1. Abuse of market power (abuse of dominant position).
2. Merger control.
3. Restrictive agreements, which includes cartel enforcement.
4. State aid; and,
5. Unfair trade practices.

---

[1] Ley Orgánica de Regulación y Control del Poder de Mercado – LORCPM. R.O. S. 555., 13 October 2011.

[2] Reglamento a la Ley Orgánica de Regulación y Control del Poder de Mercado. R.O. 697., 7 May 2012.

[3] Decision 608: rules for the protection and promotion of competition in the Andean Community, 28 March 2005. Decision 608 introduced a regional law on competition applicable to anticompetitive practices and abuse of dominant position. All sectors of economic activity are covered except when the Andean Community Commission decides to exclude a specific sector following a supported request from a Member State.

[4] Decision 616: entry into force of Decision 608 for the Republic of Ecuador, 25 July 2005. It enables Ecuador to apply Decision 608 when anticompetitive practices originate in Ecuadorian territory or in a third country affecting Ecuadorian territory. Bolivia and Ecuador may temporarily apply Decision 608 while they adopt a national competition law.

[5] Executive Decree 1614 of 27 March 2009.

2. Institutional Set-Up

The Superintendency of Market Power Control (*Superintendencia de Control del Poder de Mercado* or SCPM) is the administrative agency designated to enforce the antitrust legislation. The SCPM was created by the Competition and Market Power Law, and as such is in charge of merger enforcement. The SCPM initiated operations in September 2012.

The SCPM is headed by the Superintendent of Market Power Control. The Superintendent is appointed from a list of three qualified candidates that Ecuador's president remits to the Citizen's Participation and Social Control Council (*Consejo de Participación Ciudadana y Control Social*[6]). This council appoints the Superintendent for a fixed term of five years, which is renewable for an additional five years.

The SCPM is part of the "fifth power of the state" (Transparency and Social Control branch), and as such it is not subordinate to other branches of government. The SCPM is divided in five areas:

1. Merger Control.
2. Restrictive Agreements
3. Abuse of Market Power.
4. Economic Market Studies and Competition Promotion.
5. Unfair Trade Practices that Affect Competition.

The SCPM has branches nationwide. Merger control issues, however, are handled exclusively by SCPM headquarters in Quito.

The Competition Law and its Rules establish two organic and administrative bodies for SCPM:

1. Commission of First Instance (*Comisión de Resolución de Primera Instancia* or Commission) issues resolutions and sanctions (resolution body); and,
2. National Intendancies (*Intendencias Nacionales*) investigates competition matters (investigatory body).

3. Type of Merger Control

Ecuadorian law contemplates mixed merger control with optional notification. Merger control is usually *ex ante* with compulsory notification when one of the two thresholds are met (see below). Ecuadorian rules also allow the filing of non-mandatory, "informative" or "voluntary" filings. The non-mandatory filing is made to avoid later SCPM review of a transaction when the two thresholds have not been met, but where the transaction is executed in important markets or when the threshold criteria is close to being met.

---

6 <www.cpccs.gob.ec>.

The transaction that meets one of the two thresholds shall not be executed in Ecuador until it receives SCPM approval. The fine for closing a mandatory filing without prior authorisation is up to 12% of the local transaction's gross income, plus the possibility of having the transaction voided, as well as other actions and/or remedies.

The SCPM has been active in recent years reviewing local mergers and acquisitions. It also reviews international mergers that have an effect in Ecuador for which filings have not been made.

II. Scope of Application

1. Definition of Notifiable Transaction

Ecuadorian merger rules and SCPM case law establish a broad definition of what constitutes a notifiable transaction. They include mergers and acquisitions, acquisition of assets, joint ventures with permanent effects, acquisition of minority shareholdings and any other direct and/or indirect change of control mechanism.

2. Material Scope

The material scope of notifiable transactions is wide-ranging, since it includes all economic sectors. An exception is a transaction approved or created by a congressional act. At the same time, a possible exception can be a public partner – partnership approved by the competent administrative body. Another exception could be for acquisitions made by government entities or state-owned companies. Two filings, however, have been presented to the SCPM by a "private" regulated bank that is wholly owned by the state. In these cases the SCPM declared it was competent to review the transactions that were approved by its Commission of First Instance.

3. Geographical Scope

The geographical scope of a notifiable transaction has an effects-based approach. It includes national and/or international transactions with local nexus and/or local effect. The main local nexus is the real economic substance of one of the parties in the transaction in Ecuador and/or its local effect.

The SCPM has included in its criteria the existence of international ownership or income to determine the nexus between buyer and target. The competition authority has been actively reviewing important international transactions with local subsidiaries.

4. Thresholds

The Ecuadorian Competition Law has two criteria for mandatory filing, triggered by one of the following thresholds:

1. Before or after the economic concentration or the transaction the buyer will have or gain 30% or more of the relevant market(s); or,

2. Separate or combined gross revenue of buyer and target in Ecuador exceeds 200,000 unified basic remunerations (2019: USD 79.2 million; 2020: US$D80 million)[7], which are revised annually by the Ministry of Labour.

The filing has to be filed before closing the merger or acquisition that creates or effects a permanent change of control.

III. Procedure

1. Launch of Procedure

The procedure starts with the formal filing at the SCPM. It had a single notification form with annexes for all types of transactions (standard/complex/simple transactions). On April 2020, the Ecuadorian Competition Authority approved a fast-track system only for simple transactions. Then, *mutatis mutandis*, the main benefit for simple transactions is the merger clearance time reduces to three to six months. Normal transactions are approved within between five and ten months.

The buyer shall comply with one of the following conditions to apply the fast-track:

1. The buyer does not carry out, directly or indirectly, economic activities in Ecuador.
2. In horizontal transactions:
   a) Less than 30% of the relevant market(s) is horizontally integrated.
   b) The Herfindahl-Hirschman Index (HHI) before the transaction shall be less than 2,000 points in the relevant market(s), and after it shall not increase more than 250 points.
3. In vertical transactions:
   a) Less than 30% of the relevant market(s) is vertically integrated.
   b) The HHI result shall be less than 2,000 points in the relevant market(s).
4. That transaction involves companies at risk of bankruptcy.

The filing shall be in person. However, during COVID-19 the SCPM authorised e-filing. The Ecuadorian Competition Authority will decide if they continue using e-filing in due course.

The mandatory filing fee is calculated based on the gross income, assets and/or equity of the target in Ecuador. In most cases, the amount of the filing fee is not relevant considering the size of the transaction.

The mandatory filing shall be presented within eight calendar days of the transaction being approved by the parties with suspended effect.

---

[7] Note: banking and insurance markets have higher revenue thresholds, determined by the Market Power Control Board.

There are no restrictions regarding publicity of the approval of the merger or acquisition. For example, local stock market relevant reporting has to be made within three business days, including merger agreements.

2. Development of Procedure

Ecuadorian rules do not divide the procedure in phases. There is a one-stage investigation procedure. The Competition Law stipulates 60 business days in which to acknowledge and resolve the economic concentration. This period can be prolonged for up to 60 calendar days by the Mergers Intendancy (*Intendencia Nacional de Control de Concentraciones*). Notwithstanding, the time frame for resolving the transaction can be suspended if information is pending from the filing parties and/or third parties, including private and/or government bodies.

The investigative powers of the SCPM are those established in Article 49 of the Competition Law. The SCPM has broad powers while conducting investigations and handling filings, including the power to:

1. Subpoena any information and documents relevant to the investigation from parties and non-parties, including but not limited to financial statements, accounting books, correspondence, magnetic data, without the owner and/or holder being able to offer arguments regarding the reserved nature of the information to impede or obstruct the investigation.
2. Compel testimony of the parties and/or third parties, in the presence of legal counsel, through depositions that are conducted by designated members of the SCPM. Said depositions can be recorded to generate a complete record of the statements made.
3. Enter into the premises of the parties and/or third parties, with or without previous notice, and examine books, records and any document relevant to the investigation, as well as to take any testimony of the people that are in the premises. During the inspection, any magnetic and/or physical documents can be seized or a copy of documents can be made. Photographs or video recordings can be made if deemed necessary. In the case of raids, seizing of documents or making copies of documents that contain confidential or secret information, a judge order must be obtained in advance.

The SCPM generally calls the transaction parties and third parties to meetings and requests information. There are no specific rules for commitments, but they can be presented and discussed in the meetings with the members of the Mergers Intendancy. The parties to the transaction shall cooperate with the SCPM and other regulators, and can be called to working meetings with the Mergers Intendancy. Correspondingly, any public or private person has a duty to collaborate with the SCPM and is obliged to provide all data and information necessary for the application of the Ecuadorian Competition Law. In this sense, the law stipulates the cooperation of the different institutions of the public government and regulatory entities.

The SCPM can solicit information from foreign competition authorities, as well as other local and international authorities (e.g. tax authorities, companies authorities, stock market authorities, etc.). This is very common in international filings.

3. Conclusion of Procedure

The Mergers National Intendancy presents a final non-bidding report to the Commission of First Instance. The Commission makes the final decision regarding the filing of the transaction. It can approve, subordinate or deny the filed transaction.

The Commission delegates to the Mergers National Intendancy the monitoring of the commitments and the execution of its final decision. The Commission can also appoint a third person to supervise the execution of the commitments.

The Commission's decision can be appealed to the Superintendent by the parties to the transaction and/or by third parties that are affected by the final decision. In Ecuador, no formal intervention from the government can be made to overrule the decision, or from other entities or ministries.

The decision of the Commission of First Instance can be appealed to the Superintendent of the SCPM. The resolution of the Commission or the Superintendent can be appealed for judicial review to the Administrative Court of Appeals.

Cassation appeals by the parties and/or the SCPM are allowed. These are heard by the National Court of Justice. An extraordinary action can be filed at the Constitutional Court for final revision on *a certiorari* basis. *Certiorari* can be requested only for violations of a constitutional right and with limitations.

It is important to note that, as a general rule, the effects of the Commission's decisions are not suspended during appeals to different administrative and judicial bodies.

4. Sanctions

A mandatory filing transaction shall not be executed in Ecuador until it is approved by the Commission of First Instance. The fine for closing a mandatory filing without prior authorisation, or "gun-jumping", is up to 12% of the parties' local gross income for the transaction. Moreover, the Commission has the power to undo the transaction and impose additional conditions and/or measures. Correspondingly, failure to provide requested information by the transaction parties and/or third parties can be sanctioned with fines of up to USD 500,000.

Competition Law fines are determined by the local gross turnover of the entire company or group of companies. Article 6 of the Law defines turnover of the company as the value resulting from the total gross sale of the products and/or services of the companies during the previous year, minus the value-added tax and other final sale taxes.

In practice, fines are determined by the Commission of First Instance, which must take into account the parameters set in the Competition Law. These parameters include:

a) The dimensions and characteristics of the affected relevant market;
b) The market share of the parties of the transaction that carried out the practice or gun-jumped;
c) Effects of the conduct on the rights and legitimate interests of consumers and competitors;

d) Benefits obtained as a result of the conduct; and
e) Attenuating and extenuating circumstances related to each party responsible for the mandatory filing or illegal conduct.

IV. Substance

1. Competition Analysis

The merger review test set forth in the Competition Law touches on a combination of competition assessment, elements of public interest, market effect, consumer benefits and role of efficiencies.

The relevant SCPM analysis includes:

a) The status of the competition in the relevant market(s);
b) The degree of market power or dominant position of the parties involved in the transaction, and of their main competitors;
c) The need to develop and/or maintain competition in the market, including its structure and the actual and/or potential competitors;
d) If market power is generated or strengthened by the transaction, or will effectuate a significant decrease, distortion or obstruction of competition. It also considers whether there is a clearly foreseeable effect on competitors; and
e) Potential contributions, e.g.:
   i) Improvement to production or commercialisation of goods and/or services;
   ii) Promotion of technological progress or economic progress in the country;
   iii) Competitiveness of the national industry in the international market as long as it does not have a significant impact on the economic wellbeing of national consumers;
   iv) Welfare of Ecuadorian consumers;
   v) Compensation effect on certain markets and specific restrictive effects on competition; and
   vi) Diversification of social capital and participation of workers (this was abolished in 2017).

2. Statistics

The SCPM reviews on average 16 mandatory filing transactions and four non-mandatory (informative) filing transactions per year. The following are the statistics for merger transactions reviewed by the SCPM from 2014 to 2019:

1. Non-mandatory (informative) filing: 21.
2. Mandatory filing: 101 divided as follows:
   a) Without remedies: 83.
   b) With remedies: 18.
   c) Blocked: 1.

3. Case Law Illustration

Case: AB InBev / SABMiller Ecuador (Case SCPM-ICC-EXP-2015-040)

The Belgium-based AB InBev agreed to buy SABMiller in a USD 107 billion worldwide acquisition, the so-called "Megabrew" deal in 2016. AntiTrust Consultores & Abogados represented the target company in Ecuador.

In Ecuador, SABMiller's subsidiary, Cervecería Nacional, was the beer market – leader with 96.32% market share (2016) while AB InBev had 3.56% (2016). The acquisition included *Pilsener, Pilsener Light* and *Club* brands, the country's three top-selling beers. Cervecería Nacional was established in 1887. SABMiller acquired Cervecería Nacional from the Colombian group Santo Domingo in 2005.

On 6 May 2017, the Commission of First Instance issued its resolution and decided to subordinate the approval of the acquisition of SABMiller's subsidiary Cervecería Nacional. The Commission imposed a series of structural and behavioural remedies to maintain competition in the local beer market.

The following were the conditions and remedies:

1. Total disinvestment of the AB InBev production plant in Guayaquil (Ecuador), and total disinvestment of other assets. This was the smaller production plant between AB InBev and SABMiller.
2. The use of DINADEC S.A. (SABMiller's local distribution company acquired by the buyer) to allow access to AB InBev's nationwide distribution channel to local breweries.
3. Implement separate contracts with clients and providers to include procompetition conditions.
4. The prohibition of exclusivity clauses.
5. Create and implement an e-commerce platform for the sale of independent craft beer producers.
6. Open refrigerator space at the final sales points to craft beers and other drinks (up to 30% of refrigerator space for competitors).
7. The sale of the *Biela*, *Dorada*, *Zenda* and *Maltín* brands.
8. License the use and exploit of the *Brahma* brand, as well as production distribution and marketing of products of the brand.
9. Limit the advertising budget of the *Pilsener*, *Club*, *Budweiser*, *BUD66* and *Pony Malta* brands (main local brands).
10. Maintain jobs and job stability for workers of both companies (target and buyer in Ecuador); transfer 5% of the shares of the local company to workers through a trust (this option was removed from LORCPM Rules after this case).
11. Provide access to the bottling process and bottle design of one bottle, its production system, training and promotion to local craft breweries.

On 15 November 2017, after the remedies were approved by the Commission of First Instance, the SCPM subsequently added a new condition within the process of divestment.

The condition was the sale of the *Club* beer brand, owned by SABMiller, which had a 10% national market share. This brand has been sold in Ecuador since 1966. After a court claim by AB InBev and SABMiller, this disinvestment provision was ruled to be not mandatory and *Club* currently remains part of AB InBev's local brands. Ultimately, this acquisition was approved in Ecuador after AB InBev carried out the remedies.

The AB InBev production plant in Guayaquil and other assets were acquired by a local group of investors through the Biela corporation (CEREC Holding Company). Biela corporation control was acquired by Heineken in May 2019.

EL SALVADOR

Regina Vargas[*]
(Superintendencia de Competencia)

Abstract

In El Salvador, the merger regime is undergoing a transition period due to the adjustment of the Competition Law by the Administrative Procedure Law that came into force in 2019. The amendment is in the process of approval and substantially modifies the merger procedure and the stages within it, without prejudice to the technical, economic and legal specialty of the competition issues. Merger procedure is a single stage ex ante for all mergers that meet the criteria that the Competition Law and its Regulation establish as a notifiable merger transaction. The Competition Law encompasses all economic sectors. On a merger transaction in a regulated sector, if the board of directors authorise, deny or condition it, this decision is binding to the sectoral regulator. Failure to submit a request for authorisation of a merger carries a pecuniary sanction, notwithstanding the possibility of judicial action by the general attorney.

---

* Head of Competition Advocacy at the Superintendencia de Competencia of El Salvador since 2009. Bachelor's degree in International Business and Master Degree studies in Business Law. Expert in antitrust and trade policy.

I. Introduction

1. Brief Overview

The Competition Law in El Salvador has been in force for 15 years. The enactment of this law took approximately 12 years. With the signing of the Chapultepec Agreements in 1992, El Salvador ended a 12-year civil war. The agreements not only included the terms by which the armed conflict would end but also included structural reforms, such as modification to the judicial and electoral systems, armed forces regulation, the creation of the National Civil Police and the introduction of social and economic measures.

The economic measures of the agreements established the adoption of a Consumer Protection and Competition Law. The Consumer Protection Law had a fast-approval process in the Salvadoran Congress. The first Consumer Protection Law was enacted on 31 August 1992, published in the official gazette No 159, volume 316 and entered into force on 9 September 1992. Unfortunately, the Competition Law did not have the same expedited process. A first draft of a Competition Law was presented to Congress in 1994 and, after that first attempt, various proposals of the Competition Law were presented by different actors including think tanks, academia, consumer protection associations and the Ministry of Economy with the assistance of international organisms. However, the enactment came 12 years later on 26 November 2004.

The Salvadoran Competition Law granted a one year *vacatio legis* so that the Competition Authority, the *Superintendencia de Competencia* (SC), could be created and promote awareness among economic agents so that the Law could be implemented effectively. On 1 January 2006 the Competition Law entered into force and the SC began operations with the mandate to promote, protect and guarantee competition, by preventing and eliminating any anticompetitive practice, regardless of its nature, that restricts competition in any way or impedes access to the market to economic agents, in order to increase economic efficiency and consumer welfare.

Article 57 of the Competition Law derogated provisions on regulations and laws regarding competition, such as articles from the Criminal Code that prohibited monopolies, Commerce Code provisions that legalised certain anticompetitive practices such as agreements of under 10 years among competitors for production and market division, and sectoral regulation. The SC is the only authority that has the power to resolve competition issues.

In 2007, almost two years after the enforcement began, the Competition Law underwent some important amendments, most of them regarding the administrative sanctioning procedure for anticompetitive practices. The sanctions regime modified the amount of the fines to be imposed in relation to anticompetitive practices carried out, trying to dissuade economic agents not to engage in anticompetitive behaviour. The maximum fine is up to 6% of the total annual sales obtained by the offender during the previous fiscal year, up to 6% of the value of the assets during the fiscal year previous; or equivalent to 2–10 times the estimated gain from anticompetitive practice, whichever is higher.

Regarding merger control, the amendment introduced other fines and sanctions for those who must request merger authorisation and do not do so, for not complying with the conditions made in the final resolution authorising the merger and for those who do not comply with precautionary measures.

In February 2019, the Administrative Procedure Law (APL) came into force, allowing 18 months for public institutions to adapt their administrative procedures stated in laws and regulations that may be contradictory or opposed to the APL. The merger and administrative sanctioning procedures have undergone modifications due to the APL but the merger control procedure is the one that endured the highest number of adjustments. The reform of the Competition Law is ongoing, following the approval procedure to incorporate the adjustments necessary due to the APL[1]. The main changes in the merger control procedure are:

1. The APL mandates that all administrative procedure terms must be counted in business days, so the 90 *calendar* days' term that the Competition Law gave for a merger control review decision is now 90 *business* days, and the term can be suspended.
2. The terms of the administrative procedures, including the merger control procedure, can be suspended when there is a legal incident or if the authority requires information of the economic agents involved in the transaction or third parties that participate in the economic activity in which the transaction is taking place. The term is suspended until the information requirement is completed.
3. Two hearings have been added to the administrative procedures, one at the beginning of the procedure and one at the end, before the final decision is made.
4. Interested third parties can formally become part of the procedure when they can justify a legitimate interest.

Regarding the analysis standards, they remain similar because the changes are to the procedures and not to criteria or standards. Saying that, it remains a one-phase procedure, with the legal standard that a merger may only be cleared if it does not significantly limit competition or when there is a significant gain in efficiency, resulting in savings in direct costs and benefits for consumers that cannot be reached by means other than the merger, and guaranteeing that there will not be a reduction in market supply.

The SC has a webpage with a comprehensive information, including resolutions from the board of directors regarding anticompetitive practices and merger control, sectoral studies, opinions, educational publications, law and regulation, guidelines, interinstitutional agreements and news, among other activities to comply with and effect implementation of the Competition Law[2].

2. Institutional Set-Up

The SC is an independent institution, part of the executive branch, with administrative and budgetary autonomy to exercise the obligations and duties set in the law, by means of technical, legal and economic analysis. It has a total of 52 full-time staff members: one

---

1 While the amendment finishes the approval procedure, the SC is applying the APL and the Competition Law.

2 Superintendencia de Competencia, "Concentraciones económicas" (2020), <https://www.sc.gob.sv/index.php/concentraciones-3/>.

superintendent, 30 technical units called *intendencias*, eight support units, 11 administrative units and one secretary-general. The institutional budget for 2020 is USD 2,659,133 and it is financed entirely by the government's "General Fund of the Nation". The SC has its own separate budget, approved by the board of directors and it is submitted to the Ministry of Finance through the Ministry of Economy, the Ministry of Economy being the institution by which the SC relates with the executive branch.

The maximum authority is the board of directors, which is the decision-making body. It is composed of the superintendent, who presides over the board, and two other directors, all of them appointed by the president of the republic for a term of five years. They can be reappointed. There are three alternate directors, also appointed by the president that attend board meetings and may speak, but they not have the right to vote, with the exception of when they are substituting a director. The superintendent is the only full-time member of the SC and the rest of the board members serve part-time.

The Competition Law establishes criteria to determine who is unfit to be appointed as board member by the president of the republic. To date, the board members have come either from the academic community or from other government institutions. There has been only one appointment of a board member from the private sector, but it was ensured that the appointment complied with the provisions established in the Competition Law. There is a provision in the Competition Law that provides the causes for removal of a board member and, when a cause of removal applies, the removal process must follow due process and comply with the constitutional mandate that the affected person must have a fair trial before removal. To date, all the appointments end on the same date, except in one case when a board member died and his replacement's appointment ends three years after the other board members.

The board meets once a week, even though the Competition Law requires them to meet at least once a month or when the circumstances require it. The directors have a compensation rate for each session of the board they attend. The decisions of the board are taken by majority and all their resolutions are made public.

The superintendent is the legal representative of the SC and oversees and supervises the institutional activities. They may modify the organisation of the institution by abolishing or creating units. Since 2012, the SC is composed of three *Intendencias*: Advocacy, Economic and Investigation. The Economic Intendancy is in charge of analysing the merger transactions that are notified. The Economic Intendancy reports the finding of the merger analysis to the board who deliberates on whether to approve, condition or deny the merger.

3. Type of Merger Control

The Competition Law contains an *ex ante* mandatory merger control regimen that applies to all economic sectors without exception. Regarding the regulated sectors, the decision of the SC is binding for the institution that oversees the sector. Article 31 of the Law establishes the criteria of what should be understood by merger under the competition regime in El Salvador. The main criteria that is taken into account to define a merger by the Competition Law, is if the economic agents that are part of the transaction have been independent from each other and whether one economic agent acquires control, direct or indirect, total or partial, over the other economic agent in the transaction. The Law also establishes notifiable merger thresholds, stated in article 33.

The Regulation contains several articles which expand on various substantive aspects of the merger review, such as the mandatory pre-merger notification (article 23), concept of merger (article 18), the notification thresholds (articles 19 and 20), criteria and relevant elements to be taken into account to determine whether the merger might significantly limit competition (articles 21 and 22) and the authorisation procedure (articles 24–32). In the case of a merger that derives from a transaction performed abroad, the respective merger authorisation must be submitted before it takes place in the national territory. This will be explained with greater detail in the next section.

With the APL in force the merger control procedure underwent some changes that will be part of the Competition Law reform. It is still a one-phase procedure, with the difference that in the original text of the Competition Law there is no detail on the procedural matter for merger review but rather establishes a term of 90 days to carry out the prospective analysis established in the Competition Law and its Regulations. Once the Competition Law is reformed the merger procedure will be described. This process will be explained in section III(4).

II. Scope of Application

1. Definition of a Notifiable Transaction

To determine if the merger requires an *ex ante* notification it must comply with the legal criteria (article 31 of the Competition Law): that the economic agents have been independent from each other and entered an act, contract or agreement, with the purpose of totally or partially merging, acquiring consolidating, integrating or combining their business. The second determinant that must be considered is if one or more an economic agent who controls at least one other economic agent acquires partial or total direct or indirect control of another economic agente through any means whatsoever.

In order to determine what is a merger, the Regulation clarifies that "merger" encompasses all transactions perfected according to the Commerce Code: a merger or acquisition is any act or legal form, including judicial adjudications, actions of voluntary or forced liquidation, and inheritance or legacies, which result in the merger of enterprises, division or enterprise participation, and assets in general.

As established in article 32 of the Competition Law, for legal effect, control is understood as the capability of an economic agent to exert an influence over another by exercising property rights, or the use of all or part of the economic agent's assets or by means of agreements that grant a substantial influence in the composition or decision-making of the board and management bodies or legal representatives of the economic agent.

2. Material Scope

The Competition Law provisions, including merger control provisions, are binding to all economic agents, be they natural or legal person, state or local government, enterprises with state participation, cooperative associations, or any other organisation participating in economic activities. The only consideration that the Competition Law establishes regarding the scope of the Law are those economic activities that the Constitution and the laws reserve exclusively to the state and municipalities such as garbage collection, lighting, and parks maintenance and security, among others. When not proving the economic activities, the state and municipalities must comply with the provisions set forth in law. Regarding mergers in regulated sectors, a merger decision from the SC is necessary for the economic agent to operate.

3. Geographical Scope

The Competition Law and the Regulation do not require that the merger transaction takes place in El Salvador, but if the economic agent is going to operate in national territory they have to submit a merger notification. Regarding merger thresholds, according to SC jurisprudence the relevant assets or revenues have to be located in or obtained in El Salvador. Nonetheless, jurisprudence has developed a local nexus standard, according to which the presence of the economic agents involved in the transaction and the effects in national territory must be considered when determining whether a merger is notifiable. The SC only examines mergers if all economic agents involved in the transaction have direct or indirect presence in the jurisdiction.

In the final resolution SC-030-S/C/R-2010, 23 September 2010 – Financial Sector – Leasing Bogotá, S.A. Panama, BAC Credomatic Gece Inc:

Hence the purpose of Article 33 of the Competition Law, where it is established as a parameter, to define the operations subject to authorisation, the combination of assets or total income. The term combination is part of the economic rationality previously stated in the sense that, if in the Salvadoran territory there are no assets or income to add on the part from any of the parties involved, there would be no business combination that could have the potential to negatively affect the competitive conditions of any market in particular. Potentiality that is what gives meaning to the entire *ex ante* review process[3].

4. Thresholds

Once the criteria are met for determining whether a merger needs an *ex ante* notification or not, there is an economic threshold established in the Competition Law (article 33): in assets, 50,000 minimum urban annual wages in the industry sector; or total income exceeding 60,000 urban annual wages in the industry sector. The SC, to calculate the thresholds, must consider the minimum urban annual wage in force the day prior to the filing date. The local nexus criteria apply considering only the assets and revenues located or obtained in the national territory. The SC must add all local assets and income of the

---

3 Free translation of Resolution SC-030-S/C/R-2010.

economic agent part of the transaction. For the calculation of the income threshold, the sales of the products and services provided by the economic agents of their last fiscal year, prior to deductions of the sales discounts and tax deduction.

Table 1: Merger Thresholds

	Number of Minimum Annual Wages of the Industry	Minimum Annual Wage of the Industry in El Salvador*	Threshold in USD
Assets	50,000	USD 3,650	182,500,000
Income	60,000		219,000,000

* Executive Decree No 6, 21 December 2017, published in the Official Gazette No 240, volume 417 on 22 December 2017.

III. Procedure

With the entry into force of the APL, in February 2019, the procedural stages for merger review must be clearly established in the text of the Competition Law. It is important to clarify that even though the reform for the changes to the Competition Law from the APL have not yet been passed through Congress, it is mandatory to apply the adjusted procedure; the SC has been applying the adjusted procedure for merger control since then, meaning that it applies the APL and the Competition Law.

The merger procedure established by the Competition Law grants the SC board of directors a 90-calendar-day term to issue a decision regarding a merger notification. With the adjustment to the Competition Law, this term becomes a 90-business-day period if there is no suspension of the legal term. The suspension of the legal term takes place when information requirements are delivered by the SC to the economic agents or if the SC requires the economic agents involved in the transaction to clarify or complete the information required. In the case that a merger control decision is not taken in this term, the Competition Law establishes that it is understood that the merger has been authorised. Non-compliance with the term by the SC board of directors is one of the causes of removal of board members, established in the Competition Law.

1. Launch of Procedure

The merger control notification is a single-phase procedure and is mandatory for all the merger transactions that fall under the definition of merger and pass the thresholds established in the Competition Law. Currently there is no filing fee for merger notifications. Interested third parties can become part of the procedure when they prove they have a legitimate interest and can submit their position regarding the merger transaction that is under review. The merger notification must be presented in writing to the SC. There are still no digital channels to file a merger, due to the lack of legal instruments such as the implementation of the electronic firm law. The filing must be done before the legal act is performed, control is acquired or exercised, de facto or de jure, or assets, trusts participation, capital contributions or shares are acquired, the merger agreement is signed or successions acts are executed.

2. Development of Procedure

A merger control notification can be submitted to the SC by any of the economic agents participating in the transaction. As mentioned previously, if a merger transaction is performed abroad but the legal or material effects will take place in the national territory, a merger authorisation must be requested before the operation starts in El Salvador. The merger notification must be submitted in writing to the board of directors of the SC and must include the requirements and information established in the Competition Law and the APL[4].

Once a merger notification is received at the SC, and before it is admitted into analysis, the SC must verify whether the formal legal requirements are met. The first step is to confirm that it is a merger under the definition established in the Competition Law and if it exceeds the legal thresholds. If it is a notifiable merger, the SC has five business days to verify the compliance of the requirements established in APL and 15 business days for the verification of the requirements and information required by the Competition Law and Regulation. Once the APL amendment to the Competition Law is approved in

---

4 The competition regime in El Salvador is in transition period awaiting approval of the Competition Law reform. In the meantime, merging parties must comply with the legal requirements of the APL and the Competition law for the notification requirements.
APL requirements:
1. Clearly establish that is being submitted to the board of directors,
2. Name of the parties, permanent address or any means, electronic, magnetic or other, to receive notifications; if applicable identification of the legal representative.
3. The petition to authorise the merger transaction.
4. Details of merger transaction.
5. Signature of the interested party or its representative by any legal means permitted.
6. Place and date.
Requirements of the Competition Law and Regulation for merger notification:
1. The names of the parties that have a direct or indirect participation in the transaction.
2. Legal representative, if applicable, providing all certified legal accreditation documents. Permanent address or technical means where notice or notifications can be made.
3. Attested copies of the articles of incorporation and any amendments duly registered in the Registry of Commerce.
4. Externally audited financial statements of the preceding fiscal year of the parties.
5. Certification of the structure of capital stock prior to the merger transaction and the description of the structure of capital stock after the merger transaction.
6. The shareholding of each direct or indirect shareholder, before and after the transaction, and the persons who currently have and subsequently will have control.
7. Legal document that describes the merger transaction, its objectives and type, accompanied by the relevant information related to the transaction.
8. The structure of the merging parties' corporate groups.
9. Economic agents involved that have direct or indirect participation in holding of capital stock, administration or in any activity of other economic agents that produce or commercialise goods or services related to those provided by the merging parties.
10. Market participation of the parties.
11. Description of goods and services produced or provided by merging parties in the relevant market of the transaction.
12. List of similar goods and services to those offered by the merging parties in the national territory.

Congress, it is probable that there will be a single term in which to analyse the compliance of the formalities and legal requirements.

If requirements are not complete or are deficient, the SC must notify it to merging parties, who have 10 business days to fulfil them. If the parties involved in the transaction cannot complete the requirements in the 10 days, they may ask the SC for extension of the period. If the information is not completed in the legal period and no extension is requested by the merging parties, the notification must be declared by the board of directors of the SC as inadmissible and the parties must submit a new notification.

The legal term for merger control does not begin until the SC verifies that all the requirements and information set out in the relevant legal instruments are fulfilled. Once the analysis has started, the SC can issue a second request to the parties, and typically issues requests for information to economic agents participating in the relevant markets to have a complete overview of the transaction. The information requests suspend the legal term for mergers until all the economic agents complete the required information. The term starts running again from the point at which it was suspended, once all the requirements are fulfilled. Meanwhile, the SC can perform interviews or require technical reports.

Then, the SC has a period of 8–20 business days for information-gathering and analysis that includes classification of the confidential information. In the APL-adjusted merger procedure, the authority may hold a first hearing within 10–15 business days for merging parties, and any interested third parties to present positions, studies or reports related to the merger transaction. The information and views presented must be considered in the merger analysis. The merger parties, as well as third parties, can ask for the access to the merger file that contains the public information during all the procedure, until the file is transferred to the board of directors of the SC.

The technical team of the SC analyses and reviews all the information and documents to prepare a report with the findings for the board of directors. Once the report is finished and before the board takes the final decision, a second hearing with the merging parties and interested third parties take place. This hearing aims to communicate the findings of the analysis and whether there are any competition concerns. At this point, the parties can still submit commitments or remedies to alleviate the concerns: the SC does not have the power to negotiate them but has an obligation to take them into account in the analysis. The technical report with recommendations that is submitted to the board of directors can at this point be modified following the discussions and information presented at the second hearing.

3. Conclusion of Procedure

Finalised after the second hearing, the file is transferred to the board of directors. They can authorise, condition or deny the merger. The procedure must be completed in the 90-business-day period if there is no suspension of the term, due to information requests or legal incidents.

When a merger transaction is approved with conditions and the parties are unwilling to comply with the conditions, they can abandon the transaction, appeal the decision to the board of directors or file a new merger transaction with commitments that may alleviate or eliminate the SC's competition concerns. In 2011 América Móvil, owner of Claro, was acquiring Digicel: in this merger case the board of directors' decision added the condition for Claro to give up 20 MHz of their assigned spectrum. Said spectrum would be allocated to new competitors and in this way, will maintain the rivalry levels in the market, being that Digicel was consider a "Maverick"[5].

On the merger decision, the board of directors also issued recommendations to the General Superintendency of Electricity and Telecommunications (SIGET) to regulate and encourage the efficient use of the spectrum for mobile telephony in order to avoid its accumulation for strategically anticompetitive purposes, and to allocate the spectrum given up by Claro to a new competitor that has no relation with a mobile operator in the Salvadoran market. Recommendations were also addressed to the Consumer Defender so they can review the service quality through complaints filed by consumers and present an annual report to the SC board of directors. Claro decided not to accept the conditions and filed a new merger notification.

The second merger notification was admitted to analysis in July 2012. The technical analysis determined that there were high probabilities that the transaction would significantly limit competition in the mobile telephony market. Legal, economic, structural, technical and strategic barriers to entry were identified. A high level of market concentration was determined by the Herfindahl-Hirschman Index (HHI), the most relevant effect on competition being the accumulation of more than 50% of the spectrum concession in the country in control of one economic agent. The spectrum was divided into two different portions that were not continuous and did not offer efficiency to the service provider. Also, considering that Digicel was a "maverick"[6] in mobile telephony, who upon entry reduced prices in the service and maintained a strong commercial strategy

---

5 Superintendencia de Competencia, SC-016-S/C/R-2011: Claro-Digicel merger, <https://www.sc.gob.sv/index.php/project/solicitud-de-concentracion-economica-america-movil-y-amoviv-con-digicel-holdings-limited-sc-016-s-c-r-2011/>.

6 Free translation of decision SC-013-S/C/R-2012 – América Móvil, S.A.B. de C.V., Amov IV, S.A. de C.V. y Digicel Holdings Limited, Digicel Cayman Services Limited, *Mavericks* (September 2012).

Company that has the pre-merger ability to discipline prices based on its ability and incentive to rapidly expand the production. It can also be defined as that company that has habitually resisted obeying the rules set by the industry and aimed at promoting cooperation between competitors in setting prices or other terms of competition.

...

All legal systems agree that the basic characteristics of companies who are in that position are: a disruptive role in the market and benefit to consumers, breach of market conditions with a new technology or business model, resistance to prevailing rules in the industry that tend to establish prices or other terms of competition, independent behaviour and less predictable, among others, which may concur or exist alternatively.

...

Two of the possible effects that could be generated are analysed below of an economic concentration that includes a "maverick" company. On one hand, it can be predicted that, in the absence of efficiencies, the new company product of the merger transaction will prefer higher prices than the maverick would have preferred. If so, the merger would have removed the constraint on effective coordination and would trigger a rise in prices. About the above, it is worth asking how much this increase prices. It will depend on the preferences of the company that takes the place of the absorbed maverick. The new maverick outcome of the merger transaction may potentially favour keeping prices as low as the old maverick but this result is unlikely. On the other hand, it is also possible, but markedly less likely, that a merger involving a maverick may encourage the new economic agent product of merger to keep prices low. This second possibility is less likely because it requires the transaction to generate great savings in variable costs for the new entity (or other substantial efficiencies capable of benefiting consumers, such as providing the merged company with the ability to launch

promoting rivalry in the market with benefits to consumers, if that commercial strategy is not maintained consumer welfare may be reduced. In the unilateral conduct analysis, Claro was going to have the major market participation, having the incentive to abuse market power, being able to produce the exit of smaller competitors[7].

In the last five years, only in one merger transaction, in the beer sector, did the economic agents present a remedy proposal[8]. For the board of directors, the proposed remedies did not satisfy the competition concerns they had, deciding to impose structural and behaviour conditions. The structural conditions involved commitments from the merging parties for the next three years and required specialised monitoring. For this purpose, a monitor agent was appointed to assist SC technical staff with that task. For more detail, see section IV(3).

4. Sanctions

If a merger transaction takes place without notification, there is a fine of 5,000 minimum monthly urban wages in the industry sector. To date, two mergers transactions have been identified that did not comply with the notification, the sanction decision also included the obligation of the merged parties to submit a merger notification for authorisation to the SC. If the board of directors imposes a condition and the parties do not comply with obligations imposed in the final decision, or do so incompletely, falsely or fraudulently, there is a fine of 5,000 minimum monthly urban wages in the industry for every day of non-compliance.

For non-compliance with information requirements, the SC has a general provision in the Competition Law, that they can impose a fine of up to 10 minimum monthly urban wages in the industry for every day of delay, to the individuals, companies or institutions who deliberately or negligently fail to provide the collaboration.

Table 2: Sanction in mergers

Type of Sanction	Minimum Monthly Urban Wage USD	Sanction in Minimum Monthly Urban Wages	Sanction in USD
Not Filing Notification	304.17	Max 5,000	1,523,550
Non-Compliance Merger Conditions		Max 5,000 per day	1,523,550 per day
Not Providing Information		10	3,041.71

new products). For this reason, the evaluation of the efficiencies alleged as product of economic concentration and verify if these efficiencies are significant enough to counter lost competition.

7 Superintendencia de Competencia, SC-013-S/C/R-2012: Claro-Digicel merger, <https://www.sc.gob.sv/index.php/sala_multimedia/denegatoria-concentracion-economica-america-movil-y-amoviv-con-digicel-holdings-limited-sc-013-s-c-r-2012/>.

8 Superintendencia de Competencia, "SC condiciona concentración en mercado de cervezas" (2017) <https://www.sc.gob.sv/index.php/sc-condiciona-concentracion-en-mercado-de-cervezas/?unapproved=521&moderation-hash=649af2f7721b41abbf5338f4f455b09b#comment-521>.

IV. Substance

1. Competition Analysis

The substantive merger analysis established in the Competition Law and Regulation is a standard competition assessment where, once admitted to analysis, the criteria to be considered are to determine the relevant market where the merger will take place and produce effects, the control of the parties involved, gain in efficiencies derived from the merger transaction and if the parties involved hold a dominant position in the relevant market considering the criteria of the Competition Law; concentration level in the markets is also measured.

To determine whether the merger transaction will limit significantly competition the SC must consider, among other relevant elements: if a foreign firm acquires control of Salvadoran firms or accumulate shares in national territory, if a party involved in the merger transaction is an insolvent company[9], temporary entailments such as: consortiums and strategic alliances or corporative restructuring operations.

The SC uses the HHI to assess concentration levels. The threshold at which it determines that a market is highly concentrated is considered to be 2,500 HHI. When analysing a merger transaction, in those cases where HHI increases 200 points because of the transaction, a greater scrutiny is done in the prospective merger analysis, as it may distort competition in the market. If the merger is taking place in a regulated sector, regulatory implications are taken into account in the analysis because sometimes they may alleviate competition concerns, such as a high level of market concentration as measured by the HHI. An example is in the electricity sector, where SIGET has the general function to ensure competition but lacks enforcement powers, as it is tasked with determining conditions for fair competition in prices offered in the regulated market system. For this purpose, the Regulation on Operation for Transmission and Wholesale Market based on Production Costs regulates the determination of prices and has prevented the exercise of market power including, among others, unjustified increases in prices. If SIGET determines that there is no guarantee of competition conditions on the prices offered, article 112-E of the Electricity Law establishes that the superintendent of SIGET and the superintendent of the SC will jointly establish competition conditions on electricity prices.

When analysing a merger transaction, efficiencies play a determining role because, by the provisions in the Competition Law, when the merging parties demonstrate gains in efficiencies, the transaction cannot be refused. Mergers that can potentially generate greater adverse effects on competition will be required to demonstrate greater gains in efficiency, since these must be significant enough to serve as a counterweight to the possible adverse effects of the transaction. The Competition Law (article 34) is based on

---

9 To date there has not been a merger notification filed due to insolvent economic agent, which article 22 of the Competition Law Regulation establishes as a relevant element in merger analysis pursuant to article 34(b) of the Competition Law. The regulation of the Competition Law establishes that the insolvent economic agent must prove that it has been unsuccessful in the search for a buyer that is a non-competitor in the market.

a welfare standard[10] that includes both the benefits obtained by the merger parties and the benefits obtained directly by the consumer. Welfare to consumers is not only analysed from a price point of view, but it has a multidimensional aspect that includes product quality, timeliness and security of supply. The fact that the benefits can be transferred to consumers must be presented by the merging parties with a certain degree of certainty, for which they must indicate how they will be materialised.

2. Statistics

As shown in the statistics in Table 2, merger control notifications have increased in the last four years. The number of "procedurally incorrect" mergers stand out as the Registry of Commerce, when registering a merger, acquisition or combination of businesses, requires the economic agent to have an SC resolution, so all the mergers that do not comply with the definition and thresholds of a notifiable merger in the Competition Law are declared "procedurally incorrect" by the SC board of directors.

Table 3. Merger notification filed at the Superintendencia de Competencia de El Salvador

(elaborated with data from the SC website)

Mergers Decision	2015	2016	2017	2018	2019	Total
Authorised	1	1	4	3	1	**10**
Conditions Applied		2				**2**
Denied						**0**
Procedurally Incorrect**	4	5	8	6	7	**30**
Inadmissible*		2	2	3	5	**12**
Under Analysis					2	**2**
Total	**5**	**10**	**14**	**12**	**15**	**56**

* Inadmissible: Merger notifications that do not comply with legal requirements.

** Procedurally Incorrect: notifications that do not follow under the legal definition of merger or do not exceed the legal thresholds.

3. Case Law Illustration

In November 2015 Anheuser-Busch InBev S.A/N.V. (AB InBev) and SABMiller plc, two of the largest beer companies in the world, agreed on the worldwide acquisition by AB InBev of all the issued share capital of or that may be issued by SABMiller. In El Salvador, the merger notification was presented to the SC by the parties on

---

10 Free translation of decision SC-013-S/C/R-2012 – América Móvil, S.A.B. de C.V., Amov IV, S.A. de C.V. y Digicel Holdings Limited, Digicel Cayman Services Limited (September 2012): "As a third requirement, the Competition Law indicates that the gains in efficiency must result in cost savings and direct benefits to the consumer. The foregoing reflects that Competition is based on a welfare standard which includes both the benefits obtained by the concentrated companies and the benefits obtained by the consumer, pointing out the need to benefit directly from the article."

5 February 2016. On 1 June 2016, once the applicant complied with all the formal requirements of the Competition Law and its Regulations, the merger transaction was admitted for analysis.

The SABMiller group had a presence in El Salvador through Industrias La Constancia, S.A. de C.V. (ILC) and other subsidiaries. ILC produced, imported, and commercialised beers and other non-alcoholic beverages. AB InBev group imported beers from its subsidiaries in Guatemala and the Dominican Republic, which were distributed in Salvadoran territory through Comercializadora Interamericana S.A. de C.V and Crio Inversiones S.A. de C.V., respectively.

The merger analysis carried out by the SC revealed that the transaction would produce a significant limitation of competition in the beer market and affect consumer welfare. The consequences identified were:

1. The acquiring firm would basically become a monopolist;
2. The rivalry between the two main market competitors would disappear;
3. Reinforcement of ILC's dominant position, creating conditions favourable condition to a generalised increase of the prices for all beer brands in its portfolio; and
4. Barriers to market entry would be reinforced.

To preserve the competitive dynamics of the beer market, the SC board of directors decided to apply conditions to the merger. The main conditions imposed were:

1. Submit a divestment plan to the SC board of directors for approval;
2. Formalise relationships with suppliers and refrain from committing anti-competitive practices, and
3. Maintain the labour guarantees of its employees.

The board of directors' decision regarding the structural condition of divesting of assets was considered pertinent to prevent harm to consumers. On 1 December 2016, complying with the imposed condition, AB InBev presented for approval a divestment plan that stipulated, among other things, that it would divest (sell) the *Regia Extra* and *Supreme* beer brands (in its three presentations: *Classic*, *Red* and *Black*), within 180 working days, which could be extended for an equal period.

AB InBev and ILC signed a drawback (*maquila*) contract for the production of the beer brands that were part of the divestment plan, and for access to the ILC distribution network during a three-year transition period, which may also be extended only once for the same period. In addition, AB InBev was required to sign a "hold separate" agreement, according to which, among other things, it would have the obligation to continue offering and maintaining the commercial value of the brands as part of the divestment plan until the process was completed.

The SC board of directors ordered AB InBev and ILC to formalise business relationships with retail distributors and suppliers, to refrain from introducing clauses that would limit competition in their contracts; as an example, they had to refrain from establishing contractual clauses with bars or restaurants that prohibit them from offering rival brand products. AB InBev had to comply with the condition to maintain the labour guarantees of its employees for up to three years after the divestment was completed. This condition implied, among others, that in the event of any dismissal of employees, it must be justified and certified that it is not due to the merger.

As it is common in this type of merger transaction, to follow up on the imposed conditions an independent international company was hired to monitor the procedure. This firm reported exclusively to the SC, and its fees were covered by AB InBev. The monitoring agent was selected by the SC board of directors based on a shortlist of firms submitted by AB InBev. The requirements that were considered for the selection of the monitoring agent were: relevant experience as a monitoring agent, the quality of the methodological proposal, the availability of a suitable team to be in charge of the case and an interview with the SC technical team was taken in consideration. The selected firm was Duff & Phelps, who had accredited experience acting as a monitoring agent in the divestment process in European Commission cases in various industries such as carbonated beverages, chemistry, civil aviation, power generation, pharmaceuticals and financial services. On 6 February 2017, Duff & Phelps was appointed under oath to verify the compliance of the conditions and obligations imposed including: a) the sale of the *Suprema* brands, in their three varieties, and *Regia Extra*; b) maintenance of production volumes and the commercial value of the brands during the sale process; and c) maintenance of the labour guarantees of ILC personnel.

The divestment status of certain assets detailed in the divestment plan were follow up by the monitoring agent; as well as behavioural conditions such as: formalising business relationships with suppliers and retail distributors, upon presentation for approval of the model contracts; disclosure of sufficient information on the terms that the commercial relations were regulated with third parties; and the obligation to comply with all the conditions established in the document "Acceptance and Commitment to Fulfil Conditions". The monitoring agent had an important role in the buyer's search and selection process for the brands that were divested. The buyer of the divested beer brands that was authorised by the SC was a new economic agent that entered the beer market.

The SC technical team that reviewed the merger acted as the counterpart of the monitoring agent, maintaining direct communication. The monitoring firm presented periodic reports on progress in the implementation of the conditioning to the board of directors. All information presented by the acquiring firm was evaluated by both Duff & Phelps and the SC technical team, determining that those operating contracts and the rest of the information regarding the implementation of the conditions contained appropriate terms to contribute to the development of a competitor able to effectively challenge the market.

On June 2018, the SC board of directors approved Cervecería Salvadoreña S.A. de C.V. as a buyer of the *Regia* and *Suprema* brands and their related assets. Cervecería Salvadoreña is a Salvadoran company incorporated on 31 August 2017, whose purpose is the production, distribution and marketing of beer products, industrial supplies and products for human consumption. The company accredited its independence from AB InBev, and presented information on the experience of its managers, the hiring of key personnel and other conditions that reflect its ability to compete effectively, including investment projections for the construction and operation of a plant. This decision also included the consent to the behavioural conditions: contracts for the sale of assets, the provision of manufacturing services, distribution of beverages, provision of transition services and brand use licences, and the hold separate plan.

Since the approval given by the SC board of directors in 2018, Cervecería Salvadoreña has been responsible for implementing the strategies needed to generate competitive pressure in the beer market. The approval does not limit the SC to initiate action in the case of non-observance of any of the conditions and obligations of the merger transaction or violating the Competition Law.

HONDURAS

Marvin Francisco Discua Singh*

(Commission for the Defence and Promotion of Competition)

Abstract

In Honduras, the control of mergers began with the Competition Law. This has as its foundation the constitutional rule prohibiting monopolies and other anticompetitive conducts. The Law set up a clear objective towards promoting the markets and economic efficiency; it established a scope of wide-open application; and it created a Commission of an administrative nature and with sufficient autonomy to investigate and sanction not only prohibited conducts, but also those mergers that exceed any of the thresholds established by the Commission. The procedure related to the notification and verification of mergers contains an analysis of the market participation of the parties involved, the economic efficiencies, and the possibility of carrying out restrictive practices to free competition, among other aspects. As a result of this verification, the Commission could decide to authorise, prohibit or approve with conditions the investigated transaction. Once the final administrative channel has been exhausted, the interested parties may contest the administrative ruling issued by the Commission, sending it for judicial review.

---

* Marvin Francisco Discua Singh is currently the legal director of the Commission for the Defence and Promotion of Competition of Honduras (Commission), he has a Master's in management and public policies from the University of Chile, Santiago, a postgraduate degree in intellectual property from the University of Mérida, Venezuela, a degree as lawyer and journalist of the National Autonomous University of Honduras (UNAH). He also held other positions as: technical director of the Commission, intellectual property director and negotiator for Honduras in intellectual property for the DR-CAFTA free trade agreement and professor of the Master's degree programme in mercantile law of UNAH.

The author wants to express his gratitude for the valuable collaborations given by the economists Jorge Reyes, who kindly provided the English translation, and Jorge Borjas, who as well as providing timely observations during development, provided his unconditional support in the editing of this paper.

I. Introduction

1. Origins of the Competition Legislation

One of the key precedents to the antitrust law was the structural reform implemented in the Honduran economy in the 1990s. These took place immediately after the country was declared not eligible for international credit at the end of the 1980s.

The economic and social changes that gave rise to the Law on the Structural Ordaining of the Economy in March 1990 called for substantial changes in the public policies of that time. This implied preeminence to private initiative and the market economy, in contrast with the internal interventionist development model, for whom one of the important foundations was the Economic Regime of the 1982 Constitution of the Republic[1].

The objective of the structural adjustment was to comply with the conditions demanded by international credit institutions in order to regain credibility and to foster the economic and social development of the country, based on the new paradigms (efficiency and competition). In this way, a variety of economic liberalisation and opening of trade policies were given a boost, next to the modest deregulation processes and the privatisation of public enterprises.

This change of model implied the approval of, among others, the competition law or antitrust law. But this was put off by more than a decade. Its approval took place in December 2005[2], and it was linked to the accession to the Free Trade Agreement between the Dominican Republic, Central America and the United States of America (DR-CAFTA), which was ratified by the Honduran legislative branch (National Congress of the Republic) on March 2005.

Therefore, the DR-CAFTA and the constitutional principle set out in Article 339, paragraph 1 of the Constitution of the Republic[3] represented the factual and juridical inducement for the approval of the Law for the Defence and Promotion of Competition (the Law), so that its enforcement would have to coexist with the constitutional economic regime mentioned, characterised or inspired in the Keynesian economic theories, and logically cohabit in markets with scarce competitive dynamics or little antitrust tradition.

---

1 See Moncada S Efraín, *Temas Constitucionales* (Edigrafic 2001) 508–515: he explains that the 1982 Constitution, in force in Honduras, follows the principles and precepts of economic policies of the constitutions of 1957 and 1965. He highlights that in Honduras the model is that of "developed constitutions" as opposed to "summary or brief constitutions" such as the one in the USA. In addition, he stresses that the fundamental principles that inspired the economic system come from the Keynesian economic theories that existed at the time. This framed, among other theories, the administrative intervention of the state in the economy to correct the imbalances that took place in society.

2 The Law for the Defence and Promotion of Competition was approved on 16 December 2005, by Decree Number 357-2005 of 4 February 2006, published in the Official Journal *Diario Oficial La Gaceta* Number 30,920, <https://www.cdpc.hn/sites/default/files/Privado/marco_legal/LeydeCompetencia_Honduras.pdf>.

3 The first paragraph of Article 339 of the Constitution states that: "Monopolies, monopsonies, oligopolies, division of the market and similar practices in industrial and commercial activity are prohibited". It is worth mentioning that this was reproduced in the first recital of the Law for the Defence and Promotion of Competition.

2. The Law for the Defence and Promotion of Competition

Three general aspects of the Law are worth briefly highlighting. The first aspect is the objective of the Law: "The present law has as its objective to promote and protect the practice of free competition in order to get the efficient functioning of the market and the welfare of the consumers" (article 1).

The second aspect relates to the scope of application, which is divided in two parts: part one is about the *orden público*[4] (public order) of the Law, where it states that, "the present law is applicable to all the areas of economic activity, even when these are regulated by special laws, regulations or resolutions. The provisions of the present law are of *orden público* and there can be no allegation of customs, uses, practices or commercial stipulations against it" (article 3).

Part two is related to the persons submitted to the Law, where it states that, "the provisions herein are subject to all economic agents, or their associations, be they natural persons or legal entities, public administrative entities, municipalities, industrial, commercial, professional, for-profit and non-profit entities or other natural persons or legal entities that under any title deed, participate actively in the economic activity inside the territory of the Republic of Honduras" (article 4, paragraph 1).

Moreover, in article 4, paragraph 3 of the Law, there is the inclusion of those with legal addresses outside the Republic of Honduras, when their activities, contracts, agreements, practices, arrangements, acts or businesses produce effects in the national territory.

The third aspect is to enunciate the procedures set out in Title VII of the Law, in the following order: the Procedure to Demand Information (Chapter I); the Procedure to Sanction Practices, Acts and Conducts that are Prohibited (Chapter II); the Procedure Related to Mergers (Chapter III); the Procedure of Provisional Measures (Chapter IV) and the Publicity Regime (Chapter V).

It is worth mentioning that the application of the procedure to sanction practices, acts and conducts that are prohibited, falls upon three types of practices that are susceptible of distorting competition: the first, restrictive practices prohibited due to their nature (article 5), are the ones done between two or more competing economic agents; the second, restrictive practices to be prohibited due to their effect (article 7), are the ones done between non-competing economic agents; and the third, mergers, absorptions or mixed undertakings with potential anticompetitive effects, whose concentration of power may represent another type of restrictive commercial practices, when they are used to create a monopoly or a situation of dominant power in a given market (article 15).

Lastly, relevant to refer to the Law's rules about the procedure of exception or reduction of the payment of the fine for the case of restrictive practices and conducts that are prohibited due to their nature, from which it was derived the rule for the Administrative Leniency Programme or Procedure, to be found in the 2015 reforms of the Law[5].

---

4 *Orden público* means the wide-open application of the Law.

5 The Programme of Administrative Leniency and the Reduction of the Payment of the Fine, is found in the Reform by Addition of the Law for the Defense and Promotion of Competition, approved by Decree Number 4-2015

3. The Commission for the Defence and Promotion of Competition

The Commission for the Defence and Promotion of Competition (the Commission), in accordance with article 20 of the Law, is created as an autonomous institution, with legal status and financial wealth patrimony of its own, with functional, administrative, technical and financial independence in its internal regime and in fulfilling its functions. Its address is in Tegucigalpa, the capital of Honduras, with jurisdiction at the national level.

The superior direction is performed three commissioners that constitute the Plenary of the Commission. Article 24 of the Law states that the commissioners are nominated by the National Congress of the Republic for a period of seven years, selected from names submitted for the election of the candidates who are proposed by the organisations and institutions referred to in article 61:

> According to article 24 of the present Law, this will be managed in conformity with the following system: the candidates that the National Congress will review and select, will come from the following organisations or institutions:
>
> i. Three candidates proposed by the Honduran Private Enterprise Council (*Consejo Hondureño de la Empresa Privada – COHEP*);
> ii. Three candidates proposed by the National Convergence Forum (*Foro Nacional de Convergencia – FONAC*);
> iii. Three candidates proposed by the National Competitiveness Forum (*Comisión Nacional de Competitividad*);
> iv. Three candidates proposed by the Executive Branch (*Poder Ejecutivo*); and,
> v. Three candidates proposed by the Honduran Federation of Associations of University Professionals (*Federación de Colegios Profesionales Universitarios de Honduras – FECOPRUH*).
>
> The election of the three commissioners by the National Congress will be decided by the qualified majority of two-thirds for a period of seven years.

Among the Commission's main functions are: investigate the presence of prohibited practices and conducts established in the Law and take the measures that are deemed necessary so that these practices and conducts cease, without prejudice to applying the corresponding sanctions; and verify and investigate mergers to determine their compatibility with the Law and, when one is prohibited, dictate appropriate measures.

In order to carry out its functions, the Commission should have the necessary technical units to fulfil its action plan. The internal organisation will be ruled by a regulation[6].

---

of 11 February 2015 and published in the Official Journal *Diario Oficial La Gaceta* Number 33,737, of 23 May 2015, <https://www.cdpc.hn/sites/default/files/Privado/marco_legal/Gaceta_reglamento_Programa_Clemencia_CDPC.pdf>.

6 Article 33 of the Law states that: "The Commission will appoint a Secretary who must be elected by it and will also count with the administrative and technical units required for carrying out its functions. The internal organisation will be ruled by a Regulation."

Likewise, in order to be a commissioner, there are stipulations about inabilities, grounds for removal and restrictions. Article 29 of the Law prescribes that the commissioners will cease in their functions for the following causes:

a) Death;
b) Resignation;
c) Preventive imprisonment, substitute measures or prisoner declaration;
d) Physical or mental disability duly proven; or
e) Clear negligence shown in carrying out their functions.

Finally, article 30 establishes that retiring commissioners cannot be hired in any form within the following six months by undertakings that have been the subject of investigations processes in the last two years.

4. Mergers: Control of a Preventive Nature

Merger control process is governed by the Law, its Regulation, and the other development norms that are available to the Commission to carry out its functions. Among these functions are the ones that prohibit mergers when their objective or effect is to restrict, diminish, damage or impede free competition (article 12 of the Law). In this sense, there are norms and procedures for merger control that are characterised as being preventive and compulsory, where the analysis is done before they take place.

So, article 13, paragraph 1 of the Law, about Previous Compulsory Notification and Verification, prescribes: "Before their effects take place, mergers must be notified to the Commission by the economic agents, and they can be submitted for verification by it ..."

Additionally, it is established that: "as a result of the previous verification or investigation of the merger, the Commission may take a favourable decision, prohibit it or order conditional measures for its approval" (article 18).

II. Scope of Application

1. Definition of Merger

In conformity with article 11[7] of the Law and article 9 of the Regulation, a merger comprises any act by which there is a concentration, a merger or a consolidation of one or more economic agents.

Therefore, a merger in its different forms is understood as taking hold or the change of control of one or several undertakings, namely: taking control of share participation,

---

[7] Article 11 states that: "A merger shall be understood as taking or changing of control in one or more undertakings by means of shareholder participation, management control, merger, acquisition or any other rights on shares or nominal capital participation or debt titles that causes any type of influence in the decisions of shareholders or any act or acts done by suppliers, clients or any other economic agent by virtue of which shares, nominal capital participations, trusts or assets are clustered.

control of the administration, the merger, the acquisition of property or any other lawful right over shares or participation in capital or debt titles that causes any type of influence in decisions of undertakings, the consolidation, the integration or combination in all or in part of its businesses, or any other act by which shares, social participations, trusts funds or assets are grouped between suppliers, clients or any other economic agent.

The Regulation includes merger operations derived from judicial adjudications, acts of voluntary or forced liquidations and inheritances or legacies, because of which undertakings, divisions, or parts of the undertakings and assets merged in general (article 9, paragraph 2).

Therefore, a merger is any act, contract or legal term that implies the acquisition or change of control of an undertaking, in part or in full, by another economic agent.

2. Material Scope

According to the scope of application of the Law mentioned above (article 3), the material scope of merger operations applies to all areas of economic activities, even when they are regulated by special laws, guidelines or resolutions. It is important to point out that the Law and the Regulation do not establish exceptions.

3. Geographical Scope

The geographical scope that the Law prescribes that it applies to all persons that operate inside the national territory as well as those that are domiciled outside of the Republic of Honduras, provided that their activities, contracts, agreements, practices, arrangements, acts or businesses produce effects in the national territory (article 4, paragraphs 1 and 3).

With regard to this, the last paragraph of article 14 of the Regulation states that: "In the case of mergers derived from legal actions undertaken abroad, they should be notified before having legal or material effects in the national territory".

4. Thresholds

According to article 13 and Resolution Number 04-CDPC-2014-AÑO-IX of 6 June 2014[8], about the definition of thresholds, mergers that are subject to verification are those that meet any of the following criteria: (i) total assets exceeds the equivalent of 4,000 minimum wages; (ii) the joint participation of the economic agents involved in the merger exceeds 25% in the relevant market; or (iii) the sum of the volume of sales of the economic agents directly involved in the merger exceeds 5,000 minimum wages. Article 10 of the Regulation states that:

> To calculate the amount of the total assets according to article 13 of the Law, the Commission will have to add up the assets of all of the participating undertakings.
>
> To calculate the total amount of volume of sales as referred to in article 13 of the Law, the Commission will have to add the resulting sales of the products

8 Resolution 04-CDPC-2014-AÑO-IX, 6 June 2014, <https://www.cdpc.hn/sites/default/files/Privado/Normativas/resoluciones%20normativas/RESOLUCION%20NUEVOS%20UMBRALES%20PDF.pdf>.

and services provided or other income coming from the commercial operation of the undertakings engaged in the merger, during their last fiscal year, before deductions done on sales discounts, as well as those done on sales tax and those done on other taxes directly related to the economic activity in question.

As a specific example of the current calculation of the thresholds, the amount of total assets and the sum of the amount of the volume of sales, as it applies to manufacturing undertakings in Honduras, results in 577,428,480.00 Lempiras or 721,785,600.00 Lempiras. As at the time of writing, these are equivalent to USD 23.2 million and 29 million, respectively[9].

III. Procedure

1. Compulsory *Ex Ante* Notification and Verification

The initial stage in the procedure is the obligation to notify merger operations to the Commission. The procedure starts with the receipt of the request from any of the economic agents involved, their legal representatives or others empowered by law[10].

The notification of merger operations should be in writing and can follow one of two procedures: 1) the ordinary or relative procedure of mergers prescribed in the Law; or 2) by means of a special step or procedure to authorise Merger operations referred to in article 13 of the Regulation, issued through Resolution Number 014-CDPC-AÑO-VII[11] of 21 December 2012. In the same order, the description of these procedures is as follows:

A. Ordinary or Relative Procedure of Mergers as Prescribed in the Law

In the ordinary notification procedure, the Commission will verify the merger operations that are likely to restrict free competition, provided that they exceed the asset amounts, participation in the relevant market or exceed the volume of sales established in the Law, its Regulation and other provisions[12].

The economic agents involved in the merger operation, as foreseen in article 13 of the Law, will have to present, in addition to the authorisation request, the minimum legal

---

9 Resolution Number 04-CDPC-2014-AÑO-IX, about asset and volume of sales thresholds, indicates that these are calculated on the base of the annual average established in the Minimum Wage Table as related to the prevailing daily income, issued by the Ministry of Work and Social Security, for different productive sectors of the country.

10 The Law, article 13, last paragraph and articles 15 and 37, paragraph 2, prescribe the legal consequences of omitting the notification, not submitting it to *ex ante* verification, or in the case of an extemporaneous notification. In the case of article 13, last paragraph, it is considered a breach of the Law to start an investigation with respect to article 15 and applies successive fines in the case of an extemporaneous notification according to article 37 of the Law.

11 Resolution Number 014-CDPC-AÑO-VII, 21 December 2012, <https://www.cdpc.hn/sites/default/files/Privado/Normativas/resoluciones%20normativas/%28No%20014-2012%29%20Resoluci%C3%B3n%20Normativa%20Art%2013%20Reglamento%20LDPC.pdf>.

12 Article 21 of the Regulation provides the concerned party with the resources to consult about the legality of merger operations that do not reach the threshold amounts of assets, participation in the relevant market or volume of sales.

information required in article 22 of the Regulation[13]. They will also have to provide data and information, including the following:

- The economic agents that are participating in the merger.
- Names of legal representatives entailed by the economic agents that are participating in the merger.
- The nature and characteristics of the merger operation.
- The relevant market for the product.
- The geographically relevant market.
- The market share.
- The dynamics of the market.
- Market entry barriers.
- Investigation and development activities.
- Efficiencies derived from the merger operation.

When the information is not sufficient to do the corresponding analysis, there will be a request for additional necessary information, in conformity with article 46 of the Law. In this case, the time frame to carry out the verification is paused and will restart once the requested information has been completed.

Subsequently, the corresponding decisions will be made in order to establish the viability to authorise or not the merger operation.

B. Special Procedure to Authorise Mergers in Article 13 of the Regulation

In this special notification procedure, the Commission will approve the merger operations described in article 13 of the Regulation:

> To the effects of verification or investigation referred to in article 16 of the Law and as stated in article 13 of the Regulation of the Law, the Commission will have to approve operations in which:
>
> a) The economic agents involved in legal acts related to shares or social participations in foreign undertakings that do not acquire the control of Honduran undertakings, nor is there the accumulation in the national territory of shares, social participations, trust fund participations or in assets in general, in addition to the ones that they possess before the transaction, either directly or indirectly;
>
> b) The mergers fall upon an economic agent that encounters itself in a state of insolvency, so long as it testifies to have searched unsuccessfully for non-competing buyers;
>
> c) The merged undertakings have among them temporary ties that are used to develop a given project or to a specific aim, such as consortiums and strategic alliances, among others;

---

13 Regulation of the Law of the Commission, <https://www.cdpc.hn/sites/default/files/Privado/marco_legal/Reglamento_Ley_CDPC-2007.pdf>.

d) The mergers consist of a simple corporative restructuring, where an economic agent has directly or indirectly owned and possessed 98% of the shares or social participations of the economic agent or agents involved in the transaction for the last three years at least.

In any of the cases foreseen in article 13 of the Regulation, the concerned economic agents of the planned merger should enclose with the following information and documents with their request:

- The general information of the economic agents notifying a merger and those participating directly in it.
- Description of the merger, its objectives and types of operations, copy of the draft of the contract or document that will regulate the relationship in question.
- The remaining data and relevant documents that verify or make known the extremes related to any of the cases foreseen in article 13. For example, the economic agent that finds itself in state of insolvency should enclose the financial statements that confirm such situation, as well as information and/or documents that testify having searched for non-competing buyers.
- The Commission can require additional data or documents to verify that the merger is within the cases foreseen in article 13.
- If the Commission determines that the merger operation does not fit to what is established in article 13, it will proceed to notify the economic agents involved in the merger operation to continue with the procedure in conformity with articles 52, 53 and 54 of the Law.

C. Payment for Verification of Mergers

In attention to the Article 63-B of the Law, the economic agents obliged to notify mergers before the Commission will have to pay an amount equivalent to 0.15% of the total value of assets engaged in the merger operation, to determine whether it complies with what is established in the Law.

The amount to be paid for verification of mergers cannot be more than the equivalent of 250 monthly minimum wages. The payment receipt must be turned over to the Commission in a period of 10 working days, starting on the day following the notification of the admission of request of the merger operation in question.

The fees collected go to the General Treasury of the Republic. Then, the Ministry of Finance proceeds, on a quarterly basis, to transfer to the Commission the equivalent of the value of the amount paid for verification of mergers.

D. Limitation in the Requests for Mergers

Article 23 of the Regulation establishes that when a request for authorisation of a merger does not meet the requirements indicated in article 22 (the information that must be submitted to the verification), under article 53 of the Law[14], the parties will be called upon to complete it within a period of 10 working days. If they fail to do so, the verification will be filed without further ado.

Moreover, in article 23, paragraph 2 of the Regulation, it is warned that the merger request will be declared inadmissible if those concerned do not present the additional information required by the Commission throughout the procedure and it will be filed without more ado.

E. Publicity Related to Mergers

The publicity regime in article 56 of the Law states that the Commission will make public its resolutions by the means seemed convenient. Generally, resolutions are published in the website of the Commission (<www.cdpc.hn>) or in a newspaper with national distribution, paid for by the concerned parties and as disposed by the applicable resolution.

The merger procedure established in the Regulation also facilitates communication mechanisms, so that the Commission can request information from other related parties; including the possibility that related third parties can participate as parts of the merger procedure[15].

In addition to this, in outstanding cases regarding the procedure for failure to notify a merger, the Commission may publish a summary of the resolution of the investigating procedure, in any of the communication media.

2. Development of Procedure

Once the matter is prepared for decision, the Commission has 45 working days to issue a final resolution, from the date the request was received with all the information to carry out the verification, or if more data and information were required, the date that the Commission receives all the additional data and documents, to its satisfaction.

From this point until the conclusion of the merger verification procedure, the Commission has the Technical Directorate[16] at its disposal, which is in charge of coordinating with the Legal and Economic Directions, the elaboration and emission of the corresponding reports or decisions related to the procedure of compulsory notification and verification requests.

---

14 Article 53(2) prescribes that in all cases in which the Commission is requested to determine about a merger as foreseen in article 13, the procedure to follow is: "The Commission can request data from additional documents, within 10 working days after the request ..."

15 Article 25 of the Regulation establishes that the Commission may request information from other economic agents related to the merger, without signifying that it considers them part of the merger procedure. However, these third parties with legitimate and direct interests can intervene in the procedure, lodging complaints and bringing necessary evidence.

16 The Commission has at its disposal the following directions: Technical, Legal, Economic and Promotion of Competition. The Technical Direction is in charge of the activity of coordinating with the other directions, diverse activities derived from the different procedures.

A. Merger Decisions

Under article 19 of the Law, as a result of an *ex officio* investigation or at the request of a party, and without prejudice to the corresponding precautionary measures in accordance with article 17, once the verification or investigation of a merger has been done, the Commission can:

a) Authorise the merger operation;
b) Prohibit the merger; or,
c) Order conditional measures for its approval.

B. Corrective Measures

To remedy the anticompetitive effects of a merger operation, the Commission may impose measures that are directly tied or that are proportional to the correction of the effects or that comply with the Law. The following corrective measures can be ordered:

a) Parties to excise, alienate, sell or transfer to independent third parties rights over specified tangible or intangible assets, social participations or shares;
b) Parties to modify or transfer a specified line of production; and,
c) Parties to modify or eliminate clauses from contracts, agreements or arrangements.

C. Third-Party Participation

According to Article 25 of the Regulation, the Commission can request information from other economic agents related to the merger, without them becoming parties to the procedure. Third parties with a legitimate and direct personal concern can participate in the procedure, formulating allegations and bringing necessary proofs.

Moreover, in matters regarding the start of the sanctioning procedure for not complying with the obligation to notify a merger[17], the Commission, after ordering he respective investigation procedure, can publish a summary of the resolution with the object that any person can collaborate or present new complaints about the facts that motivated the investigation.

In this regard, article 15 of the Law, and article 59 paragraphs 4 and 5 of the Regulation, respectively, provide that:

> When a merger has not been submitted to previous verification and there is the presumption that it restricts, diminishes, damages or impedes free competition, the Commission, within a period no longer than three months after the merger has taken place or from the date in which it was known, has to initiate an investigation, be it an *ex officio* or be it at the request of a party, in which it will have to demand from the economic agents concerned the information deemed relevant to the referred investigation.

---

17 Article 55(b) of the Regulation establishes that "The Commission will initiate a procedure, be it an *ex officio* or be it at the request of a party, in the following cases: ... b) The failure to carry out the obligation to make a notification of a merger as stated in Article 13 of the Law."

A summary of the resolution can be published in any communication media when the matter is deemed relevant in the opinion of the Commission. This publication should contain, at least, the identification of the restrictive practice to free competition to be investigated and the market in which is taken place, with the aim that any person could collaborate in this investigation. By no means, there will be a revelation in the publication referred in this paragraph, of the name, denomination or trade name of the economic agents involved in the investigation.

Once the summary of the agreement is published, the persons willing to collaborate in the procedure could do it during the investigation, as well as presenting new complaints about the facts motivating the investigation.

In any of the situations in which other economic agents participate, the Commission and the third parties agree, among other obligations, to preserve the confidentiality of the information given to the administrative file in conformity with articles 32 of the Law[18] and 47 of the Regulation, depending on the case.

D. Participation of National and Foreign Entities

The Commission, in strict observance of the geographical scope of the Law, specifically with respect to the Law's character of *orden público*, may enter agreements with sector regulator entities, whose activities are regulated by special laws, regulations or resolutions, in order to coordinate the work of cooperation and vigilance in those markets and prevent the realisation of restrictive and prohibited conducts of the Law.

In this sense, the Commission, in order to carry out the merger procedure in activities regulated by special laws, can request information, technical opinions and the collaboration of regulator entities, to the effect of resolving issues related to the origin of the merger in question.

The Commission is committed to preserving the confidential character of the consultations, investigations, procedures, documents and information furnished by the other party, with the aim of preserving the concerns of natural persons or legal entities involved, the market and the activities of the organisations.

In the reciprocal cooperation and collaboration agreements with homologous international entities, without prejudice to the commitment to guard and keep the due confidentiality, the Commission and each one of the homologous agencies could agree upon the implementation of an agile and timely mechanism for mail and procedures, like permitting the reception of consultations by phone and electronic mail, among others.

3. Conclusion of Procedure

Once the Plenary of the Commission receives the reports or decisions of the Technical Directorate with respect to a request for notification of a merger, the Commission

[18] Article 32 of the Law establishes that the commissioners, civil servants and employees that divulge information about the matters known to the Commission or that exploit it for personal gain or in damage to the Commission, the State or persons, will become civilly and criminally liable.

will proceeds to do a final evaluation of all matters in the administrative file, altogether with the recommendations done by the technical economic and legal units, to the effect of making the corresponding decision in accordance with the Law and Regulation.

As set out in section III(2)(A) in relation to merger decisions, the Plenary of the Commission may decide the following:

A. Authorisation or Approval of the Planned Merger

According to article 14 of the Law, mergers that are approved by the Commission cannot be contested later, unless the approval was obtained on the basis of false information.

To fulfil the procedure, the resolution that authorises the merger should provide the reasons and the conviction elements on which Commission based its determination that the merger is consistent with the Law. In the same way, there will be a verification of the derivative or produced effects in the relevant market, as well as consideration of the gains in efficiency that convert to benefits to the consumers, among other aspects.

As described in section III(1)(B), regarding the procedure to authorise merger operations in article 13 of the Regulation, the Commission must specifically authorise the operations contained in these legal provisions.

B. Denial or Prohibition of a Merger

Article 12, paragraph 1 of the Law prescribes that there is a prohibition of mergers whose object or effect is to restrict, diminish, damage or impede free competition.

In accordance with the procedure, in the resolution denying authorisation there should be an indication of the reasons motivating the prohibition of the merger by the Commission, particularly regarding the significant limitation to competition in the market. To that effect, it must show elements related to the following: (i) verifying the existence of a notable participation in the market, to act unilaterally, leaving out the remaining competitors; (ii) lack of proofs regarding the increase in economic efficiency and the welfare of the consumer as a result of the planned merger; and, (iii) anticompetitive effects produced in the relevant market.

C. Authorisation with Conditional Measures

In view of articles 18 and 19 of the Law, and 28 of the Regulation, the Commission Plenary could authorise a merger and establish the following conditions:

a) To carry out a given conduct, or to refrain from doing it;
b) To divest or give away to third parties rights over certain assets, social participations or shares;
c) To modify, transfer or eliminate a certain line of production;
d) To modify or eliminate terms or conditions of the actions that they try to pursue;

e) To force the accomplishment of actions directed to foster the participation of competitors in the market, as well as to give access or sell goods or services to them; or
f) Anything else whose object is to avoid diminishing, damaging or impeding free competition.

D. The Commission: Sole Administrative Authority

The Plenary of the Commission functions as sole administrative authority, and there is a reconsideration recourse (*recurso de reposición*) against resolutions issued by the Commission[19]. The decision that resolves the recourse puts an end to the administrative process.

E. Judicial Hearing

Once the administrative process is exhausted, a firm resolution of the Commission may be contested in a judicial court at the Administrative Disputes Tribunal (*Tribunal de lo Contencioso Administrativo*).

F. Fulfilling or Monitoring of Conditions

Pursuit or monitoring of obligations established by the Commission in the authorisation of mergers with attached conditions, is assigned to the Technical Directorate and it is carried out by the respective technical economic and legal units.

4. Sanctions

The economic sanctions applied to mergers, according to the Law, spread out to two types of infringements, so:

A. Infringement Related to Articles 13 (last paragraph), and 15 of the Law

This type of infringement is related to investigations regarding the omission or the failure of the economic agents involved, in respect to the obligation to notify a merger; or when it has not been submitted to verification and it is determined that it restricts, diminishes, damages or impedes free competition.

The corresponding procedure for these cases can be initiated *ex officio* or at the request of a party, according to article 55(b) of the Regulation, quoted in section III(2)(C).

In these cases, the sanctions prescribed in article 37 of the Law apply, provided that it is demonstrated that there are practices or conducts prohibited according to articles 5 and 7 of the Law. To these effects, the Commission will impose a sanction per economic agent equivalent to three times the amount of the economic benefit obtained by them as a result of the unlawful conduct. If it is not possible to determine the amount of this benefit, a sanction will be set so that by no means could exceed 10% of gross profit on sales of the previous fiscal year.

---

19 In other words, administrative rulings issued by the Commission Plenary can be appealed before the Commission itself.

B. Infringements Related to Articles 37(2) and 41(3) of the Law

These sections provide a description of the following infringements and sanctions: (i) for extemporaneous notification; (ii) for failure to deliver or late delivery of the information requested by the Commission (article 37, paragraph 2 of the Law comprises both types); and, (iii) for not carrying out the corrective measures applicable to a merger act or an order to partially or totally undo a merger (article 41(3) of the Law).

The sanctions that proceed in accordance with article 41 of the Law, for the three types of infringements mentioned, depending on the case, are fines levied on the economic agents and the associations of economic agents from 1,000 to 50,000 Lempiras for each day of a delay in carrying out what was ordered, up to a maximum of 30 calendar days.

IV. Substance

1. Competition Analysis

The main purpose of competition analysis of mergers is to determine if they comply with the Law. To that effect, in accordance with article 16, the following must be considered:

a) The market share of participating economic agents and effects with respect to other competitors and buyers of goods and services, as well as to other directly related markets and economic agents;
b) If there is a possibility that the merger permits, promotes or does prohibited practices and conducts or imposes barriers to entry to new economic agents;
c) When there is a possibility that the merger facilitates a unilateral rise in prices, without other economic agents having the power to counteract it, actually or potentially; and,
d) The need of the merger as the only option to avoid the exit of the market of the productive assets of one of the economic agents participating in the merger in question.

Moreover, the analysis of merger operations will consider articles 16, 8 and 11 of the Law, about checklist items to verify and the elements comprised in the following articles of the Regulation: article 6, gains in efficiency; article 7, general rules for the analysis of the relevant market and notable market participation; and article 8, notable market participation. In this order, the economic analysis comprises the following aspects:

a) Identification of the relevant market in which the merging undertakings operate;
b) Determination of the resulting level of concentration;
c) Level of competition in the market;
d) Existence of barriers to entry to new participants;
e) Economic efficiencies derived from the operation; and,
f) Impact or effect that results when any of the involved undertakings exit the market.

In this regard, article 12 of the Regulation states:

> In order to carry out the merger analysis referred to in article 16 of the Law, the following criteria will be considered:
>
> a) Limit of the relevant market where the merger will eventually produce effects, in accordance with the criteria established in article 16(1) of the Law and article 7 of the Regulation;
> b) Limit of the relevant market where the merger will eventually produce effects with respect to competitors and consumers of the goods or services, as in other related markets and economic agents;
> c) Control of the economic agents involved in the terms established in article 11 of the Law;
> d) Notable participation in the market that could result if the merger takes place, in accord with the criteria established in article 8 of the Law and article 8 of the Regulation; and
> e) Appraisal of the gains in economic efficiency in the relevant market that may be derived from the merger, in terms of article 6 of the Regulation, the same that will have to be verified by the economic agents that make them.

2. Statistics

Since 2007 the Commission has analysed a total of 105 merger operations, of which 26.7% have been related to the commercial sector, 24.8% to the financial sector and 20.9% to the industrial sector, as can be seen in the following table and graph.

Mergers Notified to the Commission According to the Economic Sector (2007–2019)									
Year	**Commercial**	**Communications**	**Energy/ Fuels**	**Financial**	**Industrial**	**Mining**	**Health**	**Transport**	**Total**
2007	2	0	1	6	0	0	1	0	10
2008	2	0	1	10	3	0	0	0	16
2009	2	1	0	0	2	1	0	0	6
2010	3	4	1	3	2	0	0	0	13
2011	2	3	3	1	1	1	0	0	11
2012	3	1	0	1	2	0	1	0	8
2013	0	1	0	1	2	0	0	0	4
2014	0	0	0	2	1	0	0	0	3
2015	3	1	1	0	0	1	0	0	6
2016	0	0	3	1	2	1	0	0	7
2017	3	0	0	0	3	0	0	1	7
2018	6	0	1	1	3	0	0	0	11
2019	2	0	0	0	1	0	0	0	3
Total	**28**	**11**	**11**	**26**	**22**	**4**	**2**	**1**	**105**

Source: Commission for the Defence and Promotion of Competition

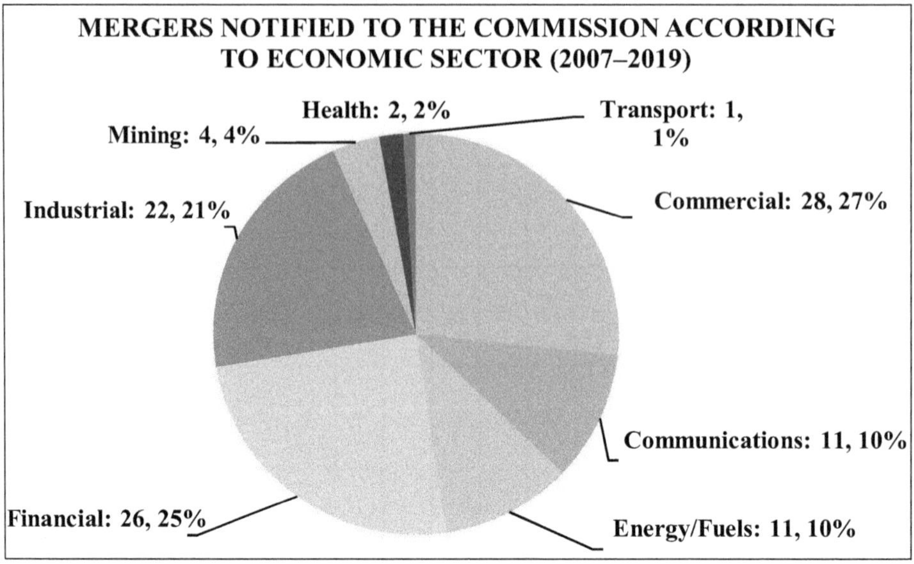

Source: Commission for the Defence and Promotion of Competition

With regard to the decisions resulting from the verifications of the merger operations, between 2007 and 2019 all operations were resolved favourably, of which 13 mergers (12.4%) have been approved with conditions.

Mergers Verified by the Commission (2007–2019)										
	2007–2010	2011	2012	2013	2014	2015	2016	2017	2018	2019
Verified and approved	45	11	8	4	3	6	7	7	11	3
Verified and approved with conditions	5	4	0	0	1	0	0	2	1	0
Denied	0	0	0	0	0	0	0	0	0	0
Appealed (*Recurso de Reposición*)	0	1	0	0	0	0	0	1	1	0

Source: Commission for the Defence and Promotion of Competition

To date there have been three appeals (2.8% of the total), one in the telecommunications sector, specifically the cable television market, and two in the industrial sector in the production and commercialisation of beer and sugar economic sectors.

3. Case Law Illustration

Merger AB InBev and SABMiller

In the case of the merger between AB InBev (purchaser) and SABMiller (seller), and the subsequent change of control of the company Cervecería Hondureña, S.A. de C.V., wholly owned by SABMiller, the Commission decided by means of the definitive case Resolution Number 014-CDPC-2016-AÑO-X of 4 August 2016, to authorise the merger operation partially, and denied it for the beer market.

Among the facts and reasons that served as the foundations for the prohibition of the merger are: (a) participation in the market will reach 92.9%, increasing the Herfindahl-Hirschman Index by 165 points, to a total of 8,672, indicating that this market will remain under a monopolistic structure; (b) the resulting economic agent will consolidate approximately 93% of the market share, facilitating an increase of prices; (c) the existence of barriers to entry with the capacity to impede the entrance of potential competitors; (d) the departure of the acquired undertaking eliminates a participant with the capacity to convert itself into an effective competitor; (e) the evidence of contentious processes about restrictive practices to competition prevents unilateral conducts whose objective is to exclude potential competitors; and, (f) the increments in efficiency proposed could not be proved and be contrasted with potential harms to the competitive process and the welfare of the consumers.

On the other hand, in Resolution Number 002-CDPC-2017-AÑO-X of 2 February 2017, dictated over the appeal presented against the partial prohibition contained in the final resolution, the Commission decided to restore and in consequence, authorise with conditions the merger in the beer market. The conditional measures aim to avoid restrictions and diminishing the welfare of consumers, and to make viable the possibility to verify or prove *ex post* the proposals about the increments in economic efficiency and the welfare of the consumers.

Next to the conduct conditions imposed, on the side of efficiency, the following obligations are to be adopted:

a) To report to the Commission, for five years, on the gains in efficiency in the product market: production, commercialisation and distribution of beer, at least, of those goods produced locally by Cervecería Hondureña, reporting at the end of each calendar year, about:
   - i. Achieved savings of resources that permit the notified economic agent, in a permanent manner, to produce the same quantity of beer at a lower cost or a greater quantity at the same cost;
   - ii. Reduction in costs if there is the production of two goods or services, jointly rather than separately;
   - iii. Significant shrinkage in administrative expenses;
   - iv. The innovation and technological transfer of commercial information;
   - v. The diminution of the cost of production or commercialisation derived from the expansion of the infrastructure or distribution network; including information about estimated improvements in terms of quality, innovation, variety and prices by means of the model cost/connect/win.

f) To make a report to the Commission, within 30 days of the date of notification of the Resolution, on data, information and/or conditions of the beer market, before the merger, to bring all the pertinent information to the Commission to verify the economic structure of Cervecería Hondureña.

To those effects, the notified economic agent must bring, among others, information about costs, prices and distribution of, at least, the goods produced locally by Cervecería Hondureña for the last five years (2012–2016); in order to be able to contrast and/or verify the efficiency and the welfare of the consumer situation, before and after the merger operation, in costs, prices and distribution of, at least, the beer produced locally by Cervecería Hondureña.

Finally, on this case, it is worth noting that the decision of the Commission about the appeal reasserts the precompetitive tendency of its resolutions. So much in this one, as in other mergers, that the Commission did not seek to prohibit mergers *per se* or to go against mergers, instead it opted to examine the possible economic efficiencies *ex post*, with the object of making a reasonable counterbalance in the face of consolidation or strengthening of the notable market participation of the purchaser.

MEXICO

Luis G García Santos Coy[*]
Carlos Mena Labarthe[**]
Mauricio Serralde Rodríguez[***]
Virginia Campás Alcalde[****]
(Creel, García Cuéllar, Aiza y Enríquez)

Abstract

The aim of this chapter is to provide an overview of merger control practice and procedure in Mexico. In particular, the chapter outlines the evolution of competition law in Mexico and sets out the current legal framework. Further, it provides guidance on the process to determine whether a transaction shall be reviewed by the Mexican Competition Authorities, the nature and criteria of Mexican thresholds and any relevant legal aspects to be considered. It addresses procedural merger control items such as a detailed description of the standard review process, legal terms to obtain clearance, potential sanctions and conclusion of the procedure. Finally, it describes the Mexican Competition Authorities' substantive competitive analysis and provides an illustration of a recent case involving a merger blocked by the Federal Economic Competition Commission in 2019 in the digital markets.

---

[*] Mr García is are a senior partner at Creel, García Cuéllar, Aiza y Enríquez. He specialises in antitrust and competition law, actively participating in all types of cases before the competition authorities, from complex pre-merger filings to investigations, administrative procedures and constitutional (Amparo) proceedings, as well as leniency applications. Mr García also regularly advises multinationals and private equity investors on acquisitions and investments in Mexico across multiple industries, including digital platforms. Mr García is a member of the Mexican Bar Association and the International Bar Association.

[**] Mr Mena is the head of the antitrust and competition practice and a partner at Creel, García Cuéllar, Aiza y Enríquez. Prior to joining the firm, Mr. Mena worked for 10 years in various positions at the Federal Competition Commission of Mexico (COFECE). He currently advises clients regarding all aspects of economic competition in Mexico. Mr Mena also has experience in coordinating proceedings in different jurisdictions, especially in Latin America. He is a lecturer at ITAM University and has published extensively on competition and regulation.

[***] Mr Serralde is a partner at Creel, García Cuéllar, Aiza y Enríquez. He specializes in antitrust and competition law, actively participating in all types of cases before the competition authorities, from pre-merger filings, to investigations, administrative procedures and constitutional (Amparo) proceedings, as well as leniency applications. He also devotes substantial time in advisory and compliance by clients with Mexican competition legal framework with respect to their operations. Mr Serralde is a member of the International Bar Association and the Mexican Bar Association.

[****] Mrs Campas is a senior associate at Creel, García Cuéllar, Aiza y Enríquez, She focuses on antitrust and competition law.

I. Introduction

1. Brief Overview

For over one hundred years, the Mexican Constitution has recognised the need to prohibit monopolies in Mexico[1]. Nonetheless, competition law was not implemented until 1993 when the first competition law entered into force (enacted in 1992), and the Federal Commission of Competition was created.

The bloom of competition legislation in Mexico occurred between 2013 and 2014 with the amendment to the Mexican Constitution (*Constitución Política de los Estados Unidos Mexicanos*, Constitution) and the enactment of the new and current competition law (*Ley Federal de Competencia Económica*, Competition Law). The referred amendment to the Constitution enabled the creation of the new Federal Economic Competition Commission (*Comisión Federal de Competencia Económica*, COFECE)[2] and the Federal Telecommunications Institute (*Instituto Federal de Telecomunicaciones*, IFT[3]; jointly with COFECE, the Competition Authorities), two relatively new autonomous agencies independent from the federal government.

Competition matters are governed by Article 28 of the Constitution, the Competition Law, and the Regulations to the Competition Law (*Disposiciones Regulatorias de la Ley Federal de Competencia Económica*; Regulations). The Competition Authorities issue their own guidelines applicable to certain matters of interest; although guidelines are not binding, they tend to provide a sense of the Competition Authorities' views. With respect to merger control, it is particularly relevant to note the existence of COFECE's guidelines (*Guia para la Notificación de Concentraciones*; Guidelines), while IFT has its own specific guidelines (*Guia para el Control de Concentraciones en los Sectores de Telecomunicaciones y Radiodifusión;* IFT Guidelines). The Guidelines and IFT Guidelines are focused on orientating economic agents during the merger control procedure.

2. Institutional Set-Up

As noted above, in Mexico there are two autonomous Competition Authorities, COFECE and IFT. For an economic agent to determine the applicable Competition Authority, it shall consider the subject matter of the case[4]. In general terms, IFT oversees matters in the broadcasting and telecommunications sectors, while COFECE is in charge of all other matters and sectors.

The Competition Authorities are autonomous public entities of the Mexican state, with their own legal personality and assets, and are independent in their decisions and

1 Mexican Constitution of 1857.

2 COFECE website, <https://www.cofece.mx/>.

3 IFT website, <http://www.ift.org.mx/>.

4 There have been cases in which part of the deal was reviewed by IFT and the rest of the same case by COFECE. For instance, UCE/CNC-004-D16. It is relevant to note that the Competition Authorities may disagree on their jurisdiction over the subject matter of the case giving rise to jurisdictional conflicts. In such circumstances, the case is brought to the courts which ultimately decide upon the competent authority to review the case.

operations. Their purpose is to guarantee free competition and free access to markets, and to prevent and investigate monopolistic practices, concentrations and other practices as set forth by the Constitution.

The plenum of commissioners is the ultimate authority within each of the Competition Authorities. The plenum is a governing body with full independence to review the cases and matters in a collegial manner and by majority of votes. It is composed of seven commissioners including a chair commissioner. Commissioners are elected for a term of nine years[5]. The Competition Authorities' chair commissioner shall be appointed by the Chamber of Senators from among the commissioners by a vote of two-thirds of the members present for a period of four years, renewable only once.

3. Type of Merger Control

The merger review process is pure *ex ante* when any of the filing thresholds is met, and suspensive in all cases. The parties cannot close a transaction prior to receiving clearance by the Competition Authorities, or the expiry of the deadline to issue a decision (if such decision has not been issued by then).

---

5 The selection procedure for commissioners is described as follows:
- The evaluation committee composed of the heads of the Bank of Mexico (Banxico), the National Institute for the Evaluation of Education (INEE) and the National Institute of Statistics and Geography (INEGI), shall issue a public call to cover the vacancy.
- The applicants shall accredit the requirements before the evaluation committee and must pass an examination of knowledge in the matter; the procedure shall observe the principles of transparency, publicity and maximum concurrence.
- For each vacancy, the committee shall send the president of the Mexican Republic a list with a minimum of three and a maximum of five candidates, who have obtained the highest passing grades. In the event that the minimum number of applicants is not met, a new public call shall be issued.
- The president of the Mexican Republic shall select from among those applicants the candidate it will propose for ratification by the Senate.
- Ratification shall be effected by a vote of two-thirds of the members of the Senate present, within a non-renewable period of 30 business days from the submission of the proposal.
- In the event that the Senate rejects the candidate proposed by the executive, the president of the republic shall submit a new proposal.

According to Article 23 of the Competition Law, commissioners might be removed due to the following severe causes:
- Undertaking employment, position or responsibilities other than those pertaining to their office as commissioner, with the exception of lecturing positions;
- Discussing matters of their responsibility with persons that represent the interests of economic agents outside the parameters set by this law;
- Participating in campaign acts of political parties as a representative of the commission;
- Failing to comply with the board of commissioners' definitive decisions;
- Using, for personal benefit or that of third parties, the confidential or reserved information at their disposal by means of their office, as well as disclosing said information in infringement of the law;
- Abstaining to resolve without a justified cause and in a recurrent manner the matters under their jurisdiction in the periods provided for in this law;
- Knowingly submitting altered or falsified information to the board of commissioners with the purpose of influencing a decision, and
- Failing to excuse themselves from participating and voting in cases where they have any direct or indirect interests.

When the internal comptroller becomes aware of circumstances which would prompt the causes of removal and considers that there are evidentiary elements, it shall immediately and without delay notify them to the Senate. The Senate then decides on the removal.

If a transaction reaches the competition thresholds, it shall not come into effect in Mexico until it has been approved by the relevant Competition Authority.

If none of the filing thresholds is met, then the transaction shall not be required to be notified to the Competition Authorities. As explained in section III(4), for unlawful concentrations not falling under the Mexican thresholds[6], the Competition Authorities will have a term of one year from closing to investigate the merger through their investigation powers.

II. Scope of Application

1. Definition of Notifiable Transaction

Merger control cases in Mexico requiring a filing to the Competition Authorities entail a "concentration". A "concentration" is broadly defined[7] as a merger, acquisition of control[8] or any other action through which corporations, associations, stock, equity interest, trusts and assets in general are combined, carried out amongst competitors, suppliers, customers or any other economic agent[9].

2. Material Scope

Mexican thresholds are applicable to any kind of transaction, regardless of the subject matter or whether there is a market share increase or acquisition of corporate control. Once monetary thresholds are reached, the transaction shall be reviewed by the competent Competition Authority.

Certain transactions are exempt from being reviewed by the Competition Authorities, namely[10]:

a) An increase in participation in a company in which the acquirer has had control since its incorporation or as a result of an authorisation by the Competition Authorities.

b) The incorporation of management, guarantee or any other type of trusts that do not result in imminent transfer of assets, partnership interests, participation units or shares to any third party other than the trustor or the trustee

6 Article 62 of the Competition Law refers to unlawful concentrations as those that "have as their purpose or effect to obstruct, diminish, harm or impede free market access and economic competition".

7 Article 61, Competition Law.

8 Although the thresholds provided in the Competition Law do not make specific mention of control, any acquisition of control should be considered as acquisition/accumulation of assets for purposes of merger control analysis.

9 Pursuant to the Competition Law, an economic agent "is any entity or individual, with or without profit, federal, state or municipal public administration agencies and entities, associations, business chambers and professional associations, trusts, or any other form of participation in economic activity". Any reference to "economic agent" shall consider the foregoing definition.

10 The exemptions are included in Article 93 of the Competition Law. Please note that these exemptions should be analysed on a case-by-case basis.

(in cases of foreclosure of a trusts estate, the transaction should be notified if any of the relevant thresholds is met).

c) Transactions over shares or partnership interests of foreign entities, as long as the participating economic agents do not acquire control over Mexican entities, nor accumulate shares in Mexico, partnership interests, participation in trusts or assets in general (in addition to those already owned, directly or indirectly)[11].

d) The acquisition by investment funds of securities in the stock markets unless the transaction allows the acquirer to acquire decisive influence over the target (without any specific limit on the percentage to be acquired).

e) Acquisitions in the stock market of less than a 10%[12] participation in the company and the acquirer does not acquire either the power to influence, directly or indirectly, the management (i.e., the right to appoint/revoke board members, managers or directors; impose decisions in shareholder meetings or equivalent bodies; maintain any interest that would allow it to exercise 10% or more of the voting rights; or influence the management, operations, strategy or key policies of the target).

f) Acquisitions by private equity funds for speculative purposes where these funds do not have portfolio companies participating, directly or indirectly, in the relevant market of the target[13]. In this case, the Regulations provide that private equity funds with speculation purposes correspond to those in which the investment or acquisition is made on behalf of the passive investors, with the sole purpose of generating a return to the investors, on the understanding that the fund shall not have the possibility (de jure or de facto), nor the intention to participate, manage or influence, directly or indirectly, in the management, operation or commercial policies of the target.

g) Corporate restructurings where the economic agents are part of the same group and there are no third parties involved.

Furthermore, and pursuant to transitory article 9 of the Federal Telecommunications and Broadcasting Law, certain transactions carried out among concessionaires within the telecommunications and broadcasting sectors where there is a preponderant agent (meeting specific conditions) shall not require a pre-merger filing and, instead, only a post-closing notice shall be submitted to the IFT, which in turn will be entitled to investigate the transaction[14].

---

11 Please note that this exemption applies even if the target has sales into Mexico, provided that there is no accumulation in Mexico of assets or shares.

12 Particularly for this case, the Regulations provide that for purposes of calculating the 10% of the capital stock of the issuer, all of the shares representing the issuer's capital stock should be considered and not just shares trading on a stock exchange.

13 Under Article 3 of the Competition Law, economic agents: "*individuals or legal entities with or without profit purposes, governmental entities of the federal, state or municipal public administration, entrepreneurial chambers, groups of professionals, trusts, or any other means or form of participation in the economic activity.*"

14 The requirements are the following:
- The so-called Dominance Index must be reduced as a consequence of the transaction and the Herfindahl-Hirschman Index must not increase more than 200 points;

3. Geographical Scope

The geographical scope of the thresholds is limited to Mexico. Transactions with effects only unfolding abroad shall not be analysed by the Mexican Competition Authorities.

In particular, the thresholds require a local nexus or effect when determining that a transaction shall be notified. Therefore, cases where there is either a price allocation to Mexico (indirectly entailing that there is an acquisition of a business in Mexico) or an accumulation in Mexico of assets, capital stock or sales/revenues, in excess of certain monetary values described below, shall be notified to the Competition Authorities for their review.

4. Thresholds

In Mexico, thresholds are purely monetary. Mexican thresholds do not consider market share increases or control, and all transactions may be subject to a filing.

A concentration shall be notified to the Competition Authorities where it reaches at least one of the following thresholds[15]:

I. The value of the transaction or series of transactions[16] that give rise to the concentration, notwithstanding the place of execution, represent within Mexico, directly or indirectly, 18 million times of the equivalent in pesos of the general Measure Unit (*Unidad de Medida y Actualización*, UMA[17]) (Mex$1,563,840,000[18]);

- The resulting economic agent shall have a market share under 20% in the sector (i.e. telecommunications or broadcasting, as opposed to the relevant market);
- The preponderant economic agent in the corresponding sector may not intervene in the transaction; and
- The transaction shall not have the purpose or effect of reducing, damaging or hindering free and open competition in the corresponding sector.

The parties to a qualifying transaction must submit a notice to the IFT within 10 business days of the closing transaction. The IFT has 90 calendar days to investigate the transaction and has authority to impose obligations on the parties to encourage competition in the market in case it finds the existence of market power in the market of telecommunications networks which provide services of voice, data or video.

15 A pre-merger filing has to be submitted before the Competition Authorities before: (1) a transaction is closed in accordance with the applicable legislation or, if applicable, the conditions precedent to which such transaction is subject are satisfied or waived; (2) the acquisition (or the direct or indirect exercise) of control over the target business, or the acquisition of assets, participation in trusts, partnership interests, or shares of other economic agent; (3) the execution of merger agreement; or (4) in the event of series of transactions, the last act is completed and as a result thereof, the monetary thresholds are reached. Concentrations derived from legal transactions carried out abroad should be notified before they produce legal or material effects in Mexico.

16 There is no rule on the time limit for a transaction to occur in order not to be considered as a series of transactions. The Guidelines define succession of acts as "the sequence or series of legal acts or operations which enable an economic agent to unite companies, shares, social parts or assets of the same economic agent or interest group". The Competition Law establishes that if a transaction involves a succession of acts (a series of transactions), it must be notified before "the culmination of the last one, due to which the amounts provided for in [article 86] are surpassed".

17 From 1 February 2020 the UMA is Mex$86.88. The UMA is adjusted each year and thus thresholds shall be updated for purposes of calculating relevant thresholds.

18 Approximately US$64 million (at Mex$24.42/US dollar) or €59 million (at Mex$26.29/Euro). For purposes of analysing the thresholds, COFECE considers the lowest exchange rate between Mexican pesos and the relevant currency of the five days prior to the closing of the transaction.

II. A single transaction, or a series of transactions, resulting in the accumulation of 35% or more of the total assets or shares of an economic agent, whose domestic assets or annual domestic sales exceed 18 million times the UMA (Mex$1,563,840,000[19]); or

III. The transaction results in (i) the direct or indirect acquisition of assets[20] (total assets as opposed to net assets) or amount of capital stock[21] in Mexico exceeding the equivalent of 8.4 million times the UMA (Mex$729,792,000[22])[23], and (ii) the joint or separate domestic total assets or annual domestic sales/revenues of all the parties to the transaction exceed, jointly or separately, the equivalent of 48 million times the UMA (Mex$4,170,240,000)[24].

Threshold I refers to the purchase price allocated specifically to Mexico or the value of the Mexican business, regardless of the value of the assets or annual sales of the target in Mexico. According to the Guidelines, in case of international transactions in which there is no value assigned or allocated to the Mexican business, threshold I shall not be applicable.

Threshold II refers to the acquisition of 35% or more of an economic agent with assets or annual sales in Mexico above a certain figure. For determining the value of total assets (as opposed to net assets), the higher figure between book value (as included in the balance sheet) and commercial value of the assets (price paid). With regard to annual sales, economic agents might consider annual net sales or revenues (as per the income statement in the financial statements).

Threshold III is aimed to capture smaller transactions, where the target has assets or capital stock in Mexico above of approximately Mex$729 million, and the parties involved in the transaction (i.e., acquirer, target and seller) have a significant size (with assets or sales in Mexico in excess of Mex$4,170 million).

III. Procedure

1. Launch of Procedure

Currently all notifications are reviewed under the standard review procedure in Mexico and all kinds of transactions follow the same course of notification procedure irrespective

---

19 Approximately US$64 million (at Mex$24.42/US dollar) or €59 million (at Mex$26.29/Euro).

20 As opposed to net assets, as reflected in the audited statements of the Mexican subsidiaries (prepared pursuant to Mexican Generally Accepted Accounting Principles, GAAP). Local counsel also suggests revising the most recent interim statements. If there are local assets held by foreign entities, a case-by-case assessment of the legal status of such assets is required to verify whether they need to be considered for jurisdictional purposes.

21 The amount of capital stock refers to amount of paid up share capital (e.g. shares), as reflected in the corporate books of the company and in the financial statements. The capital stock of all Mexican target entities needs to be considered, even if owned by foreign companies.

22 Approximately US$29 million (at Mex$24.42/US dollar) million or approximately €27 million (at Mex$26.29/Euro).

23 If only 50% of the target is acquired, only 50% of the target's assets would need to be considered under the first limb of the third threshold (but not the for the second limb of the third threshold), so this threshold reflects the percentage of investment and the size of the parties.

24 Approximately US$170 million (at Mex$24.42/US dollar) million or approximately €158 million (at Mex$26.29/Euro).

of the substance of the case. Despite the fact that the fast-track system is set forth in the Competition Law, in practice COFECE has dissuaded economic agents to pursue it due to the reasons outlined below.

In accordance with article 92 of the Competition Law, if the economic agents to a transaction provide evidence to the Competition Authorities that such transaction will not have any effect in the market (i.e., absence of overlapping and/or related activities), then an expedited review procedure might be applicable. Under this scenario, the Competition Law provides for the Competition Authorities to issue an official communication accepting to process the notification within the five business days of the date of receipt of the notification. Within 15 business days of the issue of such official communication, the Competition Authorities must clear the transaction. Should the Competition Authorities not issue a resolution within such term, constructive assent is deemed applicable.

Nonetheless, if the Competition Authorities determine that a concentration submitted under this procedure does not meet the requirement of no overlapping and/or related activities, or if the filing is not submitted with all the information required under the Competition Law, then the Competition Authorities will issue an official communication denying the expedited review procedure and initiating a standard review process. Therefore, the expedite review process poses a burden on the Competition Authorities to expeditiously and thoroughly review and confirm that the parties' activities do not have any overlap and/or relation and that the parties have submitted all required information and complied with formalities. In case there might be a relation over the parties' activities or an element of the formalities is outstanding, then the transaction shall be analysed under the standard review process.

From 24 January 2020, all notifications to COFECE shall be handled by digital channels. Further, a filing fee shall be paid prior to submitting the filing with COFECE and the amount is updated each year. As of January 2020, the filing fee is of Mex$190,020[25]. There is no filing fee with the IFT.

In relation to publicity issues arising from the notification during the procedure[26], it should be noted that after the first request for information has been issued and fully responded to; an extension to respond a request for information is granted; or the filing is accepted for process without any request for information, the Competition Authorities tend to publish in their website the name of the economic agents involved in the transaction together with the official communication channel by means of which the authorities deem the response to the request for information as complied with. In certain transactions the parties might request confidentiality over the case without the disclosure of their names, arguing that publicity might directly impact their course of business or the transaction itself, for instance in deals involving publicly traded companies when an acquisition has not been revealed to the public. The Competition Authorities might then agree to hold

---

25 Approximately US$7,780 (at Mex $24.42/US dollar) million or approximately €7,228 (at Mex $26.29/Euro).

26 The notification, exhibits, and any subsequent writ submitted to the Competition Authorities might not be accessed by any third party unless such party requests to have access to the file. In those rare cases, the third party would only have access to the non-confidential versions of each writ as submitted by the legal representatives of the parties.

the file as confidential until the transaction is made public. As for publicity issues, once the filing has been analysed and approved by the Competition Authorities, COFECE publishes a non-confidential version of the resolution in its website around one month after notification to the parties. In the public version, all confidential information from the parties appears redacted.

The obligation to file the transaction in Mexico is upon all involved parties[27]. Specifically, the Competition Law, the Regulations and the Guidelines set out that the entities or individuals directly involved in the transaction shall be the ones submitting the filing and appearing in the procedure. The Guidelines determine that in transactions where there is a transactional agreement such as the share purchase agreement, the signatories shall be deemed "directly involved". Pursuant to the Regulations, in cases with several purchasers or buyers from the same corporate group, the ultimate controlling entity of each group may appear as the notifying entity on behalf of its subsidiaries.

2. Development of Procedure

With regard to the standard review procedure, the Competition Authorities have 60 business days to review the notification and issue a resolution. This term is counted as from the date at which the Competition Authorities have a complete file with the information that they deem necessary for their analysis. Should the Competition Authorities not issue a resolution within such term, constructive assent applies

The Competition Authorities have the authority to request additional information to complete their file within the following terms:

i. Ten business days following the date of filing, to request basic information that should have been included in the initial filing (the parties will have 10 business days to submit that information and the possibility of requesting an extension of 10 additional business days to respond); and/or
ii. Fifteen business days from (1) the date of filing or (2) the date on which the request of information mentioned in (i) is satisfied, to request additional information that the Competition Authorities consider necessary to analyse the transaction (the parties have 15 business days to submit that information and may request one or more extensions for up to 40 additional business days in aggregate to respond).

Furthermore, the Competition Authorities may request additional information that they deem relevant for their analysis of the notifying parties, authorities or economic agents (third parties to the transaction)[28], that may be related to the concentration. The term to respond such requests for information is 10 business days, which can be extended in justified cases. Such requests will not restart the clock of 60 business days for the Competition Authorities' review. Should the parties not provide the information requested fully and timely, the Competition Authorities may dismiss the file.

---

27 Unless there is a legal or factual impossibility to make a joint filing, for instance, in hostile takeovers.

28 In Mexico it is getting more common for the Competition Authorities to issue market tests (open consultations), in complex transactions.

If the Competition Authorities issue a request for additional information pursuant to (i) and/or (ii) above, the 60 business days for review and resolution will start running from the date on which the Competition Authorities receive the information requested.

In particularly complex cases, the Competition Law allows the Competition Authorities' to extend the period to request additional information, and/or issue a resolution, for up to 40 additional business days.

It should be noted that pursuant to the Competition Law, provided the parties offer remedies in during the Competition Authorities' review procedure, the 60-business-day period to issue a resolution will restart from the date at which such remedies are offered.

Pursuant to the Guidelines, in international transactions or those in which the relevant markets might have a global scope, COFECE tends to cooperate and communicate with other foreign competition authorities. To this end, it is common that the Competition Authorities request waivers to discuss the substance of the case with other authorities, as well as timings and other relevant implications.

It is relevant to note that it is possible to make a carve-out only for the Mexican business and/or subsidiaries in order to close the transaction, as long as the transaction is not legally effective/closed in Mexico. In this regard, the purchaser must not acquire the shares or assets in Mexico, nor acquire control (de jure or de facto) over the target, nor the intention to participate, manage or influence, directly or indirectly, in the management, operation or commercial policies of the target. In addition, the parties will need to implement the correct mechanisms (e.g. clean rooms and non-disclosure agreements) to avoid any exchange of sensitive commercial information during this period.

3. Conclusion of Procedure

Once the case team has finalised its analysis of the matter, a draft resolution is internally prepared for the plenum's review[29]. During the plenum's meeting, one of the commissioners will present the case to the rest and they will vote in favour, imposing remedies or objecting it. The plenum of each Competition Authority issues its decisions without intervention from the government, since it is an autonomous and independent agency.

In particular, in cases where the Competition Authorities anticipate competitive concerns in the relevant market in Mexico, the Competition Authorities shall inform such concerns to the economic agents at least 10 business days before the date the case is to be included in the agenda of the plenum. This provides the economic agents with the opportunity to offer remedies or conditions to dissipate such concerns[30].

COFECE tends to be reluctant to accept post-closing divestitures or behavioural remedies since they are considered difficult to monitor. Instead, divestitures of standalone businesses or structural remedies are preferred. Should the Competition Authorities find that a transaction might have anticompetitive effects, they might request the economic

29 Usually the plenum of commissioners meets once a week.

30 As mentioned in section III(2) above, the 60-business-day period for the Competition Authorities to issue a resolution will restart as of the date at which such remedies or conditions are offered.

agents to transfer certain assets, rights, partnership interests or shares to third parties, amend the transaction documents, refrain from carrying out specific conducts, assume the obligation to carry out certain acts to promote competitors participation in the relevant market or to provide access to the relevant market.

Once the Competition Authorities issue a resolution it will be valid for a period of six months, counted from the day the resolution is notified to the parties. During the term, the parties might request only one extension for an additional term of six months (in total, the resolution could be valid for a period of one year) in justified cases. Should the parties not close the transaction within a year from obtaining the resolution, a new filing shall be required.

The parties also have the obligation to evidence closing within 30 business days after it occurred. In order to comply with the foregoing obligation, the parties shall submit transactional documents to the Competition Authorities showing proof that closing was undertaken upon the terms approved in the resolution.

The decisions issued by the Competition Authorities may be challenged before the administrative specialised Economic Competition Tribunals (*Juzgados en Materia Administrativa Especializados en Competencia Económica*) under the *amparo indirecto*. The specialised tribunals can review COFECE's decisions both in substance and form and overrule them.

4. Sanctions

In cases where a transaction reached the thresholds and the economic agents[31] fail to notify it to the Competition Authorities, the statute of limitations is of 10 years from closing. The Competition Law provides a fine of to up to 5% of the annual income in Mexico of the economic agents involved in the transaction.

If the transaction is determined to have anticompetitive effects, the Competition Authorities might order the economic agents to unwind the transaction or to take remedial steps, such as partial divestiture, to counteract the effects, in addition to imposing a fine of up to 8% of the annual income in Mexico on the economic agents involved in the transaction.

In cases where the economic agents notified their intent to carry out a transaction and during the Competition Authorities' review period the parties start implementing the deal as if it was authorised (considered gun-jumping), economic agents might be fined with up to 5% of the annual income in Mexico.

Further, during the Competition Authorities' review period, in the event the economic agents do not comply with what is requested, a fine might be imposed as an enforcement measure, for up to an amount equal to 3,000 times the UMA, which currently would amount to Mex$260,640 for each day that the economic agents fail to submit the requested documentation or information.

---

31 The term economic agents refers to the notifying parties in the notification, which may be the seller, the acquirer, and/or the target (including their controlled companies and ultimate parent companies), as applicable. The relevant turnover will be the domestic turnover/annual income of seller's and the acquirer's respective economic groups, unless it is a hostile takeover.

It is also relevant to note that, as previously mentioned, a transaction might be subject to a merger control investigation by the Competition Authorities within one year from closing, even if it falls below the thresholds set forth in the Competition Law. In that regard, any concentration whose purpose or effect is to hinder, diminish, damage, or prevent free and open competition, might be considered an unlawful concentration.

IV. Substance

1. Competition Analysis

There is no specific market share threshold in Mexico to be applied by the Competition Authorities for approving a transaction, and the analysis is undertaken from a pure competition assessment perspective.

In general terms, the Competition Authorities evaluate the relevant market involved in the transaction (upstream and downstream)[32], the economic agents that participate therein, the degree of concentration and the effects in the market. Pursuant to the Competition Law[33], the following elements shall be considered: (i) relevant market, (ii) identification of the main economic agents that supply the market in question, an analysis of their power in the relevant market and the degree of concentration (explained below); (iii) the effects of the concentration in the relevant market concerning other competitors or consumers of the goods or services, as well as regarding other related markets and economic agents; (iv) the equity participation of the involved parties in other economic agents, and the participation of other economic agents involved in the transaction, provided these economic agents participate in the relevant market; (v) arguments of the parties on the efficiencies that will result from the concentration[34], and (vi) other criteria or analytic instruments set forth in the Regulations or technical criteria. As to the degree of concentration, in 2015 and 2016, COFECE and IFT, respectively, published the *Technical criteria for the calculation and application of an Index to determine the degree of concentration in the relevant market*, based on which the Competition Authorities will carry out the

---

32 The Competition Authorities consider the possibility of substituting the product or service for others, technological possibilities, the availability of substitutes for consumers and time required for substitution, the product distribution costs, relevant inputs, complementary products and substitutes from abroad (freight, insurance, tariffs and non-tariff restrictions); costs to and ability of users to access other markets; regulatory restrictions that limit the users or consumers' access to alternative supply sources or the access of suppliers to other clients, among others.

33 Article 63 of the Competition Law.

34 In connection with what are considered as efficiencies on the market, Article 14 of the Regulations sets forth the following:
- Obtaining savings in resources that allow production of the same amount of goods to lower cost or a greater quantity of the good at the same cost, without diminishing the quality of the good;
- Cost reduction if two or more goods or services are produced jointly;
- The transfer or development of production technology;
- The reduction of the cost of production or commercialisation derived from the expansion of an infrastructure or distribution network; and
- Other efficiencies demonstrating that the net contributions to consumer welfare arising from the merger outweigh its anticompetitive effects.

analysis of the Herfindahl-Hirschman Index (HHI). The HHI aims to analyse the degree of concentration in a relevant market and the possibility for an economic agent to have substantial power in a certain relevant market.

Particularly, the HHI helps to determine whether a market is highly concentrated, when the results are closer to 10,000 points or highly atomised, are closer to 0 points. Each Competition Authority has established criteria to interpret such Index, which is comprised of three independent tests. For instance, COFECE considers that its criteria are met when: (i) the increase between the HHI prior to the transaction and post-transaction is less than 100 points; (ii) the total value of the HHI post-transaction is less than 2,000 points; or (iii) the total value of the HHI after the transaction is between 2,000 and 2,500 points, and the increase between the HHI prior to the transaction and post-transaction ranges between 100 and 150 points when the economic agent resulting from the transaction will not be among the four larger participants in the relevant market.

On the other hand, IFT considers that its criteria are met when: (i) the total value of the HHI after the transaction is less than 2,000 points; (ii) the total value of the HHI post-transaction is between 2,000 and 3,000, and the increase between the HHI prior to the transaction and post-transaction is less than 150 points; or (iii) the total value of the HHI post-transaction is less than 3,000 points and the increase between the HHI pre- and post-transaction is less than 100 points.

The Competition Authorities consider the HHI as a first approach. Nonetheless, it is important to point out that results derived from the analysis of such Index are not conclusive, as the Competition Authorities shall analyse other elements to conclude their assessment, such as, the specific characteristics of the market, market barriers, efficiencies, etc.

2. Statistics

In 2019 there were 153 merger control cases analysed by COFECE. From the 153 cases, 144 were concluded during the year and 132 approved without conditions. Of the remaining 12 cases, two cases were blocked and 10 were not approved as COFECE was not the appropriate authority to review the cases, they were withdrawn by the parties, or they were dismissed for not providing the required information.

As noted in section III(2), the Competition Authorities have 60 business days to review the notification and issue a resolution, counted from the latest of the date of filing, the response to the request for basic information or the response to the request for additional information. From the 144 cases reviewed and approved by COFECE during 2019, the average resolution timeline was 17.5 days from the date on which COFECE had a complete file.

During 2019 economic agents were able to submit a physical or electronic filing, and of the 153 cases there were only 44 submitted electronically. As from 2020, only electronic filings are allowed.

The economic sectors with more cases approved during 2019 were the (i) manufacturing industry, (ii) real estate services, (iii) transport, mail and storage, (iv) electricity, water and/or gas supply, and (v) financial and insurance services.

For merger control cases filed before IFT during 2019, there were only six cases reviewed and analysed.

3. Case Law Illustration

On November 2018, Walmart and Cornershop notified their intention to carry out a concentration and in May 2019 the transaction was blocked by COFECE. The transaction involved Walmart's acquisition of Cornershop[35], a digital platform with operations in Mexico and Chile. In Mexico, Walmart's activities are limited to operating self-service stores, supermarkets, membership price clubs, pharmacies and online shops. With regard to Cornershop, its activities are focused on logistic services of purchase and immediate delivery of products offered by self-service stores, membership price clubs and other businesses to consumers, through a website and mobile app.

COFECE defined Cornershop as a two-sided platform with two differentiated users and two mutually reliant demands. On one hand, final consumers, purchasing through the digital platform; on the other, shops and businesses that exhibit their products through the digital platform. In light of the above, the relevant market was considered by COFECE as narrow as the logistics service of exhibition, purchase and immediate delivery of goods offered by self-service and membership price clubs through the Internet and apps to consumers (end users) (the relevant market).

Surprisingly, the physical or online stores were not considered as substitutes for the services offered by the platform since there are important differences for the consumer, who must go to make a purchase in the physical stores. Where the consumer decides to go through the portal or app of the store, purchase options are naturally limited to that establishment and the delivery times are longer.

With such a narrow definition of the market in mind, only two other companies were considered as Cornershop's competitors (Rappi and Mercadoni), offering an integral service that includes the full-time attention of a shopper, purchase options in multiple stores, short delivery times and tracking of the order in real time.

COFECE considered that there was a vertical consolidation of businesses since Walmart and Cornershop participated in different levels of the same chain. Cornershop was deemed to be the leader in the narrowly defined relevant market, while Walmart the major player in the traditional business of self-service stores and membership price clubs.

COFECE analysed the effects on the market and considered that in case the transaction was to be undertaken, Walmart and Cornershop would have the capacity to establish barriers to entry, prevent third parties accessing the market or displace current competitors.

The economic agents submitted remedies to ease COFECE's concerns, including granting free access without discrimination to all shops within the digital platform, and the agreement to refrain from using Walmart's competitor's information to their own benefit. The suggested remedies were considered by COFECE as insufficient to guarantee the participation of Walmart in other platforms, access and equal treatment to the establishments operating in Cornershop and the use of the information.

---

35 COFECE case number CNT-161-2018; Mexican Competition Authority, "The Mexican Competition Authority prohibits a concentration between a retail company and a company offering logistical services to retailers (Walmart/Cornershop)" (5 June 2019), e-Competitions June 2019, Art. N° 90775.

NICARAGUA

Ernesto Rizo Pallais*
Favio Batres P**
(BLP)

Abstract

Nicaragua has been developing a merger control system since 2006, when the Promotion of Competition Law was enacted (Law 601), establishing fundamental principles on the protection of competition, market access and consumer welfare. Law 601 also created the Instituto Nacional de Promoción de la Competencia, known as Procompetencia, a governmental agency in charge of promoting and protecting competition in Nicaragua, as well as administering merger controls and process. Merger controls include filing procedures leading to an administrative resolution either authorising, conditioning or rejecting the transaction filed. The experience in Nicaragua in this field encompasses both national and international deals. Certain cases have involved different competition agencies in the region and the world. From smooth-paced filings to highly complex operations, Nicaragua has a significant practice flourishing in the merger control arena.

---

* Ernesto Rizo Pallais is a partner in the Nicaraguan office of BLP, Ernesto has over 20 years of experience in the legal field, specialising in transactions involving agribusiness, banking and finance, energy and infrastructure, and business law. Ernesto graduated from the Pontificia Universidad Javeriana in Bogotá and was a Fulbright scholar at Georgetown University where he obtained a Master's degree in banking and financial regulation.

** Favio Josué Batres P is a senior associate in the Nicaraguan office of BLP. Favio has over 15 years of experience in the legal field, specialising in business law, banking and project finance, mergers and acquisitions, competition and antitrust, competition litigation and commercial arbitration. Favio graduated from Universidad del Valle in Managua and obtained a Master's degree in business law from Universidad Centroamericana in Managua.

I. Introduction

1. Brief Overview

On 28 September 2006, the Nicaraguan National Assembly approved the Promotion of Competition Law (Law 601[1]), as part of the state's efforts to promote the economic development of the country, by encouraging good practice in competition among the diverse economic, sectoral and regional agents; regulating, conditioning and, in some cases, forbidding practices that may harm or jeopardise the free competition and the rights of consumers.

Law 601 was a novelty in Nicaraguan business law practice. It was only with this law that such concepts as relevant market, dominant position, market share and economic thresholds, among others, entered into the scope of analysis of business law practitioners when dealing with mergers and acquisitions, transfers of shares or assets, investments or divestitures and other similar corporate transactions.

A few months later, Decree No. 79-2006, Regulations to Law 601 (Regulations[2]), came into effect, providing details and specifics for the application of Law 601, including rules of procedure. These two legal measures comprised the essential framework on competition and antitrust matters in Nicaragua, impacting both the legal community and businesses alike, since certain relevant transactions have to include the merger control analysis as a new integral component[3].

Procompetencia, was formally organised in 2009, previously, the first merger control filings were conducted by Procompetencia in its role of regulator and enforcement authority. Since the enactment of Law 601, the legal framework has undergone two important amendments: the first modification included the appointment of the attorney general as the state representative in merger control cases[4]. This amendment determines that the office of the attorney general must be a part in all filings and procedures. The second change granted exclusive competence on merger control procedures to sector regulators in their respective markets[5]. Therefore, filings involving financial services, telecommunications and the energy industry are conducted within the respective regulator of each of these industries.

Merger control cases have not only increased in number in Nicaragua, but in complexity as well. Multinational economic agents carrying out worldwide transactions have cleared filing procedures in different countries in Europe, the US, Asia and Latin America and Caribbean,

---

1 Published in *La Gaceta*, Official Diary, Issue No 206, on 24 October 2006.

2 Published in *La Gaceta*, Official Diary, Issue No 10, on 15 January 2007.

3 Procompetencia has also prepared and issued guidelines (Guidelines) to file and process merger authorisation requests, which are not binding and are solely for information purposes. The guidelines may be found at: <http://procompetencia.gob.ni/wp-content/uploads/2017/09/2-Gu%C3%ADa-para-solicitud-de-concentraciones-econ%C3%B3micas.pdf>.

4 Law No 773, Amendments to Law 601, published in *La Gaceta*, Official Diary, Issue No 200, on 24 October 2011.

5 Law No 868, Amendments and Additions to Law 601, published in *La Gaceta*, Official Diary, Issue No 106, on 10 June 2014, <http://procompetencia.gob.ni/wp-content/uploads/2015/03/Ley-No.601-y-Reglamento-Refundida-20161.pdf>.

and have done so in Nicaragua as part of the requirements to implement the operation in the country, which has granted experience and efficiency to the antitrust system in Nicaragua.

After 10 years of antitrust practice in Nicaragua, we can say that the legal system has been strengthened and enhanced by the experience acquired so far by all the parties involved: Procompetencia, antitrust practitioners, economic agents and other governmental authorities participating in merger control cases, promoting and developing a free competition and antitrust culture in the country.

2. Institutional Set-Up

A. Procompetencia and its Members

Procompetencia was created as a public law institution, with independent legal status and resources, domiciled in Managua, the capital city of Nicaragua, and authorised to open branches in any other places of the country. The agency is of a technical nature and is autonomous for budgetary purposes, not linked or subordinated to a particular branch of government.

The organisation's highest authority is a board of directors, which consists of a president and three directors, each with a substitute member, who are appointed by the president of the republic and ratified by the National Assembly by absolute majority of votes. The board of directors then appoints one of its directors for the position of secretary, for a one-year term, which then rotates among the other directors.

Directors are appointed from three shortlists of candidates proposed by the *Consejo Superior de la Empresa Privada* (COSEP), which is the superior board of the private companies' chamber, the *Consejo Nicaragüense de la Micro, Pequeña y Mediana Empresa* (CONIMIPYME), which is the board for the small enterprise sector, and the *Ministerio de Fomento, Industria y Comercio* (MIFIC), the governmental branch for the promotion of industry and commerce[6].

Directors cannot be removed from their positions without justified cause, and the removal must be approved by the National Assembly after a request from the president of the republic, and after the affected party is heard following due process[7].

Sector regulators, such as the *Instituto Nicaragüense de Telecomunicaciones y Correos* (TELCOR), the regulator for telecommunication and postal services; the *Superintendencia de Bancos y de Otras Instituciones Financieras* (SIBOIF), the regulator for the banking and financial system; the *Instituto Nacional de Energía* (INE), the energy regulator; the Instituto Nicaragüense de Acueductos y Alcantarillados (INAA), the national water and sewerage services regulator; have exclusive jurisdiction over competition and mergers matters involving the economic agents in their respective sectors.

---

6 ibid., art 7.

7 ibid., arts 7 and 11. The causes to remove directors are the following: (i) incompatibility arising after the appointment as director; (ii) serious breach of obligations and functions; (iii) negligence or incompetence duly demonstrated; (iv) physical or mental disability preventing them from complying with duties; (v) non-attendance at three consecutive board meetings; (vi) conviction for certain crimes; (vii) prohibition causes.

B. The System

The agency's system is administrative in nature, with, among others, the following functions:

Conduct investigations, whether on an *ex officio* basis or following complaints filed by parties, in situations that may affect the competition in the market; admit or reject complaints; request judicial authorities to apply pre-emptive measures; issue resolutions and impose sanctions; resolve challenges; authorise, condition or reject mergers totally or partially; order a total or partial demerger[8].

Crimes against free competition are prosecuted by the state prosecutor according to the Nicaraguan Criminal Code and Criminal Procedure Code, thus Procompetencia´s actions are limited to investigating, conducting procedures and issue resolutions in the administrative stage.

3. Type of Merger Control

The type of merger control is pure *ex ante* with compulsory notification and request of authorisation[9]. When a proposed transaction meets either the market share or economic thresholds established by Law 601, then any or all of the interested parties must notify the intended transaction and request authorisation in advance, completing the filing process until the resolution is issued.

The legal and material effects of transactions executed outside Nicaragua are suspended until Procompetencia approves it locally[10].

II. Scope of Application

1. Definition of Notifiable Transaction

The following transactions are identified as "concentrations" under Law 601:

a) Acts, contracts, agreements or covenants aiming to merge, acquire, consolidate, integrate or combine the whole or partial businesses of independent economic agents, becoming non-independent agents.

b) The acquisition, by any means, total or partial, of the direct or indirect control of other economic agents by one or more economic agent already controlling others.

c) Any other agreement or act transferring, implicitly or legally, the assets of a company or the determinant influence in such company's ordinary or extraordinary administrative decisions, in favour of an economic agent[11].

---

8 ibid., art 14.
9 Regulations, art 31.
10 ibid., art 32.
11 Law 601, art 24.

Despite the above, only if these transactions meet either market share or the economic thresholds established by Law 601, do they become notifiable to Procompetencia[12].

2. Material Scope

Law 601 is applicable to any act, conduct, transaction or covenant carried out by economic agents in all sectors of the national economy, including those executed outside Nicaragua, insofar as they produce or might produce anticompetitive effects in the national market. The following aspects should be considered:

a) With respect to the governmental authority involved in regulated industries such as telecom, banking and finance, energy, etc., where each specific regulator handles and decides over competition and merger controls, Procompetencia plays a limited role, submitting a non-binding opinion on the determination of the analysed practice, and not on the technical or special aspects of the regulated sector[13]. Hence, a merger involving economic agents in any of these sectors should not clear the filing procedure with Procompetencia, since it is resolved by the corresponding regulator, and said regulator may request a non-binding opinion to Procompetencia solely on the competition matters associated with the transaction, but the decision is taken by the sectoral regulator.

b) According to Law 601, associations taking effect for a limited time to develop a specific project are not considered "concentrations" in terms of Law 601[14]. The Regulations further elaborate on this matter and establish that the following are not considered as "concentrations" according to article 26 of Law 601: (i) the temporary associations to develop a determined project or for a specific end, such as consortiums or strategic alliances, among others[15]; and (ii) the acquisition of shares or contributions in Nicaraguan entities, when the economic agents do not acquire their control, and do not accumulate in Nicaraguan territory shares, participation in companies, participation in trusts or assets in general, in addition to those directly or indirectly held before the transaction[16].

c) Those mergers of which the effect is, or might be, the reduction, restriction, harm or prevention of the economic free competition respect to equal, similar or substantially related goods or services are forbidden. However, mergers with an insolvent economic agent are excepted from this prohibition[17]. The

---

12 According to the Guidelines, a concentration implies the acquisition or control of a portion, or the whole, of an economic agent by another, by means of an agreement or covenant such as sale – purchase agreements, mergers, joint investments and others. The Guidelines also describe the analysis Procompetencia runs on a merger authorisation request, including the possibility of implementing a unilateral price-fixing practice, creation of entry barriers to new competitors, production of economic efficiencies, the relevant market in which the transaction will produce effects and the market exit of productive assets (Guidelines, note 3, 7–10).

13 ibid., art 15, as amended by Law No 868.

14 Law 601, art 26.

15 Regulations, art 29.2.

16 ibid.. art. 29.1.

17 Law 601, art 26.

Guidelines add that the insolvent economic agent must prove that non-competitors buyers were sought unsuccessfully[18].

Procompetencia may conduct investigations on a case-by-case basis and determine whether a specific transaction or operation falls within any of the scenarios described in paragraphs b and c above.

3. Geographical Scope

Law 601 is applicable to any act, conduct, transaction or covenant executed or carried out by the economic agents in all sectors of the national economy, including those performed outside Nicaragua, so long as they produce, or might produce, anticompetitive effects in the national market[19]. For these purposes, Procompetencia analyses the current situation in the local market, including market shares, competitors, consumers, suppliers, entry barriers, etc., as well as the market situation that would result from implementing the transaction, determining whether it would produce anticompetitive effects in the local market. The assessment is made during the filing process in Nicaragua if any of the thresholds described in section II(4) are met.

Likewise, transactions already executed outside Nicaragua, meeting or surpassing the Nicaraguan merger control thresholds, cannot take legal or material effects in the country until Procompetencia approves the transactions locally[20].

The Nicaraguan merger control system therefore covers both national and international transactions, with an effects-based approach which is assessed via notification to, and filing procedures with, Procompetencia in Nicaragua.

4. Thresholds

Transactions must be notified to Procompetencia when meeting or surpassing any of the following thresholds:

Market Share Threshold: When as a result of the transaction an equal or superior relevant market share of 25% is acquired or increased. This applies to all type of mergers, whether horizontal, vertical or conglomerate; however, in practice, when an economic agent involved in the transaction does not have any share or participation in any sector locally prior to the transaction, the merger could be regarded as a mere "change of ownership" making the filing unnecessary. However, a case-by-case analysis is recommended.

Economic Threshold: When the economic agents in the transaction have a combined gross income above an average of 642,857 minimum wages (currently equivalent to approx USD 120 million)[21].

Regarding the market share threshold, in practice, the economic agents provide Procompetencia with the information on their *pre-* and *post-*transaction relevant market shares,

---

18 Guidelines, note 3, 12.
19 Law 601, art 2.
20 ibid., art 32.
21 ibid., art. 25.

and Procompetencia executes an independent due diligence exercise to confirm the information, which typically includes public and governmental sources, market investigations and assessments, and communication with other antitrust enforcement agencies abroad.

On the economic threshold, the combined gross income is calculated based on all assets and income received and accrued by the economic agents during their last fiscal exercise, whether periodically, eventually or occasionally, whether in cash, goods or compensation from sales, rents or profits, originating in the sale of goods produced, manufactured, treated or purchased in the country or abroad, rendering of services, leases, sub-leases, works, compensated activities of any nature, gains or benefits produced from movable or real estate assets, capital gains and other incomes of any nature, before the corresponding tax deductions[22].

Procompetencia considers the average minimum wage and the official exchange rate of the day prior to the notification.

III. Procedure[23]

1. Launch of Procedure

The procedure is launched with the notification made to Procompetencia by any of the economic agents involved in the transaction. There is a general notification form for all transactions, the Nicaraguan antitrust agency has not developed different forms for simple or complex transactions. They are both filed using the same form with the same formalities and substantial contents in order to be processed.

Once the notification form and attachments have been admitted, Procompetencia notifies the attorney general to participate in the process as a party representing the State of Nicaragua. With the attorney general part of the process and after any incidental aspect or related matter has been cleared, the Regulations provide for a term of 30 business days to run a preliminary review of the case, if Procompetencia considers that there is no evidence indicating that the transaction may cause significant limitations to competition, then within the next five business days the transaction may be authorised[24].

The above procedure is mandatory for all notification filings, disregarding whether the transaction is simple or complex. If Procompetencia determines it cannot issue a resolution within the above time frame, then a full investigation process (phase II) follows. There is no fast-track system for simple transactions and, so far, all transactions notified have been resolved via the full investigation process.

---

22 Regulations, art 30.

23 This section describes the procedure followed by Procompetencia as the administrative authority for competition matters in general, including mergers and acquisitions. However, as previously explained, Procompetencia is not in charge of procedures nor of resolving competition issues involving regulated sectors such as telecom, banking, etc., in which the respective regulators handle and resolve these aspects. There are no specific procedures nor standards established so far by sectoral regulators for competition matters, so each transaction is subject to a case-by-case analysis.

24 Regulations, art 38.

Up to now there are no digital channels available to make online or digital filings, therefore all filings are made physically at Procompetencia's headquarters in Managua. The filing fees are as follows:

Amount of Transaction (USD Million)	Procompetencia Filing Fees (USD Thousand)
Up to 3.5	35
3.5 to 7	50
7 to 10	75
Above 10	100

Law 601 did not set out a specific deadline for filing. It nonetheless requires economic agents to notify and obtain approval in advance for their proposed transactions in events where notification is mandatory.

Economic agents may request Procompetencia to hold filed information and documents under confidentiality terms, if it has commercial value due to its secret nature; if this is the case, reasonable measures must be taken to keep all information and documentation restricted. The confidential information declared so by Procompetencia is kept in a separate record, and only the president and the personnel working on the filing may have access to it[25].

2. Development of Procedure

A. Phase I

Phase I consists of the notification filed with Procompetencia by any of the economic agents involved in the transaction as well as the first administrative decisions taken and procedures ordered by the agency[26].

Procompetencia reviews the notification and may grant 10 business days to the economic agents to correct or complete any required information. If the information

---

25 ibid., art 47.

26 According to Art. 33 of the Regulations, the notification filed must contain:

a) A request of the authorisation of the transaction;
b) Legal names of the economic agents and of those participating directly or indirectly in the transaction;
c) Information on the legal representatives and documents demonstrating their capacity and address for notices in the city of Managua;
d) Authenticated copies of articles of incorporation and by-laws of the economic agents;
e) Financial statements for the last fiscal year, certified by an authorised public accountant;
f) Certification of the *pre-* and *post*-transaction shareholder structure;
g) Description of the transaction, a draft of the transaction legal document, including any non-compete clauses and the reasons for it;
h) Mention of other economic agents participating in the companies directly involved in the transaction, participating in other entities producing or commercialising equal or similar goods to those in the notified transaction;
i) Description of the transaction's goods and services, and a list of similar goods or services produced or commercialised by other economic agents not involved in the transaction;
j) Market share of the economic agents in the transaction, and the location of their production plants and distribution centres.
k) Any other information or documentation required by Procompetencia.

or documentation requested is not corrected or completed, or if the additional information is not filed within such 10-day period, Procompetencia may reject the filing[27].

Once the filing is admitted, Procompetencia notifies the attorney general to participate in the process representing the State of Nicaragua. The agency runs a preliminary review of the case in 30 business days, and if it considers that there is no evidence indicating that the transaction may cause significant limitations to competition, then within the next five business days the agency should authorise the transaction[28].

B. Phase II

In Phase II, there are 90 business days in which to submit evidence. After the evidentiary period has concluded, a new 60-business-day period is granted for Procompetencia's personnel to prepare a draft resolution that will be submitted for the president's review. Procompetencia's president can then issue, within the next 30 days, a resolution either with a total, partial or conditioned approval, or a full rejection of the transaction.

Within the evidentiary period, additional evidence may be incorporated to the file of record. Procompetencia may conduct an independent diligence, including market investigations that may involve third parties such as competitors or consumers. The agency can also request necessary information of any foreign authorities to investigate any possible breach of Law 601[29], as well as requesting more information and documentation from the filing parties[30]. The attorney general may also request Procompetencia to obtain more evidence from the economic agents, other governmental authorities, relevant market participants, etc. With all this additional evidence, the agency will make its final decision.

3. Conclusion of Procedure

Procompetencia's final decision may be a total, partial or conditional approval of the transaction, or an outright rejection of it. If no challenges are filed against it within five business days of notification, then the agency's decision remains firm[31].

To date, in Nicaragua, all transactions filed have been approved with certain conditions imposed on the economic agents. The nature of these conditions includes the following:

a) To pursue a specific conduct or refrain from executing a specific action.
b) Transfer to third parties specific assets, rights, contributions or shares.
c) Eliminate a specific line of production.
d) Amend or eliminate certain terms or conditions from the actions to be executed.

---

27 ibid., art 34.
28 ibid., art 38.
29 Law 601, art 14(n).
30 Regulations, art 34, para 2.
31 Law 601, art 39.

e) Promote the competitors' participation in the market, as well as provide them with market access and sell them goods or services.
f) Any other conditions aimed at to avoiding harm to and hindrance of competition[32].

Compliance with these conditions or commitments is monitored by Procompetencia via periodic reviews, economic agents' reports, third party reports, *in situ* inspections, and others.

Any of the parties in the process, whether the economic agents or the attorney general, may challenge Procompetencia's resolution, via a revision recourse, to be filed within the next five business days and to be resolved by Procompetencia's president within 10 business days[33].

A further appeal can be further filed by any of the parties before Procompetencia's board of directors within the next 10 business days. Procompetencia's board of directors will resolve the appeal within 60 business days, finalising the administrative stage[34]. Any further challenge from any of the parties must be filed and resolved judicially.

4. Sanctions

Law 601 imposes a series of penalties for not notifying transactions that require filings. Penalties range from 100 minimum wages to 600 minimum wages[35] (currently approx USD 18,800–112,750).

Furthermore, if the economic agent does not provide information or fails to cooperate in timely manner in the filing process or submits incomplete or inaccurate information, they can be penalised with 15 minimum wages per day of delay (currently approx USD 2,820 per day)[36].

Additionally, for cases of undue mergers, the agency is authorised to order a total or partial demerger, or the termination of the control or the actions, as applicable[37].

IV. Substance

1. Competition Analysis

The substantive test and analysis for merger review is mainly based on a competition assessment. The Regulations set out the following criteria for assessment:

a) The relevant market where the transaction currently produces effects.
b) The portion of the relevant market where the transaction will eventually produce effects with respect to competitors and consumers, as well as other markets and other related economic agents.

---

32 Regulations, art 40.
33 Law 601, art 39.
34 ibid., art 40.
35 ibid., art 46(c).
36 ibid., art 46(d).
37 ibid., art 28(c).

c) The control of the involved economic agents.
d) Dominant position arising out of the transaction.
e) Relevant market assessment on the economic efficiencies that may derive from the transaction, which must be demonstrated by the economic agents[38].

The agency takes into account the above aspects in a transaction, along with the particularities of each case, in order to decide the total, partial or conditional authorisation, or the rejection of the transaction.

Procompetencia also analyses the procompetitive and anticompetitive effects of a transaction, analysing whether the transaction may result in the reduction, restriction, harm or prevention of free competition with respect to equal, similar or substantially related goods or services, taking into account (i) the relevant market's affected scope; (ii) the effects on competitors and clients in both the relevant and other markets, as well as in other economic agents; (iii) the control of the economic agents involved; (iv) the dominant position to arise out of the transaction; and (v) the market assessment of the economic efficiencies to be gained from the transaction[39].

2. Statistics[40]

Year	Cases Analysed	Cases Concluded	Type of Decisions	Average Time to Resolve	Economic Sector
2017	4	3	Approved with conditions	120 business days, approx.	Commerce, tourism and agrichemicals
2018	0	1 (started in 2017)	Approved with conditions	360 business days, approx. (resolved with revision recourse)	Agrichemicals, commerce
2019[41]	2	0	N/A	N/A	Pharmaceuticals, commerce

3. Case Law Illustration

Decision number: Concentration No 0002-2012.

Parties: Nestlé, S.A. (buyer), and Pfizer Inc. (seller).

Industry: Infant dairy formula business line.

38 Regulations, art 28.

39 These are the standard aspects considered by Procompetencia when analysing mergers and acquisitions. There are no standards established so far by sectoral regulators where Procompetencia is not in charge of processing and resolving competition matters, being those cases subject to a case-by-case analysis.

40 Information provided by Procompetencia at authors' request.

41 One of the cases initiated in 2019 concluded in March 2020, it was approved with conditions in 90 business days, approx., and corresponds to the commercial sector. The other case is still ongoing.

Brief description of the transaction: In 2012, Nestlé, a Swiss corporation with an operating branch in Nicaragua, acquired the infant dairy formula business line of Pfizer, a US corporation (Business), in a transaction involving more than 40 countries around the world, including Nicaragua. Before the transaction, Nestlé had a relevant market share in Nicaragua greater than the 25% threshold established in Law 601, while Pfizer's share was lesser than such threshold and its business was conducted through a local authorised distributor. Since the transaction would increase Nestlé's market share, the transaction was subject to filing with Procompetencia, which would decide on whether to authorise, condition or reject the transaction for Nicaragua.

Relevant issues discussed: Possible adverse effects in a highly sensitive market given the nature of the Business involved, including the reduction of competition in the market, an eventual price-fixing emerging power, refusal of commercial treatment with certain economic agents and the possible consequences on consumers, amongst others.

Analysis: The Business was identified as highly concentrated in the country, which would be even more concentrated as a result of the transaction, strengthening the buyer's dominant position in the market. Certain factors, such as the consumer's medical-prescribed choice of products, a local ban to advertise breastfeeding substitutes, and consumer brand loyalty were found as elements that would make difficult the timely entry of a competitor that might have a bearing in the market to discipline the emerging concentrated entity.

However, Procompetencia determined that such risks could be diminished by implementing certain measures, such as, amongst others: (i) ensuring the existence of an effective and independent competitor; (ii) maintenance of economic feasibility, distribution channels, trade of products and competitivity of the Business in the country; (iii) strengthening of breastfeeding education as well as the technical capabilities of the governmental branches in this area.

Final decision: Procompetencia approved the transaction subject to the following conditions: the buyer should (i) commence a divestment process of the Business, transferring to a third party the involved assets as well as licensing the use of trademarks, assigning permits, inventories, etc.; (ii) maintain and expand the distribution channels; (iii) cooperate in the breastfeeding education campaigns and financing educational materials; (iv) cooperate, financially, with the improvement of food-related laboratories and other facilities of the corresponding governmental branches, and; (v) comply with environmental and breastfeeding substitutes laws and regulations.

PANAMA

Jorge Molina Mendoza[*]

(Fabrega Molino)

Abstract

Despite the fact that Panama enacted its first antitrust laws in 1966, the protection of commercial competition has been anticipated, constitutionally, since at least 1946. Since then, the power to determine the legality of restrictive practices in market competition has been bestowed upon public tribunals, so that any one person may contest any and all acts considered violations of antitrust laws, among them contracts pertaining to mergers. Current legislation, in effect from 2007, creates an institutional system to protect market competition, headed by an administrative entity specialised in these matters, with the power to exert control over mergers. Nevertheless, this control is characterised as explicitly voluntary, since the law does not demand that merger operations are notified ex ante before any governmental authority. Therefore, the Panamanian system for the control of mergers reveals itself to be sui generis, because though it relieves mergers from the obligation to notify themselves, regardless of the amount of resources involved, it allows for voluntary notification. In the event that this notification does not take place, the ex post merger control of the tribunals stands as valid.

[*] Jorge Molina Mendoza is senior partner in Fabrega Molino and is head of the litigation and arbitration group. He is a former appeal judge on antitrust matters.

I. Introduction

The following are the ideas that, from a purely analytical perspective, outline Panamanian regulation for the protection of economic competition in its merger regulation component, which operates, as is known, mainly on the horizontal operations of mergers and acquisitions. In this chapter we will use "merger" and "economic concentration" as synonyms. The reason for this is that in jurisdictions belonging to the civil law tradition, they are known as *economic concentrations*, while in the common law system they are known as *mergers*, although they are in fact the same thing. As this publication is in English, the use of these terms as synonyms avoids confusion. The reader should consider the size of the economic system of Panama. According to official statistics, Panama has a population of about 4 million people, with a gross domestic product close to US$68 billion in 2019. The economic system is organised around three main economic activity clusters: transport and logistic activities led by the Panama Canal, financial activities and the growing tourism industry. Thus, the regulations over mergers are not as strict as in other countries. Actually, the economic system, by default, has a higher rate of concentration markets.

1. Brief Overview

The current Panamanian Constitution, dated 1972, establishes in Articles 295[1] and 298[2] free competition as a value to which our society wanted to grant durability.

Article 295 contains the prohibition of any contract, agreement or act that is aimed at restricting or preventing free trade and competition, as these may monopolise the market to the detriment of the consumer and small businesses. The origin of this law goes back to the 1946 Constitution, specifically Article 236, since the content of this last article was reproduced verbatim by the 1972 Constitution. The forecast of the 1946 Constitution is very interesting in regard to this prohibition, mainly due to the fact that the model of economic development existing at that date was that of "import substitution". Using high tariffs to protect the development of the national industry, this protection compensated with price control, especially on basic goods and services. This, in turn, did not generate competition incentives, but rather configured monopolistic or oligopolistic structures. Notwithstanding this, the 1946 Constitution incorporated free competition law into the constitutional text as a basic element of the Panamanian economic system. Here it is useful to consider the provisions of Article 295 of the current Constitution.

---

1 Political Constitution, Article 295:
Any combination, contract or action that tends to restrict or prevent free trade and competition and that has monopoly effects to the detriment of the public is prohibited in commerce and industry. Belonging to these conducts are practices such as exploiting a sole natural or legal person, series or chains of retail merchant establishments, in a way that makes it ruinous or tends to eliminate competition from the small merchant or industrialist. There will be popular action to challenge in court the conclusion of any combination, contract or action that aims to establish monopolistic practices. The Law will regulate this matter.

2 Political Constitution, Article 298: "The State shall ensure free economic competition and free competition in the markets. The laws will establish the modalities and conditions that guarantee these principles."

A first point to consider is the consequences of the constitutionalisation of antitrust laws. When referring to antitrust we mean free competition as public policy; this is understood as the state decision that will give scope and depth to competition. However, since there is a constitutional rule, the result is that, regardless of the orientation that economic policy may take, it will dictate a parameter from which it cannot be separated, which corresponds to the constitutional development of the protection of competition contained in Article 295 of the Panamanian Constitution. That is, regardless of the direction that economic policy may take, access to markets and the prohibition of unreasonable private restrictions on competition must prevail. Now in Panama's case, by constitutional mandate, two matters are added to the essential core of the constitutional protection of competition: consumer protection against restrictive competition practices and small business protection. Thus, the rest of the objectives that are intended to be added in a legal instrument to develop a free competition policy may or may not be included, but the newly listed ones seem to be mandatory.

Regarding the legal competition regime, the first rule was Law No 29 of 1996 (L29). With L29, the Panamanian state took a diametrically opposed turn with respect to antitrust. L29 is the first antitrust regulation adopted, constituting a competition protection regime. Thus, the state allows the interaction of supply and demand to flow as price-fixing mechanisms, which restores to the consumer its rational and decision-making power.

L29 included a structure that prohibited restraint practices, composed in turn of three elements: prohibition of collusion or cartels (horizontal restraint practices), prohibition of abuse of the dominant position (vertical restraint practices), and prohibition of mergers considered restrictive to competition (mergers). The objectives proposed in L29 were mainly those of economic efficiency, consumer protection, equality of economic agents and the free market as the basis for our economic system.

L29 was replaced by Law No 45 of 2007 (L45)[3], which "dictates rules on consumer protection and defence of competition and other provisions". This is the current Panamanian antitrust law[4]. Through this law the Authority for Consumer Protection and Defence of Competition (ACODECO) was created, and this regulation serves as the main material for the chapter contained in Executive Decree No 8-A of 2009 (D8-A)[5], as well as the guide issued for the analysis of economic concentrations, known as the Guide for the Control of Economic Concentrations (Guide)[6].

2. Institutional Set-Up

We now consider the public entities involved in the competition protection system, along with their respective powers. In order to clearly expose the make-up of the system in

---

3 Authority for Consumer Protection and Defence of Competition: Laws and Regulations, <http://www.acodeco.gob.pa/acodeco/view.php?arbol=2&sec=1&pagi=0>.

4 Law No 36 was issued in 2018. This statute regulates mergers in the in the mobile phone sector. Its rules actually refer to L45. See note 3.

5 Laws and Regulations, note 3.

6 ibid.

question, it is necessary to return to the Panamanian constitutional norm. Article 295 of the Constitution establishes, in its last paragraph, that "there will open popular action to challenge in court the conclusion of any combination, contract or action that has as its object the establishment of monopolistic practices". This means that control of restrictive competition practices falls in the judicial field, which explains why it is not ACODECO that has jurisdiction to declare the illegality of said conduct. On the other hand, Article 298 of the Constitution ascribes to the state the duty of ensuring "free economic competition and free competition in the markets". Thus, the state is obliged to perform this public function. To satisfy that constitutional mandate, ACODECO was created, and assigned with the stewardship of the administrative component of Panamanian antitrust. This means that two entities take part in the competition protection system: ACODECO, at administrative level, and the judicial branch, through the competent courts, at judicial level.

A. Administrative Government of Panama Antitrust

We have mentioned almost from the beginning of this chapter that ACODECO has an essential role in the system that protects and defends competitive commerce in Panama. This entity was created by means of L45, and possesses nationwide jurisdiction. It is a decentralised, administrative government entity, meaning that it is not attached to the executive branch, and thus can act independently. ACODECO's director must be a university graduate and have a minimum of seven years of experience in commerce, customer service, financial services or other related fields.

The National Directory of Commerce, itself a division of ACODECO, is directly responsible for protecting the rights of commercial enterprises, and reports back to the administrative head of ACODECO. In merger cases, the national director of antitrust affairs acts as an entity of the first instance, while ACODECO's head administrator functions as an authority of the second instance. The administrator is appointed for a term of seven years, as a measure to guarantee their active independence. This period is, intentionally, two years longer than the presidential term, with the intention to make the administrator transcend the political influence of the election cycle. The administrator is designated by the current Panamanian president, and must be ratified before the National Assembly. Once their election has been ratified, the administrator can only be removed if their actions are deemed worthy of removal according to laws established by ACODECO. Behaviour worthy of removal from the position include such things as the permanent inability to fulfil their function, crimes against the state or national heritage, lack of integrity in the exercise of their responsibilities, disregard for what the laws forbids them from doing and general negligence. The decision on removal of the administrator falls to the Third Chamber of the Supreme Court, who holds a destitution trial to enact the administrator's removal.

Decisions about the *verification* of merger procedures are adopted by the national director of antitrust affairs, providing the merger parties with an appeal determined by the head administrator at ACODECO. After this appeal is exhausted, the decision of ACODECO remains final.

In addition to the protection and defence of competition, ACODECO has other duties, such as consumer protection, among others within the field of economic competition.

Among the duties that L45 attributes to ACODECO, regarding antitrust, are the following:

a) To investigate and sanction, within the limits of its jurisdiction, the actions and conducts prohibited by L45.
b) To advocate for free competition before economic agents, associations, educational institutions, non-profit entities, civil society organisations and the Public Administration, through which it may recommend, through technical-legal reports, the adoption or modification of any procedure or requirement of any sector of the national economy, or carry out studies in order to promote and strengthen competition in the market.
c) To be aware of the queries that economic agents and consumers submit for consideration, to carry out studies on market behaviour to detect distortions in the market economy system and to promote the elimination of such practices through their disclosure or the recommendation of legislative or administrative measures aimed at their correction.
d) To issue an opinion on their own initiative or at the request of municipalities, autonomous or semi-autonomous institutions and state institutions in general, when free competition or protection may be affected by their decisions, acts or draft laws.
e) To cease, at any stage of the investigation carried out at the administrative headquarters or after the judicial process has been promoted before the competent authority, the investigation or withdrawal of the judicial process, by carrying out transactions, after complying with the legal requirements, provided that the investigated or sued economic agents accept measures regarding the conduct or acts investigated, including criminal clauses that guarantee compliance with the agreement.
f) To investigate and verify monopolistic, anticompetitive or discriminatory practices by companies or entities that provide public services, in accordance with the provisions of this law and in accordance with the regulations and sectoral laws applicable to the public service in question. For this, ACODECO will request the support and collaboration of the technical personnel of the National Authority of Public Services.
g) To verify concentrations, in cases in which the parties to a concentration go before it *ex ante*.

This range of powers is complemented by the procedural authority that is granted to ACODECO, so that procedurally, it can institute judicial processes to obtain a declaration of illegality of conduct that it considers representative of restrictive practices of competition or illegal concentrations, as well as the capacity to integrate as a third party in processes not initiated by it, based on the use of popular action established in the Constitution to exercise the control of legality of prohibited antitrust behaviours.

Review of the listed or referred competences attributed to ACODECO serves to conclude that it can act as an investigating entity of conducts that may include activities prohibited by L45, as well as requiring a declaration of illegality before the competent courts, without excluding the corresponding sanctions. Finally, it is important to point out the power of ACODECO to sign a cooperation agreement with companies investigated for breach of antitrust rules. In these cases, ACODECO can reach an agreement and supervise the parties to confirm compliance avoiding judicial proceedings. These agreements can avoid or mitigate fines[7].

B. Judicial Component of the Antitrust System

Again, we must return to Article 295 of the Constitution. There it is established, among other things, that control of behaviours that may conflict with the protective regulations of competition rests with the judicial branch. In order to comply with this constitutional provision, L45 creates judicial offices, whose jurisdiction mainly revolves around the market dynamics.

The structure of these judicial seats follows that of the judicial branch, which in general terms is as follows: the first level comprises municipal courts. At the second level, are the circuit courts, which, in addition to exercising powers granted to them in the first instance, hear appeals from the municipal courts. The third level is made up of the higher courts, whose basic purpose is to be the *ad quem* of cases attributed in the first instance to the circuit courts. At the final level there is the Supreme Court of Justice, which hears extraordinary appeals (cassation). The list of powers that are attributed to the courts related to the antitrust regime are as follows:

a) Municipal courts do not hold jurisdiction over antitrust legality control.
b) Circuit courts: hear, in the first instance, cases generated by the infringement of the system of practices, vertical and horizontal restraints of competition, both in declarative claims and in convictions. Additionally, they are competent to authorise for ACODECO the practice of evidence as pre-trial discovery.
c) Superior court: hear appeals filed against the sentences handed down by the circuit courts. In addition, they will hear, uniquely, the challenges to acts constituting illegal mergers.
d) Civil Chamber of the Supreme Court of Justice, will hear the extraordinary appeal that is brought against the ruling handed down, such as *a quo* and *ad quem*, by the Superior Court.

As can be seen, the Panamanian antitrust authorities, has a heterogeneous nature (mixed), since it involves administrative and judicial entities. With this description, it is appropriate to address the matter of concentration regulation.

3. Type of Merger Control

As a general rule, there is no obligation to notify mergers. In any case, the legality of any particular merger is of an *ex post* nature, and as such attributed to the corresponding judges. This does not mean that there are no illegal mergers. These are included in what we call the rules of illegality, consisting of those "whose effect is or may be to

---

[7] <http://www.acodeco.gob.pa/acodeco/view.php?arbol=2&sec=3&pagi=0>.

decrease, restrict, damage or unreasonably prevent free economic competition and free competition with respect to the same, similar or substantially related goods or services"[8].

These circumstances give Panama a *sui generis* merger control. Before explaining this statement, it is important to clarify that formal legal control is under the judicial branch and is *ex post*. For this reason, the official definition of merger control is a judicial control. Having said that, it must also be said that ACODECO has an essential role in the antitrust system and in merger control specifically. It is because of this that ACODECO has the competence to hear the merging parties in what is known as *verification*. The justification for verification is to incentivise the merging parties to go voluntarily to ACODECO in order to review the merger in its legal aspects. Tis procedure is voluntary and there are no sanctions whether the parties choose to enter verification or not. The benefits produced for submitting the merger to verification begins once ACODECO has granted a favourable opinion to the merger. Therefore it cannot be challenged at all. This is important, because in the Panamanian antitrust system anybody is entitled to challenge all kinds of mergers. So, the risk of facing a challenge at any moment, up to the end of the statute of limitations, could be significant.

As seen, Panama has a type of control merger *sui generis*. The formal control operates as an *ex post* judicial trial, and the parties can go to ACODECO *ex ante* to obtain a favourable opinion, and thus approval of the merger.

II. Scope of Application

1. Definition of Notifiable Transaction

Pursuant to the general rule, there is no obligation to notify merger transactions. But the parties can go, voluntarily, to verification in order to obtain protection over their operation. In this context, the merger could be defined as horizontal merger, vertical merger or conglomerate merger[9].

It is worth noting that the antitrust regulations, in merger matters, are fundamentally dedicated to horizontal mergers. However, the regulations do foresee and apply loosely to vertical mergers, and even extend to conglomerate mergers. For this reason, our comments have grounds over the horizontal mergers.

L45 incorporates a definition of merger at article 21, which due to the importance it has for our work, we now reproduce:

> Article 21. Concept and prohibitions. A merger is understood to be the merger, acquisition of control or any act by which companies, associations, shares, trusts, establishments or assets in general are grouped, which is car-

---

8 L45, art 21, para 2.

9 According to the Guide, horizontal mergers take place between competitors, vertical mergers are made between clients' or suppliers' products or services, and conglomerates are those that occur between parties that have no obvious financial relationship. Guide, para 40.

> ried out between suppliers or potential suppliers, between clients or potential clients, and other competing economic agents or potential competitors among themselves. At the time of verifying the effect, the acquisition or merger may be taken into consideration if said economic concentration promotes and/or presents, within its objectives, the increase in the production or distribution of goods and/or services for the domestic market or international, fosters technical or economic progress or drives the competitive development of an industry or sector. In these cases, the benefits must be verifiable.
>
> Mergers whose effect is or may be to decrease, restrict, damage or unreasonably prevent free economic competition and free competition with respect to the same, similar or substantially related goods or services are prohibited.
>
> For the purposes of this chapter, the accidental associations that are made for a defined time to develop a certain project are not considered as prohibited mergers, as well as mergers between competitors or non-competitors that do not generate harmful effects for the competition and the market.
>
> Likewise, prohibited mergers are not considered to be those that fall on an economic agent that has systematically incurred losses and lost market share in a way that threatens its permanence in said market, provided that it proves to have unsuccessfully sought non-competing buyers. This matter will be regulated by the Guide.

Our conclusion, after examining the content of article 21, is that the legislator included much more than the definition of mergers. This provision contains several rules, which due to their relevance, we consider of interest to specify:

i. Establishment of the main characteristics of mergers: the first thing to note is that it is more than a definition of mergers. Article 21 contains a description of the ways in which the legislator understands how a merger can be configured. This definition is descriptive and not conceptual. It highlights from the first paragraph of the rule, where mergers are defined, that the parameters established there are the elements that perfect, constitute or configure a merger under Panamanian antitrust law: the union of rights or assets under the same control.
ii. Establishment of the prohibition rule: mergers, according article 21, are not generally prohibited. Only those that restrict competition in an unreasonable way are prohibited. Therefore, the prohibition rule examines the irrationality of the merger in question.
iii. The establishment of the rule of reason for the examination of legality of mergers.
iv. The verification of a merger in order to examine the degree of reasonableness, and thereby verify that it does not incur the parameters that would make it illegal (discussed below).

It is through these components that mergers in Panama are regulated. For this reason, the rest of the norms that L45 contains are related to the referenced elements.

2. Material Scope

A. Objectives of Panamanian Antitrust

L45 is the main instrument in competition policy of the Panamanian state. It establishes the institutional and regulatory system for market protection, as well as that of the consumer and users. Both substantive and procedural rules are established. Article 1 sets out the purposes of the law, which can be referred to as market efficiency and consumer protection. Both antitrust objectives lead to the prices achieved in the markets being the result of the purest interaction of supply and demand for goods and services, repressing those business practices that may affect the spontaneous price level. The importance of the above lies in the fact that Panamanian antitrust does not look for objectives other than those mentioned, so the protection of small and medium-sized companies, protection against the power of companies derived mainly from their size, or guardianship of employment levels are not part of the regulations.

B. Subjective Scope of Panamanian Antitrust

The general rule is that L45 applies to both nationals and foreigners, public entities and private equity companies, and even non-profit organisations. The exception to the rule is made up of four specific cases:

i. Collective labour agreements;
ii. Upholding of rights derived from intellectual property;
iii. Activities that the Constitution has reserved to the state, and that the state itself executes; and
iv. Those actions declared by the Cabinet Council to be of *public interest.*

From the context given in Article 3 of L45, it seems to be that only a situation of extreme abnormality would merit a public interest exception. L45 would have to constitute a faculty of the Cabinet Council to exempt a certain restrictive practice of competition, to the detriment of the rest of the competitors and the public, which conflicts, among other things, with the equality that should govern all acts that emanate from authority. And, further, without a doubt, the use of this power does not constitute a discretionary act of the Cabinet Council, with which it is subject to the control of legality attributed in our country to the Contentious – Administrative Jurisdiction, whose competence is exclusive to the Third Chamber of the Supreme Court of Justice, which is exercised in a single instance.

Specifically, regarding mergers, there are the following exceptions:

a) Accidental associations between competitors, to develop a certain project and for a defined time.
b) Formation of associations between competitors or non-competitors that do not affect competition or the market.
c) The doctrine of the failing firm or failing company.

3. Geographical Scope

Panama is a unitary republic. Therefore, all statutes apply throughout the country. In antitrust matters, the general rule is that L45 applies when the restrictive practice of competition has effect in the Panamanian jurisdiction. In the antitrust context, its territorial effects clause does not emphasise its application in the place of the conclusion of the act or contract that implements or constitutes the restrictive practice of competition, but the element that allows its application is that the violating act has effect in the Panamanian territory. Mergers fall under this rule[10].

4. Thresholds

Given that in Panama the general rule does not require notification to any authority, there are no quantitative nor qualitative thresholds. As an important issue the statute of limitation on the merger is three years, which enters in effect as soon as the merger has material effect.

III. Procedure

As mentioned, the *sui generis* type of merger control implies the need to explain both systems: the verification process exercised by ACODECO and the judicial trial for merger challenge.

1. Control Executed by ACODECO through the Verification Process

In simple terms, verification is the faculty attributed to ACODECO so that *ex ante* the coming into effect of the concentration in question, it decides on its legality. At this point it is necessary to return to the general rule: that in Panama, concentrations are allowed, regardless of their magnitude, be it quantitative or qualitative. Therefore, the companies involved in a concentration are not obliged to notify ACODECO or any other authority of the celebration or existence of the concentration in question. This causes ACODECO, in principle, to play a passive role vis-à-vis the concentrations, as it does not have competence or function to prevent them. For this situation, L45 encourages the participants in a concentration to consult ACODECO prior to the celebration or coming into effect of said operation; that is verification.

According to L45, if as a result of the verification ACODECO is favourable to the concentration, because it finds, after analysis, that in terms of efficiency it generates benefits, or at least, is neutral for the effects of the market, the concentration cannot be challenged before the competent courts for a declaration of its illicitness. This is equivalent, in material terms, to a declaration of legality of the concentration, to which is added the effect of *res judicata*. Although the regulations do not establish the latter, due to the impossibility of being contested once the concentration is verified by a favourable

---

10 L45, art 2.

opinion of ACODECO, only the court may be sued for defects in its confirmation, such as a falsehood provided by the parties to the concentration or that the information provided was not complete.

A. Launch of Procedure

Since verification is voluntary, the parties involved in the merger must present themselves to ACODECO in order to be verified. This consists of a petition, from the parties to ACODECO, requesting that the merger is awarded a favourable opinion. To do this, the parties must present, as a minimum, the following:

i. A description of the companies and representatives involved in the merger.
ii. Copy of the articles of incorporation and good standings of the companies involved.
iii. Financial statements, from as recent as the previous year, certified by a public accountant.
iv. Description of the capital structure of the companies involved, before and after the transaction merger.
v. Description of the transaction merger, its objectives, and a copy of the draft.
vi. Copies of relevant analysis and value-assessment on the business or investment project that the parties consider essential to the successful realisation of the merger.
vii. Precise, detailed plans of the times and stages at which the merger will take place.
viii. A non-competition clause detailing how the parties involved are bound to not compete against each other in the market, and to justify their existence.
ix. Description of the business, assets or service activity that the merger companies provide, as well as data on their participation in the market.
x. Description, when applicable, of the importance of the cost of transportation of the company's products, from the production facility to the designated points of commerce.
xi. Acknowledgement of the legal barriers, economic or otherwise, to entry in the market in which the merger companies intend to participate.
xii. A report, if the information is available, of the companies that have entered and exited the market within the last three years.
xiii. To divulge, when applicable, influences that the companies involved in the merger may possess over other companies that have already been integrated into the production chain.
xiv. Reference the main providers and clients of the economic agents involved in the merger.

The D8-A regulates the verification procedure, and highlights that ACODECO has 60 calendar days to issue its concept, with the characteristic that upon expiry of said term without ACODECO's pronouncement, a positive administrative silence will operate, taking the said silence as equivalent to an approval from ACODECO.

Once ACODECO has confirmed that the information delivered by the parties involved is thorough and complete, it will issue a confirmation that it holds the documentation necessary to perform a verification examination, and begins a 60-day countdown within which the examination must be completed. Before this confirmation, no timeline is announced.

B. Development of Procedure

ACODECO will perform a competition examination of the merger. This consists of an economic analysis of the merger, including how its execution would affect the market. The examination will take into account, foremost, the determination of the relevant market that may be affected by the merger, the *a priori* and *a posteriori* existence of substantial power on the part of the parties involved in the merger and, finally, a cost and benefit analysis, in economic terms, of the transaction merger.

During this time period, ACODECO does not usually issue any kind of communication. It is actually not expected to. In the best case scenario, if required, it will request new information from the involved parties. The confidentiality of the information provided rests solely with ACODECO.

C. Conclusion of Procedure

Along the same lines, the result from ACODECO can be favourable, conditional or unfavourable. In this sense, the entity may establish concentration measures, so that if these are not observed by its parties, the approval is not valid. The ACODECO decision is made, as previously stated, by the national director of antitrust affairs, and it can be challenged before the administrator in the form of an appeal remedy. When ACODECO does not approve the merger, it does not amount to a declaration of unlawfulness. This is because the jurisdiction to declare a merger illegal belongs to the ordinary jurisdiction, the civil branch, through the competent courts.

As a particular note, in the event of the merging parties deciding not to submit to a verification, ACODECO can begin an investigation, *sua sponte*, in order to collect evidence to file a lawsuit with the intent that the Superior Court declares the merger illegal. In this case, ACODECO is not obliged to serve the commencement of the investigation on the parties. In practice, ACODECO usually serves the process and requests documents and information from the parties. They are not obligated to cooperate with the investigation and may decide not to participate. However, attorneys usually recommend the parties to cooperate with ACODECO in the interest of starting the defence of the merger. So, this investigation is useful to file proof in order to clarify the facts and prove the efficiency defence, or a defence based on other grounds, like the non-existence of substantial power, or to discuss the definition of the market, or negotiate with ACODECO the measures that it can consider in order to not challenge the merger or convert the investigation to the verification process. In this latter context, ACODECO could enter an agreement with the parties regarding the conditions that it imposes in order to grant favourable opinion to the merger and end the administrative proceedings.

D. Sanctions

Since merger verification is voluntary, and since the objective is to obtain a favourable opinion from ACODECO, it is in its rights to determine, in case that it deems it, that the merger does not deserve a favourable opinion, thus denying it. From this, there comes no sanction of any kind. Given that the verification is *ex ante*, ACODECO may grant an unfavourable opinion, which does not impact the legality of the merger. However, even in these circumstances, ACODECO may not appeal to any tribunal to declare the merger illegal, as it does not exist. What ACODECO can do, instead, is initiate and conduct an investigation for the supposed illegality of the merger denied. The result of that investigation is ACODECO's decision to file a claim again the parties involved in the merger. It requires that the merger has been concluded. Under L45 ACODECO may enact provisional measures to suspend the execution of those mergers. After ACODECO issues this kind of act, it must appear before the Superior Court and file a formal claim against the merger. Once the Superior Court had received the claim, it has the power to keep or lift the measure taken by ACODECO.

2. Judicial Trial for Merger Challenge

According to the antitrust law, control of the legality of the concentrations falls to the judicial branch, through the competent courts.

A. Launch of Procedure

First and foremost, the venue for carrying these kinds of cases is the Third Superior Court of Justice, of the judicial district of Panama, in Panama City. This judicial office has jurisdiction in this matter within the entire territory of the Republic of Panama. As the Panamanian Constitution establishes that any person can challenge any act related to the violation of antitrust laws, any person can present a lawsuit demanding for a particular merger to be declared illegal.

The process by which the judicial challenge of the merger is provided is of sole instance, which is why the sentence that decides it does not admit ordinary remedies. The judicial decision can only be challenged through the extraordinary appeal process (cassation), heard by the First Chamber of the Supreme Court.

B. Development of Procedure

This process follows the model established by US federal rules. It is characterised by the following stages:

i. The lawsuit can be filed by anyone, since the challenge is conceived as a group action.
ii. After the claim has been presented and replied, a hearing is held (preliminary hearing), the purpose of which is to organise the dispute and examine its scope, in order to determine which facts must be proven and which party assumes its burden of proof, as well as fixing the number of expert witnesses that each party will present.

iii. Subsequently, the merits hearing is held. The witnesses that each party offers are presented, together with documents, expert witness reports, judicial inspections or reports that the parties wish to propose.
iv. After the previous session, another hearing is held, in order for the parties to present their closing arguments.
v. The final act is the ruling by the court.
vi. It is anticipated that the parties can manage the production and collection of information as evidence, or evidence itself, through "discovery" process, also a concept of American origin.
vii. There is no rule to indicate which is the test or standard used by the Superior Court to analyse the legality of the challenged merger. This question could be treated as a lack of regulation, and in this case the Superior Court will apply the Guide. So, the Guide is the rules that the Superior Court will employ in ruling the case.

C. Conclusion of Procedure

The Superior Court decision must contain the decision of the claim included in the lawsuit filed to contest the merger. It will contain the declaration of illegality or the decision to dismiss the claim on the contested concentration. However, and as a different matter from ordinary civil procedures, the principle of coherence is flexible. This is because when resolving a claim of illegality of the contested concentration, the Superior Court can enact *sua sponte* decree measures that condition the legality of the concentration. These measures would be the same measures that ACODECO can order within the *verification* process. It must also decide on whether or not to grant the damages claimed.

D. Sanctions

If a merger is considered illegal by the Superior Court, two types of sanctions apply. The first is the imposition of a fine by ACODECO. This fine will be up to the sum of US$250,000, and can only be imposed when the sentence that decrees the illegal merger is final.

The other sanction that implies that the merger is declared illegal is the ruling based on the doctrine of treble damages. It is important to note that this condemnation is considered a sanction, due to its nature of punitive damage, since the general rule in Panama is that there are no punitive damages. In the event that the damages ruling is obtained by reason of a challenge action at the request of ACODECO, said damages would be for the people who actually suffered loss.

In the event that the judicial process to challenge the merger begins as a result of a denouncement made before ACODECO, which in turn conducts out an investigation that ends with the decision to file a lawsuit with the Superior Court to contest the merger, L45 provides a reward equal to 25% of the fine imposed for the illegal merger. This reward will belong to whoever made the denouncement. It should be noted that this person does not participate in the merger challenge.

IV. Substance

1. Competition Analysis

In the verification process, through the rule of reason approach, based on the information presented by the interested party, ACODECO carries out an efficiency examination, on the following points[11]:

i. Relevant market: The delimitation of the relevant market for concentrations is linked by mandate of article 28 of L45, with the provisions of articles 8 and 18. The analysis is carried out to determine the relevant market has two parameters; the product market and the geographic market.
ii. Substantial power of the parties to the concentration in the relevant market: similar to the relevant market, the regulation of substantial power is linked to concentrations pursuant to article 19 of L45, by mandate of article 28. The analysis of substantial power is carried out based on the concentration that exists before and after the operation in question. The degree of concentration is calculated through the concurrence of two analytical tools, the Herfindahl-Hirschman index and the Dominance index.
iii. Effects of concentration on the rest of the market, specifically, on barriers to entry for new competitors.

This element belonging to the economic analysis of the mergers is specified by two precise extremes: the capacity that the corresponding business entity has after the concentration operation to abuse its position, and the possibility that the merger allows the resulting business entity to conduct collusive practices.

According to the Guide, a company's ability to abuse its post-merger market position will depend on the degree of effective market competition that other companies outside the merger may hold. The Guide defines this situation as the capacity for rival enterprises to "sustain aggressive measures to maintain or increase their market share"[12].

Instead of listing scenarios that may avoid this situation, ACODECO highlights, in the Guide, three specific events that allow the exercise of market power over the company resulting from the merger (insiders): the absence of alternative competitors; markets without substitute products; and the event that the merger may generate a verticalisation that could increase the cost of competition for businesses outside the merger.

As to the increase in possibilities for collusive conducts, the Guide establishes that this scenario will depend on the level of business stability found in the rest of the competitors in the market. This way, if effective market competition is not impacted severely by the merger, this stability has potential to create collusive agreements, especially because the condition of stability facilitates the supervision of the agreements by the parties involved.

---

11 All these elements are in the Guide, note 7.

12 See Guide, note 7, para 152.

2. Statistics

Due to the size of the Panamanian economy, there are few merger operations. However, there were some cases in 2019, all managed by ACODECO, meaning that during 2019 there was no judicial challenge to merger operations.

We found four cases; three from the verification process, and one from an investigation carried out by ACODECO[13].

The cases filed to the verification process were the following:

No	Parties	Activity	Decision
1	Distribuidora Petro Hielo, S.A., Oasis Tropical, S.A. (vendor) and Hielo Ameglio, S.A. (buyer)	Ice markers	Conditioned
2	Western Excellence, Inc. (vendor) and DMPTY, Inc. (buyer)	Ice cream	Favourable opinion
3	Cable Onda, S.A. (vendor) and Telefónica Móviles de Panamá, S.A. (buyer)	Cable TV	Favourable opinion

3. Case Law Illustration

To offer a case law illustration we will cite the only case that was conditioned in order to get concept favourable as an output of the verification instance by ACODECO. The description of the case is the following:

i. Parties: The vendor was Petro Hielo, S.A. and Oasis Tropical, S.A. and buyer was Hielo Ameglio, S.A[14].
ii. Type of agreement: acquisition of 100% of the shares of both vendor companies.
iii. Act issued by ACODECO: Resolution No DNLC-HCE-004-19 of 3 April 2019.
iv. Description of market: Ice makers.
v. Brief description of transaction: The vendor was a single economic agent split into two different companies duly by the vertical integration to serve the market. Market share's vendors join them as the second party of all companies which participated in this market. The buyer was the third. The parties of the share purchase agreement agreed a no-competition clause with a duration of five years.
vi. Analysis made by ACODECO:
    a) The share purchase agreement places the buyer in a position capable of performing vertical restrictive practices of competition: as a result of

---

13 See <http://www.acodeco.gob.pa/acodeco/view.php?arbol=1&sec=11&pagi=0>.
14 ibid.

calculations made by ACODECO about the position a company might occupy after a merger, it reflects an increment in the degree of integration into the production chain. This, on general principle, would mean an advantage that would impede the entry of new competitors into the market, and therefore the emergence of restrictive vertical practices from the competitors. Nevertheless, in the time prior to the merger, if new brands and distributors entered the pertinent market, which may not be significant enough to affect the competition of the insiders, the position the merger will result in will not alter the conditions that will allow the entry of new competitors. Within this phenomenon, risk is mitigated by the increase in the degree of vertical integration produced by the merger.

b) According to ACODECO, in the market in which the merger operates, there existed an effective rivalry between its members, since in the time around when the merger was executed, outsider competition could be reliably observed. There is constancy in the incident of market strategies on the part of outsider companies to generate larger market shares, via the concurrence of pre-existing routes and strategies, as well as entrepreneurship on to new routes;

c) In the latter years new economic agents had entered the relevant market;

d) Due to the grade of effectiveness of the competition the power of the market reached by the buyer is not allowed to incur vertical restriction practices.

The conjunction of described elements in points a) and b) denote a level of market competition sufficient to impede unilateral behaviour on the part of the company resulting from the merger.

vii. Condition imposed by ACODECO: ACODECO's objection was for the time of the non-compete agreement. ACODECO agreed with a deadline of three years. The parties accepted the condition imposed by ACODECO.

PARAGUAY

Cynthia Andino*

(Independent consultant on competition and commerce)

Abstract

The National Constitution of Paraguay, in force since 1992, establishes competition as part of its legal framework. Later, the Competition Defence Act was enacted on 2013 (Law No 4956/2013) and its Rules on 2014, which regulates merger and acquisitions control. Law No 4956 created the National Competition Commission (CONACOM) as the national independent and autonomous administrative competition authority. It has two bodies, the board of directors and the Investigations Bureau. The Competition Defence Act allows for an ex post or ex ante mandatory economic concentration filing. In practice, all filings have been filed ex post. The evaluation of a concentration filing is carried out in two stages. The first stage has a timeframe of 30 business days. In this "fast-track" stage, CONACOM can authorise economic concentrations compatible with the market that do not raise or imply a significant obstacle to effective competition. The second stage has a time frame of 60 business days for more complicated matters. The competition law contemplates structural and/or behavioural remedies. The fines for gun-jumping include the imposition of conditions to do or stop doing an act, conditions to stop the effects of prohibited conducts contrary to the public interest, fines, nullification of the economic concentration and/or other measures the authority deems proper.

---

* Cynthia Andino is an independent consultant on competition and commerce. She holds a Master's in droit des affaires, University of Strasbourg and a European Master's in transnational trade law and finance, University of Deusto and University of Tilburg. Mrs Andino participated in the Commission that drafted Paraguay's Competition Defence Act and was Paraguay's coordinator for UNCTAD's COMPAL programme. She participated in the Trade Defence and Competition Commission of MERCOSUR, and the negotiation group for the EU – MERCOSUR Trade Agreement Competition and Trade Remedies Chapters. The author thanks the contribution of Charles Reeves and David Sperber. She also expresses gratitude to the members of UNCTAD's delegation and the foreign national authorities who supported the Ministry of Industry and Commerce (MIC) during the law-making process.

I. Introduction

1. Brief Overview

The National Constitution of Paraguay, in force since 1992[1], establishes the following:

> **Article 107 – Competition**
>
> Everyone has the right to engage in lawful economic activity of their choice, within a regime of equal opportunities. Market competition is guaranteed. The creation of monopolies and the artificial rise or fall of prices or breach of competition, usury and unauthorised trade that creates harm will not be allowed and will be sanctioned by the Criminal Law.

The technical assistance of the UN Conference on Trade and Development (UNCTAD) helped set the groundwork for the enactment of the Paraguayan Competition Defence Act (*Ley de Defensa de la Competencia*). In 2009 UNCTAD sent a work mission[2] to raise public and private awareness of the need to adopt a competition law. The mission was received by the then president of the Republic of Paraguay, as well the minister and vice-minister of the Ministry of Industry and Commerce (MIC), the author, the MIC director of standards and trade negotiations, various authorities from the Department of Competition, and UNCTAD Competition and Consumer Defence, members of the Basque Court of Defense of Competition (TVDC), a representative of the Administrative Council for Economic Defence of Brazil (CADE) and a representative of the National Economic Prosecutor's Office of Chile (FNE).

The UNCTAD mission presented to the Paraguayan president the need for competition legislation and regulation, and laid forth the benefits such regulation generates for commerce, the market and consumer welfare. Subsequently, meetings with Congress (*Congreso de la Nación*), as well as seminars and workshops, were held. The mission's work was complemented by the contributions of experts with the academy and representatives of the private sector.

USAID provided technical assistance in 2010. Paraguay also received visits of experts from Federal Trade Commission (FTC) and the Competition Court of Chile (TDLC)[3]. These missions also raised awareness for competition regulation with legislative members and advisers, academia, private corporations and the general public.

The first bill of the Paraguayan Competition Defence Act was submitted by the MIC to Congress in 2003. While well received, it was not allowed a floor vote. Among other draft bills, a preliminary bill drafted by the private sector[4] was subsequently submitted to Congress in 2010.

---

1 Paraguay Carta Magna. In force on 20 June 1992.

2 UNCTAD, 3rd Annual Conference of the COMPAL Programme (Lima, 20–22 June 2012), <unctadcompal.org/wp-content/uploads/2017/03/LIBRO-DE-PONENCIAS-III-CONF-ANUAL-COMPAL-jun-2012.pdf>. The delegates were Hassan Qaqaya, Pierre Horna (UNCTAD), Juan Luis Crucelegui, Joseba Andoni Bikandi (TVDC), Fernando Furlan (CADE) and Monica Salamanca (FNE).

3 The delegates were Armando Irizarry and Ellen Connelly (FTC) and Javier Velozo (TDLC).

4 "Feprinco presentó propuesta sobre ley de competencia" (*Diario ABC*, 19 April 2010) <www.abc.com.py/edicion-impresa/economia/feprinco-presento-propuesta-sobre-ley-de-competencia-92122.html>.

Starting in 2011, the MIC, in collaboration with the private sector and UNCTAD, presented a new preliminary draft bill of the Competition Defence Act to Congress. However, some sectors and the NGO *Base Investigaciones sociales*[5], objected to this bill. They argued that it was harmful to the general interest and that it was prepared by the private sector. This preliminary draft bill was subsequently modified and approved. It was enacted on 25 June 2013 as Law No 4956/2013, the Competition Defence Act. The Rules regulating the Competition Defence Act were enacted on 14 April 2014. Lastly, CONACOM issued a Manual on Filing Concentration Transactions[6] and a filing fee form[7].

2. Institutional Set-Up

Law No 4956 created the National Competition Commission (CONACOM) as the national administrative competition authority. Although CONACOM is part of the executive branch under the MIC, it enjoys full autonomy and independence, and it is not subordinate to the MIC. The relationship between the two institutions is relegated to the MIC's presentation of the list of candidates to the executive branch for the designation of CONACOM authorities.

CONACOM has a public administrative nature. Its decisions can only be revised though reconsideration or reinstatement. Appeals are heard by the Administrative Court of Appeals (*Tribunal de Cuentas*).

Law No 4956 establishes two organic and administrative bodies for CONACOM:

a) The board of directors (*Directorio*) issues resolutions and sanctions (resolution body); and,
b) The Investigations Bureau (*Dirección de Investigación*) investigates competition matters (investigatory body).

The board of directors is comprised of three members. They shall be lawyers, economists, accountants or business administrators, and are appointed by the executive branch. The Board of Qualifications (*Junta de Calificaciones*) selects candidates from a list of applicants submitted by the MIC and approved by the executive branch. Board members serve a six-year term. They can be reappointed for a second term.

The Investigations Bureau is presided by a director. The director is appointed in the same fashion as the members of the board of directors. The director serves for a five-year term and apparently can be reappointed indefinitely.

---

5 See BASE Investigaciones sociales, "Proyecto de Ley de Defensa de la Competencia en realidad defiende a las Corporaciones" <<www.baseis.org.py/proyecto-de-ley-de-defensa-de-la-competencia-en-realidad-defiende-a-las-corporaciones/>; Aún no se presenta ley de competencia que garantice beneficios al consumidor (*Diario ABC*, 13 June 2010), *<www.abc.com.py/edicion-impresa/economia/aun-no-se-presenta-ley--de-competencia-que-garantice-beneficios-al-consumidor-116336.html>.*

6 CONACOM, Resolution 34, 31 May 2019.

7 CONACOM, Resolution 56, 31 October 2019.

The procedure for confirming the shortlist of members for the board of directors is unusual, as the Board of Qualifications[8] is made up of four representatives from the public sector and four from the private sector. The Board of Qualifications was created at the request of the private Federation of Production, Industry and Commerce (Feprinco).

The board of directors' main functions are:

a) Deciding cases within its subject matter jurisdiction.
b) Ordering the instruction of anticompetitive cases.
c) Authorising, conditioning, or denying economic concentration operations subject to Law No 4956.
d) Sanctioning violations of Law No 4956.

3. Type of Merger Control

The regulatory mechanism for the control of commercial operations in Paraguay is *ex post*[9], as Article 14 mandates:

> "Concentration operations shall be notified and registered in the Registry of Concentrations of the Competition Authority within 10 days of their execution, running from the following day of the date of the written agreement, or the publication of the purchase offer, exchange or acquisition of a controlling interest when at least one of the two circumstances are met …".

Notwithstanding, Article 14 of the Rules states that: "natural or legal persons may request prior authorisation of a concentration operation. In such event, the rules on notification, evaluation and decision of the board of directors are applied according to the Law and these Rules."

Thus Paraguay allows for both *ex post* and *ex ante* filings of economic concentrations. In practice, however, the parties in economic concentrations file *ex post.* It is worth noting that Paraguayan regulations do not contemplate the suspension of concentration activities during the investigation stage.

II. Scope of Application

1. Definition of Notifiable Transaction

The notifiable transactions include: mergers, acquisitions, purchase of assets, change of control, consortiums or joint ventures and the like. In cases when two or more of these transactions have taken place during two years between the same participants, it

8 Nicaragua has a similar structure, however, it is unusual and contrary to international doctrine that the private sector participates directly in the selection of Competition Authority members, since this could compromise its independence and generate conflicts of interest. For this reason, and pursuant to the Voluntary Peer Review of Competition Law and Policy of Nicaragua by UNCTAD in 2013 (UNCTAD/DITC/CLP/2013/2), it was recommended that Nicaragua modify its appointment mechanism for members of *Procompetencia*.

9 During discussions of the draft of the Defence Competition Act the MIC recommended *ex ante* filling, but this was not accepted by the private sector.

will be considered to be a single concentration operation carried out on the date of the last transaction.

2. Material Scope

Economic concentration regulation includes all sectors. Exceptions include the holding shares or financial securities for up to one year. Decisions by the public authority in cases of bankruptcy, insolvency, liquidation, suspension of payments, or other similar procedure are also considered to be exceptions.

3. Geographical Scope

The geographical scope of economic concentration control is at national or regional level.

4. Thresholds

Pursuant to Article 14, the non-cumulative filing thresholds are:

a) Acquire or increase a [market] share equal to or greater than 45% of the national market for a given product or service, or of a geographic market defined within it; [or]

b) The total gross income in the Republic of Paraguay of all the participating parties of a concentration, in the terms of the previous article, in excess of 100,000 (one hundred thousand) monthly minimum wages of the last year[10].

III. Procedure

1. Launch of Procedure

Article 14.3(a) establishes that the two parties shall file an economic concentration when both parties gain or have joint control (or similar), such as in joint purchases, consortiums, joint ventures, associations or mergers. Article 15 of the Rules determines that in the event of an acquisition of control, the buyer or acquiring party shall make the concentration operation filing.

Concentration operations must be notified and registered in the Registry of Concentrations of the Competition Authority within 10 days of execution, running from the day following the date of the written agreement, or the publication of the purchase offer, swap or acquisition of a controlling interest when at least one of the two aforementioned thresholds has been met. Digital filings are not possible.

The filing fee is calculated based on the transaction's value from 0.1% to 0.005%. The minimum percentage applies to higher values. We compared other Latin American jurisdictions and constitutes a very small fee amount. For example, a USD 20 million transaction will pay 0.005% or USD 1,000.

---

10 On 1 January 2020 the monthly minimum wage was ₲2,192.839 = USD 336.

2. Development of Procedure

The evaluation of a concentration filing is carried out in two stages. The first stage has a time frame of 30 business days. In this fast-track stage, CONACOM can authorise economic concentrations compatible with the market when they do not raise or imply a significant obstacle to effective competition. The second stage has a time frame of 60 business days.

CONACOM subsequently has a term of 90 business days to resolve the concentration operation. It can either authorise, subordinate with conditions or deny it. If CONACOM has not issued a ruling within this 90-day period, the operation will be deemed to have been tacitly approved.

Law No 4956/2013 does not establish an extension for the 90-day period. The Rules, however, establish that if CONACOM requests additional information during the second stage, an additional term of 15 business days (renewable for an additional 15 days) will be granted for these purposes. Therefore, upon a CONACOM request for additional information, an extension of up to 30 business days may be granted. Thus, the second phase may have a duration of up to 90 business days, and the entire procedure could have a duration of up to 120 business days.

CONACOM may request the following information:

a) Information on the objectives, aims, economic and financial foundations of the transaction.
b) Detailed information on the products and services involved in the transaction.
c) Detailed information on the relevant market(s) affected by the transaction.
d) Information on competitors and the degree of competition existing in the relevant market(s).
e) Information on the origin of the products and/or services produced or marketed.
f) Information of customers or consumers, the production process and the installed capacity.
g) Costs of production, distribution, sale and supplies.
h) Information on distribution and marketing, distribution channels, prices and transportation costs.
i) Information on foreign trade and consumption, tariffs, duties and other import restrictions on the market(s) of the products and/or services involved in the transaction.
j) Information on the elements that determine barriers of entry and exit, the ease or difficulty of access to the market of the transaction.
k) Detailed description of the effects of the transaction on the market(s) for the products and/or services involved, as well as the economic efficiencies generated by it.
l) Any additional information that CONACOM deems necessary for the analysis of the effects of the transaction on competition.

Correspondingly, any public or private person has a duty to collaborate with CONACOM and is obliged to provide all data and information necessary for the application of the Competition Defence Act.

In this sense, the law stipulates the cooperation of the different institutions of public government and regulatory entities. Foreign cooperation with international organisations is stipulated in the Rules through CONACOM's International Relations and Cooperation division.

3. Conclusion of Procedure

CONACOM, in the first stage (fast track) of the evaluation of the filing, may approve economic concentrations that evidently do not represent a significant obstacle to effective competition.

In the case of a second stage, and after the compatibility analysis period of the filing, the board of directors by resolution will either:

a) Authorise the transaction; or,
b) Subordinate the authorisation of the transaction to the fulfilment of conditions and/or measures; or,
c) Reject the transaction.

The Rules establish that CONACOM may subordinate the authorisation to the fulfilment of measures for those transactions that pose an obstacle to effective competition in the market, since the consequences directly derived from it are offset by the gains of economic efficiency generated. On the other hand, it is important that an increase in the market quota by the buyer does not constitute conclusive evidence about the incompatibility of the transaction.

As mentioned before, if the board of directors does not resolve a matter within the prescribed time frame the transaction is approved by affirmative administrative silence.

As for remedies, CONACOM may impose structural and behavioural conditions, which shall be proportional to the objective sought. The remedies are directly linked to overcoming the creation or strengthening of a dominant position in the relevant market(s), which could later create an obstacle to competition.

The head of the Department of Concentrations Control (*Jefe del Departamento de Control de Concentraciones*) is in charge of monitoring compliance with imposed remedies.

The board of directors decisions can only be revised though reconsideration or reinstatement, although its decisions can be appealed at the Administrative Court of Appeals (*Tribunal de Cuentas*).

4. Sanctions

In the event of gun-jumping, CONACOM will automatically request the parties to notify the transaction within 20 business days. The Rules clarify that gun-jumping can be fined with the following:

a) The imposition of conditions or obligations to do or stop doing an act;
b) Stopping or removing the effects of prohibited conduct contrary to the public interest;

c) Fines equivalent to 150% of profits gained through the illegal conduct or up to 20% of the gross turnover of the sale (excluding taxes) of products of the infringing practice in the relevant market in the last 12 months. These fines may not be less than the advantage obtained, when it is quantifiable;
d) Nullification of the economic concentration or transaction; and/or
e) Any other measures authorised by Law N 4956.

All persons, public or private, are subject to a duty of cooperation with CONACOM and are obliged to provide the requested information. So, failure or refusal to deliver such information is punishable with a fine to public entities. The fines, according with the Rules for non-compliance with the information requirement includes public and private persons. The fine may be between 10 and 300 daily minimum wages[11], depending on the relevance of the information required. This fine can be repeatedly doubled until the information is provided.

IV. Substance

1. Competition Analysis

The following will be taken into account in the evaluation of an economic concentration:

a) The structure of relevant markets.
b) The necessity to preserve and develop effective competition in markets.
c) The actual or potential competition from competitors located in or outside Paraguay.
d) The market situation of the participating competitors, as well as their economic and financial strength. The availability of suppliers and access to supply sources or markets.
e) The existence of de facto or legal obstacles to accessing said markets.
f) The evolution of the supply and demand of the products and/or services of the relevant market.
g) The interests of intermediate and final consumers.
h) The evolution of technical or economic progress, provided that this is for the benefit of consumers and does not constitute an obstacle to competition.

The following considerations, amongst others, can be taken into account when conducting the compatibility analysis of a transaction within the market:

a) If the transaction produces a concentration increase in the relevant market, and as result, the concentrated market generates levels that pose an obstacle to effective competition.
b) If the transaction facilitates conducts or practices that pose an obstacle to effective competition, as well as entry barriers to new competitors, by creating or reinforcing a dominant position in the relevant market.

---

11 Approximately USD 129 – 3,877 as at 1 January 2020. Modified by Decree 3488 of 26 March 2020.

c) If the transaction has, or may have, the purpose of unduly displacing other persons from the relevant market, or prevents them from accessing it, especially in economic concentration operations between persons located at different stages of vertical competition.

As per the analysis of economic efficiency gains produced by an economic concentration, the following will be taken into account:

a) Production efficiencies related to cost reduction; and,
b) Dynamic efficiencies related to the development of new or better products.

The filing party shall have the burden of proof to demonstrate the gains in economic efficiency.

2. Statistics

Although CONACOM was created by Law No 4956 in 2013, the board of directors was not appointed until 31 July 2015[12], following a problem between some local television channels who stated they were not working[13]. The first resolution issued by CONACOM was its Code of Ethics in 2015. Until April 2016, the Institution did not have its own physical space to operate or a website.

The following are the statistics on concentration filings and decisions (from CONACOM's website):

- 2017 – 8 filings: 1 resolved with remedies, 1 denial, 1 non-submission (gun-jumping), and 6 grants of authorisation.
- 2018 – 4 filings: 1 resolved with remedies and 3 grants of authorisation.
- 2019 – 2 filings: 2 resolved with remedies.

Since CONACOM initiated its operations it has resolved 14 filings: 9 authorised without remedies, 4 authorised with remedies, 1 non-submission (gun-jumping) and 1 denial.

3. Case Law Illustration

A. Coca-Cola Acquires AdeS and AdeZ[14]

The CocaCola Company and Coca-Cola Femsa S.A.B. de C. V. acquired AdeS/AdeZ trademarks, which was owned by Unilever Paraguay[15]. It is a ready-to-drink juice with trademarks AdeS/AdeZ. In Paraguay, the transaction was fully analysed during the second stage. CONACOM analysed trademarks, raw material, supply, components and inventory, and the domain name (<ades.com.py>). The AdeS product is mainly a soya drink with juice flavour.

---

12 Presidential decree No 3842, 31 July 2015, <www.presidencia.gov.py/archivos/documentos/DECRETO3842_9njxlzw3.pdf>.

13 "Defensor de la competencia-todavia-no-opera" (*Diario ABC*, 22 September 2015), <www.abc.com.py/edicion-impresa/economia/defensor-de-la-competencia-todavia-no-opera-1410443.html>.

14 CONACOM, Resolution No 1/2017, 23 February 2017, <www.conacom.gov.py/ambitos-de-actuacion>.

15 Ingrid Rojas, "Coca-Cola obtiene autorizacion para adquisicion de AdeS en Paraguay asistida por Berkemeyer" (Lexlatin, 13 March 2017), <lexlatin.com/portal/noticias/coca-cola-obtiene-autorizacion-para-adquisicion-de-ades-en-paraguay-asistida-por>.

On 15 June 2016 the Buyer presented an acquisition filing at CONACOM. The transaction was fully evaluated during the second stage. CONACOM analysed these elements to determine the relevant market and the products substitution:

a) Nutritional content and function of the product and the competitors.
b) Product formula.
c) Marketing and sales.
d) Final consumers' desire.
e) Distribution channels.
f) Competitors and their production capacity.
g) Barriers to entry.
h) CONACOM confirmed they did not have the history of the relevant market products substitution, cross-elasticity, consumers habits and final clients' opinion.

The buyer claimed that AdeS was not a substitutive product of other juices. Nevertheless, CONACOM disagreed and declared the "ready-to-drink juices" as the relevant market. The relevant market has at least four main competitors. After the acquisition, the buyer will have more than 50% of the ready-to-drink juices market. Since the main distribution channel of this product is supermarket retail, and the competitors have power to compete with the acquiring company, no remedies were ordered[16].

In this case the Investigations Bureau issued its opinion recommending the authorisation of this concentration operation with remedies[17]. The board, however, concluded that due to the substitutability of the analysed products the case did not present future competition problems or the creation of a dominant position. Thus remedies cannot be imposed in the absence of competition problems.

B. Copetrol Acquired Petrobras Gas Stations in Paraguay[18]

This section includes a summary based on public information and CONACOM's Resolution 3/2019. Corporación Paraguaya Distribuidora de Derivados del Petróleo S.A. (Copetrol) a producer and distributor of fuels and lubricants acquired control of stock (purchase of assets[19]) of Petroleum Brasileiro SA (Petrobras, through its subsidiary Paraguay Energy S.A (PE) in Paraguay).

CONACOM's analysis included the following:

a) Market share.
b) Number and capacity of its competitors.
c) The products and brands of the parties, as well as their participation and growth in the relevant market.
d) Substitute products and barriers to entry.

---

16 CONACOM, Resolution No 1/2017, note 15.

17 CONACOM, PARECER/DI/N01, 16 February 2017.

18 CONACOM, Resolution No 3/2019, 5 January 2019, <www.conacom.gov.py/ambitos-de-actuacion>.

19 This terminology was used by the buyer in the filing.

e) The infrastructure and installation capacity for the provision of the relevant markets' services.
f) Product distribution and sales channels.
g) The ability of potential competition to exist in the short term.
h) The existence or creation of a dominant position.
i) Other efficiencies.

It should be noted that according to the public version of the Investigations Bureau's report on this transaction[20], paragraph 240 states that: "… if the dominance persists in the relevant markets, this Bureau is of the opinion that the analysed transaction is incompatible with Law No 4956/13."

Notwithstanding the above, and as a principle of law, the opinion of the Investigations Bureau is not binding on the board of directors decision-making and is not obliged to agree with the findings in the investigators' report. This is what happened in this case.

The amount of the transaction was approximately USD 383.5 million. It was concluded on 27 June 2018. The filing was made to CONACOM on 11 July 2018. Since the transaction surpassed the threshold of more than 100,000 minimum wage salaries (approx. USD 33,600.000) it was fully analysed by CONACOM. On 5 February 2019, CONACOM authorised Copetrol's acquisition of all PE shares and determined the behavioural and structural conditions and remedies.

Structural remedies:

a) Copetrol cannot combine the Copetrol and Petrobras brands in more than 50% of the gas service stations in the different cities of the country.

Behavioural remedies:

b) Copetrol and PE shall maintain suggested retail prices for naphtha, diesel and special alcohol products in certain cities.
c) Copetrol and PE shall maintain sales prices established by certain municipalities for Diesel III or C products, and may not sell above these sales prices to the public.
d) Copetrol and PE shall maintain the offer of oil and gas freight services in market conditions
e) Copetrol and PE shall keep offering oil and gas tank storage services in market conditions.

These remedies are for a three-year period.

Paraguay's former Secretary of Finance, economist Cesar Barreto[21], affirmed that Copetrol will gain 30% of the relevant national market after closing the transaction. It will serve as an important benchmark and player. He also mentioned that the brands

---

20 CONACOM, PARECER/DI/N01/2019.

21 "Analista estima que copetrol" (*Diario Última Hora*, 2 July 2018), <www.ultimahora.com/analista-estima-que-copetrol-n1303089.html>.

will continue to operate independently and there will be no merger of the distinctive signs. The former secretary indicated that: "There will be vertical integration throughout the distribution channels. We are going to have three or four large groups that are going to manage 60% of the market, and six to seven small companies that will have an important role as well."

This acquisition is considered one of the largest private sector financial transactions in the history of Paraguay, with a value of USD 383.5 million. Before the transaction, PE had 197 gas service stations and Copetrol had 355 gas service stations nationwide. Thus after the transaction it now operates 552 gas service stations in the country.

According to Copetrol administrators, despite the purchase of 100% of PE shares, both brands will continue to operate independently. The share package, however, will correspond to Copetrol as sole owner. Some analysts consider that after the transaction Copetrol became the leader of this relevant market of the sale of gas and hydrocarbons[22].

C. Copetrol Acquired Axion in Paraguay[23]

On 1 February 2019 Copetrol signed an agreement to acquire the assets of gas retailer Axion Energy Paraguay S.R.L[24]. (Axion), a subsidiary of Pan American Energy S.L., Argentina Branch (PAE) based in Paraguay. This purchase of assets occurred after Copetrol's acquisition of Petrobras on June 2018. It was authorised by CONACOM in February 2019. Axion had 3% of the market share in 2018 with 40 gas service stations[25].

On 6 December 2019, CONACOM authorised (with remedies) the economic concentration. The remedies are:

Structural remedies:

a) Limit on the number of gas service stations that operate under any of the trademarks of Copetrol Group to a maximum of 50% of the total gas service stations that operate in Asunción.

Behavioural remedies:

b) Copetrol Group shall maintain the suggested retail prices for gasoline, special diesel and alcohol, and retail prices for type III or C diesel, for all service stations operating with one of its trademarks in the greater Asunción area.

---

22 *Diario La Nación*, 27 June 2018),

23 CONACOM, Resolution No. 29/2019, 6 December 2019, <www.conacom.gov.py/ambitos-de-actuacion>.

24 Ingrid Rojas, "Copetrol subscribe acuerdo para adquirir activos de Axion Energy en Paraguay" (LexLatin, 25 February 2019), <lexlatin.com/noticias/copetrol-suscribe-acuerdo-para-adquirir-activos-de-axion-energy-en-paraguay>.

25 Revista Plus. 26 February 2019. <www.revistaplus.com.py/2019/02/26/copetrol-compra-todas-las-estaciones-de-servicio-de-axion-energy-en-paraguay/. Cronista. <www.cronista.com/apertura-negocio/empresas/Axion-Energy-vende-todas-sus-estaciones-de-servicio-en-Paraguay-20190225-0005.html

c) Copetrol Group shall continue to offer sale prices to third parties under conditions no less favourable than those offered to companies within its group.
d) Copetrol Group shall continue offering tank storage services under market conditions without discrimination.

Such remedies will be valid for three years from its compliance date.

In our opinion, CONACOM should have imposed a prohibition on Copetrol acquiring the same or similar assets in Paraguay for at least three years after the approval the PE's acquisition in February 2019, in order to maintain competition in the relevant market and revise the competition effect in the market.

Copetrol Group argued that the transaction will provide possible benefits to final consumers through lower prices. But they do not explain how the economic efficiency gain will benefit consumers or how their specific plans will reduce prices for consumers.

In regard to the remedies imposed in the second concentration, CONACOM affirmed these conditions seek to compensate for the possible obstacles that the acquisition could bring to competition. They also state that in the course of the case the buyer has not proven the alleged benefits that this transaction will generate for consumers. Therefore, the board of directors rule out the existence of benefits that compensate the competition problem created by the merger.

In this sense, and given the current scenario, after the two economic concentrations Copetrol Group increased its market power considerably and become the market leader in less than one year. Although the different trademarks and gas stations operate independently, they are controlled by a single group. CONACOM has a duty to supervise that this does not affect competition and that all remedies are fulfilled. In both transactions behavioural remedies prevailed, which require an allocation of additional supervision resources. It is for this reason that behavioural remedies are not the most common decision handed down by the authorities.

Copetrol Group held 552 gas service stations after the PE transaction. It added 40 gas service stations after the Axion transaction. With 592 gas service stations as of 2019, Copetrol Group currently controls 57.4% of the country's sales market share, 53.6% of Paraguay's gas service stations, and has thus increased its dominant position. It should be noted that according to CONACOM, Copetrol Group also has structural links with its direct competitor (Barcos y Rodados) in the Argentine company Delta Patagonia S.A. Although this relationship occurs in different geographical area, the effect is felt in the same product market in which both companies operate in Paraguay. This relationship has to be closely reviewed by CONACOM so it does not represent a barrier to entry for new future competitors or violate anticompetitive agreements.

Lastly, we note that on 14 November 2019 the Investigations Bureau concluded that the Axion transaction reinforces the dominant position of Copetrol Group in the gas and liquid fuel sales market through its gas stations in Asunción and therefore violates Paraguay's Competition Defence Act[26].

---

[26] CONACOM, PARECER/DI/DCC/028/2019.

V. Conclusion

The main aim of Paraguay's competition rules is to ensure market competition, not to directly protect consumers, reasoning that market competition itself benefits consumers. CONACOM's control of economic concentrations is therefore a vital part of the competition regime as a prevention tool against possible negative effects on competition and, primarily, to limit the undue increase of market power by economic parties.

Although Paraguay's antitrust regulations are relatively new, it is evident that merger control investigations are being carried out in accordance with the law. Despite its shortcomings, especially *ex post* filings, the regime has had salutary effects. However, without mandatory *ex ante* filing notifications, the Regulations have to date never been applied by notifying parties. We also recommend that Article 14's 45% market share threshold be loosened to 30% as is stipulated in other Latin American and European Union regulations. On the other hand, one of the strengths of the Paraguayan Competition Defence Act is the two stages for mandatory filing transactions, including the fast-track route for simple cases.

Finally, we have analysed Copetrol cases and the remedies imposed. Its strategy is to be a leader in the relevant gas market, and it has direct agreements with its main competitor Barcos y Rodados. It is vital that CONACOM revises its conduct to prevent future competition problems.

This author also concludes CONACOM should impose a behavioural remedy on Copetrol to block its acquisitions or control transactions in the same markets for three years. This remedy seeks to mitigate possible new concentration transactions to protect competition.

PERU

Luis José Diez Canseco Núñez[*]
Camila Chamorro Poma[**]
Dario Morales Herrera[***]

(DiezCanseco)

Abstract

Competition Law in Peru has been in place for almost 30 years. Merger control was first enacted in 1997 but was limited to the electricity sector. In November 2019, general merger control legislation was approved by means of Emergency Decree 013-2019, which in May 2020 was amended by Legislative Decree 1510. This legislation will enter into force on 1 March 2021 and, subject to evaluation, will be valid until late February 2026. The new merger legislation expands its application to all Peruvian economic activities including the electricity sector.

* Luis José Diez Canseco Núñez: Lawyer from the Pontifical Catholic University of Peru (PUCP). Master in comparative law and visiting scholar at George Washington University Law School. Fulbright and Hubert H Humphrey Scholar. Dean of the Law School of the Technological University of Peru (UTP). Professor of law at PUCP. Former president of the Tribunal of Justice of the Andean Community, international officer at the WIPO and UNCTAD, general coordinator of the competitiveness programme of the Presidency of the Council of Ministers and the World Bank, member of the competition tribunal of Indecopi, consultant of the Inter-American Development Bank and the World Bank. Name Partner at DiezCanseco.

** Camila Chamorro Poma: Bachelor in Law of the National University of San Marcos (UNMSM). Student at the Master's programme in economics and public policy at UNMSM. Worked at the Technical Secretariat of the Specialised Chamber for the Elimination of Bureaucratic Barriers of Indecopi. Member of the winning team of the Peruvian Antitrust Moot Court Competition 2018. Associate at DiezCanseco.

*** Dario Morales Herrera: Bachelor in Law of UNMSM. Student of the Master's programme in business law at UNMSM. Worked at the Technical Secretariat of the Commission for the Defence of Free Competition of Indecopi. Member of the winning team of the Peruvian Antitrust Moot Court Competition 2018. Associate at DiezCanseco. Member of the Competition and Regulation Institute.

I. Introduction[1]

1. Brief Overview

Peru's first competition law was Legislative Decree 701 (DL 701), enacted in the early 1990s, followed by the creation of the National Institute for the Defence of Free Competition and the Protection of Intellectual Property (Indecopi). This law and its amendments, only included control of anticompetitive conduct; thus only sanctioning restrictive agreements and abuse of dominant position. It did not include merger control.

In 2008, DL 701 was replaced by new competition legislation which was enacted through Legislative Decree 1034 approving the Repression of Anticompetitive Conducts. This new legislation restructured Peruvian competition legislation but did not include merger control. Legislative Decree 1034 was partially modified in 2015 and 2018 in various matters related to restrictive practices but, once again, merger control rules were not introduced.

By the end of 1997, Law 26876 was issued concerning merger control. It is referred to as the Electricity Sector Anti-Monopoly and Anti-Oligopoly Law (Electricity Sector Concentration Law). This law will be in force until February 2021, when it will be superseded by Emergency Decree 013-2019, as amended. Law 26876 introduced a prior notification system for mergers in the mentioned sector.

Following lengthy discussions taking more than 20 years, as well as several unsuccessful legislative initiative, Emergency Decree 13-2019 was published in November 2019, setting up a prior notification system for business concentration operations (the Merger Control Law). This law, which for the first time establishes a general regime of merger control in Peru, was expected to enter into force in August 2020, but Legislative

---

1 Disclaimer: this chapter was updated until 14 September 2020. On 24 August 2020, the Consumer Commission of the Peruvian Congress adopted a proposal recommending the Congress Plenary to issue a new law to replace the Merger Control legislation. The proposed text is almost similar to the Emergency Decree 019-2019 as amended by Legislative Decree 1510, but some changes are introduced:

- Calculation of the thresholds includes, in addition to sales and income of the companies, the value of their assets.
- Thresholds must be increased or decreased only by law from Congress.
- Indecopi carries out the merger control of the companies in the financial system, even in case of systemic risk, without prejudice to the prudential control of the financial regulators.
- Prior control will be mandatory in those cases in which the thresholds are exceeded. In all other cases it will be voluntary.
- The Technical Secretariat of the Commission may investigate mergers that do not exceed the thresholds are capable to seriously affect competition.
- The Merger Control Law regulations will be issued by the Presidency of the Council of Ministers instead of the Ministry of Economy and Finance within 15 days of its enactment.
- The date of entry into force of the law is anticipated but still subject to the issuance of its regulations.
- The validity of the law will be indeterminate and no longer for only 5 years.

In general terms, the Consumer Commission intends to reinforce the Peruvian merger control system and legitimize its legislation by replacing the Emergency Decree 019-2019 as amended by Legislative Decree 1510, which has a validity of 5 years, by a law with unlimited duration. The proposal is currently awaiting to be submitted to the Congress Plenary which will finally decide whether to enact the recommended changes.

Decree 1510 delayed it until 1 March 2021. This legislation, subject to evaluation of its enforcement, will remain in force until late February 2026.

It is to be noted that the publication of the regulations for the implementation of Emergency Decree 013-2019 was also delayed from the originally planned date in the middle of 2020 to the end of the year. Because of this, this paper will only refer to the text of the law.

2. Institutional Set-Up

Indecopi is an administrative authority whose legal nature is that of a specialised technical agency, which provides it with an important margin of independence. Moreover, by means of its organisational law, Legislative Decree 1033 and the Organisational Law of the Executive, Law 29158, it is formally attached to the presidency of the Council of Ministers instead of to a particular sector or ministry, making Indecopi one of the highest ranks within the public administration and allowing it to enjoy functional, technical, economic, budgetary and administrative autonomy.

Despite the fact that Indecopi has carried out remarkable and increasingly rigorous work in the field of free competition, there is currently a debate as to whether it should be granted the status of autonomous constitutional body, so that it can enjoy a higher level of independence – even from the executive branch – and guarantee the constitutional mandates entrusted to it: defence of free competition, repression of unfair competition, protection of consumers, protection of intellectual property, elimination of bureaucratic barriers and safeguarding of the subsidiary role of the state.

3. Type of Merger Control

The forthcoming Merger Control Law establishes a prior notification system to control transactions that involve business concentration among different companies. Indeed, it establishes a mandatory notification regime. Therefore, operations falling within the scope of application of the law (following a threshold system) will not have any legal effect unless they are approved by Indecopi. In order to safeguard these provisions, infringements such as the failure to comply with the duty to notify or to execute operations without authorisation will be punished with monetary penalties.

Prior to formal notification, economic operators are given the possibility of consulting the authority for guidance, individually or jointly, on the existence of the duty to notify a transaction or on the information to be submitted. It should be noted that Indecopi's response to these consultations is not binding. The provisions of the new Merger Control Law will be complemented with a Regulation prepared by the Ministry of Economy and Finance and guidelines that may be approved by the Commission for the Defence of Free Competition, none of which have yet been published.

II. Scope of Application

1. Merger Control Law

A. Definition of Notifiable Transaction

This section will develop the content given to the concept of merger, in accordance with the Merger Control Law.

In this regard, Peruvian law provides a broad scope of action by defining the act of merger as any act or operation that implies a transfer or change in the permanent control of an undertaking or part of it, by reason of the acquisition of shares, participations, or through any other contract or legal figure that confers direct or indirect control of an undertaking.

Likewise, the acquisition of productive assets from any company that carries out activities in the sector, or any other act, contract or legal figure including legacies, by virtue of which companies, associations, shares, social parts, trusts or assets in general are concentrated, carried out between competitors, suppliers, clients, shareholders or any other economic agents, is included in the definition.

To this end, Article 5 of DU 013-2019 offers some examples:

- A merger of two or more economic agents, which were independent before the operation, whatever the form of corporate organisation of the merging entities or of the entity resulting from the merger.
- The setting-up by two or more economic operators who are independent of each other of a joint venture, a joint association, the use or usufruct of shares and/or holdings, management contracts, share syndication contracts or any other similar contractual arrangement involving the acquisition of joint control over one or more economic operators, in such a way that the said economic operator performs on a permanent basis the functions of an autonomous economic entity.
- The acquisition by one or more economic operators, directly or indirectly, of rights enabling them, individually or jointly, to exercise control over all or part of one or more economic operators.
- Finally, a set of actions or transactions among the same economic agents in a period of two years will be considered a single transaction, for which it must be notified before the execution of the last transaction by which the threshold is surpassed.

The rule is also precise in delimiting which acts or operations of business concentration are excluded from the scope of application of the law, as follows:

- Corporate growth of an economic agent as a result of operations carried out exclusively within the same economic group.
- Internal corporate growth of an economic agent, regardless of whether it occurs through its own investment or with resources from third parties who do not participate directly or indirectly in the market.

- Corporate growth of an economic agent that does not produce effects on the markets within the national territory, in part or whole.
- Control acquired over an economic operator as a result of a temporary mandate conferred by legislation concerning the expiry or termination of a concession, asset restructuring, insolvency, composition with creditors or other similar procedure.
- Where credit institutions or other financial or insurance or capital market institutions whose normal business is dealing and trading in securities, for their own account or for the account of others, temporarily hold shares or holdings that they have acquired in an undertaking with a view to reselling them, provided that they do not exercise the voting rights attached to those shares or holdings with a view to determining the competitive behaviour of that undertaking.
- The acquisition of rights by an economic operator who has not previously participated in the relevant market or related markets, which allows it to exercise control over all or part of an economic operator who participates in any of these markets, under the terms established in the regulations of the emergency decree.

B. Material and Geographical Scope

The Merger Control Law affects acts of business concentration that produce effects in all or part of the national territory, including acts of concentration that are carried out abroad and directly or indirectly link economic agents that develop economic activities in the country.

It also includes economic agents that offer or demand goods or services on the market and carry out acts of concentration that produce or may produce anticompetitive effects in all or part of the national territory.

It is important to highlight that in cases of business concentration operations that include companies in the financial system that take deposits from the public, or insurance companies that present relevant and imminent risks that compromise the solidity or stability of the referred companies or of the systems they integrate, only prior control by the Superintendence of Banking, Insurance and Private Pension Fund Management Companies (SBS) is required, given the nature and reserved character of these businesses, which must be determined by the SBS.

C. Thresholds

The Merger Control Law indicates that the thresholds from which a business concentration is subject to the *ex ante* control procedure are as follows:

- When the total sum of the value of sales or annual gross income in the country of the companies involved in the operation has reached during the fiscal year prior to that in which the operation is reported, a value equal to or greater than 118,000 ITU, equivalent to USD 495,600,000.
- When the value of annual sales or gross revenues in the country of at least two of the companies involved in the business concentration have reached,

during the fiscal year prior to that in which the operation is reported, a value equal to or greater than 18,000 ITU each, equivalent to USD 75,600,000.

2. Concentrations Law in the Electricity Sector

A. Definition of Notifiable Transaction

A business concentration is defined as the performance of the following acts: merger; formation of a joint venture; direct or indirect acquisition of control over other undertakings by means of the acquisition of shares, holdings, or through any other contract or legal form conferring direct or indirect control over an undertaking, including the conclusion of joint venture contracts, joint ventures, use or usufruct of shares and/or holdings, management contracts and contracts for the syndication of shares, or any other similar and/or analogous business collaboration contract with similar consequences.

Likewise, this includes the acquisition of productive assets of any company that develops activities in the sector; or any other act, contract or legal figure including legacies, by virtue of which companies, associations, shares, social parts, trusts or assets in general are concentrated, that is carried out between competitors, suppliers, clients, shareholders or any other economic agent.

B. Material and Geographical Scope

The Law on Concentrations in the Electricity Sector entrusts the Commission for the Defence of Free Competition of Indecopi with the review and prior authorisation of business concentration operations or mergers in the electricity sector, of a vertical or horizontal nature, in order to avoid possible negative impacts on competition in the sector.

Therefore, those acts of merger that, despite being carried out abroad, directly or indirectly involve companies that generate and/or transmit and/or distribute electrical energy in the national territory, are subject to the rules of said law. Likewise, the shareholders of a company domiciled in Peru, linked to companies that participate directly in the act of concentration, are obliged to comply with this law, and are subject to the sanctions contemplated therein.

C. Thresholds

Prior authorisation shall be requested for acts of concentration directly or indirectly involving undertakings engaged in the generation and/or transmission and/or distribution of electricity which, prior to or following the act giving rise to the request for authorisation, jointly or separately, hold a percentage equal to or greater than 15% of the market in acts of horizontal concentration.

In the case of acts of vertical concentration, those that involve, directly or indirectly, companies that carry out activities of generation and/or transmission and/or distribution of electrical energy that have, before or after the act that originated the request for authorisation, a percentage equal to or greater than 5% of any of the markets involved.

III. Procedure

1. Merger Control Law

A. Launch of Procedure

The Merger Control Law, the general rule governing merger control procedures, has not yet established a notification system. To date, its regulations have yet to be issued. Nevertheless, it introduced the possibility for its further regulations to set up a simplified notification system for transactions with a lower risk to harm competition.

B. Development of Procedure

Deadlines

The Technical Secretariat reviews the application for authorisation of the operation and notifies the parties of compliance with the requirements within 10 working days. The period for rectification is 10 working days.

In the first phase of the assessment, the period for the Commission to determine whether the merger falls within the scope of the rule and has potential restrictive effects on competition is 30 working days.

The second phase assessment of the operation will not exceed 90 working days, but may be extended by up to 30 additional working days.

Powers of competition authority

The competent authority is Indecopi. As for the competent bodies, the Commission for the Defence of Free Competition is the one that evaluates and resolves in the first instance and may: a) authorise, establish conditions or deny concentration acts; b) issue orders or mandates regarding concentration acts; c) issue guidelines on the interpretation of the rules of the Merger Control Law; d) request from the regulatory bodies a non-binding report on the level of concentration in the relevant markets including a technical opinion on the possible effects of the operation under evaluation. It may also issue interim or corrective measures such as dissolution of the transaction, or disposal of all shares or assets, and enforcement measures for failure to comply with corrective measures.

On the other hand, the Technical Secretariat of the Committee for the Defence of Free Competition is the instructional body in charge of conducting and investigating the procedures of prior control and preliminary investigative actions to initiate a sanctioning procedure. Thus, it has the following functions: a) to carry out inquiries and preliminary investigations; b) to instruct the procedure, carrying out investigations and acting as evidence; c) to initiate *ex officio* or at the request of a party the investigation and sanctioning procedure; d) to carry out studies and publish reports; e) to draw up proposals for guidelines; and f) to carry out training activities and disseminate regulations.

For the analysis of the concentration, the Technical Secretariat and the Commission will take into account internationally recognised factors such as market structure, real or potential competition, evolution of the offer and demand, entry barriers, economic and finance power of the undertakings involved in the operation, whether it may create or reinforce market power. By means of DL 1510, it has also included in this analysis the grave economic situation of one of the undertakings, thus allowing the failure firm defence.

Finally, the Specialised Chamber for the Defence of Competition of the Indecopi Tribunal is the body that decides in second and final instance appeals against decisions issued by the Commission.

Commitments

Economic operators may submit to the authority a proposal for commitments in order to avoid or mitigate the possible effects of the merger. If the authority accepts the proposal, it authorises the operation subject to those commitments and closes the procedure.

The procedure is suspended until the authority reaches a decision on the proposal for up to 15 working days. By common agreement, it may be suspended for an additional period of 15 and 30 working days in the first and second phases.

Specific rules on commitments will be laid down in the Regulation.

Cooperation with regulators and other authorities

The authority may request information from other entities. If such information is essential for the resolution of the procedure, the deadline for resolution may be suspended for a maximum of 10 working days, which may be extended by five additional working days.

Regulators are required to provide a non-binding report on the level of concentration in the market for which they are responsible, indicating their technical opinion on the effects of the merger.

In the case of economic agents regulated and supervised by the SBS or the Superintendency of the Securities Market, prior control of merger operations is carried out by Indecopi; however, the authorisation will require the approval of both Indecopi and the respective superintendency.

Cooperation with national or international entities

Cooperation among the authority and other entities, whether national or foreign, can be carried out to ensure a proper enforcement of the legislation through a memorandum of understanding or interinstitutional agreements.

C. Conclusion of Procedure:

According to the Merger Control Act:

The authority shall issue a decision terminating the control procedure, expressing its decision to authorise the operation, to authorise it with conditions or to refuse it.

If the authority does not issue an express pronouncement within the period, the request for authorisation will be considered approved.

According to the third provision, Indecopi's decisions on prior control of operations may be challenged in court through a contentious – administrative action.

If the authority authorises a concentration subject to the fulfilment of conditions, it will establish a period for its review, after which it will determine whether to maintain it, to render it ineffective or to modify it. Notwithstanding this, when a variation in the conditions of competition is found within this period, the authority may review the condition imposed *ex officio*. At any time, economic agents may request the authority to waive or modify the condition, in accordance with the regulations yet to be issued.

D. Sanctions

The Merger Control Law, in accordance with Legislative Decree 1034, provides the following:

Failure to submit the request for authorisation constitutes a minor infringement, punishable by a fine of up to 500 ITU (USD 630,000).

Failure by the authority to comply with the information requirement within the time limit constitutes a minor offence, punishable by a fine of up to 500 ITU (USD 630,000). It may not exceed 8% of the sales or gross income of the offender or its economic group, relating to all its economic activities for the previous fiscal year.

The implementation of the concentration before it is submitted to the control procedure, before the authority issues its decision or before positive administrative silence occurs, constitutes a serious infringement, punishable by a fine of up to 1,000 ITU (USD 1,260,000). It may not exceed 10% of the sales or gross income received by the offender or his economic group, relating to all his economic activities, for the previous year.

The provision of incomplete, incorrect, adulterated, misleading or false information to the authority, or simply the refusal to provide information, constitutes a very serious infringement, punishable by a fine of more than 1,000 ITU (USD 1,260,000). It may not exceed 12% of the sales or gross income received by the offender or his economic group, relating to all his economic activities for the previous year.

2. Concentrations Law in the Electricity Sector

A. Launch of Procedure

The Electricity Sector Merger Law and its Regulation, approved by Supreme Decree 017-98-ITINCI, provide the following with respect to the initiation of the procedure:

Notification system

There is a system of notifications. However, it has not provided for a fast track for the analysis of transactions.

Single/various notification forms

With respect to the forms of notification, there is a standard form of notification. These Regulations have not contemplated the possibility of notification by digital channels.

Filing fees

The rate applicable for the control procedures of operations in this sector amounts to 0.1% of the value of the operation up to a maximum of 50 ITU (USD 63,000).

Filing deadline

The notification must be made before the acts of merger are carried out. Until all the required information has been submitted, notification shall not be deemed effective.

Publicity issues

All information submitted during the pre-notification procedure shall be considered confidential and be treated as confidential.

The technical report and the resolutions may be published while protecting the commercial and/or industrial secrets of the companies.

B. Development of Procedure

Deadlines

Within five days of submission of the notification, the Technical Secretariat verifies the information submitted. In case there is any omission, it will grant a maximum period of five days for correction.

The Commission or Technical Secretariat may request additional information within 10 days, which must be provided within a maximum period of 10 days. Likewise, within 20 days of expiry of that period, the Technical Secretariat shall submit to the Commission its opinion on the effects of the operation and, if appropriate, recommend measures or sanctions.

For its part, the Commission shall have a period of 30 days to issue its decision, counting from the expiry of the period to submit additional information or from the receipt of such information. However, where further analysis of the compatibility of the operation with the market is necessary, the Commission may extend the deadline for a further 30 days without any possibility of extension.

Powers of competition authority

The Electricity Sector Merger Law and its Regulations provide general powers to the organs of the competition authority. Thus, it is the responsibility of the Free Competition Commission in the first instance, and the Competition Tribunal in the second instance, to hear and resolve concentration and sanction procedures.

Commitments

At any stage of the *ex ante* evaluation procedure and before the final decision, the Commission or the court may propose amendments to the operation, to which applicants may commit themselves. In addition, if it considers appropriate, or in order to ensure compliance with commitments, the Commission may make authorisation subject to compliance with certain conditions.

Cooperation with regulators and other authorities

The Supervisory Agency for Investment in Energy and Mines – Osinergmin is the entity in charge of determining the percentages of market participation of electricity generation, transmission and/or distribution companies. The Commission, the Chamber or the Technical Secretariat may request from the Electricity Tariff Commission, the Ministry of Energy and Mines, the Osinergmin and/or any other public body a report on technical aspects of the markets and services and/or products related to the notified operation.

C. Conclusion of Procedure

The Commission may declare the application for authorisation inadmissible (when the operation is outside the scope of the law), authorise the operation or disapprove it. If the authority does not issue a statement within the initial 30-day period, it must be understood that the transaction is not compatible with the market and that the application has been rejected.

Although the Law on Concentrations in the Electricity Sector does not expressly state this, according to Article 64 of Legislative Decree 807, the resolutions of the Indecopi tribunal can be challenged before the judiciary.

Neither the Act nor the associated Regulations make specific provision for the monitoring of conditions imposed. However, Article 32 of the Regulations does state that failure to comply with them entails revocation of the authorisation.

D. Sanctions

Failure to submit a request for authorisation of a concentration before it is carried out, failure to submit the information required by the authority within the time limit or providing fraudulent information may be punished by a fine of up to 500 ITU (USD 630,000).

Notwithstanding the above, a fine not exceeding 10% of the sales or gross receipts for the year preceding the decision of the Commission or board may be imposed when the operation is carried out without prior authorisation, after notification but before the decision of the Commission or board, despite having been declared incompatible by the authority, or when it does not comply with the conditions set by the authority.

IV. Substance

1. Competition Analysis

The Merger Control Law establishes that the analysis should focus on the structure of the market involved, the levels of actual or potential competition and the evolution of supply and demand, as well as the number of participants in the market. Likewise, the authority must take into consideration the economic power of the companies involved, the existence of entry barriers, the possible generation of efficiencies as a result of the concentration and the severe crisis situation of any of the merging companies.

On the other hand, the analysis under the Law on Concentrations in the Electricity Sector seeks to establish whether the concentration would have the effect of diminishing, damaging or preventing free competition in the relevant markets. For this purpose, the level of participation of the companies in the market, the number of competitors, and the perspectives of economic and technological development will be taken into consideration. It will also take into account any barriers to entry that may arise, the unification of different sectors of the production chains and how the concentration will impact users.

2. Statistics

Table 1 lists the business concentration operations that required authorisation by Indecopi since the effective date of the Law on Concentrations in the Electricity Sector.

Table 1: Concentration Operations in the Electricity Sector

Approved without conditions	Approved with conditions	Denied	Total
17	2	0	19

Source: Resolutions of CLC-Indecopi (1997–2019)

3. Case Law Illustration

The main case in Peru is one regarding the sale of shares of Peruvian Opportunity Company S.A.C. (POC) carried out under the Merger Law in the electricity sector. The case was processed under File 002-2019/CLC-CON, reaching a decision through Resolution 007-2020/CLC-INDECOPI on 27 March 2020.

The parties in this case were China Yangtze Power International (Hong Kong) Co Limited (CYPC), as purchaser, and Sempra Americas Bermuda Ltd (Sempra), as seller. In this regard, there was a sale of the shares of POC, which allowed CYPC to obtain control of Luz del Sur S.A.A. (Luz del Sur) and Inland Energy S.A.C. (Inland).

The relevance of the case lies in the fact that Luz del Sur was the main distributor of electricity to Peruvian users, so the impact of this operation on the energy market is extremely important. With this transaction, CYPC would have the largest share in the market for the distribution of electricity to residential users, in addition to having a significant share in the market for electricity generation, while it already had electricity generators to which Inland has been added.

Indecopi's main concern was the possibility that Luz del Sur would decide to acquire electricity only from generating companies linked to CYPC's economic group, ignoring other companies. In order to alleviate this possible anticompetitive effect, the decision taken was to approve the concentration on the condition that any acquisition of electricity by Luz del Sur be made through open tenders in which generating companies from different economic groups may participate.

Final note (Information until September 14th, 2020)

On August 24, 2020, the Consumer Commission of the Peruvian Congress adopted a proposal recommending the Congress Plenary to issue a new law to replace the Merger Control legislation. The proposed text is almost similar to the Emergency Decree 019-2019 as amended by Legislative Decree 1510, but some changes are introduced:

- Calculation of the thresholds includes, in addition to sales and income of the companies, the value of their assets.
- Thresholds must be increased or decreased only by law from Congress.
- Indecopi carries out the merger control of the companies in the financial system, even in case of systemic risk, without prejudice to the prudential control of the financial regulators.
- Prior control will be mandatory in those cases in which the thresholds are exceeded. In all other cases it will be voluntary.
- The Technical Secretariat of the Commission may investigate mergers that do not exceed the thresholds are capable to seriously affect competition.
- The Merger Control Law regulations will be issued by the Presidency of the Council of Ministers instead of the Ministry of Economy and Finance within 15 days of its enactment.
- The date of entry into force of the law is anticipated but still subject to the issuance of its regulations.
- The validity of the law will be indeterminate and no longer for only 5 years.

In general terms, the Consumer Commission intends to reinforce the Peruvian merger control system and legitimize its legislation by replacing the Emergency Decree 019-2019 as amended by Legislative Decree 1510, which has a validity of 5 years, by a law with unlimited duration. The proposal is currently awaiting to be submitted to the Congress Plenary which will finally decide whether to enact the recommended changes.

URUGUAY

Luciana Macedo*
Natalia Jul**
(Uruguay Competition Commission)

Abstract

Uruguay's mergers control regime has recently been modified. The reform of Act No 18.159, by Act No 19.833 was approved on September 2019. The rules on the substantive analysis of mergers and acquisitions have changed. The reform establishes the obligation to ask for authorisation when operations meet certain thresholds, before they are conducted. The Competition Commission can authorise, deny or condition the operation to remedies. The Commission can intervene in cases where a merger may have anticompetitive effects, such as the establishment or consolidation of market power, or the facilitation of coordination among competitors. An abbreviated procedure and a complex one are planned. The abbreviated procedure will correspond to those operations that, due to their impact, do not represent an obstacle to competition. If the evidence suggests to the competition authority that the operation is considered to have a negative impact on competition in the relevant market, a second stage of analysis will be carried out, in which additional information may be requested from the parties or from third parties. The parties can propose commitments to mitigate the negative effects on competition such as structural or conduct remedies, which could be modified by the competition authority. In addition, the authority may make commitment proposals for the authorisation of the operation.

---

* Economist specialising in competition policy and regulation of network industries. In 2003 she achieved a MSc in economic regulation and competition from City University, London. President of the Competition Commission in Uruguay since 2019. Commissioner of the Competition Commission in Uruguay since 2009. Lecturer of competition policy at the Catholic University of Uruguay since 2019.

** Lawyer specialising in competition policy, and utilities regulation. Member of the Competition Commission in Uruguay. Appointed as a commissioner in 2017. She previously worked as a lawyer with extensive experience in private sector, holding positions of responsibility and advising the management bodies of recognised companies. Lecturer of competition law at the Catholic University of Uruguay since 2019.

I. Introduction

1. Brief Overview

The first competition rules in Uruguay were stated in articles 13, 14 and 15 of Act No 17.243 of 29 June 2000, which were complemented by articles 157 and 158 of Act No 17.296 of 21 June 2001, and regulated by Decree No 86/001.

Uruguayan doctrine understood that such regulations were insufficient, both formally and substantially. In addition, the authority that was in charge of competition law (Competition Defence Area under control of the General Direction of Commerce of the Ministry of Economic Affairs and Finance) did not have enough strength in terms of independence to be able to act. This institutional design did not allow the area to educate through its decisions on the importance of the rules on defence of competition to economic agents and consumers.

In the period between 2000 and 2005, a "Special Commission" was created to study legislative solutions regarding freedom of commerce in Uruguay. After the creation of this Commission, it was resolved to request a professor specialised in commercial law of the University of the Republic of Uruguay to draft a project about competition law.

Due to an overwhelming majority in the deputies chamber the project was approved. However when the project arrived to the senators' chamber, it was not approved. Although the rules on defence of competition are of paramount importance for a market economy, reaching the end of the legislature in 2005, the chances of the law being sanctioned were exhausted.

Between 2005 and 2010, substantial progress was made in the legislature regarding this topic. The executive authority sent a project that substantially reproduces the contributions made in the previous period.

Act No. 18.159 about Promotion and Defence of Competition was adopted in 2007. It was an improvement over the previous dispersed articles in different laws. It established a more coherent set of rules that contain the core elements of all competition legislation, and the new legal framework gave greater autonomy to the enforcement agency. At the time of promulgation, the priority of the law was to investigate anticompetitive conduct rather than analyse mergers.

The main value protected by Uruguayan competition law is consumer welfare. In fact, article 1 of Act No 18.159 states: "This law is of a public nature and its purpose is to encourage the welfare of current and future consumers and users by promoting and defending competition, stimulating economic efficiency and ensuring free and equal market access to companies and products."

The legal sources of Act No 18.159 were:

- US Sherman Antitrust Act 1890.
- US Clayton Act 1914.
- EU Treaty of Rome 1957.

- Spanish Act No 15/2007, 2007.
- Argentinian Act 1999.

In addition, an important background of Act No 18.159 is the prevailing legislation on the MERCOSUR, especially the *Protocolo de Fortaleza* decision No 18/96 which establishes the importance of the freedom of market and the prohibition of anticompetitive practices.

2. Institutional Set-Up

The Promotion and Defence of Competition Commission is a decentralised authority of the Ministry of Economic Affairs and Finance. Being a decentralised authority means that the Commission has decision-making powers. However, all its decisions are subject to appeal before the Ministry.

The Commission is composed of three members appointed by the executive branch, acting in the Council of Ministers. They have a term of six years and can be reappointed. The appointments do not follow the political cycle, in order to assure independence. Its president represents the Commission. Each member serves as president for two years, on a rotating basis. The Commission adopts its decisions on the investigations and other issues as a collegial body in ordinary and special meetings.

3. Type of Merger Control

According to Act No 18.159, mergers and acquisitions do not require competition authority approval. Those operations require a previous notification to the authority, providing certain mandatory information requested. Articles 7 to 9 of Act No 18.159 establish the obligation to notify, 10 days before they are conducted, those operations that meet certain thresholds.

Decree No 404/007 regulates the notification procedure and requirements; there are also guidelines issued by the Commission. However, the Commission does not have the authority to prohibit an operation or to condition it subject to the fulfilment of certain commitments.

Article 9 of Act No 18.159 provides that previous approval is required only when a monopoly results from the merger.

Uruguay's merger control regime has recently been modified. The reform of Act No 18.159 by Act No 19.833 was approved on September 2019. The rules on the substantive analysis of mergers and acquisitions have changed. The Commission can intervene in cases where a concentration may have anticompetitive effects, such as the establishment or consolidation of market power, or the facilitation of coordination among competitors.

Article 3 of Act No 19.833 establishes an obligation to ask for authorisation when operations meet certain thresholds, before they are conducted. The Commission can authorise, deny or condition the operation to remedies. The law considers a six-month period before the introduction of the new regime in order to regulate the procedure. That is why the new regime will be in place in mid-April.

The Commission has a period of 60 days to analyse the effects of the merger and issue a resolution.

The Commission is working on the regulatory decree as well as on the elaboration of guidelines and manuals for the substantive analysis and remedies.

II. Scope of Application

1. Definition of Notifiable Transaction

Article 7 of Act No 18.159 provides that acts of mergers can include "transactions involving a change in the structure of control over the participating companies through: company mergers, the acquisition of corporate equities, equity interests or shares, the acquisition of commercial, industrial or civil establishments, the total or partial acquisition of business assets, and any other kind of legal transactions that involve the full or partial transfer of control of economic units or companies".

2. Material Scope

There are three industry-specific regulators that have competition powers. These regulated sectors are financial services, communications services and energy-gas-water services, and the regulators are, respectively, the Central Bank of Uruguay, Regulatory Authority for Communication Services (URSEC) and the Regulatory Authority for Energy and Water Services (URSEA).

The legislative interest was in not omitting the existence of specific regulators in specific areas of the economic activity and assigned these the same powers as the Commission, obviously limited to the scope of their respective organic and functional areas of specialisation. In addition, article 27 of Act No 18.159 gives the possibility to specific regulatory organs to make non-binding queries to the Commission.

3. Geographical Scope

According to article 3 of Act No 18.159, all natural and legal persons, public and private, national and foreign, who carry out economic activities with or without profit, in the Uruguayan territory, are obliged to be governed by the principles of free competition.

Those who carry out economic activities abroad are also obliged, as long as these activities fully or partially display their effects in the Uruguayan territory.

4. Thresholds

The thresholds are (at least one of both): i) when because of the merger, the companies participating in the merger reach 50% or more of the market share in the relevant market; ii) when the annual gross revenue in Uruguay, of all participants of the merger, is at least 750 million Indexed Units (equivalent to USD 90 million at time of writing).

The thresholds have been modified. Following international best practice recommendations, the market share threshold was eliminated. The reason for this was to set clear and simple thresholds based on objective information.

According to article 3 of Act No 19.833, authorisation is required when the annual gross revenue in Uruguay of all the participants in the merger is at least 600 Indexed Units (equivalent to USD 70 million).

III. Procedure

1. Launch of Procedure

Prior to the enactment of Act No 19.833, major mergers and acquisitions did not require administrative authorisation or approval, except in cases where, as a result of the transaction, a monopoly was formed over the relevant market.

Decree No 404/007 and Resolution No 39/010 issued by the Commission regulate the administrative procedure regarding competition. Currently the Commission is working on the elaboration of the procedure for authorisation of economic concentrations that will come into full effect in mid-April 2020.

There will be a standard notification form for all operations. The possibility of notifying by digital channels is not planned for the moment. The competition authority can request additional information of the parties in the cases that are considered complex after the prior evaluation.

2. Development of Procedure

An abbreviated procedure and a simplified one are planned. The abbreviated procedure will correspond to those merger operations that, due to their impact, do not represent an obstacle to competition. At this stage the competition authority may: a) establish that the information is incomplete and/or insufficient for continuing with its analysis; b) authorise the operation; or c) determine the need for further analysis and move to the second stage, planned for complex operations.

If the evidence suggests to the competition authority that the operation is considered to have a negative impact on competition in the relevant market, a second stage of analysis will be carried out, in which additional information may be requested from the parties or third parties. The second stage includes publicising the operation so that third parties can make claims about possible changes or impacts on the conditions of competition in the affected markets.

After the second stage of evaluation the competition authority may: a) authorise the operation; b) authorise the operation subject to the fulfilment of certain commitments; c) deny the authorisation.

The parties can propose commitments to mitigate the negative effects on competition such as structural or conduct remedies, which could be modified by the competition authority. The authority may also make commitment proposals for the authorisation of the operation. The Commission will establish a compliance schedule.

3. Conclusion of Procedure

Decisions of the Competition Commission are subject to appeal before the Ministry of Economic Affairs and Finance.

In addition, final decisions issued by the Commission may be challenged in Administrative Court. The court is not specialised in this field. It is a general court for matters of public law that hears petitions for the annulment of final administrative decisions on grounds of legality.

4. Sanctions

Operations done without requesting for the authorisation from the Competence Authority will not produce legal effects, notwithstanding the sanctions that the competition authority is entitled to impose, in terms of articles 17 and 19 of Act No 18.159.

The competition authority can impose sanctions if:

a) The merger is not reported properly and on time.
b) The requirements set out in the merger decision are not met.
c) The merger is not authorised, but the parties continue with the operation.

Sanctions are established in article 17 of Act No 18.159.

The Commission may impose the following sanctions:

a) Warning.
b) Warning with publication of the resolution, at the expense of offender, in two national newspapers.
c) Fine to be determined between 100,000 IU and a maximum amount of the higher of the following:
   i. 20 million IU.
   ii. The equivalent of 10% of the annual turnover of the offender.
   iii. The equivalent of three times the damage caused by the anticompetitive practice, if determinable.

For the purposes of its determination, the following will be taken into account: material damage caused; degree of participation of those responsible; intent; repeat offender status; and attitude assumed during the development of administrative actions.

Sanctions may be applied in cases where the provisions established in articles 7 and 9 of the law being regulated are not complied with.

In the case of concerted practices between competitors, it will be considered as a special mitigation the complaint made by one of the members of the agreement or the contribution it provides to obtain evidence sufficient for the sanction of the remaining offenders.

IV. Substance

1. Competition Analysis

The analysis of mergers seeks to verify whether a position of power in the market will be acquired or consolidated as a result of the transaction and if the transaction has the effect of restricting competition. The analysis considers as well if the merger can facilitate coordination among competitors. The competition authority will consider in the analysis the relevant market definition, the degree of concentration, the existence of entry barriers and the impact on upstream and downstream competition.

Efficiency gains are also analysed. The parties to the transaction must provide the information regarding efficiency gains. The efficiencies must be directly attributable to the concentration; they should not be achievable in a less restrictive way for competition and the benefits must be passed on to consumers.

2. Statistics

N/A.

3. Case Law Illustration

N/A.

VENEZUELA

Alejandro Gallotti*

(LEĜA)

Abstract

Mergers and acquisitions in Venezuela are formally regulated by the typical parameters of "free competition" through the Antitrust Law. However, the Venezuelan economy does not operate in practice within these principles, as a series of law decrees enacted since 1999 have transformed the legal framework of the Venezuelan economy to a system of economic control by the national government. The merger and acquisition regime should, in theory, operate within the parameters of the Antitrust Law and other special rules, where the transaction or business cannot represent a prohibited practice, and especially cannot result in an economic concentration or other figure that has negative effects on the relevant market. Although there is an authority on the matter, the Antitrust Superintendence, and a current legal regime, in practice the Superintendence appears diminished by the policy of price controls and industry control that the national executive develops. In fact, since the creation of the Antitrust Superintendence in 2014, there have been no publications on merger and acquisition decisions. The Superintendence's website has been inoperative for over a year, and procedures are not proceeding rapidly. Although it is possible to take legal action against the Superintendence, either for its decisions or its omissions, in practice judicial power is severely questionable since it lacks independence and follows the policies imposed by the Chavismo regime. All this makes the subject under study a question of theory versus practice.

---

* Public law and foreign investment protection specialist. Constitutional law and public law professor. Independent researcher at Georgetown University (Washington DC). Junior partner at LEĜA.

I. Introduction

1. Brief Overview

Venezuela currently operates within an economic system of market control by government authorities, actions that are carried out through various bodies such as the Antitrust Superintendence, the National Superintendence for the Defence of Socioeconomic Rights, and other administrative units of the national executive. Price regulations, the imposition of profit margins, nationalisation of industries and the constant threat to private property, all supported by a state policy of generalised subsidies through oil revenues, are the most common characteristics of the Venezuelan economy of the last 20 years. However, this was not the case before the arrival of the ideological movement known as "*Chavismo*".

A. Venezuelan Economic Regulation in the Second Half of the 20th Century

We could say that the democratic era of Venezuela began in 1958[1], with its constitutional antecedent the Constitution of 1961 whose Article 96 *et seq.* established that citizens could engage in the lucrative activity of their choice, without more limitations than those provided in the legal system, the prohibition of monopolies, the guarantee of private initiative and the protection of private property. This, however, had its ups and downs in the following decades where the nationalisation of the oil industry in 1975, as well as habitual policies for the control of prices of basic products, marked a mixed system of economy, where economic freedom prevailed, but the state reserved most of the wealth (the gross domestic product was based mainly on oil, an activity controlled by the state) and reserved the possibility of setting prices for essential products, using as arguments national security, social justice, public health or other reasons of social interest.

Towards the end of the 1980s and beginning of the 1990s, Venezuela sought to resume the path of decentralisation and deregulation of both the powers of the national government and the economic activities controlled by it. Thus, various regulations were approved, such as the Law on the Decentralisation and Transfer of Competences of the Public Sector; the participation of the private sector in services of general interest such as electricity and telephony, as well as industrial sectors, were fully admitted. Thus, on 13 January 1992, the Law to Promote and Protect the Exercise of Free Competition was passed through the National Congress, which correlatively counted on the creation of the Superintendence for the promotion and protection of free competition known as *Procompetencia*, aimed at preventing and punishing abuses within the market. Moreover, *coups d'état* (1989 and 1992 the most notorious) and political instability also increased, leading to a situation that would begin to diminish the country's public institutions, and an increase in poverty and deterioration in quality of life began to be felt.

---

1 There were brief democratic periods before 1958, but it is from 1958 that a lasting democracy began.

B. Venezuelan Economic Regulation in the 21st Century

The legal advances observed during the 1990s began to suffer setbacks with the arrival in 1999 of the so-called *Chavismo*[2]. The following 10 years would see a very large range of products with prices fixed by the national executive (although it was the practice of previous governments, under *Chavismo* it became much more extensive and common, and economic agents were also punished with severe prison terms), innumerable reforms in economic matters (generally through presidential decrees of legal rank), repeated attacks on private property and, especially, the imposition in 2003 of the so-called "foreign currency exchange control regime" through which all economic activities of the country would be directly or indirectly affected by a generalised subsidy, which was financed with the highest oil prices observed in Venezuelan history, from 2005 to 2014. Although the Constitution of 1999 (NC) (replacing that of 1961) continued to contemplate, in Article 112 *et seq.*, economic freedom, private initiative and private property rights, these became the first constitutional rights repeatedly and continuously ignored and violated by the new government, which at the time of writing has been in power for 21 years.

All these legislative reforms in the economic sector and the usual practice of confiscation of movable and immovable property, as well as the foreign currency exchange control regime, ended up in the Decree-Law of Fair Costs and Prices of 2011 that would later be repealed through the Organic Decree-Law of Fair Prices (OLFP) of 2013 (reformed on several occasions), where the government began to regulate the cost structures and profit margins for economic activities carried out in Venezuela (with exceptions provided in special laws, such as hydrocarbons, banking, the stock market etc.), imposing a profit margin that could not be more than 30% over the cost structure.

In 2014, through presidential Decree 1.415, the Antitrust Decree-Law (Antitrust Law) was issued[3] (repealing the Law to Promote and Protect the Exercise of Free Competition of 1992), with regulations that largely complied with the economic standards of a free-market competition regime. However, the existence of the foreign currency exchange control regime (still in force back then[4]), general price-fixing practice, the profit margin limit and the control of various economic and industrial activities by the state have made the current framework of Venezuelan free competition little applied in practice.

Certainly the legal regime of "fair prices" is not the regulatory framework of free competition in Venezuela: this framework corresponds to the Antitrust Law. It is not reasonable to refer to the Antitrust Law without considering the entire legal – economic context that governs in Venezuela, since, in Venezuela, free competition is a purely formal matter (provided for in the NC and the Antitrust Law), and in practice the economic framework operates within a set of state control norms executed through practices that deny all legal security and due process provisions provided in our national regulations and international human rights conventions.

---

2 Movement of the former president Hugo R Chávez Frías and Nicolás Maduro Moros.

3 Special Official Gazette No 6,151, 18 November 2014.

4 Abrogated in 2019.

Those economic regulations have brought about a significant reduction in free competition, as economic agents do not have enough room for manoeuvre because economic conditions have been reducing the number of productive companies as a result of a lack of raw materials (three-quarters of gross domestic product has disappeared), the inconvenience of access to foreign currency (reducing imports of any kind) and the absence of legal protection for both domestic and foreign companies, where economic agents cannot assess the risks of new investments, keeping their cost structure to a minimum and putting all their effort into preserving their business in a country where inflation (inflation in Venezuela reached 1,698,488.2% in 2018[5] and 7,374% in 2019[6]) and the devaluation of the bolivar has been reducing the purchasing power of producers, merchants, providers and consumers.

Since August 2017, the National Constituent Assembly (NCA), created unilaterally by Nicolás Maduro, issues the country's normative acts, usurping the powers of the Venezuelan legislative power[7]. Since then, the NCA has issued different types of decrees and laws such as the national budget law (an exclusive attribution of the parliament[8]), the Constitutional Law of Agreed Prices[9] (APL) and more recently, in January 2020, a profound reform of the tax framework, including the organic tax code and the value-added tax law[10], all without parliament, the only competent authority to issue laws in these matters[11].

In 2018 the national government created a new currency called the *petro* (without the authorisation of the National Assembly and outside constitutional scenarios), applied since 2019. The government indicates that the petro is a cryptocurrency, but as it has been implemented within absolute obscurity, the government has not provided information and public access to the platform and algorithms used for its creation, is difficult to consider it a cryptocurrency because the government is the issuer and the value is also set by the government[12]. To date, we do not have official information about foreign currency or cryptocurrency exchange operations with the petro, but the government is using it for public pension payments, and it is intended to demand the payment of some taxes with petros. The devaluation of the bolivar – the only legal currency in Venezuela – was over 90% in 2019[13].

Venezuela has been suffering a *de facto* economic dollarisation, where around 50% of transactions have been carried out in US dollars and other foreign currencies during 2019 and 2020[14]. Moreover, during late 2019 and early 2020, a certain *de facto* economic

---

5 Extra-official information from National Assembly Deputy Rafael Guzman, see "Venezuela cierra 2018 con una inflación del 1.698.488,2%" (*Noticias Bancarias*, 11 January 2019), <https://noticiasbancarias.com/economia-y-finanzas/11/01/2019/venezuela-cierra-2018-con-una-inflacion-del-1-698-4882/172036.html>.

6 See National Assembly official website, <http://www.asambleanacional.gob.ve/noticias/angel-alvarado-la-inflacion-en-venezuela-cerro-en-mas-de-7374-en-2019> accessed 30 January 2020

7 NC, Articles 347 and 348.

8 NC, Articles 203 *et seq.*

9 Extraordinary Official Gazette No 6.342, 22 November 2017.

10 Extraordinary Official Gazette No 6.507, 29 January 2020.

11 NC, Articles 201 *et seq.*

12 A Gallotti, "Venezuela" in Aidan Synnott (ed), *The Public Competition Enforcement Review* (Edn 12 The Law Reviews, 2020).

13 Information obtained through <https://www.notitarde.com/devaluacion-del-bolivar-arrecia-desde-comienzos-de-noviembre/> accessed 30 January 2020.

14 See "Maduro says 'thank God' for dollarization in Venezuela" (*Reuters*, 17 November 2019) <https://www.reuters.com/article/us-venezuela-economy-idUSKBN1XR0RV> accessed 1 February 2020.

deregulation was observed (there were no relevant legal reforms, but it did appear that the government was withdrawing from the private economy), which led to a small improvement in access to certain consumer goods, particularly in Caracas.

However, since March 2020, a new onslaught on government economic control and price-fixing began – using the dollar as a parameter – where the shortage of gasoline, continued failure of electricity service and low oil prices (accentuated by the Covid-19 crisis), as well as the Office of Foreign Assets Control sanctions against individuals and public entities who are part of the Nicolás Maduro regime. These make recovery of the Venezuelan economy practically unthinkable this year.

2. Institutional Set-Up

The Antitrust Superintendence is the main authority in free competition. It is considered an administrative unit of the National Executive Power with budgetary autonomy but without legal personality (it is part of the state legal entity). It has the power to investigate and enforce antitrust law. The superintendent is directly appointed by the president of the republic[15].

The Antitrust Superintendence has the power to investigate whether there has been an infringement of the Antitrust Law, either by acting on a complaint or on its initiative. However, before reaching a decision, the Superintendence must have sufficient evidence upon which to base its conclusions.

3. Type of Merger Control

Businesses combine mainly through: (i) mergers with other businesses; (ii) purchase of capital stock or shares of private companies or, in the case of publicly traded companies, through tender offers (public offers for acquisition as regulated in Securities Market Law); and (iii) acquisition of assets or going concerns. Businesses may also combine through joint ventures whereby two or more companies put up capital stock to incorporate a new business entity for a specific purpose.

Notification is optional. There is no need to suspend the operation in the general regime for merger control, but if the final decision of the authority is that the transaction is not allowed, there could be an investigation and an order to unwind a merger.

II. Scope of Application

1. Definition of Notifiable Transaction

The purpose of the Antitrust Law, as established in its article 1, is to promote, protect and regulate fair economic competition to ensure democratisation of productive economic activity with social equality, strengthen national sovereignty and foster endogenous and

15 Antitrust Law, art 21.

sustainable development, to satisfy social needs and build a fair, free, solidary and co-responsible society through the prohibition and sanctioning of monopolistic and oligopolistic behaviours, such as abuse of dominant position, agreed-upon claims, economic concentration, and any other anticompetitive or fraudulent practices.

Article 3 states that the following are excluded from the application of the law: grassroots organisations of popular power governed by the Organic Law of the Communal Economic System; public or mixed strategic companies; and national state-owned companies for the provision of public services.

The Antitrust Law prohibits economic concentrations that may cause or enhance a dominant position in all or part of a market, or that may generate negative effects on competition or the democratisation of production, distribution or commercialisation of goods and services.

Small and medium-sized enterprises, cooperatives and companies that form part of the communal economic system[16] are exempt from this prohibition. The law maintains the voluntary reporting status in cases of economic concentrations.

The Guidelines for Economic Concentration Assessment (1999) define a concentration as a merger of previously independent undertakings, acquisition of sole control over another undertaking or acquisition of joint control in a full-function concentrative joint venture or existing undertaking. Thus, the Antitrust Law defines "control" as a decisive influence over the activities of a company.

Besides the antitrust regime, government or stock exchange filings will be necessary depending on the structure used for the business combination. Merger agreements also need to be filed before the Commercial Registry Office where both the combining businesses are registered, along with the necessary corporate and shareholder approvals of the transaction. If businesses combine through a tender offer made to the shareholders of a publicly traded company, the purchaser is required to file advance notices and a prospectus with the National Securities Superintendence before publicising the tender offer[17].

2. Material Scope

Generally, all economic agents of a public or private nature, national or foreign, with or without profit, who carry out economic activities in the national territory or group are regulated.

As well as the businesses in circumstances mentioned in section II(1), transactions in the insurance, finance/banking, and telecommunications sectors require prior authorisation from sector-specific regulatory bodies.

In the downstream, midstream, and upstream sectors of petrochemical activities and the oil sector, private participation is permitted only in association with state-owned

---

16 An economic model that encourages domestic production to transition from the "capitalist rentier state" to the "socialist economic productive system".

17 Jorge Acedo-Prato and Victoria Montero, "Venezuela" in Alan M Klein (ed), *Getting the Deal Through: Mergers & Acquisitions 2017* (Law Business Research 2017).

companies that hold more than 50%[18]. In the gas industry, such restriction is not legally present. However, in practice, the government has imposed the same restriction.

According to the Gold Law, private participation is permitted only in association with state-owned companies holding more than 55% of capital stock. All the gold must be sold to the Central Bank of Venezuela (CBV).

The Regulations to the Insurance Activity require that any transfer of shares of an insurance company shall be notified to the Superintendence of Insurance within 15 days of the execution of the transfer entries in the company's shareholder registry book.

The Banking Sector Law provides that all acquisitions of the capital stock of a bank or financial institution shall be authorised by the Banking Superintendence[19].

If we refer exclusively to the Antitrust Law, all economic activities – except for those excluded in article 3 – are subject to possible investigations by the Antitrust Superintendence. Under article 28.2 of the Antitrust Law, the Superintendence has the power to carry out the necessary investigations to verify the existence of restrictive competition practices and open files related to said practices.

However, we must remember that economic activities and their markets (except those regulated by special laws) are subject to the OLFP and the APL, which in many cases represent a direct or indirect effect on the free competition regime described in the Antitrust Law.

Moreover, the Venezuelan framework presents many special regulations for certain industries. If an economic activity or industry has no special regulation, it will automatically be regulated by the OLFP (article 2) and the APL. Some of the most regulated industries and economic activities in Venezuela (with its regulatory bodies) are:

i. Oil industry: Ministry of Popular Power for Oil and Energy and Petróleos de Venezuela S.A. (PDVSA);
ii. Banking sector: Banking Superintendence;
iii. Mining industry: Ministry of Popular Power for Mining;
iv. Insurance activity: Superintendence of Insurance Activity;
v. Telecommunications: Ministry of Popular Power for Communications and the National Commission of Telecommunications (CONATEL)[20];
vi. Cement industry: Venezuelan Corporation of Cement;
vii. Electric power: Ministry of Popular Power for Electric Power and Corporación Eléctrica Nacional S.A (CORPOELEC);
viii. Healthcare: Ministry of Popular Power for Health and other public entities.

---

18 Nicolás Maduro's regime started in 2020 a *de facto* privatisation plan for the oil industry in Venezuela. There is no detailed and public information.

19 This is an obligation of the target entity rather than the purchaser.

20 CONATEL is a decentralised public entity in charge of the control and supervision of telecommunications (television, radio, internet, subscription television, etc.). Despite its special legal nature, is an entity under the control of the Nicolás Maduro regime.

It is also relevant to consider that a lot of the specially regulated industries are developed by public or mixed strategic companies or national state-owned companies[21]. Additionally, the banking sector is considered a public service, under article 8 of the Institutions of the Banking Sector Law, and the same applies for electricity, provision of domestic gas and many economic activities of public interest (including telecommunications, construction, sale of food, medicines, some care products).

3. Geographical Scope

Article 3 of the Antitrust Law indicates that the subjects of an application are natural or legal persons of a public or private nature, national or foreign, with or without profit, "who carry out economic activities in the national territory or group …". Thus, considering that the Antitrust Law tries to avoid negative effects within the market[22], if a transaction (national or international) is capable of affecting the Venezuelan market, it will be regulated by the aforementioned provisions.

4. Thresholds

The analysis of the threshold for economic concentration transactions is equivalent to 120,000 tax units (TU) (1 TU = 1,500 bolivars[23]). It is measured in terms of the domestic business volume of the companies involved:

i. Mergers of previously independent enterprises;
ii. Full-function joint ventures;
iii. Transactions as a result of which one or more entities directly or indirectly gain control over one or more previously independent enterprises, or parts thereof, through the acquisition of equity, assets or otherwise;
iv. The acquisition of productive assets or commercial funds;
v. Any other act, contract or legal figure by which companies, divisions, parts of companies, commercial funds or assets, in general, may be concentrated.

Considering the TU value and the foreign currency exchange rate (approximately 194,000 bolivars per USD[24]), 120,000 TU is 180,000,000 bolivars, roughly USD 927 (at the time of writing). Certainly, this is a very small value and a consequence of the hyperinflation and devaluation of the Venezuelan currency. The TU value to be used for turnover calculation purposes is the one in effect at the time the merger takes place.

The annual turnover is calculated by adding sales revenues for the last financial year of the parties minus the sum of sales discounts, value-added tax, and other taxes related to the business taxes.

---

21 Oil and mining are the most common cases.

22 Article 10: "Economic concentrations that produce or reinforce a dominant position in all or part of the market, or that may generate effects contrary to effective competition, democratisation in the production, distribution and commercialisation of goods and services are prohibited …"

23 SENIAT Administrative Providence published through Official Gazette No 41.839, 13 March 2019.

24 As at 22 May 2020 <http://www.bcv.org.ve/tasas-informativas-sistema-bancario>.

For purposes of calculating the thresholds, the revenues of all companies belonging to the same economic group of the parties in Venezuela must be taken into account. The economic group would be comprised of companies controlled by the parties in Venezuela. Only local sales are considered to calculate the annual turnover.

Foreign-to-foreign exemption: There must be a local nexus, such as a presence (branch office or subsidiary) or assets in Venezuela for the merger control regime to apply.

III. Procedure

1. Launch of Procedure

As mentioned before, the Antitrust Law does not require a previous notification (voluntary notification) and there is no need to suspend the operation in the general regime for merger control, but if the final decision of the authority is that the transaction is not allowed, there could be an investigation and an order to unwind a merger.

Nevertheless, the Superintendence, *ex officio* or at the request of third parties, may open an investigation within five years of the consummation of the transaction. If the merger has restrictive effects on competition, the Superintendence can order the dissolution of the transaction, divestiture or the imposition of fines of up to 20% of the gross sales of the offending party for the previous year.

If the economic agent decides to file a notification it just needs to complete a regular form and file it before the authority. There is a filing fee, a stamp tax to be paid, which will depend on the length of the brief to be filed. Currently, it is not more than USD 100, but considering the hyperinflation and the economic situation this could change at any time.

Administrative procedures in free competition matters are developed through the provisions of the Antitrust Law and supplemented by the Organic Law of Administrative Procedures (OLAP). In the case of mergers and acquisitions, the OLAP ordinary procedure is usually followed.

There is the possibility of developing administrative procedures by electronic means in accordance with several legal acts, like the Decree with the Force of Law on Data Messages and Electronic Signatures, the Decree with Rank, Value and Force of Law on Electronic Access and Exchange of Data, Information and Documents between the Organs and Entities of the State and the Law of Info-Government.

These laws provide the possibility of telematics and digital procedures, where private parties have the right to receive notifications through email. However, the Antitrust Superintendence digital platform (its website) is not operational for the development of administrative procedures. In consequence, the administrative procedures before the Superintendence must be followed in writing.

2. Development of Procedure

In accordance with the ordinary OLAP procedure it lasts 4 months. It may be extended for two more months. However, investigations can take more time (even up to one year). There is no consequence if the authority exceeds the review period, however, in the absence of a response, an interested party may take legal action against the administrative authority to obtain a response.

Article 34 of the Antitrust Law indicates that the authority ahs the widest powers of investigation and inspection including the following:

i. Call to Summon any person to testify in relation to the alleged infraction;
ii. Require any person to submit documents or information that may be related to the alleged infringement;
iii. Examine, in the course of inquiries, books and accounting documents;
iv. Call, through the press, for any person who can supply information concerning the alleged infringement.

Third parties can participate if they manifest and demonstrate that they have a legitimate interest in the procedure.

Since the creation of the Antitrust Superintendence at the end of 2014, no decisions have been published on this matter, however, in the past it was normal to observe Procompetencia's cooperation with other organisations (public and private), as well as the request for cooperation by Procompetencia with other organisations or entities.

3. Conclusion of Procedure

In the resolution that brings a procedure to a conclusion, the Antitrust Superintendence shall resolve upon the existence or non-existence of prohibited practices under the Antitrust Law. If the existence of prohibited practices is determined, the Antitrust Superintendence, following article 38, can:

i. Order the cessation of the prohibited practices within a given time;
ii. Impose certain conditions or obligations on the infringer;
iii. Order the elimination of the effects of prohibited practices; and
iv. Impose sanctions provided by the Antitrust Law.

The lack of payment of a fine or payments made after the deadline has expired for that purpose results in an obligation to pay default interest until clearance of the debt. The interest rate is calculated at 6% over the average rediscount rate established by CBV during the delay period.

The Superintendence may impose on undertakings any behavioural or structural remedies that are proportionate to the gravity of the infringement committed. Penalties start with the prohibition of the anticompetitive agreement and a fine that shall not exceed 10% of the total turnover in the preceding business year.

In the case of a decision of a public law authority, judicial review must be carried out through the contentious – administrative courts, where it is possible to claim for nullity, as well as damages, to demand a review of the act of the Superintendence and request annulment of the administrative act.

4. Sanctions

As no notification is required there are no sanctions in this regard.

In the case of filing false or misleading information the law establishes that the Superintendence will impose fines. However, the law does not establish the amount of the fines.

IV. Substance

1. Competition Analysis

As already explained, the substantive test consists of verifying the existence of conducts, practices, agreements, arrangements, contracts or decisions which prevent, restrict, distort or limit free competition.

This general prohibition is also applied to mergers and acquisitions, and the following may be highlighted as particular assumptions: agreements or conventions, concluded directly or through unions, associations, federations, cooperatives and other groups subjects to application of the Law, that restrict or obstruct economic competition among its members.

Prohibition of economic concentrations that produce or strengthen a dominant position[25] in all or part of the market or which generate effects contrary to effective competition, adding as part of this prohibition those which cause effects contrary to "the democratisation of the production, distribution, and marketing of goods and services".

2. Statistics

Unfortunately, there are no official statistics available for the public, nor published decisions on procedures carried out by the antitrust regulatory authority since 2014. The website is not operational at the time of writing this article. As far as our practice is concerned, there are no known cases related to merger control in the past recent years[26].

3. Case Law Illustration

As previously explained, there are no known cases in this matter since 2014, however, we proceed to present the last case of which we were aware:

Year: 2014

Parties: [restricted]

Industry: Telecommunications

---

[25] 1. When a certain economic activity is carried out by a single person or group of persons linked to each other, both in their capacity as purchasers and as sellers and both in their capacity as providers of services and in their capacity as users of services. 2. Where there is more than one person carrying out a certain type of activity, there is no effective competition between them.

[26] At least, the authors have not been notified of any cases.

An administrative resolution issued by the Protection and Promotion of the Free Competition Superintendence (now the Antitrust Superintendence) at the request of CONATEL within an administrative process initiated before CONATEL at the request of the Venezuelan company, SNV (subsidiary of a US company), a telecommunications services operator in Venezuela, to obtain authorisation for an operation to be carried out by its parent company – which amounted to the creation of a third telecommunications company to operate in the US – jointly with a Japanese telecommunications services operator (SJC).

- Although the transaction was to be completed outside Venezuelan jurisdiction and did not directly affect the company located in Venezuela (SNV), it did involve companies that were shareholders of the company (its parent company), by legal mandate, so it was mandatory to request CONATEL's approval.
- Following the Fifth Final Provision of the Organic Telecommunications Law, all operations involving direct or indirect changes in the shares and financial control of telecommunications service operators must obtain prior approval from CONATEL. To issue a resolution, CONATEL must first submit this request to the evaluation of the Antitrust Superintendence. The opinion issued by the Antitrust Superintendence has binding effects.

The Antitrust Superintendence considered that the constitution by SNV and SJC of a third company to provide telecommunications services in the United States did not affect the Venezuelan market and could offer efficiencies such as the strengthening of the local subsidiary (SNV) and the expansion of its services that to date was only as an internet access service provider.

The transaction was duly authorised.

CARIBBEAN COMMUNITY REGION

Taimoon Stewart*
(The University of the West Indies)

Marc Jones*
(CARICOM Competition Commission)

Abstract

The chapter offers an insight into the current status of competition regimes in the Caribbean Community (CARICOM). Only four of the 15 member states have competition legislation and institutional arrangements; in addition, there is a regional competition framework and commission. The designs of the national commissions are a mixture of administrative and prosecutorial enforcement models, with the regional commission being a purely administrative model. Only two of the national legislations have merger provisions and, of these, only one has been enforced, the other being proclaimed very recently. An examination of the national statutes reveals some significant differences, for instance, exemptions for the financial and telecommunications sectors in Trinidad and Tobago. Moreover, issues around the enforceability of the regional framework abound. This chapter provides details of the two merger regimes with further details of that in Barbados, the country with a merger enforcement track record. Two cases from the region are presented. In the first, the Jamaica Fair Trading Commission applied the general prohibition on anticompetitive agreements to review a merger. The case study traces the legal challenges and judgments. The second case is one that was investigated and ruled on by the Barbados Fair Trading Commission (BFTC).

---

* Taimoon Stewart is Associate Senior Fellow at the University of the West Indies, St Augustine Campus, Trinidad and Tobago, and a consultant in competition law specialising in developing countries and small economy issues.

** Marc Jones is an attorney-at-law who specialises in Competition Law. He is currently Senior Legal Counsel at the CARICOM Competition Commission based in Paramaribo, Suriname. The views expressed in this chapter do not represent an official view of the CCC or its Commissioners.

I. Introduction

1. Brief Overview

A. State of Play of Legislation

Of the 15 Member States (MS)[1] in the Caribbean Community (CARICOM), only four have passed competition legislation and only two of those include merger control provisions. The countries with competition laws and enforcement institutions are Jamaica, Barbados, Guyana and Trinidad & Tobago (T&T); only Barbados and T&T's statutes include merger control provisions. However, there are draft bills in the Organisation of Eastern Caribbean States (OECS)[2], and in The Bahamas, Belize and Suriname, all of which contain merger control provisions. The only MS of CARICOM that does not have a draft bill is Haiti. In addition to national laws, there is a regional competition policy that applies in relation to cross-border anticompetitive conducts within the CARICOM Single Market and Economy (CSME). However, the regional competition policy contained in Chapter VIII of the Revised Treaty of Chaguaramas (RTC), the legal instrument for the creation of the CSME, does not currently contain merger control provisions.

The draft bill to amend Jamaica's Fair Competition Act (1993) (JFCA) includes merger control provisions. Guyana has a draft merger control bill that has been published for comment. Finally, there is a draft model bill on competition, which contains draft merger control provisions, for the CSME countries which includes all CARICOM MS except The Bahamas. This indicates that all countries in CARICOM (except Haiti) are making progress in introducing competition legislation that includes merger control provisions. However, progress on advancing the legislative programme has been slow in the region and there is currently a Sub-Committee of the Reconvened Task Force on Competition Policy in the CARICOM Single Market & Economy to consider the practicalities of a single competition entity within the Community[3].

B. Legal Sources: Hard Law

The earliest competition law in the region is the JFCA 1993, introduced as part of a structural adjustment conditionality programme linked to World Bank/IMF financial assistance to the government. The drafters of this law were heavily influenced by the competition laws of various jurisdictions including the European Union, Canada, Australia and New Zealand. The JFCA prohibits anticompetitive agreements and abuse of dominance but does not contain merger review provisions. However, a very interesting

---

1 Member states are Antigua & Barbuda, The Bahamas, Barbados, Belize, Dominica, Grenada, Guyana, Haiti, Jamaica, Montserrat, St Kitts & Nevis, St Lucia, St Vincent & the Grenadines, Suriname and Trinidad & Tobago.

2 Members of the OECS are Antigua & Barbuda, Dominica, Grenada, Montserrat, St Kitts & Nevis, St Lucia and St Vincent & the Grenadines.

3 BFTC, *Annual Report* (2018) <<https://www.ftc.gov.bb/library/2018-ftc_annual_report.pdf>, p 17.

case culminating in the Privy Council's[4] decision in 2017 provides legal interpretation on the scope of the Jamaica Fair Trading Commission's jurisdiction to investigate proposed mergers and the legal basis for such investigation. This case is reported in detail below.

The move to deepen regional integration in CARICOM led to the creation of the CSME. There was recognition that rules on competition were necessary in the CSME to ensure that the expected gains to be had by removal of trade barriers were not diminished by private sector anticompetitive conducts[5]. It is interesting to note that while Protocol VIII on Competition Policy was being drafted and negotiated in the Council for Trade and Economic Development (COTED) in the 1990s, a parallel discussion was taking place in the Working Group for Competition Policy that preceded negotiations of the Free Trade Area of the Americas (suspended in 2003)[6]. The government officials from CARICOM countries who attended these meetings would have had the opportunity to gain some understanding of competition law and its benefits from the discussions in the group, particularly the interventions of delegates from mature competition jurisdictions such as the US, Canada, Mexico, Chile and others[7]. This would have influenced the discussions and negotiations in COTED on provisions in Protocol VIII, which became Chapter VIII of the RTC.

Chapter VIII contains the regional competition policy and institutional arrangements which form the international framework for the enforcement of rules of competition in relation to cross-border business conducted in the CSME. As well as establishing the CARICOM Competition Commission (CCC) as the regional competition authority, Chapter VIII also requires MS to enact national competition legislation and establish national competition authorities. The Chapter specifies the broad rules for competition, the types of prohibitions that should apply under national competition legislation, and the procedures for CCC investigations. Similarly, the Chapter also indicates minimum standards for the enactment of harmonised consumer protection legislation by the MS.

There is a view that the CCC directly enforces the rules of competition in Chapter VIII in relation to anticompetitive cross-border conduct. There is, however, another view that the CCC enforces the rules of competition stated in that Chapter, *as they have been implemented in national competition legislation*[8]. On the second view, enforcement of the regional rules in relation to private firms would, therefore, depend on whether the MS have enacted national competition legislation as required under Chapter VIII. Both views may be supported on the language of several treaty articles as well as the CCC's Rules of Procedure 2011. In this regard, although the issue has arisen before the regional court, that is, the Caribbean Court of Justice (CCJ), there is not yet a conclusive judgment on the point[9]. For present purposes,

---

4 The final court of appeal for Jamaica is the Privy Council of the UK. The Caribbean Court of Justice (CCJ) is intended to replace the Privy Council, as the final court of appeal for CSME member states, however, only four countries have signed up to the CCJ: Guyana, Barbados, Belize and Dominica. The Privy Council remains the highest court of appeal for the rest of CARICOM.

5 RTC Chapter VIII, Article 169.

6 Gleaned from my participation in the FTAA negotiations as Vice-president of the Negotiating Group on Competition Policy (NGCP), during which time I also attended working group meetings in CARICOM in preparation for negotiation sessions.

7 ibid. Observed as I chaired meetings of the NGCP.

8 See CCC Rules of Procedure 2011, Part II, rule 4(1).

9 *Trinidad Cement Limited v Competition Commission* [2012] CCJ 4 (OJ), [48].

if the second-mentioned view is ultimately adopted, it could raise further issues in terms of enforcement, in that at present only four MS have enacted national competition legislation. Moreover, there are significant differences in the legislation, even among those four MS. For example, the Trinidad & Tobago Fair Trading Act (TTFTA) expressly exempts the T&T financial sector from its application whereas the other statutes do not.

Barbados was the first country to act on the obligation in the RTC to legislate competition provisions, passing the Barbados Fair Competition Act (BFCA) (2002), which includes merger control provisions. Statutory Instruments Supplement No. 61 to the Act, the Fair Competition (Merger) Rules, 2009, outlines the merger application process, the determination of applications, merger investigation fees, approval of mergers and, finally, the appeal process.

T&T and Guyana followed, passing the TTFTA 2006, and the Guyana Competition and Fair Trading Act 2006 (GCFTA), respectively. T&T proclaimed part of its law in 2012 which allowed it to set up the Trinidad & Tobago Fair Trading Commission (2014), but did not proclaim the rest of its law until February 2020. As such, no enforcement has yet taken place.

While not a member of CARICOM, it is of interest to note the new legislation on competition law in Curacao. The Curacao Competition Act (CCA) entered into force in 2017. It contains provisions prohibiting anticompetitive agreements and abuse of dominance, and an obligation to notify concentrations (i.e. mergers and acquisitions)[10] subject to meeting the following threshold: (i) the combined aggregate turnover of the parties involved in the previous calendar year exceeded ANG 125 million (approx €60 million) and (ii) at least two of the parties achieved a turnover in Curacao of ANG 15 million (approx €7 million) or more of the aggregate in the previous calendar year. A concentration must also be notified if it creates or reinforces a market share of 30% or more in any of the relevant markets in Curacao.

When notifying, firms are required to provide information about the nature of the concentration, market conditions and, if possible, the expected effects of the merger (Article 5.4(1))[11]. Interestingly, the CCA only provides for an obligation to notify and does not contain a system of merger control. This allows the Fair Trading Authority Curacao (FTAC) to monitor concentrations and their effects. The FTAC is required to publish detailed rules about the information that is to be provided when notifying (Article 5.4(2)). The FTAC intends to review the provisions on concentrations in a few years and decide whether to include a merger approval system[12].

---

10 **Chapter 5 – concentrations** Article 5.1 1: "The term 'concentration' shall be understood to mean: (a) the merger of two or more previously independent undertakings; (b) the acquisition of direct or indirect control by: (i) one or more natural persons or legal entities who/which already control at least one undertaking, or; (ii) one or more undertakings of the whole or parts of one or more other undertakings, through the acquisition of participating interests in the capital or assets, pursuant to an agreement, or by any other means.
2. The creation of a joint undertaking shall qualify as a concentration within the meaning of the first paragraph, subparagraph (b)(i), if the joint undertaking performs all the functions of an autonomous economic entity on a sustained basis.
3. Cooperation between undertakings which is institutionalised in the form of a joint venture qualifies as a joint undertaking.

11 National Ordinance on Competition, Official Bulletin [2016 Nr 16], <https://ftac.cw/en/regulations/national-ordinance-on-competition/>.

12 Marieke Bredenoord-Spoek, "Curaçao Competition Act entered into force on 1 September 2017", *Stibbe Competition Law newsletter* (October 2017) <https://www.stibbe.com/en/news/2017/october/cura%c3%a7ao-competition-act-entered-into-force-on-1-september-2017?jurisdiction=222f8a598f86442d8dfbd59c596eb0a3>.

C. Guidelines: Soft Law

With regard to merger control regulation, the BFTC has published two guidelines in relation to mergers, as follows: *The Fair Trading Commission's Merger Investigation Procedures* and *The Setting of a Merger Threshold: No Simple Matter.* Having only recently fully proclaimed its competition legislation, T&T has not as yet published any guidelines to interpret the merger provisions in its law or any procedural guide.

D. Applicable Texts and Useful Links

Barbados: Merger regulation provisions in the BFCA are found in Part III, sections 20–23.
https://www.ftc.gov.bb/library/CAP326B.pdf

Barbados: Guidelines for merger investigations can be found in the following:
https://www.ftc.gov.bb/library/fair_competition_merger_rules_2009_si105.pdf
https://www.ftc.gov.bb/library/fair_competition_merger_fees_regulations_2009_si104.pdf
https://www.ftc.gov.bb/index.php?option=com_content&task=view&id=88&Itemid=28

Trinidad & Tobago: The TTFTA provides merger rules in Part III, sections 13–16.
http://tandtftc.org/wp-content/uploads/2017/01/Fair-Trading-Act-2006.pdf

Jamaica: JFCA and the Consumer Protection Act
https://jftc.gov.jm/wp-content/uploads/2017/08/Fair-Competition-Act.pdf
https://www.cac.gov.jm/portal/index.php/consumer-laws/79-the-laws/105-the-consumer-protection-act

Guyana: GCFTA and Guyana Consumer Affairs Act
https://ccac.gov.gy/wp-content/uploads/2018/08/Competition-and-Fair-Trading-Cap-90-07.pdf
https://gcci.gy/legal-docs/
https://ccac.gov.gy/wp-content/uploads/2018/08/Consumer-Affairs-Act.pdf

CARICOM: Regional Competition Policy (Chapter VIII, RTC)
https://caricom.org/documents/4906-revised_treaty-text.pdf

Competition Commissions websites in CARICOM:
JFTC: https://jftc.gov.jm/
BFTC: https://www.ftc.gov.bb/
GCCAC: https://ccac.gov.gy/
TTFTC: http://tandtftc.org/
CCC: https://www.caricomcompetitioncommission.com/en/

2. Institutional Set-Up

A. *Structure of Agency*

There are four national competition commissions in CARICOM: Jamaica Fair Trading Commission (JFTC) (1993); BFTC (2002), Guyana Competition and Consumer Affairs Commission (GCCAC) (2011), and T&T Fair Trading Commission (TTFTC) (2014), and one regional commission, the CCC (2008).

The CCC follows a pure administrative enforcement model with separate investigative and adjudicative arms. On the other hand, three of the national commissions, the JFTC, BFTC and GCCAC are mixed administrative and prosecutorial models, and the TTFTC is purely prosecutorial. All four national commissions are constituted with an investigative arm and a board of commissioners which is separate from the investigative arm. In all cases, the board is not empowered to make final determinations. Rather, the Commission's report and recommendation go to the High Court for final determination in enforcement proceedings. Notably, there are differences in the mix of administrative and prosecutorial powers in relation to each of the commissions, as explained below:

JFTC: The JFTC's Board of Commissioners vets the investigative report and decides whether to close the case, or to secure a consent agreement with the offending firm(s), or to proceed with a court application for enforcement. If a court application is filed, the Supreme Court then adjudicates, sanctions and enforces. Part VIII of the JFCA states that *if the Court is satisfied* [authors' emphasis] on an application by the JFTC that any person has contravened any obligations or prohibitions in the Act, or has failed to comply with any direction of the JFTC, the Court may exercise any powers referred to in section 47 (power to fine or grant injunction). Thus, the JFTC has to first satisfy the Court that there has been a breach of the JFCA, therefore in effect, leaving the final, legally binding determination to the Court. In that regard, it is partially an administrative model, having a Board that makes an agency decision on whether there has been an infringement, but because this decision is not a final determination, it is also partially a prosecutorial model.

The nature of court determinations as distinct from the decision of the competition commission was explained in *Jamaica Stock Exchange v JFTC* [2001][13], where the Court opined:

> It seems reasonably clear that the powers to effect any sanction for disobedience to the FTC's orders fall within the jurisdiction of the Court. The following section 47 dispels any conclusion that the orders given by the FTC after its determination of the complaint, is in any way akin to an injunction. That is so, because one of the powers of the Court, when satisfied that the directions of the FTC have not been complied with, is the power to issue an injunction to restrain the person from engaging in such conduct[14].

---

13 Jamaica Supreme Court Civil Appeal No. 92/97, judgment delivered on 29 January 2001, <https://jftc.gov.jm/wp-content/uploads/2017/08/Jamaica-Stock-Exchange-vs.-The-Fair-Trading-Commission-January-2001.pdf>.

14 ibid 28. In this case, the Jamaica Stock Exchange challenged the validity of jurisdiction of the JFTC in this sector since it is governed by provisions of the Securities Act. Further, the Stock Exchange claimed that there was no clear distinction between the investigative and adjudicative arms of the JFTC, that this was a breach of natural justice, and that the JFTC's action was *ultra vires*. Section 46 of the JFCA vests enforcement power in the

Moreover, the non-binding nature of JFTC decisions, as usually contained in its staff reports, was further emphasised by the court in *Cable & Wireless Jamaica Ltd v Digicel (Jamaica) Limited* [2010][15]. In this case, the claimant Cable & Wireless sought to rely on a JFTC staff report which supported its allegation of abuse of a dominant position against Digicel. In ruling on the admissibility of the report in those court proceedings, the Court opined that: "I am therefore of the view that this Report falls into a different category from a finding of a tribunal or expert administrative body. So what exactly is the nature of this Report? In my view it consists largely of opinion evidence, as opposed to evidence of the relevant facts"[16].

BFTC: Section 6 of the BFCA gives the BFTC Board the power to declare certain practices to be abuse of a dominant position, prohibit anticompetitive actions and prohibit acquisition of one company or its assets by another company. In the case of abuse of dominance, section 17 of the BFCA requires the BFCA to notify the enterprise of its finding accompanied by a copy of the report, and to direct the enterprise to cease the abusive practice within a specified period. Part VII, section 36, speaks to the process of appeal against the BFTC's findings. This might at first glance appear to be adjudicative powers. But, the BFCA must be read in conjunction with the Barbados Fair Trading Commission Act (BFTCA), which provides specific guidelines for legally enforcing the decision of the BFTC if the business fails to comply. This was clarified in the Barbados Court of Appeal's Judgment in *Fair Trading Commission v Barbados National Oil Co Ltd* [2015][17]. In that judgment, the Barbados Court of Appeal interpreted section 37 of the BFCA in conjunction with section 31(1)(b) of the BFTCA, and opined that section 37 of the BFCA refers to the High Court, that the BFTC has to apply to the Court in the case of a person not following its directives, and the court *has to be satisfied that any person has contravened the BFCA*, and can impose fines and order payment of compensation to persons harmed. Importantly, the Court of Appeal specified that the proceedings of the High Court are by way of a hearing on the findings of the BFTC and not a review of those findings. A final determination can only be made in proceedings under section 37 of the BFCA.

GCCAC: The GCCAC also has wide ranging powers of investigation and, like the BFTC, it can declare certain business practices to be abuses of dominant position, prohibit anti-competitive behaviour, order termination of an agreement, prohibit the carrying out of an agreement, and order cease and desist from any form or conduct that has or is likely to have as its object or effect the lessening of competition (s 7(1) GCFTA). However, Part VII, section 47 of the GCFTA states that "... if the High Court [is] satisfied on an application by the Commission that any enterprise contravened any of the Provisions of this Act, the High Court may exercise any of the powers referred to in Section 48", that is, to fine and grant injunction.

courts, stating that once the court is satisfied on an application from the JFTC that any person has contravened the law, then the court may exercise the powers specified in section 47, that is, to fine the person and to grant an injunction restraining the offending person from engaging in the conduct. As a result of this judgement, the JFTC does an investigation and produces a report with recommendations, but it is not legally binding.

15 Jamaica Supreme Court, Claim Number 2009 HCV 05568, judgment delivered on 2 September 2010.

16 ibid [45].

17 Barbados Court of Appeal, Civil Appeal No 20 of 2009, judgment delivered 25 February 2015.

In sum, the JFTC, BFTC, and GCCAC exhibit mixed administrative and prosecutorial models, having a structure that includes an investigative arm and a board of commissioners who can make an agency decision, but those agency decisions do not constitute final determinations, and the High Court or Supreme Court, as the case may be, must be satisfied that a breach has taken place, and can exercise power of sanctioning the offenders or issuing injunctions. In all jurisdictions, there is the right of appeal against the High Court/Supreme Court decisions to the Court of Appeal in the domestic jurisdiction whose decisions can be further appealed to the final appellate court, the Privy Council for some MS and the CCJ for others[18].

TTFTC: The TTFTC is a purely prosecutorial commission, with the Board not given any power of adjudication in the legislation. Nor is the Board given powers similar to the JFTC, BFTC and CCAC to prohibit anticompetitive behaviour or issue cease and desist orders, even though not legally binding. Section 6 of the TTFTA states: "For the purposes of discharging its functions under section 5 [investigate, disseminate information to the public, research and advocacy], the Commission may make application to the Court for the determination of a contravention of this Act." Sections 16(2), 17(3), 19(1)(b), and 25 reinforce the obligation on the part of the TTFTC to apply to the Court for determination and sanctioning.

By section 23 the TTFTC is given the right, in the case of an abuse of monopoly power, to prepare a report, submit it to the enterprise concerned, and request the enterprise to cease the abusive practice within six months. This is the only provision of the TTFTA that allows the TTFTC to issue a "directive". Section 44(1) states that the Court shall have jurisdiction to hear and determine applications made by the TTFTC for an Order to prohibit anticompetitive mergers or conducts and review any decisions made by the TTFTC at the request of any party, and appeals made by the Regulated Industries Commission or any company falling within the Regulated Industries Commission's purview. Section 44(2) gives the Court the power to impose fines.

CCC: The CCC follows a purely administrative model. Its structure is bifurcated with separate monitoring and investigation arms and separate adjudication, with one Board of seven commissioners which split into panels for each function as needed after appropriate conflict of interest declarations. Article 174(3) of the RTC states: "The Commission may, on the basis of its investigations, make determinations regarding the compatibility of business conduct with the rules of competition and other related provisions of the Treaty." Article 174(4) gives the CCC the power to order termination or nullification of agreements, conducts or decisions prohibited by the Treaty, direct the enterprise to cease and desist from anticompetitive conduct, including measures to overcome the effects of abuse of dominance, order payment of compensation to persons affected and impose fines for breaches of the rules of competition. While CCC decisions are appealable to the CCJ, the nature of the process would be a review of the record of the CCC's findings, not a rehearing as in the case of the national commissions.

All national commissions are empowered to initiate investigations on their own initiative, or at the request of interested persons. (JFCA s 5(1)(a); BFCA s 5(1)(b); TTFTA s 5(1)(a); GCFTA s 6(1)(c)).

---

18 See note 4.

In the case of the CCC, the procedure is more complex. A MS may request the CCC to undertake an investigation "where it has reason to believe that business conduct by an enterprise located in another MS prejudices trade and prevents, restricts, or distorts competition in the territory of the requesting MS" (RTC, Art 175(1)). The COTED may also request an investigation where it "has reason to believe that business conduct by an enterprise in the CSME prejudices trade and prevents, restricts or distorts competition within the CSME and has or is likely to have cross-border effects" (RTC Art 175(2)). In terms of self-initiation powers, the CCC may request a MS to do a preliminary examination of the business conduct of an enterprise, and if the CCC is not satisfied, it may initiate its own examination. However, if there is disagreement between the CCC and the MS as to who has jurisdiction, it must be referred to COTED for a decision.

The JFTC, BFTC and GCCAC, are multifunctional agencies, and enforce both Competition Law and Consumer Protection Law. The structure of the BFTC is different, in that its purview includes Competition, Consumer Protection, and Utility Regulation. The TTFTC enforces only Competition Law. The CCC also enforces competition law, but is further entrusted with obligations under the RTC to provide support to MSs in the promotion of consumer welfare and the protection of consumer interests (RTC Art 186).

The **JFTC** was established in 1993. The minimum number of Commissioners is three and maximum is five (JFCA, Schedule, s 1.1). There are currently five Commissioners who vet the investigative report in a case, provide an opinion, and decide whether to submit the report to the Court for determination, negotiate a consent agreement with the offending firm, or close the case. The Commissioners have the power to summon and examine witnesses, to call for and examine documents, and to administer oaths. Where they find that an arrangement has contravened sections 17, 20 or 33 of the Act, they may prohibit the arrangement. For prohibitions under sections 20 and 33, they may also direct the enterprise concerned to take steps that are necessary to overcome any anticompetitive effects resulting from the arrangement[19]. However, while de jure the Board of Commissioners has these powers, since the *Jamaica Stock Exchange* case they have not in fact summoned witnesses or adjudicated[20]. Enforcement proceedings in the Supreme Court, are instead commenced where there is non-compliance with a JFTC decision as contained in its report. Decisions of the Supreme Court can be appealed to the Court of Appeal. The final appellate court is the Privy Council in the UK.

The investigative division is headed by an Executive Director who is an *ex officio* member of the JFTC. He is supported by an Executive Secretary. There are three subdivisions within the investigative division: legal, administrative and economic. The legal section headed by a Senior Legal Counsel with three legal officers and one research officer – legal; the administrative section is headed by a general manager, with an information systems administrator, an accountant, two senior secretaries, a receptionist/telephone operator and an office attendant. The economic section is headed by a Competition Bureau Chief, two competition analysts and two research officers. The JFTC enforces the JFCA, which contains both competition and consumer protection provisions. By way

19 JFTC, "Functions and Powers" <<https://jftc.gov.jm/about-us/functions-and-powers/>.

20 Interview by Dr. Stewart with the Executive Director of the JFTC on January 15, 2020.

of Cabinet decision of the Government of Jamaica in June 2018, a new entity is being created which amalgamates the functions of the Consumer Affairs Commission with that of the JFTC. This process was scheduled to be completed in 2020. The JFTC distinguishes between technical staff and those who provide ancillary functions such as finance and accountancy. The total number of technical staff at present (March 2020) is 10. Combined with other staff, the number is 16.

The **BFTC** evolved from the original Public Utilities Board set up in 1955, which was operational until 2001 when it was reconstituted into the BFTC. The newly constituted BFTC is multifunctional with a portfolio that combines Consumer Protection, Fair Competition, and Utility Regulation. Each of these is a separate division within the BFTC. The BFTC enforces the following Acts: Fair Trading Commission Act, CAP. 326B; Fair Competition Act, CAP. 326C; Consumer Protection Act, CAP. 326D; Utilities Regulation Act, CAP. 282; and certain provisions of the Telecommunications Act, CAP. 282B; Barbados Water Authority Act, CAP. 274A; and the Electric Light and Power Act, CAP. 278[21].

The eight Commissioners are responsible for adjudicating on regulatory applications, issuing orders, initiating prosecution if necessary, and making determinations. However, as explained above, the High Court has the power to make final determinations in competition matters: decisions of the commissioners are not final in competition matters and firms can choose to comply with orders or not. In the case of non-compliance, the case is submitted to the High Court. Decisions of the High Court can be appealed to the Court of Appeal, and the final appellate court for Barbados is the CCJ.

The Chief Executive Officer (CEO) heads the administrative/investigative arm, is an *ex officio* member of the BFTC, and is responsible for administering the legislation under the purview of the BFTC and for supervision of the staff and work programme. There is a Director appointed to head each division: Utility Regulation, Fair Competition and Consumer Protection. The General Legal Counsel provides legal advice to all divisions of the BFTC[22]. The total number of technical staff is 14, of which three are in the competition division.

The **Guyana** Competition Commission was established in 2010, but after the passing of the Consumer Affairs Act (CAA) of 2011, the Commission was renamed the **Competition and Consumer Affairs Commission**, in compliance with section 4 of this Act, and the purview of the GCCAC was extended to enforcing the CAA as well as the GCFTA. There are currently four Commissioners (including the Chairman), an even number. In this regard, the Chairman may cast the deciding vote in the event of a tie. In the past the Commission was in a situation where two Commissioners had to recuse themselves in a matter due to a potential conflict of interest, resulting in no quorum.

The GCCAC has two units, the Competition Unit and the Consumer Affairs Unit. At present the Competition Unit has two staff members: (1) a competition policy officer, who heads the unit; and (2) an analyst or economist. The Consumers Affairs Unit employs two

---

21 BFTC, "Legislation" <https://www.ftc.gov.bb/index.php?option=com_content&task=view&id=18&Itemid=68>.

22 BFTC, "About Us" <https://www.ftc.gov.bb/index.php?option=com_content&task=view&id=30&Itemid=50>.

investigators and two economist/analysts along with the head of the unit: the consumer affairs officer. The unit is supported by two consumer affairs representatives and one senior consumer affairs representative. Both units are under the guidance of the office of the Director and support staff. The GCCAC is also supported by a communications and a finance specialist.

The Commissioners determine that an agreement or trade practice is anti-competitive (s 22(1) GCFTA), and determines the amount of third-party compensation (s 22(2)). In the case of an abuse of dominance, the GCCAC can notify the enterprise of its finding, direct it to cease abusive practice immediately or within a time period agreed, not more than six months. Firms are directed to immediately cease the abusive conduct in the case of tied selling. The GCCAC can prohibit market restriction or exclusive dealing and order the supplier to take such action needed to restore competition. All these powers are subject to Court adjudication in the instance where the firm refuses to obey, as the GCCACs directives are not final.

The TTFTC is still nascent, given that the law was only fully proclaimed in February 2020. The TTFTC is now preparing to enforce the law. There are five Commissioners at present and five members of staff: the Executive Director, the Secretary to the Board, one investigator, , a clerical/accountant assistant and an administrative assistant. It is evident that the TTFTC is still understaffed, and vacant positions include a senior legal counsel, an investigator and an IT/information systems administrator. The Executive Director is responsible for supervising the work and the staff of the TTFTC.

B. Procedure for Appointments and Link to Branch of Government

Jamaica: The JFTC is currently linked to the Ministry of Industry, Commerce, Agriculture and Fisheries. JFTC Commissioners are appointed by this Ministry for a period of three years and can be reappointed for another three years. The Executive Director is appointed by the Commissioners, holds the position for seven years and may be reappointed for periods not exceeding five years at a time. The Executive Director, heads of divisions and other staff members are appointed by the JFTC.

Barbados: The BFTCA provides guidelines for appointments. BFTC Commissioners are appointed by the Minister of Industry, International Business, Commerce and Small Business Development for a period of five years and the appointment can be renewed. The Board of Commissioners, with the approval of the Minister, appoints a CEO for a term not exceeding five years and this appointment is eligible for renewal. The CEO is an *ex officio* member of the BFTC. The BFTC, with the approval of the Minister, appoints the following positions: Director of Utility Regulation, Director of Consumer Protection and Director of Fair Competition. Each serves for a term of five years and each is eligible for reappointment. The BFTC appoints other members of staff.

Guyana: The First Schedule of the GCFTA outlines the procedures for appointments. There shall be no fewer than three and no more than five Commissioners of the GCCAC who are appointed for a period of three years by the Minister of Business and approved by the Cabinet; they are eligible for reappointment for another three years. At present there are four Commissioners. The Minister appoints the Chairman of the GCCAC. The Secretary of the Commission is appointed by the Commissioners, and the GCCAC seal is kept in the custody of the Secretary. The Director is appointed by the Minister as well. The Director is an *ex officio* member of the Board.

Trinidad and Tobago: TTFTC Commissioners are appointed by the President of the Republic of Trinidad and Tobago; the Chairman of the TTFTC is also appointed by the President. The TTFTA allows appointment of not less than three and no more than five Commissioners for a period not exceeding five years. The current Commissioners are appointed for a period of three years and are eligible for reappointment for a further three years. The TTFTA specifies that appointments of Commissioners shall not all expire at the same time. Of the five Commissioners, one can be appointed by the Regulated Industries Commission. The Executive Director is appointed by the Board of Commissioners.

CARICOM: Commissioners of the CCC are appointed by the Regional Judicial and Legal Services Commission (RJLSC) for a period of five years. The RJLSC may determine to renew the commissioner's tenure for a further period of five years.

At present there are seven Commissioners. The Executive Director is appointed by the Board of the Commission and while there is no statutory period for the appointment, contracts are usually for three years for all staff, and approved by the Board. There are currently three technical staff in the Commission, one Senior Economist, one Economist and one Senior Legal Counsel.

C. Links to Government Branch

The four national commissions are linked to a ministry of government (listed below) and each law outlines the relationship that should exist between the commission and the government through the relevant ministry. In all four cases, the relevant minister provides guidance for the operations of the commission and may make regulations and policy on the advice of the commission. All four Commissions must submit audited accounts, estimates of revenue and expenditure for the next financial year, and an annual report on the general activities of the commission. The Minister, upon approval of these reports, is responsible for submitting to Parliament for approval. The commissions are therefore dependent on the ministry for their financing. In the case of the GCCAC, for instance, the commission receives a monthly subvention from the ministry for monthly expenses including salaries; the relevant minister is also responsible for taking overseas travel for staff to cabinet for approval.

The following are the ministries to which commissions are linked:

JFTC: Ministry of Industry, Commerce, Agriculture and Fisheries.

BFTC: Ministry of Industry, International Business and Small Business Development.

TTFTC: Ministry of Trade and Industry.

GCCAC: Ministry of Business.

CCC: The regional commission is linked to CARICOM bodies, which are the COTED and the Community Council of Ministers (CCOM). COTED approves the work programme of the CCC for each fiscal year and the CCC reports on work programmes to COTED. The CCC may also make recommendations to COTED to enhance the effectiveness of the competition policy in the region (RTC Art 173.3(b)). The CCC submits audited financials to CCOM who approves the CCC budget on the recommendation of COTED. Under Article 182 of the RTC, COTED is given the powers to develop and establish appropriate policies and rules of competition within CARICOM, including special rules for particular sectors. Where such rules are being developed, COTED can suspend or exclude the application of the rules of competition (Art 177 RTC) to those sectors pending the adoption of the relevant rules (Art 183(1)), or to any sector or enterprise or group of enterprises in the public interest (Art 183(2)).

3. Type of Merger Control

A. Pure Ex Ante

Merger provisions in the BFCA are to be found in sections 20–23. It is a pure *ex ante* regime with a threshold for triggering compulsory notification:

> 20 (1) From the commencement of this Act, all mergers by an enterprise that
> a) by itself controls; or
> b) together with any other enterprise with which it intends to effect the merger is likely to control not less than 40 per cent of any market or such other amount of the market as the Minister may be order prescribe are prohibited *unless permitted by the Commission in accordance with this section.* [authors' emphasis.]

Such enterprises desirous of effecting a merger shall apply to the BFTC for permission to effect the merger, providing the prescribed information. This provision includes any public bid for control of an entity.

The merger provisions in the TTFTA are to be found in Part III, sections 13–16. Like the BFCA, it is also a pure *ex ante* regime with compulsory notification, but the threshold differs from that of Barbados, since it is a monetary sum, rather than a market share:

> 14 (1) Subject to the provisions of this section from the commencement of this Act –
> a) all anti-competitive mergers are prohibited; and
> b) enterprises shall not enter into a merger unless they obtain permission from the Commission where-
> (i) their assets exceed fifty million dollars [TTD, at current exchange rate: USD 7.1 million];
> (ii) at least one of the enterprises carries on or intends to carry on business in Trinidad and Tobago.

The threshold could be varied by the Minister by Order, but if this variation exceeds 50%, the relevant Order shall be subject to affirmative resolution of Parliament (s 14(4) & (5))

> 14.4 The Minister may by Order vary the asset limit specified in subsection (1)(b)(i).

B. Suspensory Effects of Transaction

In the case of Barbados, the BFCA, section 22(1) states:

> Where the Commission is of the opinion that enterprises have, without obtaining the permission of the Commission under Section 21, structured themselves in such a way as to constitute a merger within the meaning of this Act the Commission may by notice in writing direct the enterprises concerned to determine the merger within such time as is specified in the direction.

Subsection 2 prescribes that, before giving a direction, the BFTC shall give the enterprises an opportunity to be heard. Subsection 3 states that where an enterprise fails to comply with a direction under subsection (1), the BFTC shall apply to the Court for an Order against the enterprise.

In the case of T&T, the TTFTA, section 16(1), provides for the TTFTC to initiate an investigation where it has reason to believe that two or more enterprises have merged without permission for the merger. By subsection (2), after such an investigation, if the TTFTC is of the opinion that the enterprises have indeed merged within the meaning of the TTFTA without the permission as required under s 14, the TTFTC may apply to the Court for an Order for divestment of assets. However, subsection (3) allows that, before such an application to the Court, the TTFTC and the enterprise may agree to divest within an agreed period, part of their combined business or operations, if the TTFTC is satisfied that such divestment would make the merger less likely to reduce competition in T&T.

Although both provisions do not expressly provide for the suspensory effects of notification, they are nonetheless designed to address "gun-jumping" by merging parties, which may refer to either the failure to notify a notifiable merger transaction or the premature implementation of a merger before the competition authority can render its decision. On the latter point, the presence of these provisions in the statutes could indicate, at least impliedly, that compulsory notification under both regimes may be intended to have suspensory effect in as much as the merging parties would not be allowed to implement the transaction without permission. It is, however, also observed that the foregoing provisions may not capture partial implementation conduct before a decision is rendered, that is, steps taken by the merging parties which progress the transaction without fully constituting the merger.

II. Scope of Application

1. Definition of Notifiable Transaction

The BFCA requires notification where two or more firms intend to merge and their combined assets meet the threshold in the law. Section 2 defines merger as:

> a) The cessation of two or more enterprises from being distinct, whether by amalgamation, by one or more enterprises acquiring control over another or otherwise; or

b) The engagement in a joint venture between enterprises which results in two or more enterprises ceasing to be distinct entities.

Section 23 of the BFCA also captures interlocking directorates: "where a director serves on a board of directors of two or more companies that are significant competitors and the director's conduct has the effect of welding together the policies of those companies in such a way as to reduce significantly competition between or to eliminate competition, the Commission shall direct that the director serve on not more than one board of the relevant companies."

Similarly, the TTFTA requires notification where firms intend to merge and they meet the threshold specified in the law. Part III, section 13(1) of the TTFTA defines merger as follows: "

Merger means the cessation of two or more enterprises from being distinct whether by purchase or lease of shares or assets, amalgamation, combination, joint venture or any other means through which influence over the policy of another enterprise is acquired."

The TTFTA also captures interlocking directorates as well. Section 15 provides: "where a director serves on the Board of Directors of two or more companies that are competitors and the director is likely to weld together the policies of those companies in a way that would reduce or eliminate competition between them, the companies in which he serves as director shall, subject to section 14(1)(b) apply to the Commission for permission to merge." The reference to section 14(1)(b) means that this provision applies to those interlocks where the companies meet the threshold for notification, that is, assets in excess of TTD 50 million [approximately USD 7.1 million] and presence in the jurisdiction.

Overall the foregoing provisions indicate that the merger control regimes of Barbados and T&T capture transactions in a variety of legal forms. The provisions outlined above capture amalgamations, acquisitions of majority shareholdings, joint ventures and interlocking directorates. There may, however, be divergence in the regimes with regard to acquisitions of minority shareholdings. In this regard, the definition of merger under the BFCA may not capture such acquisitions on the ground that it requires amalgamation, acquisition of "control" or other like conduct. While the legislation does not define "control", acquisitions of minority shareholdings are not traditionally understood as conferring control[23]. In contrast, the definition of merger under the TTFTA references the acquisition of "influence". Although influence is not defined in the legislation, this could nonetheless indicate that the regime in T&T is capable of capturing those acquisitions of minority shareholdings that confer something less than control.

---

23 Although in light of the Privy Council's decision in *Fair Trading Commission v Digicel Jamaica Limited* (2017), it is arguable that s 13(2) of the BFCA could afford jurisdiction to review an acquisition of a minority shareholding where it is likely to have the effect of preventing, restricting or distorting competition. But note that because such an acquisition is not captured under the formal merger regime, procedural obligations such as notification requirements and remedies such as divestiture may not apply. See discussion of the Digicel/ Claro decision in the Case Law Illustration section.

2. Material Scope

The BFCA covers all economic sectors, goods and services, and includes public utility enterprises. Section 3(2): "This Act applies to an enterprise that supplies any utility service set out in the Second Schedule to the Fair Trading Commission Act". The Second Schedule of the BFTCA lists electricity, water, sewerage, domestic and international telecommunications, and distribution of natural gas.

The TTFTA is different in that there are substantial exceptions.

Section 3:

> (1): This Act shall not apply to –
> (g) companies which fall within the purview of the Telecommunications Authority Act, 2001;
> (h) banks and non-bank financial institutions which fall within the purview of the Securities Industry Act, 1995; or
> (i) such other business or activity declared by the Minister by Order subject to affirmative resolution of Parliament.
> (2) The Act shall apply to service providers within the meaning of the Regulated Industries Commission Act, 1998[24] save that the responsibility for enforcement of this Act in respect of service providers shall be that of the Regulated Industries Commission
> (3) Where a merger or an anti-competitive agreement would fall within the purview of the Commission in circumstances where any of the companies involved is a service provider, the Regulated Industries Commission shall not make any decision before it consults with the Commission.

It is important to note that although there are sectoral exceptions in the TTFTA, mergers and acquisitions in the financial and telecommunications sectors are subject to regulatory reviews under the relevant sector-specific legislation, for example, the Telecommunications Act. In that regard, the goals and methodologies of these regulatory reviews will be guided by the sector-specific legislation, and may thus entail some differences from a competition law review.

3. Geographical Scope

The BFCA refers to any market affected in the national jurisdiction. Section 2(6): "For the purposes of this Act, the effect on competition in a market shall be determined by reference to all factors that affect competition in that market, *including competition from goods or services supplied or likely to be supplied by persons not resident or carrying on business in Barbados.*" [authors' emphasis.]

24 The Regulated Industries Commission Act defines "service provider" to means any entity, including a statutory authority or a company incorporated under the Companies Act, listed in the First Schedule (the names of the companies providing services in T&T are listed in the first schedule) and licensed to provide a service listed in the Second Schedule (supply of electricity, distribution of electricity, supply of water, distribution of water, provision of sewerage and waste-water services).

While the Barbadian courts have not yet ruled on whether the BFCA permits extraterritorial application, the above reference in section 2(6) to competition from goods and services supplied or likely to be supplied by non-residents could tentatively provide a basis for arguing that the BFCA is able to capture mergers implemented outside of Barbados but which affect more than 40% of the market within the jurisdiction[25]. In practice, however, the BFTC interprets its jurisdiction to extend to mergers where at least one party has a local presence/nexus and which satisfy the notification threshold with respect to market share in the jurisdiction[26].

In the case of TTFTA, the law specifies in section 14(1)(b)(ii) that at least one of the enterprises carries on or intends to carry on business in T&T. This implies that regional and international enterprises would qualify for merger notification where that requirement is satisfied.

4. Thresholds

The threshold specified in the BFCA is "no less than 40 per cent of the market". The guidelines issued by the BFTC, *The Setting of a Merger Threshold: No Simple Matter*, explain that the rationale behind the threshold specified in the BFCA is to target firms whose merger has the potential to significantly lessen competition. Those that are so small that they do not significantly alter the existing concentration of related markets will not present a potential for the lessening of competition. Otherwise, too many inconsequential mergers will have to be scrutinised, placing a burden on the BFTC.

According to the BFTC's guidelines, the BFTC gauges the general size (gross output value) of the industries and the sizes (gross turnover) of the respective firms in those industries in order to compute a nominal value threshold that ensures that all potentially dominant mergers can be reviewed. In setting a threshold based on percentile of relevant market, the guidelines posit that various domestic industries differ vastly in size and this makes it difficult to have a nominal dollar threshold that caters to firms across all sectors. Rather, the BFCA opted for a percentage estimate which would vary in nominal value from sector to sector.

Further, in setting the threshold the drafters of the BFCA took into account the small size of the market and distinguished between the non-traded sector and the export sector. As such, there was particular concern that firms and industries in the non-tradeable sector that wish to merge could be scrutinised. In Barbados, such industries are construction, utilities, distribution, mining, quarrying, transport, storage and communications. On the other hand, mergers in products that are largely destined for international markets (tourism, manufacturing and non-sugar agriculture), may want to be encouraged to increase their concentration of power and likewise their opportunity to penetrate overseas markets.

The TTFTA section 14(1)(b)(i) gives a threshold of TTD 50 million dollars [approximately USD 7.1 million]. The TTFTC has not published any guidelines as yet on the rationale for the monetary threshold or for the sum chosen.

---

25 Although this argument is not free from difficulty, one of which would be the traditional presumption against extraterritoriality in statutory interpretation.

26 Gleaned from communication with BFTC staff.

III. Procedure

1. Launch of Procedure

In the Barbados merger control regime, BFCA section 20(1) (a) & (b) applies to all mergers by an enterprise, that by itself or together with any other enterprise with which it intends to effect the merger is likely to control not less than 40% of the market. This includes any public bid for the control of an entity (s 20(4)).

Notification must be done prior to any steps being taken to structure the merger within the meaning of the BFCA (s 2 as quoted above). However, there is no specific deadline for submission of an application for approval of a proposed merger.

The application must be accompanied by the prescribed information (s 20(3)), which is set out in Fair Competition (Merger) Rules 2009 (FCMR)[27]. Merging parties are required to submit separate applications. There is only one application procedure at present, so there is no fast track in place. It is a standard application form, regardless of complexity of the transaction. There are no provisions currently for electronic submission of an application but the BFTC is currently exploring the possibility of setting up an e-filing system and have on occasion requested parties to make electronic submissions.

Section 2 of the FCMR requires the applicant to submit to the BFTC the merger application form set out in the schedule; a merger proposal; copies of any agreements or any other contracts on which the merger is based; a copy of resolutions of the board of directors of any enterprise involved in the merger with respect to the acceptance of a merger proposal; for each of the merging enterprises, three copies of the most recent annual financial reports, if any, and the annual accounts; a list of all other regulatory bodies which will be affected by the proposed merger; copies of applications made to other regulatory bodies; and a list of the notified mergers involving any of the merging enterprises in any other country during the last five years.

On the matter of the fees payable, it is observed that there are two fees associated with the process from filing through to investigation. Section 2(1)(b) of the FCMR stipulates that a "merger application fee" should be paid to the BFTC at the time of submitting the merger application. Once the BFTC conducts a merger investigation it is further entitled under section 4 of the FCMR to charge a "merger investigation fee".

The quantum of both fees is set out in the Fair Trading Commission (Fair Competition Merger Fees) Regulations 2009. Under these regulations the "merger application fee" is a flat fee of $500 per application. However, the "merger investigation fee" is a variable fee, which depends on the outcome of the BFTC's investigation. The variable "merger investigation fee" is structured as follows, for two categories of mergers:

a) Category 1 – Where a merger is not likely to harm competition, that is, a merger with a marginal competition effect or a positive competition effect; or

---

27 Supplement to Official Gazette No 82, 10 September 2009.

b) Category 2 – Where a merger is likely to harm competition, that is, a merger with a significant negative competition effect.

Merger investigation fees payable are as follows: Category 1 merger where the total combined assets of that merger:

a) Do not exceed BBD 5 million: BBD 5,000[28];
b) Exceed BBD 5 million but do not exceed BBD 20 million: BBD 7,500;
c) Exceed BBD 20 million: BBD10,000.

Merger investigation fees applicable to Category 2 mergers where the total combined assets of that merger:

a) Do not exceed BBD 5 million: BBD 20,000;
b) Exceeds BBD 5 million but does not exceed BBD 20 million: BBD 30,000;
c) Exceeds BBD 20 million: BBD 40,000.

Section 2 of the FCMR requires submission of the merger application form set out in the Schedule to the Rules. This is a single application form, but requires the provision of detailed information upon which the BFTC could assess the impact of the proposed merger on market structure and competition.

BFCA section 20(5) requires that within three months after the receipt of the application or as soon as practicable thereafter, the BFTC shall determine whether to grant or refuse permission and shall notify the applicant in writing of its determination.

TTFTC procedural rules have not yet been implemented for merger investigations. The TTFTA does not specify that filing fees can be charged, and it is generally observed that, unlike the BFTC, the TTFTC is not expressly empowered to charge fees for services rendered under the statute.

2. Development of Procedure

The guidelines issued by the BFTC, *Merger Investigation Procedures* provide transparency on the procedures followed by the BFTC in dealing with a merger application. There are two phases: a preliminary analysis and a formal enquiry.

In **Phase 1** of the procedure the BFTC does a preliminary analysis by reviewing the merger application in accordance with the 40% market share threshold in order to determine if the transaction requires an investigation. This involves a determination of the specific market(s) for consideration by a review of the information provided by the firms on the various products and services, and the geographic area over which their products are distributed. The BFTC then makes a determination of the relevant percentage market share(s) of the enterprise(s) pre- and post-merger in each market affected by calculating the volume of output supplied by the enterprises relative to the total market. If the result of this preliminary analysis is that the merged enterprises do not control in excess of

---

28 The Barbados dollar exchange rate is BBD 2 = USD 1.

the threshold market share as determined by the BFCA, the applicants would be notified by letter that the proposed merger falls outside the jurisdiction of the BFTC and therefore does not require permission.

Phase 2 of the procedure is triggered if the preliminary analysis indicates that the combined enterprise will control an amount equal to or greater than the 40% threshold market share. The applicants will be formally notified of the intention of the BFTC to investigate the proposed merger to determine the extent to which it affects competition in the domestic market. The Guidelines states that the BFTC shall allow itself a maximum period of 90 business days to conduct an investigation into the arrangement, inclusive of the preliminary analysis.

The powers of the BFTC in merger investigations are similar to its general powers in any other competition investigation. These are the powers under sections 26–28 of the BFTCA to: hold inquiries, administer oaths, summon and examine witnesses, compel production of documents, examine any document so produced, require documents to be verified by affidavit, adjourn investigations and inspect goods and business premises. Notably, although the BFTC has search and seizure powers, these are only exercisable upon permission of the courts.

The position with regard to investigative powers is similar in the TTFTC, although more of its powers require the prior permission of the courts. In this regard, under sections 8 and 9 of the TTFTA, the TTFTC can require production of documents, verification of documents by affidavit, summon witnesses and exercise search and seizure. However, with the exception of verification of documents by affidavit, the TTFTC must apply to the courts before exercising those powers.

3. Conclusion of Procedure

There are four possible outcomes to the investigation by the BFTC:

- If the BFTC finds that the merger would not affect competition adversely or be detrimental to consumers, the BFTC shall grant permission for the merger to proceed.
- If the finding is that the merger will adversely affect competition but the merging parties can convincingly demonstrate that the transaction will produce significant cost efficiencies which will be shared with consumers in the form of lower prices, improved quality of products, etc. the merger is likely to be permitted.

  Section 21(1)(a) of the BFCA: "the merger is likely to bring about gains in real as distinct from pecuniary efficiencies that are greater than or more than offset the effects of any limitations on competition that result or are likely to result from the merger … The burden of proof is on the merging firms to demonstrate that if the merger is not completed, it is not likely that the relevant efficiency gains would be realised by means that would limit competition to a lesser degree than the merger …"

  This section also allows for a failing firm defence. Section 21(1)(b) "… one of the parties to the merger is faced with actual or imminent financial failure, and the merger represents the least anticompetitive among the known alternative uses for the assets of the failing business."

Section 21(2)(b): "The firms must prove that reasonable steps have been taken within the recent past to identify alternative purchasers for the assets of the failing business and describe in detail the results of the search for alternative purchasers."

- However, if the merger is likely to adversely affect competition or be detrimental to consumers without sufficient redeeming efficiency benefits, the BFTC may direct the enterprises within an agreed period to divest specific interests or part of the combined operation, if the BFTC is satisfied that such divestment would make the merger less likely to lessen competition or to adversely affect the interests of consumers or the economy. Section 21(3)(b)(ii) requires the relevant parties to enter into legally enforceable agreements as specified by the BFTC.
- Finally, if the BFTC considers that the likely anticompetitive effects of the merger cannot be remedied, or where no prudent divestment arrangement can be negotiated, then the merger is likely to be prohibited (BFCA s 213(a)).

These outcomes of the BFTC's merger investigation are not final, and are subject to judicial control as stipulated under the BFCA and BFTCA. Indeed, as earlier indicated, it is the courts in Barbados that are empowered in enforcement proceedings under the BFCA to make final legal determinations in competition matters, which includes determinations in merger investigations. Moreover, prior to the commencement of enforcement proceedings, merging parties are afforded a 15-day period from service of the BFTC's findings on them to challenge those findings by way of appeal to a Judge in Chambers of the High Court under section 36 BFCA. Such an appeal is by way of a review of the record on which the BFTC's decision is made (as distinct from a rehearing which would apply in enforcement proceedings as distinct from appeal proceedings), and the Judge in Chambers is empowered to "confirm, modify or reverse" any of the BFTC's findings. It should also be noted that under section 37 of the BFTCA it is open to merging parties to appeal "questions of law" to the High Court. This may contemplate, for example, a complaint that the BFTC did not observe natural justice requirements in arriving at a decision[29].

TTFTC merger procedures are outlined in the TTFTA sections 14(2) & (3), 15 and 16. Section 14(2) requires the TTFTC to "... make its determination whether to grant permission or not and to inform the applicant enterprise of its determination". The section provides that this determination should be made within one month of receipt of an application for permission to merge. This time limit may be changed by Order of the Minister. Before granting permission, the TTFTC must satisfy itself that the proposed merger would not affect competition or would not be detrimental to the consumer or the economy (s 14(3)(a)). By 14(3)(b), the TTFTC must consult with the Securities Exchange Commission to ensure that the procedure under the Securities Industry Act 1995 for mergers has been followed. The TTFTA does not apply to banks and non-bank

---

29 *Fair Trading Commission v Barbados National Oil Co Ltd* [2015], see n. 19, supra.

financial institutions which fall within the purview of the Securities Industry Act 1995 (s 3(1)(g)).

Section 15 of the TTFTA requires that if a director serves on the Board of Directors of two or more companies that are competitors and the director is likely to weld together the policies of those companies in a way that would reduce or eliminate competition between them, the companies in which he serves as director shall apply to the TTFTC for permission to merge if they meet the threshold of TTD 50 million [approx USD 7.1 million] and at least one of the enterprises carries on or intends to carry on business in T&T.

Where the TTFTC has reason to believe that two or more enterprises have merged without obtaining permission, it shall initiate an investigation (s 16(1)). Where after investigation, the TTFTC is of the opinion that enterprises have structured themselves in a way that they have merged within the meaning of Part III of the TTFTA, without permission of the TTFTC as required under section 14, the TTFTC may apply to the Court for an Order for divestment (s 16(2)). However, by section 16(3), the enterprise may agree that it will divest within an agreed period, parts of its combined business or operations, if the TTFTC is satisfied that such divestment would make the merger less likely to lessen competition in T&T.

In the TTFTC context, because the authority to make decisions under the statute is vested in the courts, "judicial review" in this context would contemplate an appeal from a decision of the High Court, which is the first instance court, to the Court of Appeal. This is provided by section 46 of the TTFTA.

4. Sanctions

In Barbados, firms can be sanctioned for *not filing an application* according to the rules: FCMR section 3(4) An enterprise that contravenes this rule (the requirements for application for permission to merge) is guilty of an offence and is liable on conviction on indictment:

a) in the case of an individual, to a fine of BBD 150,000 or to imprisonment for a term of 6 months or to both; or
b) in the case of a corporate entity, to a fine of BBD 500,000.

If an enterprise fails to comply with instructions to divest interests or part of its combined business or operations, the enterprise is guilty of an offence and is liable on conviction on indictment to a fine of BBD 500,000 or up to 10% of the turnover of the enterprise for the financial year preceding the date of the commission of the offence, whichever is the greater (s 20(9)).

In the case of **T&T**, section 16(4) of the TTFTA states that an enterprise which fails to keep the undertaking [to divest business or operations] given under subsection (3) is liable upon summary conviction to a fine of TTD 25,000 (approx USD 3,500) and to further fine of TTD 1,000 each day the offence continues (USD 140).

There are also sanctions for failure to provide requested information, which apply generally to competition investigations. In this regard, section 45 of the BFTCA sanctions the wilful refusal or failure to provide information requested by the BFTC with penalties of BBD 50,000 (approx USD 25,000) in the first instance and BBD 10,000 dollars (approx USD 5,000) for each day or part thereof that the offence continues.

In a similar vein, the TTFTA under section 12 sanctions the obstruction of competition investigations with a penalty of TTD 5000 dollars and two years' imprisonment.

IV. Substance

1. Competition Analysis

The substantive tests for merger review, as stated in both the BFCA and TTFTA, are as follows:

Section 20(6) BFCA:

> Before granting permission the Commission shall conduct an investigation into the proposed merger in order to satisfy itself that the proposed merger would not affect competition adversely or be detrimental to consumers or the economy.

Section 13(2) TTFTA:

> An anticompetitive merger is a merger which restricts or distorts competition in a market.

The language of both statutory provisions indicates that the substantive test for review is primarily a competitive effects test. Although it is observed that in practice there may not be a strict distinction between this test and some considerations under a dominance test. Indeed as the summary of the Sagicor General/Harmony General case from the BFTC indicates, considerations of post-merger dominance will be relevant in practice.

The BFCA section 20(7) and the *Merger Investigation Procedures* guidelines provide guidance to the BFTC in conducting the investigation. The BFTC will give consideration to:

- The structure of the markets likely to be affected by the proposed merger including the number and size of competitors in the various product markets before and after the merger and the barriers to entry that will impact on these market structures.
- The degree of control exercised by the enterprises, particularly the economic and financial power of the enterprises; and the extent to which the merged enterprises will have the market power to raise prices unilaterally or will have incentives to enter into collusive arrangements with the other market participants.

- The availability of alternatives to the services or goods provided by the enterprises concerned in the merger, i.e., the degree to which following the merger there will be an adequate supply of alternatives to the goods and services provided by the merging parties.
- The likely effect of the proposed merger on consumers and the economy; or the degree to which there will be improvements in the quality and delivery of goods and services supplied in the market, and the extent to which reduction in costs are passed directly to the consumer in reduced prices or indirectly through strategic investments.
- The actual or potential competition from other enterprises and the likelihood of detriment to competition, i.e. the impact of the merger on the productivity and viability of the existing market participants and potential new entrants.

The merger application form set out in the schedule to the Rules of the FCMR requires firms to submit detailed information that would allow the BFTC to conduct an investigation based on the guidance provided in the BFCA (above). These include the following:

(a) Each applicant is required to give contact information, names and positions of senior officers, ownership and control, and nature of all relevant businesses conducted and the reasons for the merger. In addition, the firm must provide details of all relevant group relationships, associated enterprises, degrees of dependency and percentages of holdings. In the case of acquisition of shares in another enterprise, the amount of the shares to be acquired and the total shares owned in it by the purchaser or any related enterprise must be declared.

(b) Firms applying for merger clearance must provide financial details of total turnover for the last financial year for each enterprise engaged in the merger in Barbados, and each relevant group of enterprises worldwide, and the gross worldwide assets of each of the enterprises engaged in the merger as at the last financial year.

(c) The merger proposal that accompanies the application must provide information on the method used to effect the merger, whether by acquisition of assets, shares, amalgamation, combination or the acquisition of an interest in a combination. Details are to be provided on the factors upon which the proposed merger is conditional, the consideration given and received by the enterprises which are parties to the merger, whether any of the merging enterprises will cease to be distinct as a result of the merger.

(d) The firms are also required to provide details of the product or service market to be affected, the geographic markets to be affected by the merger whether international, regional or national. The applicants must provide an estimate of the value and volume of each of the markets, the turnover and market shares of the merging enterprises in each relevant market, and the names of and market shares of all competitors with over 5% of the market share.

(e) Applicants must also identify the barriers or restrictions to new entry into the relevant markets to be affected by the merger whether legal, regulatory or economic. Information on the nature and extent of any vertical links involving or between merging enterprises in the relevant markets to be affected by the merger.

(f) The FCRM (s 3(i)) places the burden on the applicants to provide reasons why the proposed merger will not affect competition adversely or be detrimental to consumers or the economy. In that regard, firms should identify the structure of the markets likely to be affected by the proposed merger; the degree of control exercised by the enterprises concerned in the proposed merger, in the market, and particularly the economic and financial power of the enterprises; the availability of alternatives to the services or goods provided by the enterprises concerned in the merger; the likely effect of the proposed merger on consumers and the economy; and the actual or potential competition from other enterprises and the likelihood of detriment to competition.

(g) The firms must also provide information for a claim of efficiency gains: the reason why the merger is likely to bring about gains in real efficiencies and as distinct from pecuniary efficiencies that are greater than or more than offset the effects of any limitation on competition that results or are likely to result from the merger. Details are to be provided on the quantitative estimate of the real efficiencies that are likely to result from the merger, the quantitative estimate of the likely effects of the limitation upon competition that is likely to result from the merger, and the reasons why the proposed merger represents the least anticompetitive known alternative uses of assets where one of the parties to the proposed merger is faced with actual or imminent financial failure.

2. Statistics (BFTC)

Numbers of merger cases notified: 20

Number of cases allowed: 15

Number of cases that required remedies: 4

Number of cases disallowed: 1

3. Case Law Illustration

A. *Case Law 1: Fair Trading Commission v Digicel Jamaica Ltd & Anor*[30]

Facts: This case is the first, and so far only, merger-related competition case that has been litigated at all tiers of a national court system anywhere in CARICOM. It originated in the 2011 merger between two Jamaican telecommunications firms, Digicel Jamaica Limited (Digicel) and Oceanic Digital Jamaica Limited (Claro) (collectively, the merging parties).

---

30 [2017] UKPC 28.

The merger in the telecommunications industry was underpinned by a stock purchase agreement by which Digicel agreed to acquire Claro's business inclusive of its telecommunications licence and spectrum. The result was that Digicel wholly acquired Claro, and the latter would exit the Jamaican telecommunications market. The transfer of Claro's telecommunications operations, inclusive of its licence and spectrum, to Digicel was approved by the relevant minister acting under change of control provisions in the sector-specific legislation, that is, section 17 of the Telecommunications Act (TCA).

In the absence of a formal merger control regime under the Fair Competition Act (FCA), the JFTC investigated the merger under the general provision in the legislation that addresses anticompetitive agreements, section 17 FCA. The primary conclusion of the investigation was that because the merger would result in the removal of Claro as a significant competitor of Digicel, thereby strengthening the latter's dominance; the transaction was likely to create or increase incentives for anticompetitive conduct[31]. The JFTC did acknowledge that there could be some procompetitive benefits, but it considered that these would not sufficiently offset the likely anticompetitive effects

On the basis of that view, the JFTC recommended that the merger should not be approved. The merging parties, however, implemented the merger on the basis of the earlier ministerial approval under the sector-specific legislation. The JFTC commenced legal proceedings in the Jamaican Supreme Court, alleging breach of the competition legislation. Several issues arose in the Supreme Court proceedings, which included whether the JFTC had jurisdiction under section 17 FCA to investigate the merger in the absence of specific statutory provision for merger control, as well as whether the grant of ministerial approval under the sector-specific legislation precluded the application of the competition legislation. The Supreme Court decided in favour of JFTC jurisdiction, observing that the competition legislation *does not exclude mergers* from its application. The Court also ruled that the merger was subject to both the competition legislation and the sector-specific legislation.

The merging parties appealed to the Jamaican Court of Appeal where they argued that the focus of section 17 FCA is concerted conduct. In their view, the provision applied to agreements that relate to conduct between two parties where the parties would remain independent after implementation. For the merging parties, section 17 FCA was designed to address the risk of ongoing concertation between firms. The merging parties relied on the European Court of Justice's decision in *British American Tobacco and R J Reynolds Industries Inc v Commission of the European Communities* (*BAT & Reynolds*[32]) in support of this argument, on the basis that Article 85 of the Treaty Establishing the European Community (TEEC) had been applied to a joint venture agreement in which the parties remained independent after implementation.

Building on that argument, the merging parties further submitted that section 17 FCA did not apply to agreements that affected market structure by removing one of the parties,

---

31 JFTC Staff Report, "Investigation into the Acquisition of Oceanic Digital (Jamaica) Limited by Digicel Jamaica Limited" (non-confidential version), (8 December 2011).

32 Joined Cases C-142/84 & C156/84

because the remaining party could therefore not engage in concerted conduct with itself. Accordingly, they submitted that section 17 FCA did not apply to their stock purchase agreement because post-merger there would not be two parties but only one that would remain in the market. The remaining party, Digicel, would be incapable of engaging in concertation with itself within the scope of section 17 FCA.

On the relationship between competition legislation and sector-specific legislation, the merging parties argued that the two statutes were in conflict because the merger had been approved by the relevant minister under the sector-specific legislation whereas under the competition legislation the merger could be rendered unenforceable if the JFTC's challenge was successful. On the merging parties' view, this statutory conflict should be resolved in favour of disapplying the competition legislation on the ground that its application would result in unjustifiable business inconvenience, which would be contrary to the legislative intent in regulating mergers in the telecommunications industry.

The JFTC opposed and countered that section 17 FCA applied generally to any agreement that was likely to have anticompetitive effects in a market, regardless of whether or not the parties remained independent. For the JFTC, therefore, section 17 FCA applied to the stock purchase agreement because in its view the agreement was likely to have such an effect in relevant markets in the telecommunications industry. The JFTC also argued that the merger was subject to both competition legislation and sector-specific legislation on the basis that it is commercially foreseeable that such a transaction would be subject to multiple regulatory reviews. Consequently, there was no conflict or unjustifiable business inconvenience where the merger is prohibited because it did not satisfy all regulatory requirements.

The Court of Appeal accepted the arguments of the merging parties, and in reversing the Supreme Court's decision, the Court of Appeal ruled that section 17 FCA did not apply because the merger resulted in Claro's removal from the market, with the result that there could be no risk of concerted conduct that could attract the application of the provision. The Court of Appeal also found that the application of both sector-specific legislation and competition legislation to the merger could produce conflicting outcomes, and it therefore ruled that the competition legislation could not apply on the ground that its application would result in unjustifiable business inconvenience, contrary to legislative intent. The JFTC appealed to Jamaica's highest court, the UK Privy Council.

Issues: Among other issues, the Privy Council had to address the following:

1. Whether the prohibition on anticompetitive agreements in section 17 FCA affords jurisdiction to control mergers?
2. Whether competition legislation, in this case section 17 FCA, should apply to a merger in a regulated sector where it has been approved under the sector-specific legislation, in this case section 17 TCA?

Rules: The legal framework for resolving the issue not only included the language of the FCA and TCA, but also Articles 101 and 102 of the Treaty on the Functioning of the European Union (TFEU). The TFEU was relevant because the germane provisions in the Jamaican legislation are generally derived from the competition regime prescribed under the TFEU and its predecessor treaties. On this basis European case law, which applied the predecessor treaty articles of 101 and 102 (aArticles 85 and 86 TEEC), to corporate acquisitions was also applicable.

Analysis: The parties renewed their respective arguments at the Privy Council. The Privy Council preferred the arguments of the JFTC. In so doing, they interpreted the language of section 17 FCA as not limiting the provision to agreements that provided for concerted conduct after implementation. Instead, the Privy Council reasoned that the provision applied to "*any agreement* containing provisions having as their purpose or *likely effect* the substantial lessening of competition in the relevant market" [authors' emphasis]. On this basis, the Privy Council decided that: "An agreement by which two competitors merge is an agreement falling within subsection (1) [of s 17 FCA], because the reduction in the number of significant competitors in a market is self-evidently likely to have the effect of lessening competition."

In addressing the merging parties' argument on *BAT & Reynolds*, the Privy Council accepted that it was one where Article 85 TEEC was applied in a situation where the parties remained independent after implementation of the relevant agreement. The Privy Council, however, rejected that as a constraint on the application of Article 85 to mergers. Having regard to the language of section 17 FCA, they took the view that the provision was "arguably broader" than Article 85. More importantly, they read the *BAT & Reynolds* case as permitting the application of Article 85, and by extension section 17 FCA, to an agreement regardless of whether or not the parties remained independent after implementation.

On the relationship between the statutes, the Privy Council decided that application of the competition legislation to the merger in question was not precluded by the prior ministerial approval under the sector-specific legislation. The Privy Council reasoned that: (1) Both statutes generally apply to the telecommunications industry, with the competition legislation supplying relevant regulatory tools to address competition, such as merger control, which are not available under the sector-specific legislation; (2) Ministerial approval of the merger under the sector-specific legislation could not therefore have addressed the relevant competition issues; and (3) Legality of the merger depends on compliance with multiple regulatory regimes, not just one.

Conclusions: The Privy Council reversed the Court of Appeal's decision and restored the Supreme Court's decision in favour of JFTC jurisdiction over the merging parties, on the basis of section 17 FCA.

Commentary: The decision may be considered ground-breaking in two respects. It is the first decision in CARICOM to derive a general jurisdiction to discipline mergers and acquisitions under competition legislation in the absence of a specific grant of such jurisdiction by the legislator. Indeed, the Privy Council recognised this in declaring the applicability of section 17 FCA to mergers "... even if this result was not intended ..."

More importantly, the decision is also ground-breaking beyond the CARICOM context because it extends the reach of the anticompetitive agreements provision not just to acquisitions, which had been the case in the EU context, but also to outright mergers. Prior to the adoption in 1989 of a formal merger control regime under Council

Regulation 4064/89 EEC, the two leading European Court of Justice judgments on the subject spoke to the application of either Article 85 or 86 TEEC to acquisitions, as opposed to mergers.

In that regard, *Europemballage Corporation and Continental Can Co Inc v Commission of the European Communities* (*Continental Can*[33]) concerned the acquisition of a controlling interest in a competitor; whereas *BAT and Reynolds* concerned the acquisition of a non-controlling interest. In both cases, the target of the acquisition remained legally distinct, even if not economically so. In contrast, the stock purchase agreement between Digicel and Claro resulted in an amalgamation of the two companies into one, thus ending the legal distinction between them. The obliteration of that constraint from the prior case law is an evolutionary step. It means that section 17 FCA, as well equivalent statutory provisions in CARICOM, could, where there is no formal merger control regime, afford jurisdiction to review various economic concentrations whether they take the legal form of an acquisition of a controlling or non-controlling interest, or outright merger.

There are limitations in the applicability of the anticompetitive agreement provisions to mergers and acquisitions as well. At the outset, section 17 FCA with its focus on "agreements" is unlikely to afford jurisdiction to review and control non-consensual mergers and acquisitions, for example, takeovers on the stock exchange. Another relevant limitation is in terms of remedies. While section 17 FCA could afford jurisdiction to review, the ability of the JFTC and the court to control problematic mergers and acquisitions is limited. If the JFTC takes the view that a merger or acquisition is likely to have anticompetitive effect, short of applying to the court the options open to it would be to: (1) decide that the merger or acquisition is exempted under subsection 17(4), but as has been observed in relation to Article 85 TEEC[34], those exemptions are not readily applicable to most mergers or acquisitions; (2) authorise the merger or acquisition pursuant to section 29 FCA, but this depends on satisfying a rather amorphous public interest test; or (3) negotiate a consent agreement, but this depends on the willingness of the merging parties to accept constraints on their conduct.

The remedies open to the court on a finding of breach of section 17 FCA are even more limited. The court can declare the merger or acquisition agreement unenforceable under subsection 17(3) and impose a monetary penalty under section 47 FCA. This, however, may be of minimal remedial value where the merger or acquisition has been implemented or where the firms view the penalty as "a cost of doing business". Where the merger or acquisition is not yet implemented – it is observed that section 17 FCA does not require prior notification, much less a standstill obligation – the court could grant an injunction to restrain implementation. Similarly this may be of minimal remedial value, depending on the progress of the transaction by the time a competition assessment is completed and an application for an injunction is granted.

Apart from these options, traditional merger remedies, particularly divestiture, are for the most part not available under section 17 FCA. This is unsurprising given that the provision may not have been designed for merger control. The foregoing limitations

---

33 Case C-6/72

34 Karen Banks, "Mergers and Partial Mergers Under EEC Law" [1987] 11(2) Fordham International L J, 255–309

suggest that while the Privy Council's decision usefully adds merger review to the JFTC's regulatory toolbox, it is not an adequate substitute for a formal merger control regime with transparent, effective rules tailored to the realities of mergers and acquisitions.

The decision also adds some nuance in the CARICOM context to the relationship between competition legislation and sector-specific legislation. The discourse around this relationship traditionally involves consideration of which legislation to apply to a given transaction. This is often resolved by way of two general approaches to statutory interpretation. The first approach is to examine the statutes for express language that could indicate that the application of one of them to the transaction was meant to be excluded. This approach did not find favour with any of the courts in this case because no such language could be found.

The second approach is to invoke the doctrine of implied repeal which, based on a finding of statutory conflict, leads to one of the statutes being disapplied to the transaction. In this case, although not explicitly finding that there was an implied repeal of the competition legislation, the Jamaican Court of Appeal's approach in dis-applying same to the merger is reminiscent of the doctrine.

The Privy Council's decision indicates another consideration under which both statutes can be applied, even where the sector-specific legislation partially addresses competition concerns. On this approach, both competition legislation and sector-specific legislation are to be applied in a complementary manner, with the former filling a perceived regulatory gap regarding competition in the latter. This approach was perhaps possible because it was reasonably clear that the sector-specific legislation in this case, that is, the TCA, established a regulatory regime that contemplated competition. The position may be different in a case where the sector-specific legislation establishes a regulatory regime that does not contemplate competition. Nonetheless, the approach of the Privy Council is useful especially for young competition law jurisdictions such as those in CARICOM, which are still grappling with the relationship between competition policy and other industrial or trade policies.

B. Case Law 2: Sagicor General/Harmony General (2019)

Applicable Provision: Section 20 of the Fair Competition Act, CAP.326C of the Laws of Barbados

The Parties: The acquisition by Sagicor General Insurance Limited (Sagicor) of the entire issued share capital of Harmony General Insurance Company Limited constituting the sale and reinsurance of non-life insurance services in Barbados.

Sagicor, the purchaser, is a member of the Sagicor Group Limited, a conglomerate offering life, annuity, group and individual health insurance. The company is listed on the stock exchanges of Barbados, T&T, and London. Originally set up in 1840, Sagicor Group acquired Barbados Mutual Life Assurance Society, and thereafter, Sagicor Financial Corporation (SFC) was established. Two subsidiaries of SFC, Sagicor Life Inc. and Sagicor General Insurance Inc., were established.

The vendor, Harmony General Insurance Limited (Harmony), was established in 1996 in Barbados and provided all classes of general insurance.

Transaction: In May of 2018, the BFTC became aware that Sagicor informed policy holders of the likelihood of that company taking over the policies of Harmony. The BFTC subsequently initiated a preliminary investigation to calculate the shares of Sagicor and determined that the transaction met the statutory threshold for notification and that Sagicor should have sought permission from BFTC before proceeding. However, in the meantime (September 2018), the companies "jumped the gun" and completed the amalgamation without notifying the BFTC and applying for approval. The BFTC notified them that, pursuant to section 20 and 22(1) of the BFCA, there was a possible contravention of the BFCA. In December 2018, the BFTC received an application from the merged entity, and it reviewed the transaction under section 22 of the BFCA, which empowers it to address mergers that have been implemented in breach of the requirement to first obtain permission to merge.

Sagicor offered as the explanation for the transaction the need to create a more profitable entity because of the years of declining premium rates which led to a significant reduction in underwriting profits, and a decline in investment income due to low interest rates. The firm argued that the amalgamation would strengthen the company and this would benefit policy holders and the industry, as it was important in this industry to be financially sound.

Analysis: The investigative procedure followed the guide provided in the BFCA section 20.7(a) – (e). The BFTC first identified the product and geographic markets, and identified the competitors in the relevant market, calculated market share, assessed barriers to entry, and assessed the effect on competition of the merger. The BFTC was in a position to assess the actual effects/changes to competition since the merger was completed in September 2019. In conducting the investigation, the BFTC interviewed third-party market participants: insurance companies, brokers, agents, and their views on the effects of the merger on consumers and the insurance industry were taken into account in the analysis. The BFTC also took into account the fact that the Financial Services Commission vetted and approved the transaction. In defining the product and geographic markets, the BFTC drew heavily on case law from the EU, US and other jurisdictions on mergers in this industry and the reasoning that went into defining the relevant market.

The geographical market was defined to be national, since there were strong national dimensions to the information needed before coverage could be offered, and also, there was no cross-border selling in this industry in Barbados. Distribution channels for insurance products were all national.

Product market was more complex to define, but the BFTC relied on reasoning from cases in other jurisdictions, applied where appropriate to the case in hand. They found that the EU traditionally distinguished between general insurance, life insurance and reinsurance. In *Commercial Union/General Accident*, the EU court asserted that within life and non-life insurance, there could be many sub-products that are not interchangeable, and therefore could be separate product markets. However, the European Commission chose not to follow this narrow approach, and rather, left the definition of the relevant geographic and product market open. Similarly, in *Generali CEE/AS*, the European Commission[35] chose not to provide precise product market definition for non-life insurance products because of the multiple dimensions from which the general insurance market can be defined.

The BFTC investigators concluded that the most practical approach to employ in defining the relevant product market would be to differentiate between life and non-life insurance even though sub-products in different types of insurance were not substitutable (e.g., home insurance and motor insurance). However, like the European Commission, it chose to leave the definition open rather than specific to different types of insurance products. It was guided by the assertion that if a broader definition is reflective of the relevant market, analysis of individual submarkets may be superfluous. In regard to supply-side interchangeability, providers can offer with little constraint, components of coverage as add-ons or stand-alone: burglary, business interruption, public liability etc. Barriers to entry were deemed to be relatively low, requiring the usual basic information for company registration, but specifically, information on reinsurance agreements, the creation of a statutory fund of BBD 250,000 and a statutory deposit of BBD 1 million for long-term business. Taking these factors into consideration, the relevant product market was deemed to be the market for non-life (general) insurance in Barbados.

***Competitive Analysis*:** The BFTC considered the three variables that are used to characterise company performance in the insurance industry: gross premiums (the amount an insurance company expect to receive over the life of a policy term), net premiums (income received for assuming risk minus expenses associated with providing coverage under a policy), and earned premiums (insurance premiums paid in instalments). The investigators chose to use gross written premiums as the unit of measure in determining market share among general insurance companies in Barbados. Data on total gross premiums written for the period 2014–2018 was collected from the Financial Services Commission and its annual report.

There were 16 companies in the general insurance market prior to the transaction. Each of the insurance companies interviewed indicated that there was likely to be no anti-competitive concerns or effect as a result of the transaction, that the industry was competitive, and that companies compete through premium offerings. The prevailing view was that the amalgamation would increase the company's financial stability, thereby strengthening its ability to pay claims. Finally, post-transaction, there has not been any recorded significant changes within the general insurance market.

The BFTC concluded that entry into the general insurance market would be timely, likely and sufficient to deter or counteract any possible effects from the transaction. Additionally, consumers have the ability to switch between companies, cancel policies at any given time with few implications for cost. In respect to subproducts in the general insurance market, a general insurance licence allowed a company to offer whatever category of general insurance it desired, and the products offered by a company are entirely at the discretion of the company.

---

35 COMP/M.9056, Generali CEE/AS.

The investigators found little difference between pre- and post-merger Herfindahl-Hirschman Index: 1280 and 1372 respectively, with 1500 being the threshold for high concentration. This small change indicates that the transaction is unlikely to have adverse competitive effects and requires no further analysis.

The presumption of dominance, 40% of market share, was not met, as no company in the market had a market share that exceeded 25%. Having merged, Sagicor/Harmony had a market share of approximately 10–20%, and in respect of each product segment, Sagicor/Harmony controlled no more than 10–20%.

The BFTC concluded that there was no evidence of likely competitive harm arising from the merger transaction, as the market appeared competitive, the transaction did not present competitive concerns, and therefore did not lessen competition in the general insurance industry in Barbados.

Final Decision: The Fair Trading Commission, pursuant to section 20(5) of the Fair Competition Act, CAP.326C, determined that the result of the acquisition by Sagicor of the common shares and assets of Harmony and the physical location at Harmony Hall, St Michael, did not lessen competition in the market for general insurance in Barbados, and accordingly approved the transaction without condition under section 20 of the BFCA.

Comment: The findings of the investigation indicated that the merger did not meet the threshold for notification in the first place, but that was only verifiable after applying the rule-of-reason procedure in a full investigation.

Even though the company jumped the gun, and was therefore liable to a fine of BBD 250,000 or 10% of its yearly turnover in the preceding year, the BFTC adopted a lenient approach. This is in keeping with the BFTC's general approach to dealing with anticompetitive conducts through persuasion rather than punitive action. Given that the regime is still young, and firms are learning the rules, the BFTC has been quite successful in gaining compliance through this approach.

BIOGRAPHIES

Cynthia Andino

Cynthia Andino is an independent consultant on competition and commerce. She holds a master's in business law from the University of Strasbourg and a European Master's in transnational trade law and finance from the University of Deusto and University of Tilburg. Mrs Andino participated in the commission that drafted Paraguay's Competition Defence Act and was Paraguay's coordinator for UNCTAD's COMPAL programme. She participated in the Trade Defence and Competition Commission of MERCOSUR, and the negotiation group for the EU – MERCOSUR Trade Agreement Competition and Trade Remedies Chapters.

Favio Batres P

Favio Josué Batres P is a senior associate in the Nicaraguan office of BLP. Favio has over 15 years of experience in the legal field, specialising in business law, banking and project finance, mergers and acquisitions, competition and antitrust, competition litigation and commercial arbitration. Favio graduated from Universidad del Valle in Managua and obtained a master's degree in business law from Universidad Centroamericana in Managua.

Paula Bauer

Paula Bauer is a partner at C.R.&F. Rojas Abogados. She initially joined in 2002 until 2007, and rejoined in early 2013. Mrs Bauer obtained her law degree in 2000 from Universidad Católica Boliviana 'San Pablo' in La Paz. She earned a number of diplomas in intellectual property law on courses hosted by the World Trade Organization and is currently a member of Bolivian Industrial Property Association. Mrs Bauer has contributed to the World Bank's publication '*Doing Business in 2006: Creating Jobs*'.

Paulo Burnier da Silveira

Paulo Burnier da Silveira is a senior competition expert at the Organization for Economic Cooperation and Development (OECD) and a visiting professor at Sciences Po Paris. He is also a former commissioner at the Brazilian Competition Authority (CADE), former chief editor of the Brazilian Competition Journal, and a professor at the University of Brasilia (currently on leave). He holds a PhD from the University of Paris and has several publications in the field of competition law including '*Global Competition Enforcement*' (Kluwer 2019) and '*Competition Law and Policy in Latin America*' (Kluwer 2017).

Virginia Campás Alcalde

Virginia Campás is a senior associate at Creel, García Cuéllar, Aiza y Enríquez. She focuses on antitrust and competition law.

Vinicius Marques de Carvalho

Vinicius Marques de Carvalho is the founding partner of Vinicius Marques de Carvalho Advogados and professor of commercial law at the University of São Paulo. He is a former President of the Brazilian Competition Authority (CADE), former Secretary of the Brazilian Secretariat of Economic Law and former commissioner of CADE. He holds a bachelor's degree in law from the

University of São Paulo and PhDs in law from the University of São Paulo and the University of Paris-1 (Panthéon-Sorbonne).

Camila Chamorro Poma

Camila Chamorro Poma is an associate at DiezCanseco. She holds a bachelors in law from the National University of San Marcos (UNMSM). She was a student at the master's programme in economics and public policy at UNMSM. She worked at the Technical Secretariat of the Specialised Chamber for the Elimination of Bureaucratic Barriers of the Peruvian Competition Authority (Indecopi). She was a member of the winning team of the Peruvian Antitrust Moot Court Competition 2018.

Luis Diez Canseco Núñez

Luis José Diez Canseco Núñez is a name partner at DiezCanseco. He is a lawyer from the Pontifical Catholic University of Peru (PUCP). He holds a master's degree in comparative law and was a visiting scholar at George Washington University Law School. He was a Fulbright and Hubert H Humphrey Scholar. Luis was Dean of the Law School of the Technological University of Peru (UTP), and is currently a professor of law at PUCP. He was the former president of the Tribunal of Justice of the Andean Community, international officer at the WIPO and UNCTAD, general coordinator of the competitiveness programme of the Presidency of the Council of Ministers and the World Bank, member of the competition tribunal of Indecopi, and consultant for the Inter-American Development Bank and the World Bank.

Marvin Francisco Discua Singh

Marvin Francisco Discua Singh is currently the legal director of the Honduran Competition Authority (CDPC). He has a Master's in management and public policy from the University of Chile, Santiago, a postgraduate degree in intellectual property from the University of Mérida, Venezuela, and a degree as lawyer and journalist of the National Autonomous University of Honduras (UNAH). He previously held other positions as technical director of the Commission, intellectual property director and negotiator for Honduras in intellectual property for the DR-CAFTA free trade agreement, as well as professor of the Master's degree programme in mercantile law of UNAH.

Alejandro Gallotti

Alejandro Gallotti is a junior partner at LEĜA. He is a public law and foreign investment protection specialist. He is a constitutional law and public law professor, and an independent researcher at Georgetown University, Washington DC.

Luis García Santos Coy

Luis García is the head of the antitrust and competition practice area at Creel, García Cuéllar, Aiza y Enríquez. He specialises in antitrust and competition law, actively participating in all types of cases before the competition authorities, from complex pre-merger filings to investigations, administrative procedures and constitutional (Amparo) proceedings, as well as leniency applications. Mr García also regularly advises multinationals and private equity investors on acquisitions and investments in Mexico across multiple industries, including digital platforms. Mr García is a member of the Mexican Bar Association and the International Bar Association.

Marc Jones

Marc Jones is an attorney-at-law who specialises in competition law. He is currently the senior legal counsel at the Carribean Community Competition Authority (CARICOM) based in Paramaribo, Suriname.

Natalia Jul

Natalia Jul is a member of the Uruguayan Competition Authority, where she was appointed as a commissioner in 2017. She is a lawyer specialising in competition policy, and utilities regulation She previously worked as a lawyer with extensive experience in private sector, holding positions of responsibility and advising the management bodies of recognised companies. She is a lecturer of competition law at the Catholic University of Uruguay since 2019.

Luciana Macedo

Luciana Macedo is the President of the Uruguayan Competition Authority since 2019. She is commissioner of the Authority since 2009. She is an economist specialising in competition policy and regulation of network industries. In 2003 she achieved a MSc in economic regulation and competition from City University, London. She is a lecturer of competition policy at the Catholic University of Uruguay since 2019.

Pablo Márquez

Pablo Márquez is a partner at Márquez Barrera Castañeda Ramírez. He holds a PhD from Oxford University and a master's degree from Harvard University. He is a professor of law at Universidad Javeriana in Colombia. Pablo has over 20 years of experience in competition law and ICT. He was the chairman of the Commission for Communications Regulation and Superintendent for Antitrust at the Colombian Competition Authority. Pablo has won several awards, such as the Caldas Award from the Colombian Central Bank, the Medal of Merit in Telecoms from the Government of Colombia and the Robert Cooter Award in Law and Economics.

Marcela Mattiuzzo

Marcela Mattiuzzo is partner at VMCA. She holds a master's degree in constitutional law from the University of São Paulo and is currently pursuing a PhD in commercial law at the same institution. She was adviser and chief of staff at the Office of the President at CADE.

Carlos Mena Labarthe

Carlos Mena Labarthe is a partner at Creel, García Cuéllar, Aiza y Enríquez. Prior to joining the firm, Mr. Mena worked for 10 years in various positions at the Mexican Competition Authority (COFECE). He currently advises clients regarding all aspects of economic competition in Mexico. Mr Mena also has experience in coordinating proceedings in different jurisdictions, especially in Latin America. He is a lecturer at ITAM University and has published extensively on competition and regulation.

Jorge Molina Mendoza

Jorge Molina Mendoza is senior partner in Fabrega Molino and is head of the litigation and arbitration group. He is a former appeal judge on antitrust matters.

Darío Morales Herrera

Dario Morales Herrera is an associate at DiezCanseco. He holds a bachelor in law of UNMSM. He was a student of the master's programme in business law at UNMSM. He worked at the Technical Secretariat of the Peruvian Competition Authority (Indecopi). He was a member of the winning team of the Peruvian Antitrust Moot Court Competition 2018.

Angélica Noboa Págan

Angélica Noboa is a founding partner of the law firm Noboa Pagán Abogados of the Dominican Republic and is Knowledge Manager at Baker McKenzie Mexico, where she currently resides. Admitted to practice in the Dominican Republic, she has extensive practice in competition, telecommunications and energy law, and is a specialist in business law. She is a professor of competition law at the OMG Institute. She graduated from the Universidad Iberoamericana (UNIBE) in 1987. She is a candidate for a master's degree in corporate law from the Universidad Anáhuac Mexico Norte.

Ernesto Rizo Pallais

Ernesto Rizo Pallais is a partner in the Nicaraguan office of BLP. Ernesto has over 20 years of experience in the legal field, specialising in transactions involving agribusiness, banking and finance, energy and infrastructure, and business law. Ernesto graduated from the Pontificia Universidad Javeriana in Bogotá and was a Fulbright scholar at Georgetown University where he obtained a master's degree in banking and financial regulation.

Diego Rojas

Diego Rojas is managing partner at C.R.&F. Rojas Abogados. He studied at Marlborough College, before obtaining his law degree with an honours distinction from Universidad Católica Boliviana Law School. He was admitted to practice in 1997. Diego holds a postgraduate degree in corporate law from the Universidad Andina Simón Bolivar, a postgraduate degree in oil and gas law from the Universidad Privada de Santa Cruz de la Sierra, a postgraduate degree in conciliation and arbitration from the Universidad Aquino de Bolivia, and holds an LLM from the University of Chicago Law School, where he won an award for negotiation skills.

Maria Eduarda Scott

Maria Eduarda Scott is an associate at Vinicius Marques de Carvalho Advogados. She holds a bachelor's degree in law from the University of São Paulo and a bachelor's degree in public administration from Fundação Getulio Vargas.

Mauricio Serralde Rodríguez

Mauricio Serralde is a partner at Creel, García Cuéllar, Aiza y Enríquez. He specializes in antitrust and competition law, actively participating in all types of cases before the competition authorities, from pre-merger filings, to investigations, administrative procedures and constitutional (Amparo) proceedings, as well as leniency applications. He also devotes substantial time in advisory and compliance by clients with Mexican competition legal framework with respect to their operations. Mr Serralde is a member of the International Bar Association and the Mexican Bar Association.

Pamela Sittenfeld

Pamela Sittenfeld is an adviser to the Ministry of Foreign Trade of Costa Rica, and coordinator of the national team in charge of presenting to the Competition Committee of the Organization for Economic Cooperation and Development in the accession process of Costa Rica. She is an attorney. She graduated from the Universidad de Costa Rica, and has an Msc in Regulation and Competition from the LSE in London. She has been a consultant for Central American companies and international organisations at the local law firm BLP. She was also a professor of competition law at La Salle University, a member of the board of the National Regulator of Public Services (ARESEP) and the National Council for the Supervision of the Financial System (CONASSIF). She was also executive director of and legal adviser to the Costa Rican Commission to Promote Competition (COPROCOM).

David A. Sperber Vilhelm

David A Sperber Vilhelm is a partner at AntiTrust Consultores & Abogados, Quito. Before joining the firm, he served as the first National Competition Director at MIPRO. He teaches competition law at Universidad Internacional del Ecuador. He holds a JD from Pontificia Universidad Católica del Ecuador, an LLM from Harvard Law School and a PhD from Universidad de Barcelona.

Taimoon Stewart

Taimoon Stewart is an associate senior fellow at the University of the West Indies, St Augustine Campus, Trinidad and Tobago, and a consultant in competition law specialising in developing countries and small economy issues.

Pablo Trevisán

Pablo Trevisán is the founder of the IDC – Instituto de Derecho de la Competencia. Until February 2020, he was Commissioner of the Argentine Competition Authority (CNDC). Drafter of the Argentine Competition Act 27,442, enacted in May 2018.

Regina Vargas

Regina Vargas is the head of competition advocacy at the Competition Authority of El Salvador since 2009. She holds a bachelor's degree in international business and a master's degree in business law. She is an expert in antitrust and trade policy.

Uri Weinstok

Uri Weinstok is the head of the antitrust and competition practice at BLP. His experience includes filing and approval of mergers, representation in filing complaints and defending against investigations by the authorities, and the conduct of audits and compliance programs that help prevent and avoid anticompetitive behaviour. For more than 10 years he was a member of the Costa Rican Competition Authority (COPROCOM), and he was also its President. He has been an international consultant for the Organisation for Economic Co-operation and Development, the World Bank, and the United Nations Conference on Trade and Development. He obtained his law degree at the University of Costa Rica (1996), and a postgraduate diploma on EU Competition Law at King's College, University of London (2001).

Mario Ybar

Mario Ybar is Director of the Competition Practice at Garrigues, Chile. Previously, he was Deputy National Prosecutor and first Head of the Mergers Unit at the Chilean Competition Authority (FNE).

www.ingramcontent.com/pod-product-compliance
Ingram Content Group UK Ltd.
Pitfield, Milton Keynes, MK11 3LW, UK
UKHW020241290926
15470UKWH00002B/670

9 781939 007223